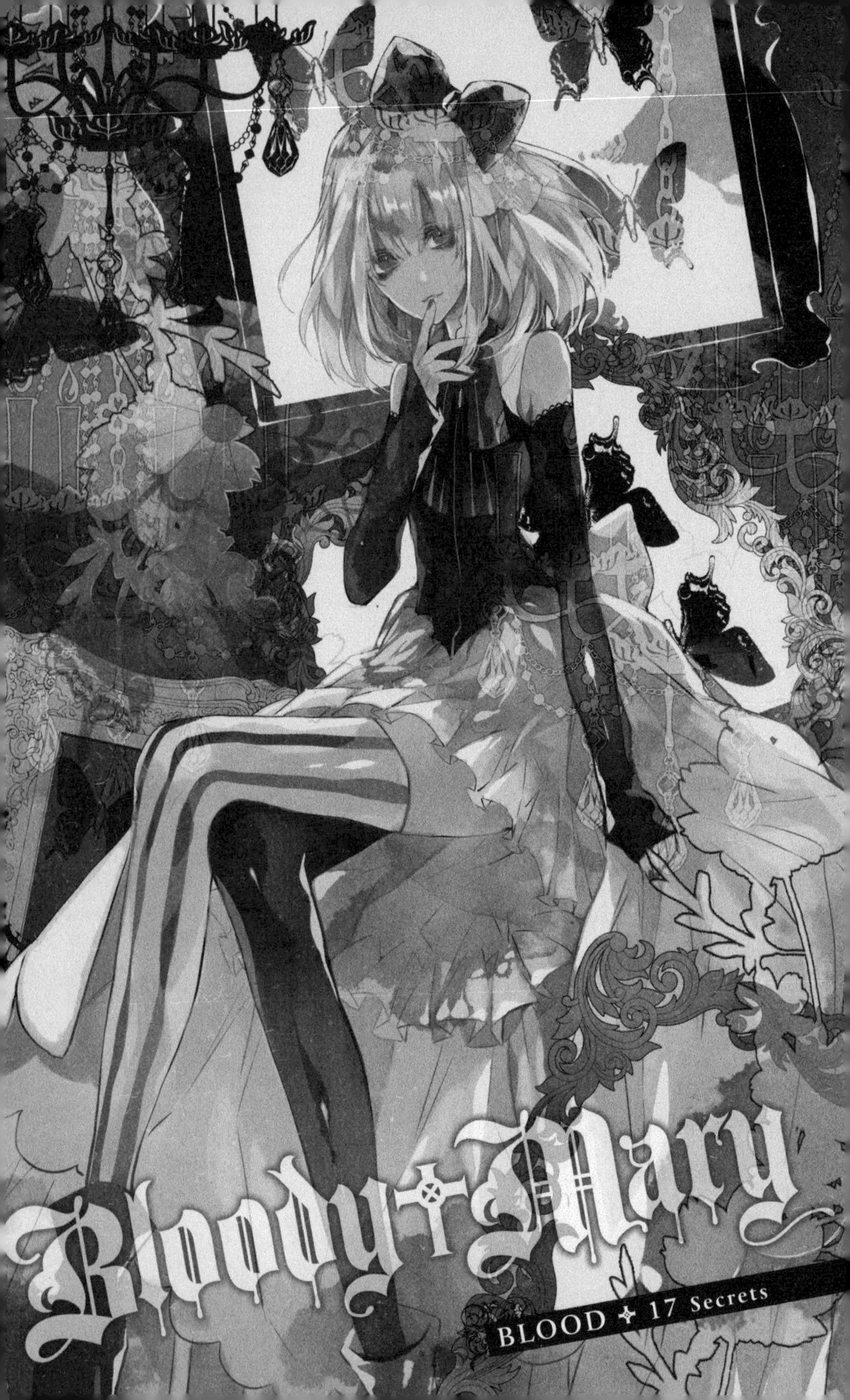
Bloody+Mary
BLOOD + 17 Secrets

Bloody+Mary

5 contents

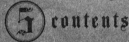

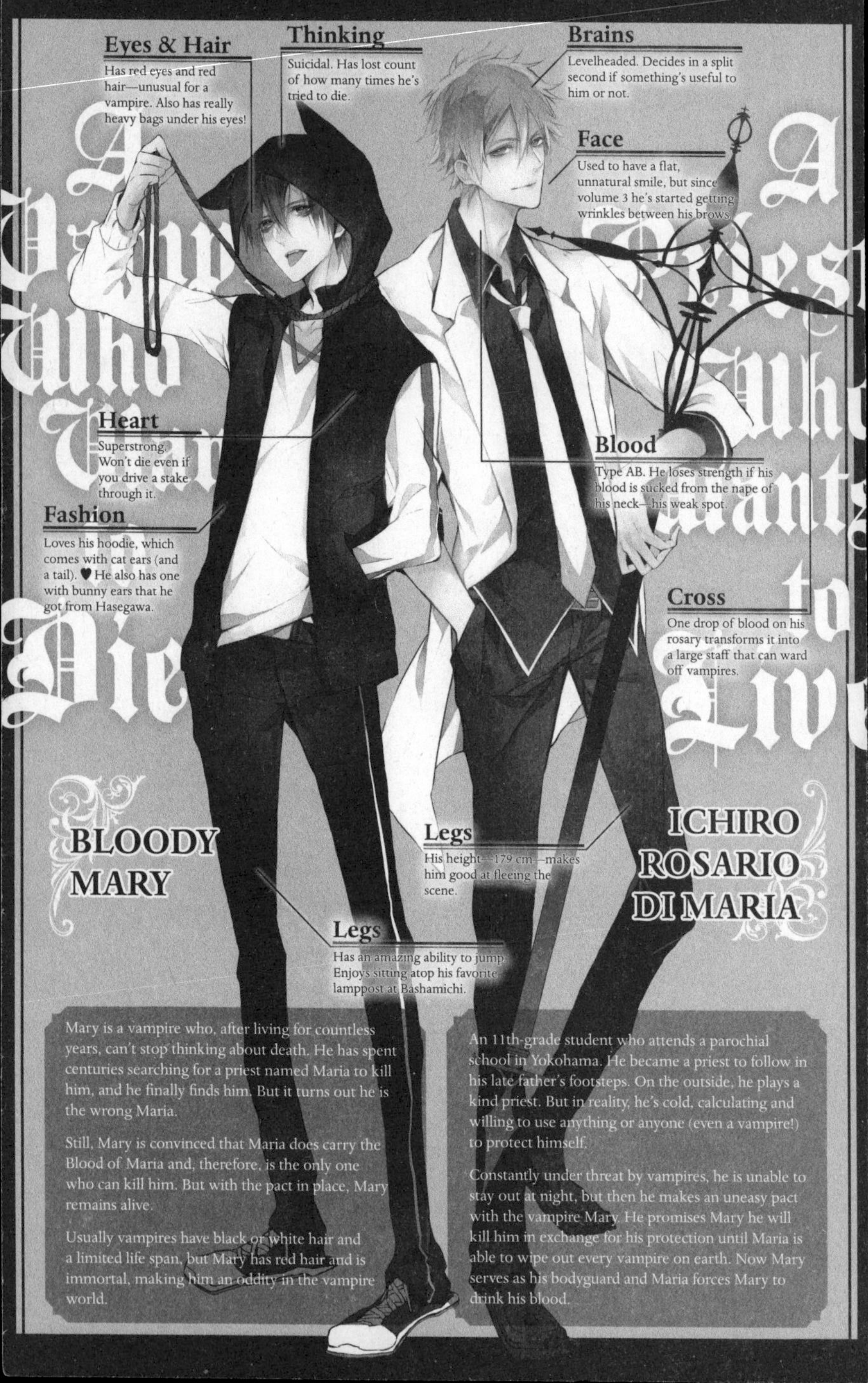
A Vampire Who Wants to Die
A Priest Who Wants to Live
Eyes & Hair
Has red eyes and red hair—unusual for a vampire. Also has really heavy bags under his eyes!
Thinking
Suicidal. Has lost count of how many times he's tried to die.
Brains
Levelheaded. Decides in a split second if something's useful to him or not.
Face
Used to have a flat, unnatural smile, but since volume 3 he's started getting wrinkles between his brows.
Heart
Superstrong. Won't die even if you drive a stake through it.
Blood
Type AB. He loses strength if his blood is sucked from the nape of his neck—his weak spot.
Fashion
Loves his hoodie, which comes with cat ears (and a tail). ♥ He also has one with bunny ears that he got from Hasegawa.
Cross
One drop of blood on his rosary transforms it into a large staff that can ward off vampires.
BLOODY MARY
Legs
His height—179 cm—makes him good at fleeing the scene.
ICHIRO ROSARIO DI MARIA
Legs
Has an amazing ability to jump. Enjoys sitting atop his favorite lamppost at Bashamichi.

Mary is a vampire who, after living for countless years, can't stop thinking about death. He has spent centuries searching for a priest named Maria to kill him, and he finally finds him. But it turns out he is the wrong Maria.

Still, Mary is convinced that Maria does carry the Blood of Maria and, therefore, is the only one who can kill him. But with the pact in place, Mary remains alive.

Usually vampires have black or white hair and a limited life span, but Mary has red hair and is immortal, making him an oddity in the vampire world.

An 11th-grade student who attends a parochial school in Yokohama. He became a priest to follow in his late father's footsteps. On the outside, he plays a kind priest. But in reality, he's cold, calculating and willing to use anything or anyone (even a vampire!) to protect himself.

Constantly under threat by vampires, he is unable to stay out at night, but then he makes an uneasy pact with the vampire Mary. He promises Mary he will kill him in exchange for his protection until Maria is able to wipe out every vampire on earth. Now Mary serves as his bodyguard and Maria forces Mary to drink his blood.

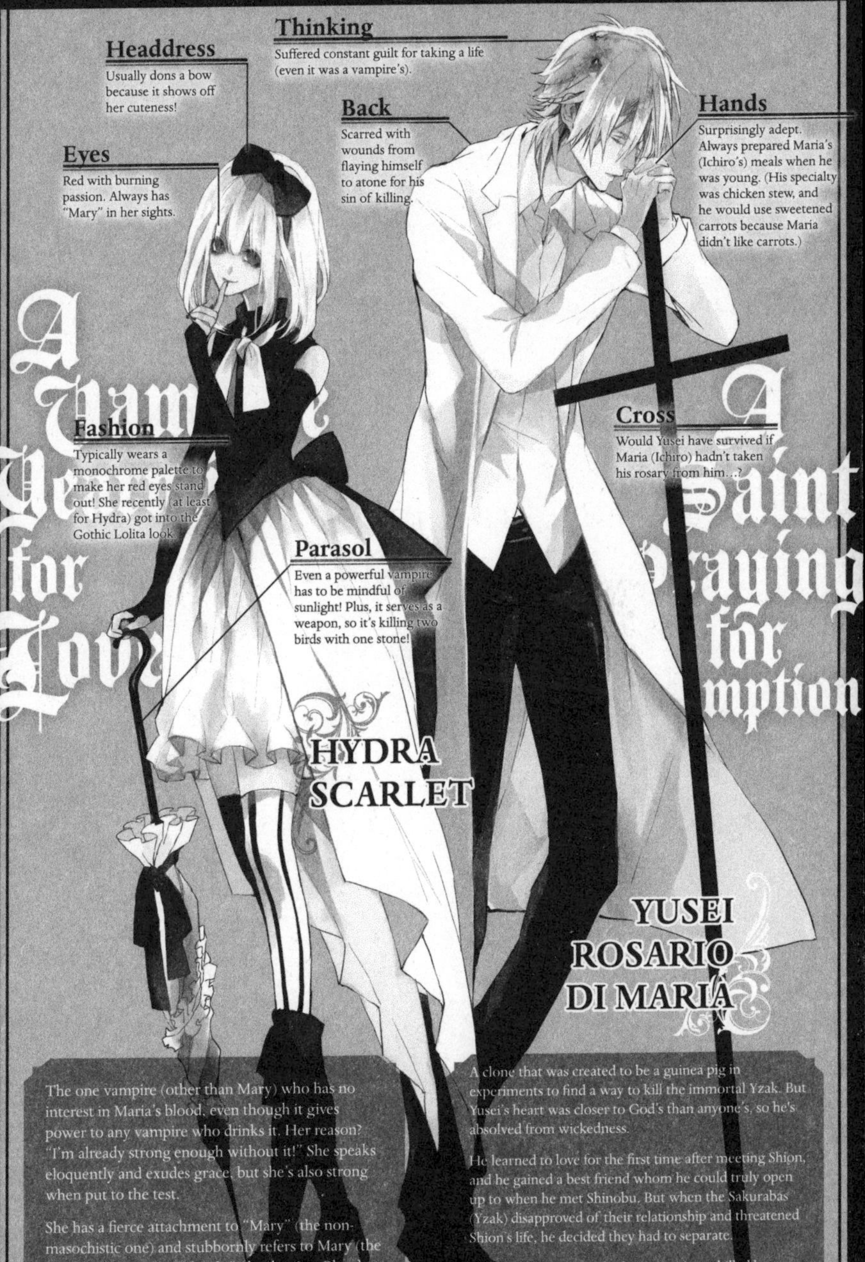
Thinking
Suffered constant guilt for taking a life (even it was a vampire's).
Headdress
Usually dons a bow because it shows off her cuteness!
Back
Scarred with wounds from flaying himself to atone for his sin of killing.
Hands
Surprisingly adept. Always prepared Maria's (Ichiro's) meals when he was young. (His specialty was chicken stew, and he would use sweetened carrots because Maria didn't like carrots.)
Eyes
Red with burning passion. Always has "Mary" in her sights.
Fashion
Typically wears a monochrome palette to make her red eyes stand out! She recently (at least for Hydra) got into the Gothic Lolita look.
Cross
Would Yusei have survived if Maria (Ichiro) hadn't taken his rosary from him...?
Parasol
Even a powerful vampire has to be mindful of sunlight! Plus, it serves as a weapon, so it's killing two birds with one stone!
HYDRA SCARLET
YUSEI ROSARIO DI MARIA

The one vampire (other than Mary) who has no interest in Maria's blood, even though it gives power to any vampire who drinks it. Her reason? "I'm already strong enough without it!" She speaks eloquently and exudes grace, but she's also strong when put to the test.

She has a fierce attachment to "Mary" (the non-masochistic one) and stubbornly refers to Mary (the masochistic one) as "Bloody." She despises Bloody and wishes he were dead!

A clone that was created to be a guinea pig in experiments to find a way to kill the immortal Yzak. But Yusei's heart was closer to God's than anyone's, so he's absolved from wickedness.

He learned to love for the first time after meeting Shion, and he gained a best friend whom he could truly open up to when he met Shinobu. But when the Sakurabas (Yzak) disapproved of their relationship and threatened Shion's life, he decided they had to separate.

After parting ways with Shion, Yusei was killed by a mysterious red-haired vampire, but no one knows who it was.

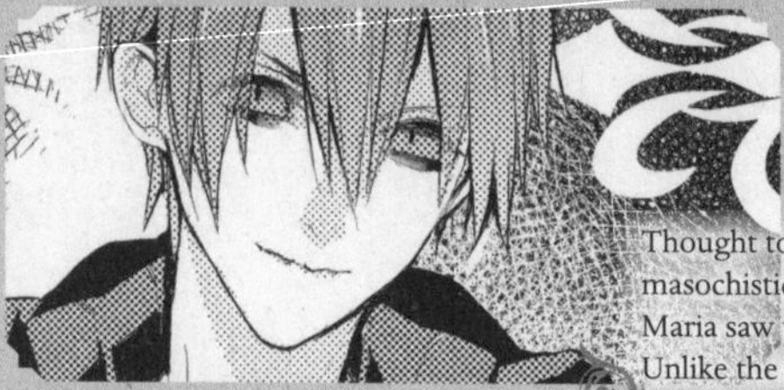

"MARY"

Thought to be an alter ego of Mary (the masochistic one). He's the red-haired vampire that Maria saw when he witnessed his father's murder. Unlike the regular (masochistic) Mary, this "Mary" doesn't wear his hoodie up (thus, no cat ears). He speaks with an attitude, isn't an idiot and definitely isn't a masochist! ← Key difference!

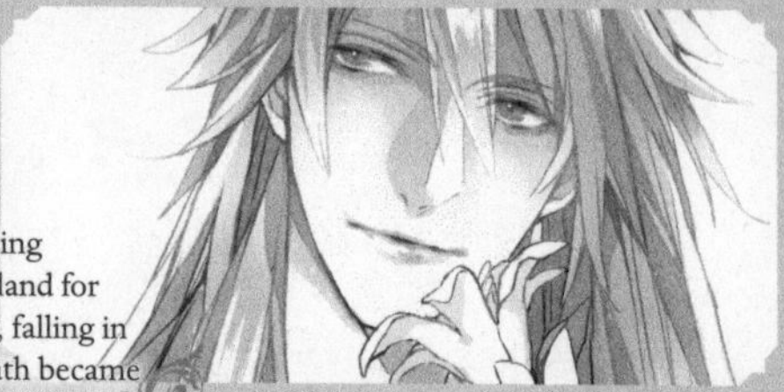

YZAK

Spent centuries of his immortal life exorcising vampires and was revered throughout England for all the lives he saved. But after meeting Yui, falling in love, and then losing her, joining her in death became his one and only goal. These mad thoughts drove him to create his clone Yusei and conduct countless death experiments on him.

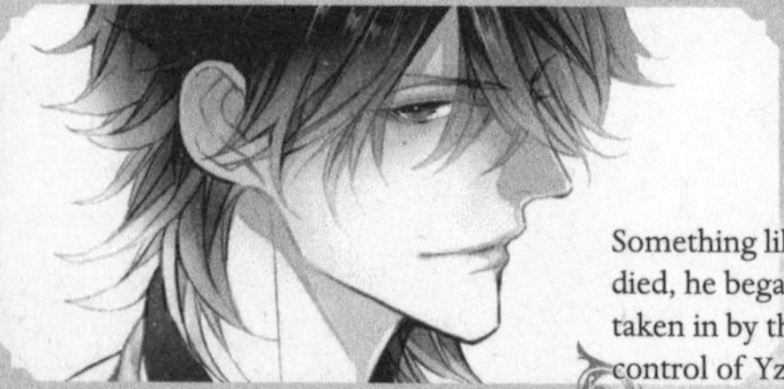

TAKUMI SAKURABA

Something like an older brother to Maria. After Yusei died, he began to look out for Maria, who had been taken in by the Sakurabas. He was once under the control of Yzak and betrayed Maria, but now he's intent on uncovering the dubious actions of Yzak and the Sakuraba family. He's guided by a strong sense of right and wrong.

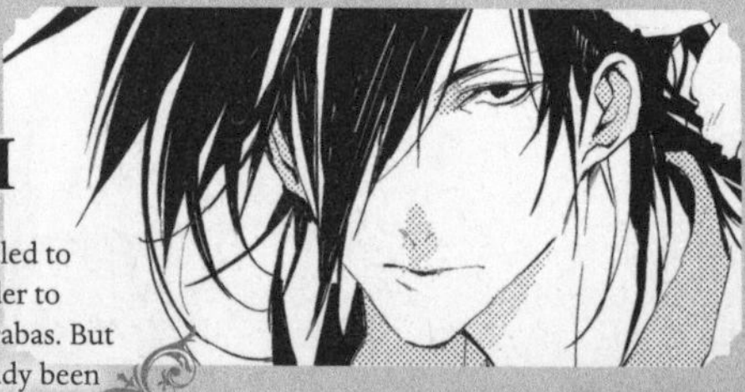

SHINOBU YUKI

Maria's uncle (his mother's brother). Traveled to England to undergo intense training in order to protect Yusei from vampires and the Sakurabas. But when he returned to Japan, Yusei had already been killed, so now he does whatever he can to protect Maria instead.

Bloody†Mary

SO, BASICALLY, THIS ISN'T REALLY A YOKOHOMA STORY ANYMORE— *Mmph*

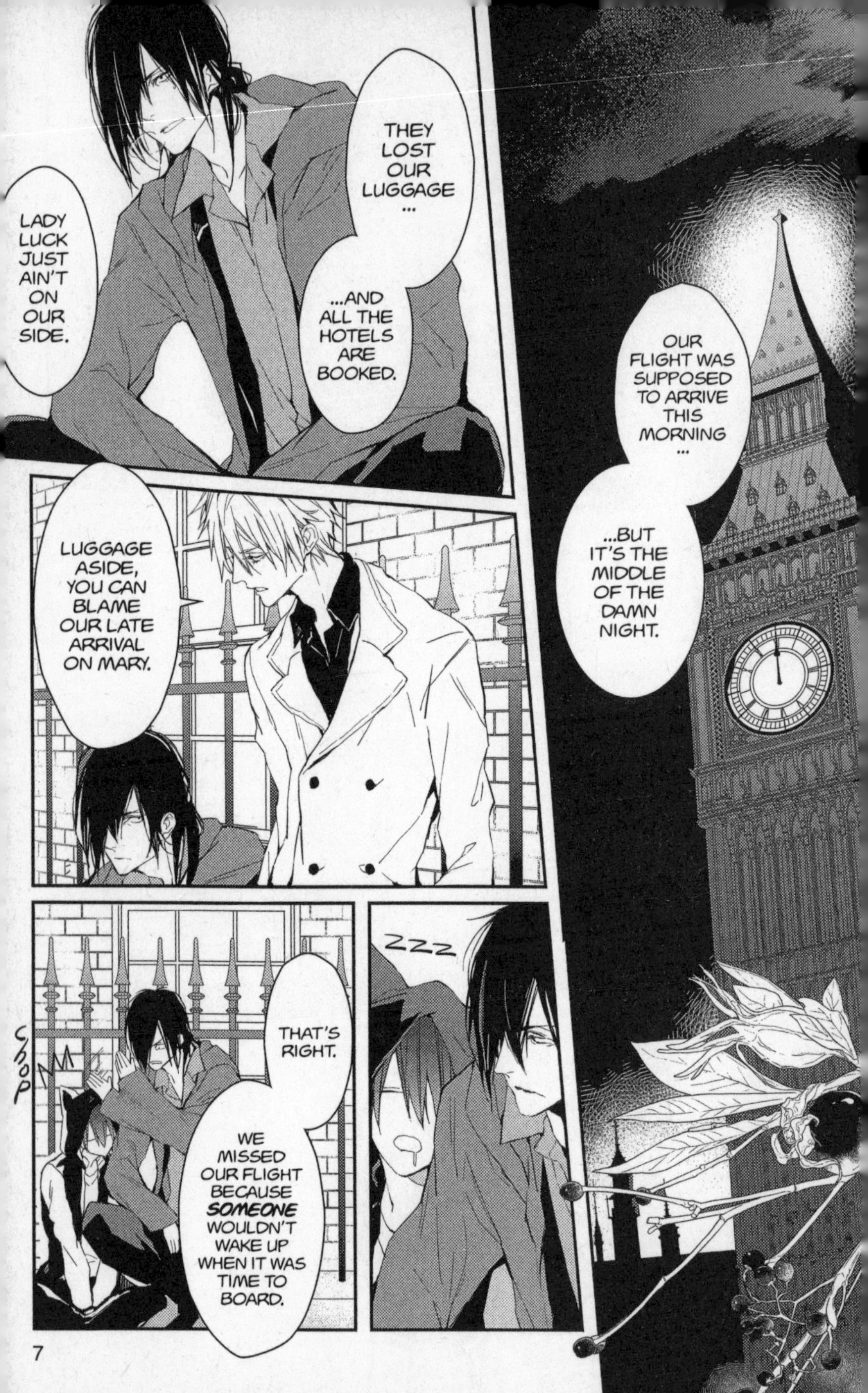
OUR FLIGHT WAS SUPPOSED TO ARRIVE THIS MORNING...
...BUT IT'S THE MIDDLE OF THE DAMN NIGHT.
THEY LOST OUR LUGGAGE...
...AND ALL THE HOTELS ARE BOOKED.
LADY LUCK JUST AIN'T ON OUR SIDE.
LUGGAGE ASIDE, YOU CAN BLAME OUR LATE ARRIVAL ON MARY.
ZZZ
THAT'S RIGHT.
WE MISSED OUR FLIGHT BECAUSE ***SOMEONE*** WOULDN'T WAKE UP WHEN IT WAS TIME TO BOARD.
CHOP

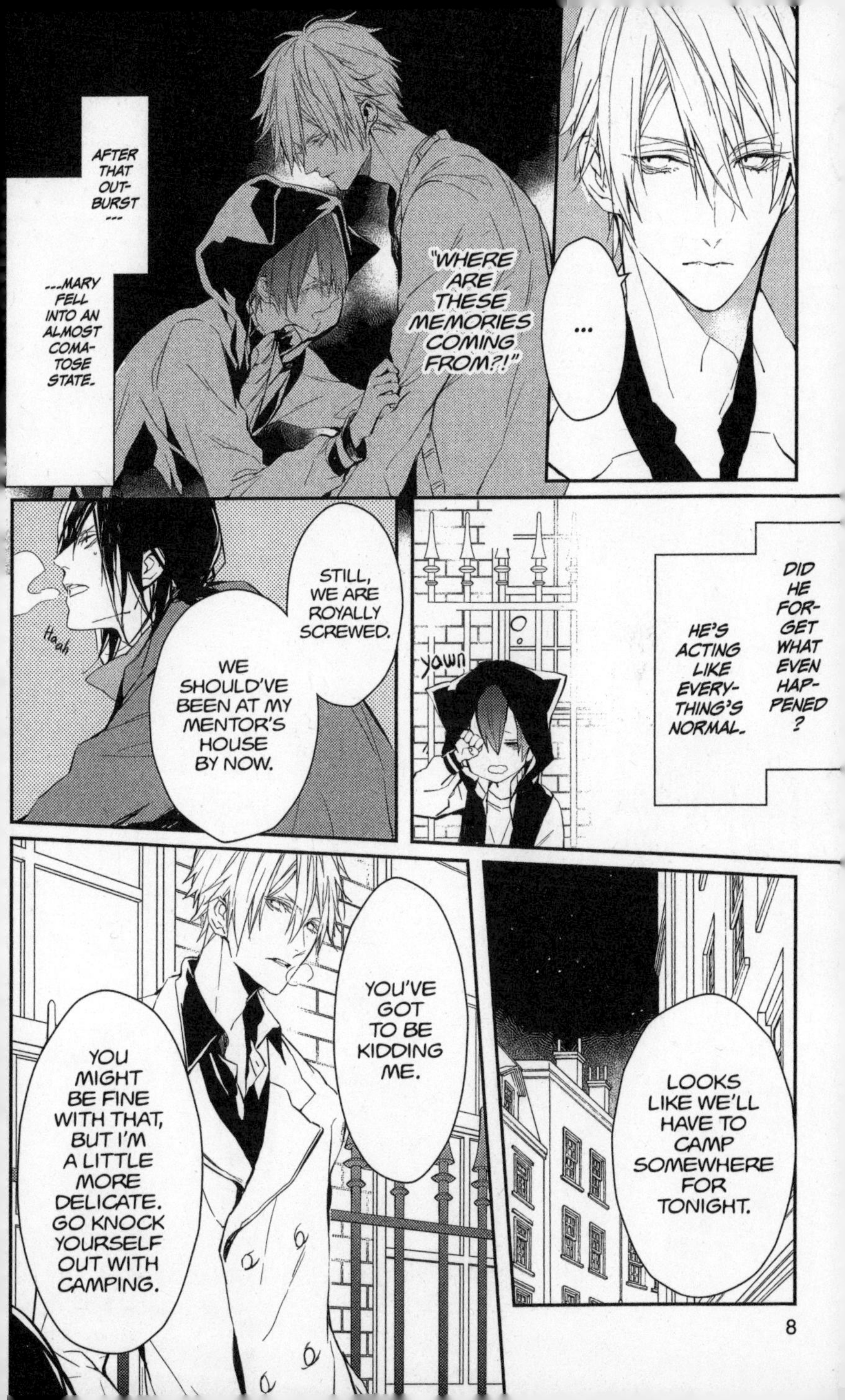
...
AFTER THAT OUT-BURST---
"WHERE ARE THESE MEMORIES COMING FROM?!"
---MARY FELL INTO AN ALMOST COMA-TOSE STATE.
DID HE FOR-GET WHAT EVEN HAP-PENED?
HE'S ACTING LIKE EVERY-THING'S NORMAL.
yawn
STILL, WE ARE ROYALLY SCREWED.
WE SHOULD'VE BEEN AT MY MENTOR'S HOUSE BY NOW.
Haah
LOOKS LIKE WE'LL HAVE TO CAMP SOMEWHERE FOR TONIGHT.
YOU'VE GOT TO BE KIDDING ME.
YOU MIGHT BE FINE WITH THAT, BUT I'M A LITTLE MORE DELICATE. GO KNOCK YOURSELF OUT WITH CAMPING.

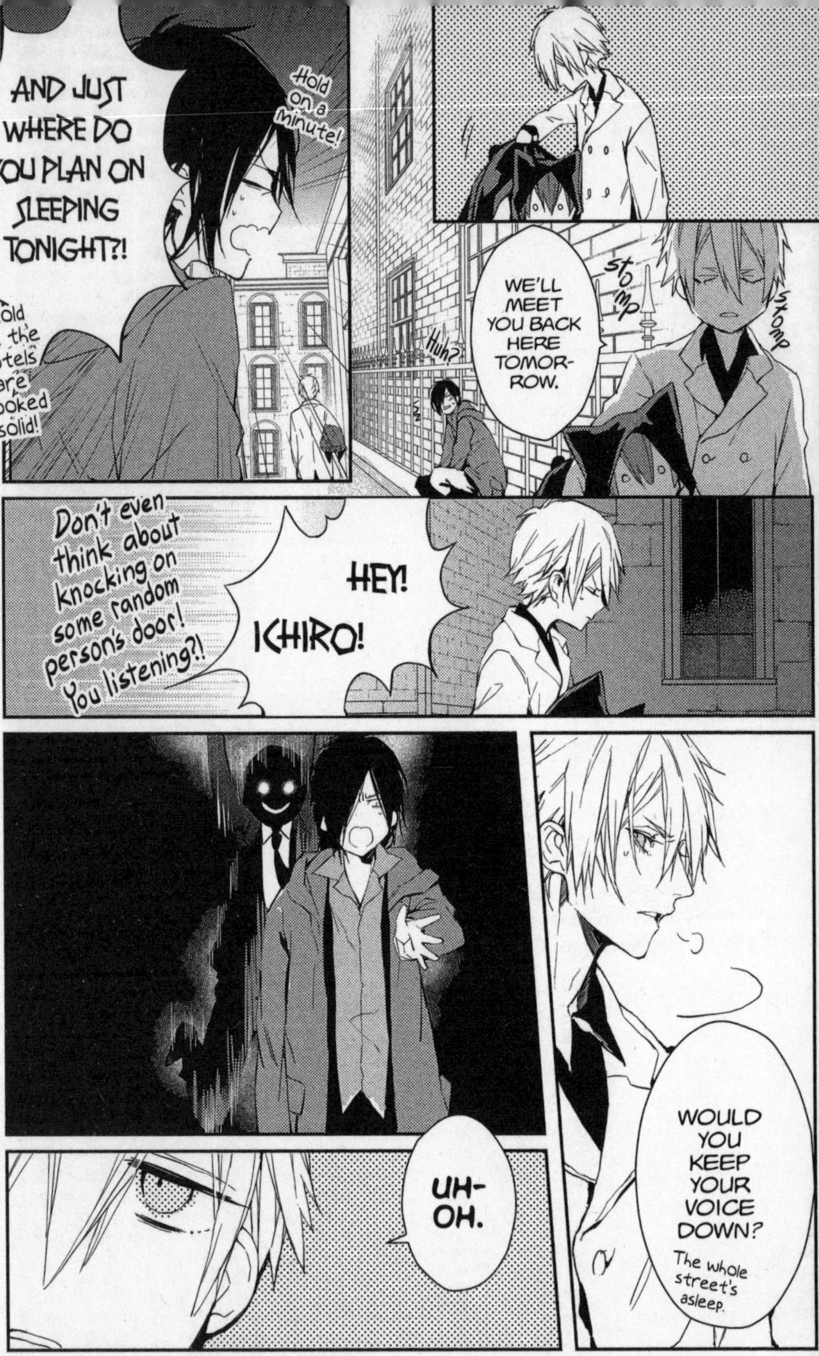
stomp
WE'LL MEET YOU BACK HERE TOMORROW.
Huh?
stomp
AND JUST WHERE DO YOU PLAN ON SLEEPING TONIGHT?!
Hold on a minute!
I told you the hotels are booked solid!
HEY! ICHIRO!
Don't even think about knocking on some random person's door! You listening?!
WOULD YOU KEEP YOUR VOICE DOWN?
The whole street's asleep.
UH-OH.

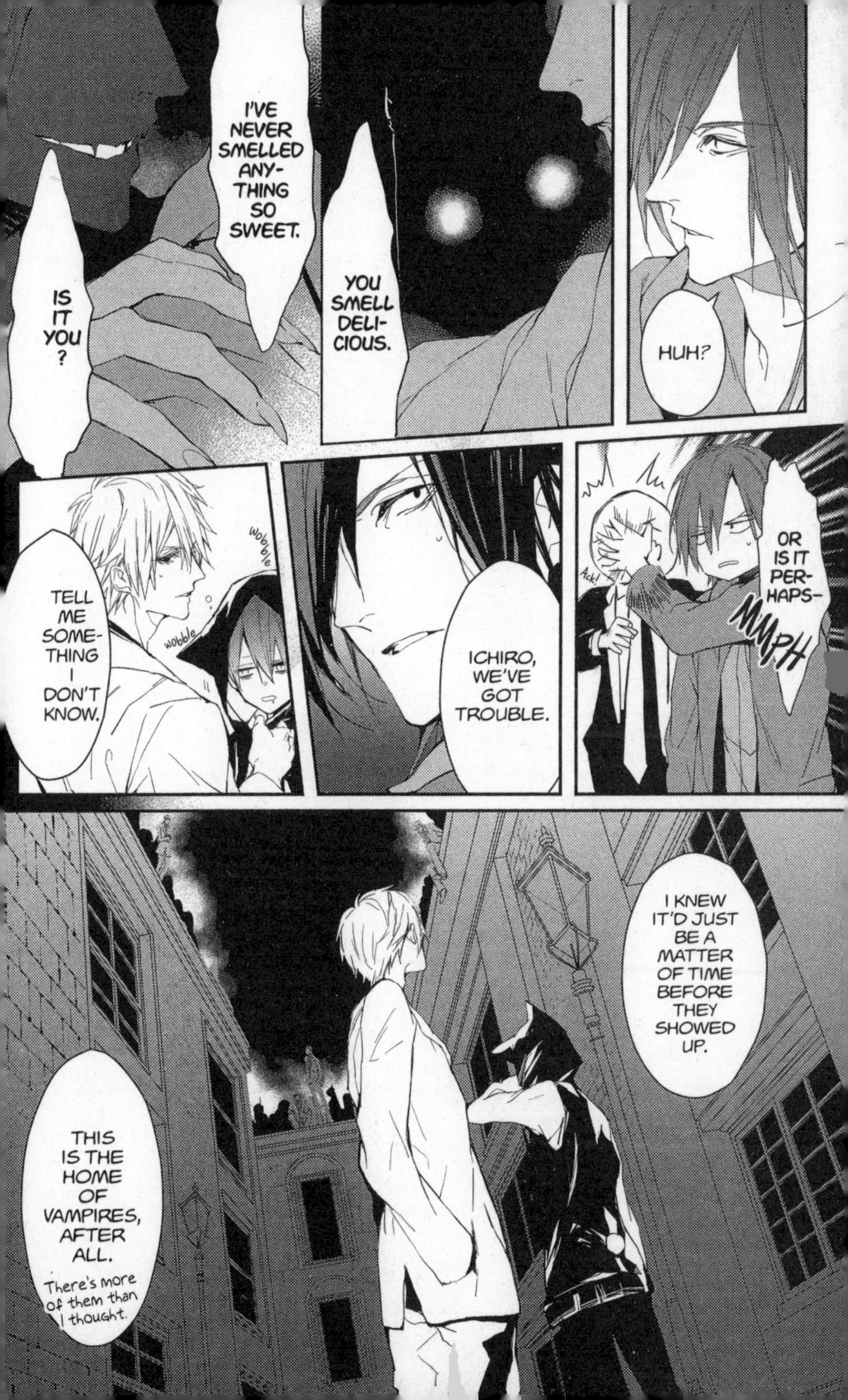
HUH?
YOU SMELL DELICIOUS.
I'VE NEVER SMELLED ANYTHING SO SWEET.
IS IT YOU?
OR IS IT PERHAPS—
MMPH
Ack!
ICHIRO, WE'VE GOT TROUBLE.
wobble
wobble
TELL ME SOMETHING I DON'T KNOW.
I KNEW IT'D JUST BE A MATTER OF TIME BEFORE THEY SHOWED UP.
THIS IS THE HOME OF VAMPIRES, AFTER ALL.
There's more of them than I thought.

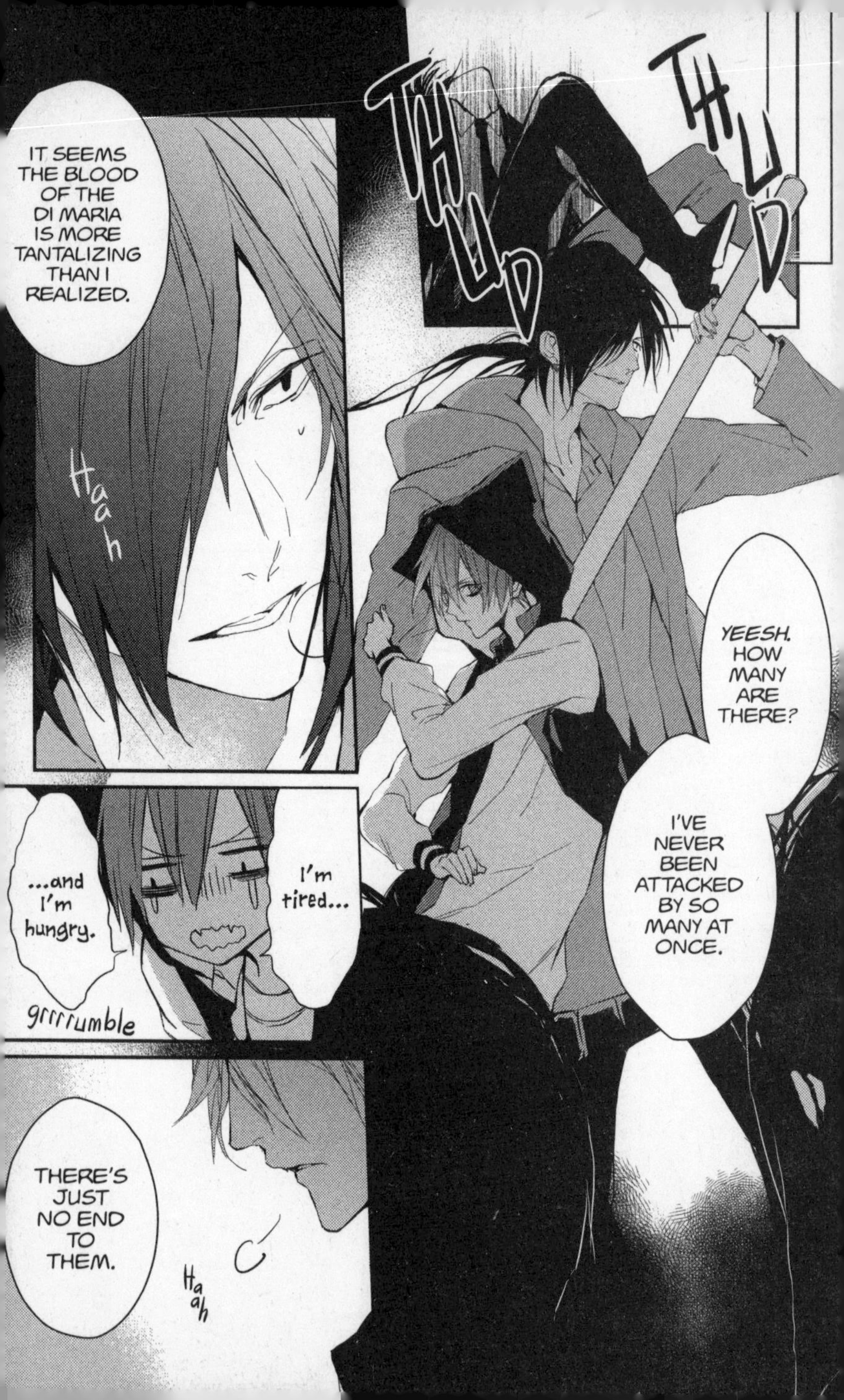
THUD
THUD
YEESH. HOW MANY ARE THERE?
I'VE NEVER BEEN ATTACKED BY SO MANY AT ONCE.
IT SEEMS THE BLOOD OF THE DI MARIA IS MORE TANTALIZING THAN I REALIZED.
Haah
I'm tired...
...and I'm hungry.
grrrrumble
THERE'S JUST NO END TO THEM.
Haah

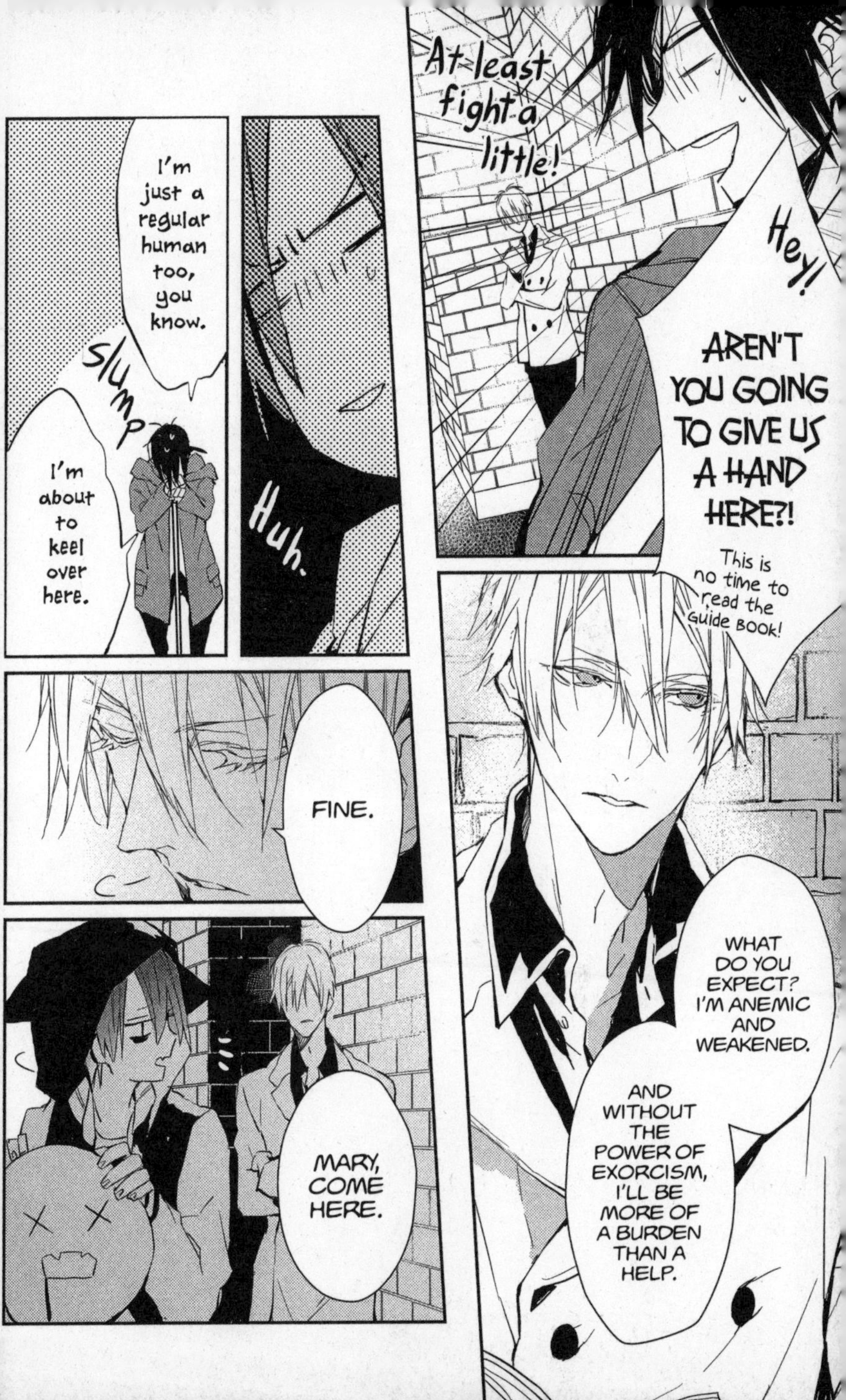
At least fight a little!
Hey!
AREN'T YOU GOING TO GIVE US A HAND HERE?!
This is no time to read the Guide Book!
WHAT DO YOU EXPECT? I'M ANEMIC AND WEAKENED.
AND WITHOUT THE POWER OF EXORCISM, I'LL BE MORE OF A BURDEN THAN A HELP.
Huh.
I'm just a regular human too, you know.
slump
I'm about to keel over here.
FINE.
MARY, COME HERE.

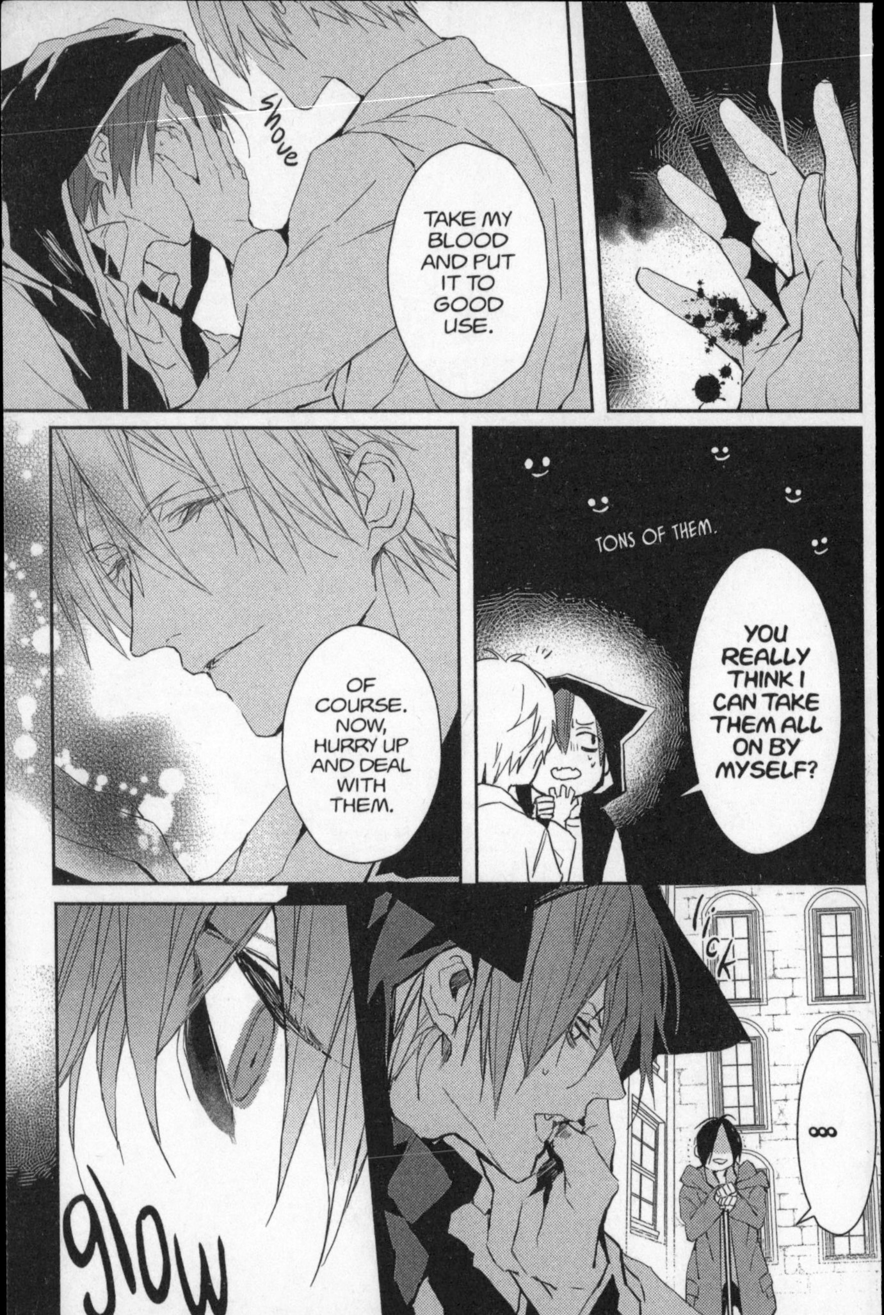
shove
TAKE MY BLOOD AND PUT IT TO GOOD USE.
TONS OF THEM.
YOU REALLY THINK I CAN TAKE THEM ALL ON BY MYSELF?
OF COURSE. NOW, HURRY UP AND DEAL WITH THEM.
lick
...
glow

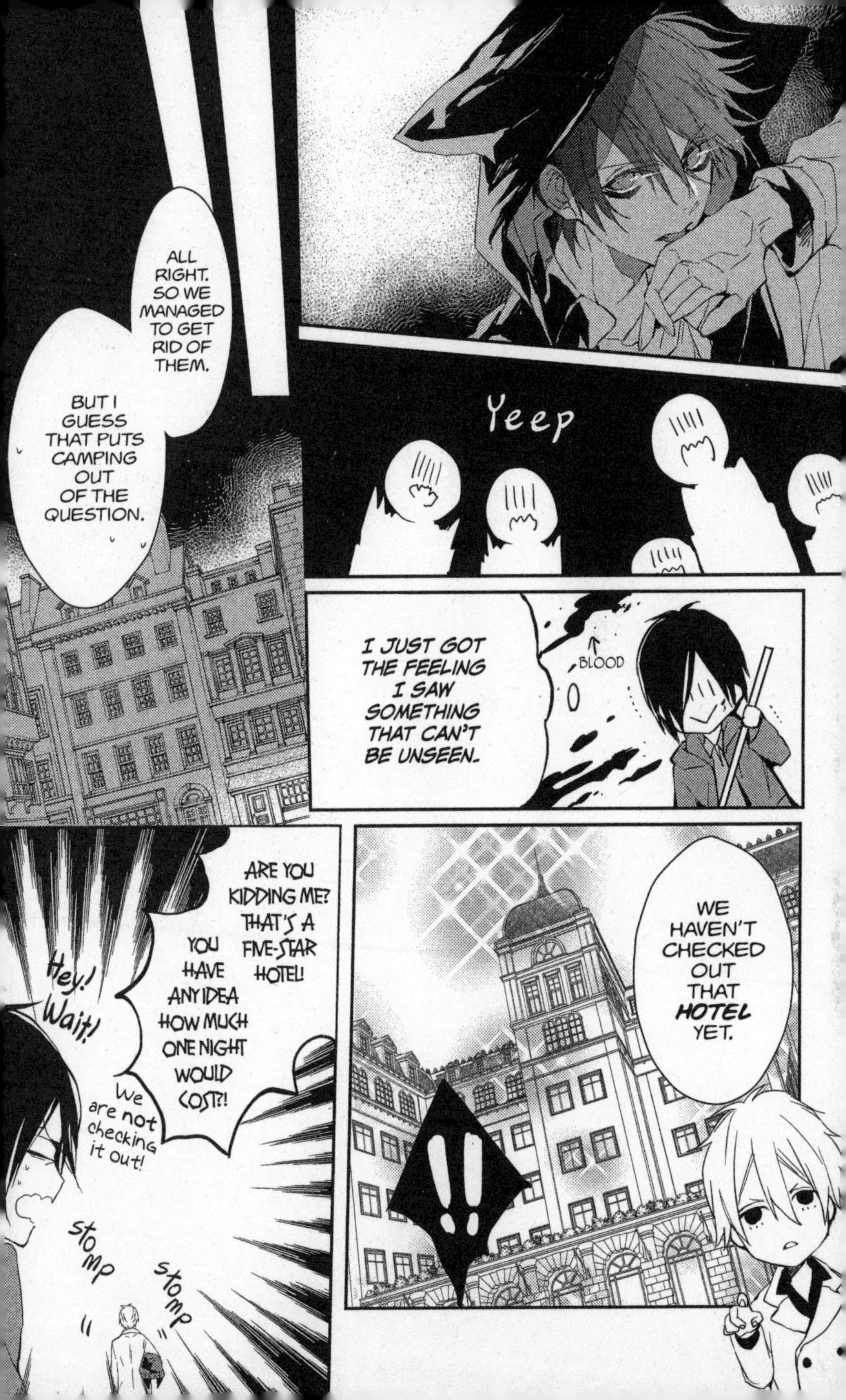
Yeep
I JUST GOT THE FEELING I SAW SOMETHING THAT CAN'T BE UNSEEN...
BLOOD
ALL RIGHT. SO WE MANAGED TO GET RID OF THEM.
BUT I GUESS THAT PUTS CAMPING OUT OF THE QUESTION.
WE HAVEN'T CHECKED OUT THAT HOTEL YET.
Hey! Wait!
ARE YOU KIDDING ME? THAT'S A FIVE-STAR HOTEL!
YOU HAVE ANY IDEA HOW MUCH ONE NIGHT WOULD COST?!
We are not checking it out!
stomp
stomp

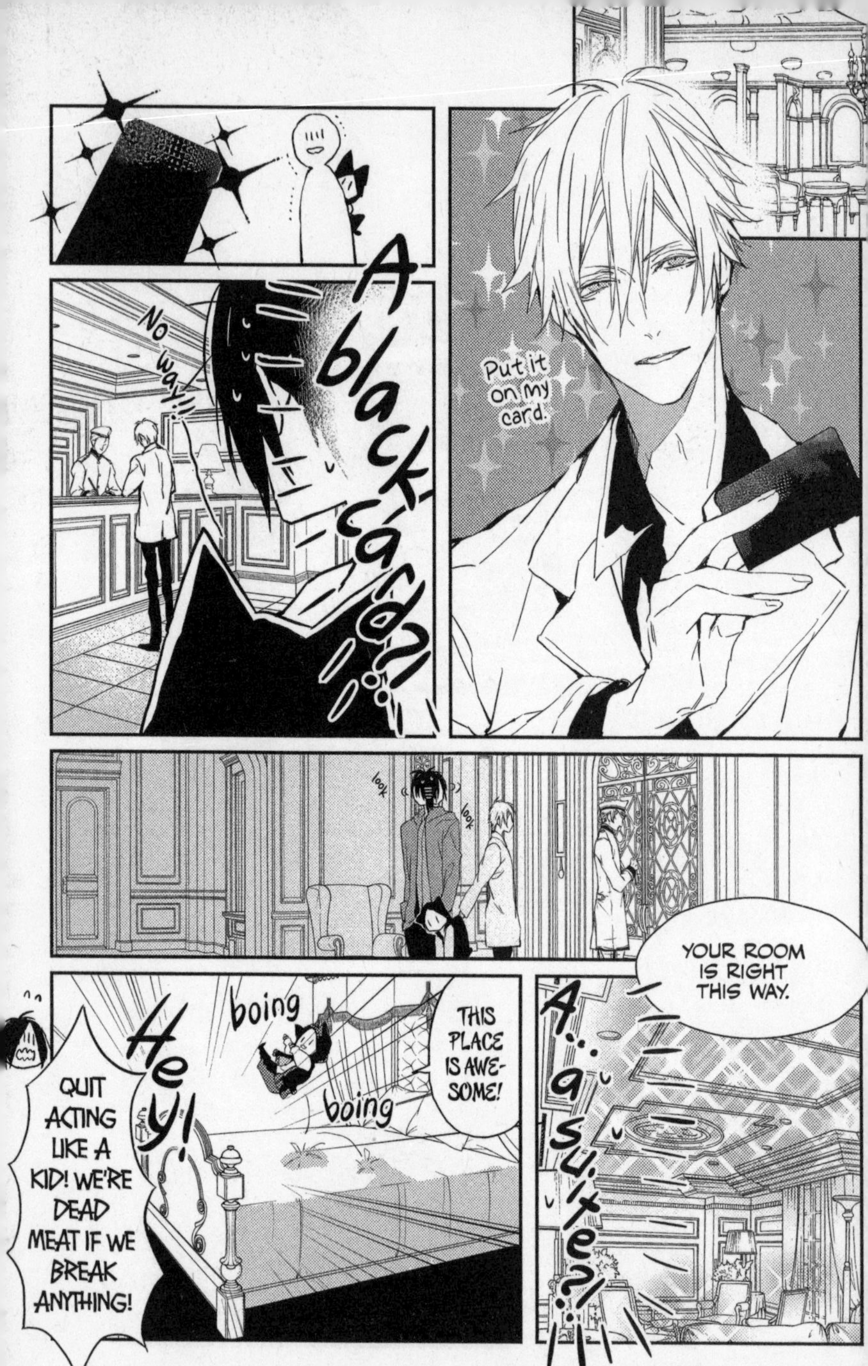
Put it on my card.
A black card?!
No way...!
look
look
YOUR ROOM IS RIGHT THIS WAY.
A... a suite?!
THIS PLACE IS AWESOME!
boing
boing
Hey!
QUIT ACTING LIKE A KID! WE'RE DEAD MEAT IF WE BREAK ANYTHING!

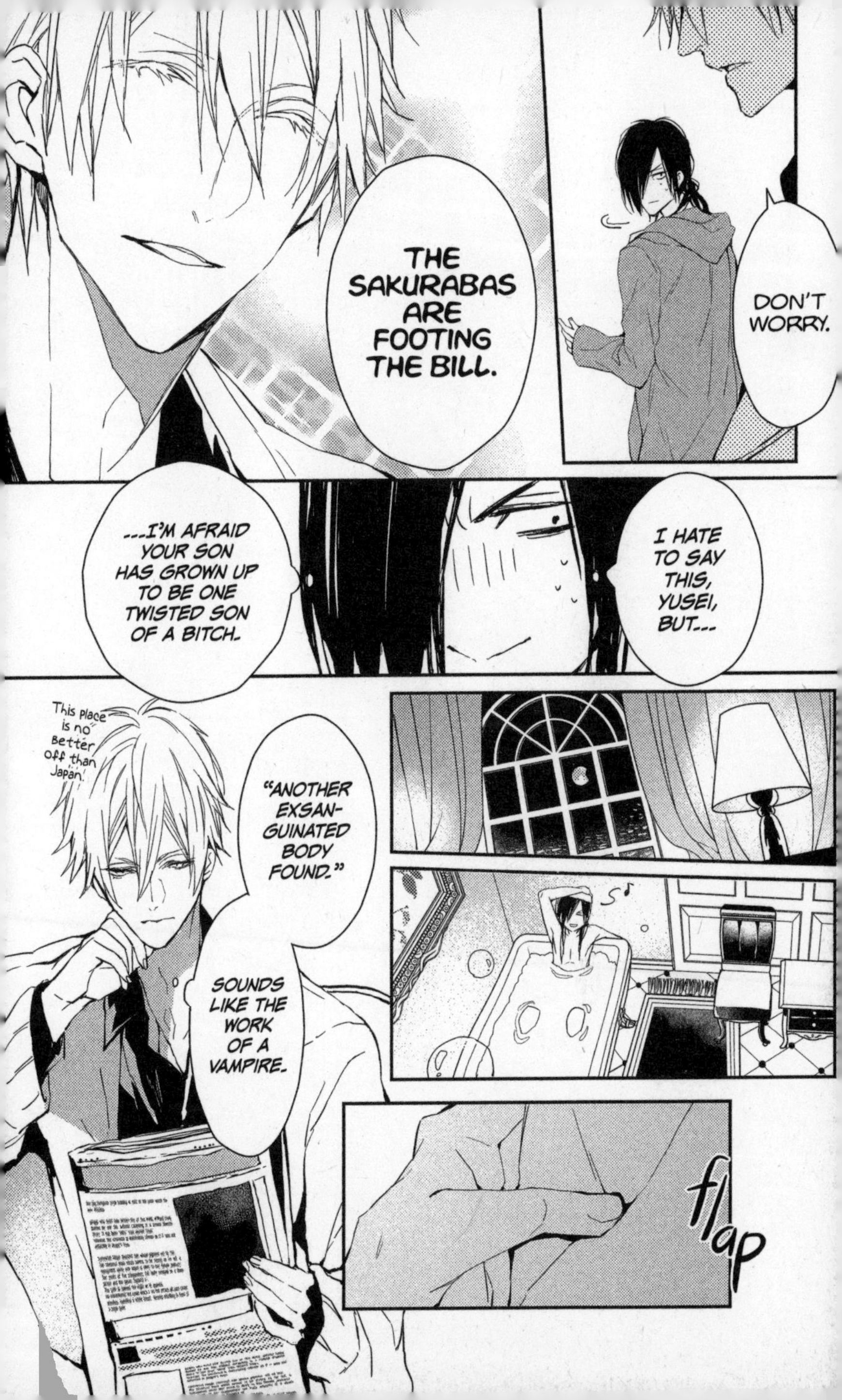
DON'T WORRY.
THE SAKURABAS ARE FOOTING THE BILL.
I HATE TO SAY THIS, YUSEI, BUT...
...I'M AFRAID YOUR SON HAS GROWN UP TO BE ONE TWISTED SON OF A BITCH.
flap
"ANOTHER EXSAN-GUINATED BODY FOUND."
This place is no better off than Japan.
SOUNDS LIKE THE WORK OF A VAMPIRE.

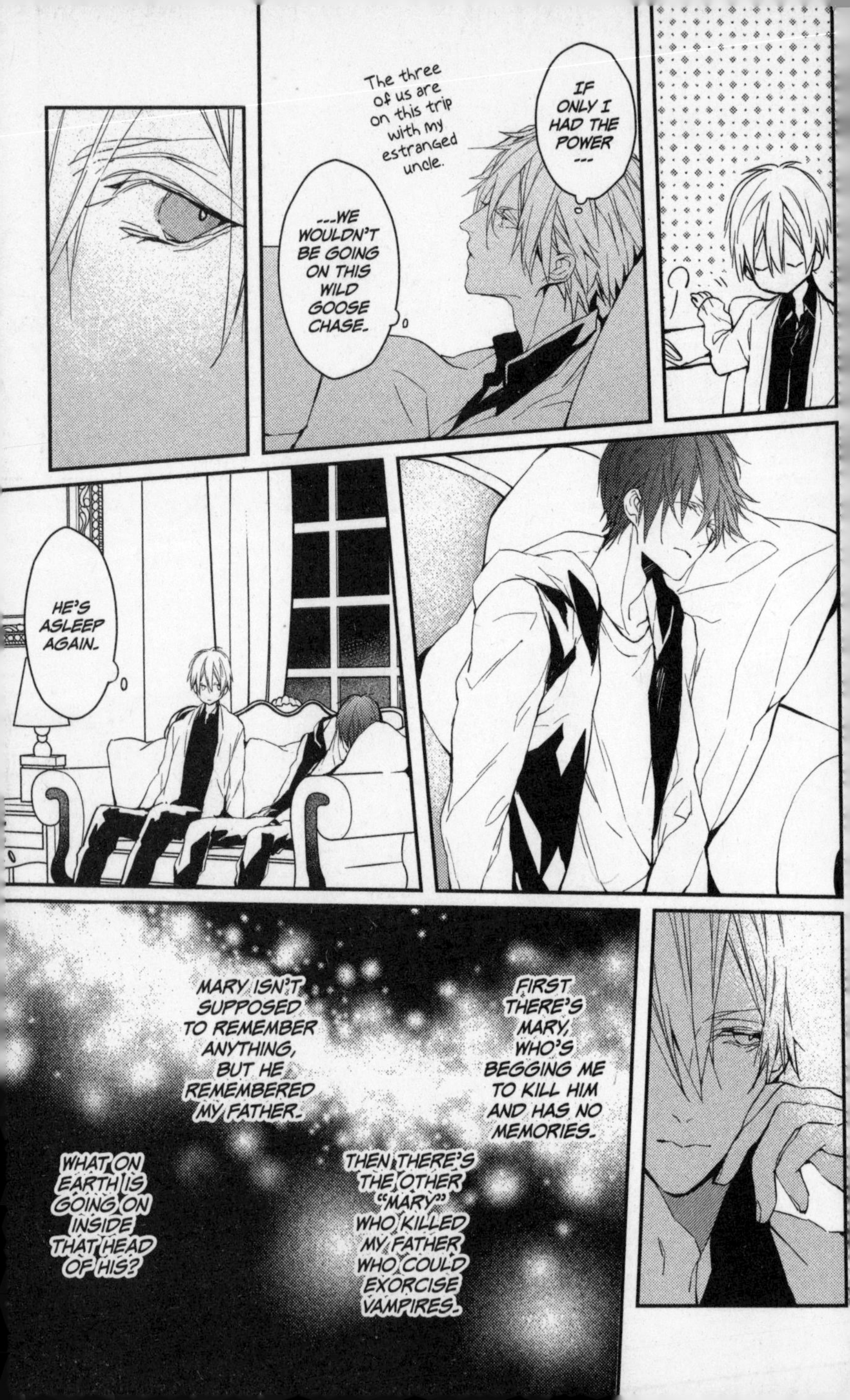
IF ONLY I HAD THE POWER ---
The three of us are on this trip with my estranged uncle.
---WE WOULDN'T BE GOING ON THIS WILD GOOSE CHASE.
HE'S ASLEEP AGAIN.
FIRST THERE'S MARY, WHO'S BEGGING ME TO KILL HIM AND HAS NO MEMORIES.
MARY ISN'T SUPPOSED TO REMEMBER ANYTHING, BUT HE REMEMBERED MY FATHER.
THEN THERE'S THE OTHER "MARY" WHO KILLED MY FATHER WHO COULD EXORCISE VAMPIRES.
WHAT ON EARTH IS GOING ON INSIDE THAT HEAD OF HIS?

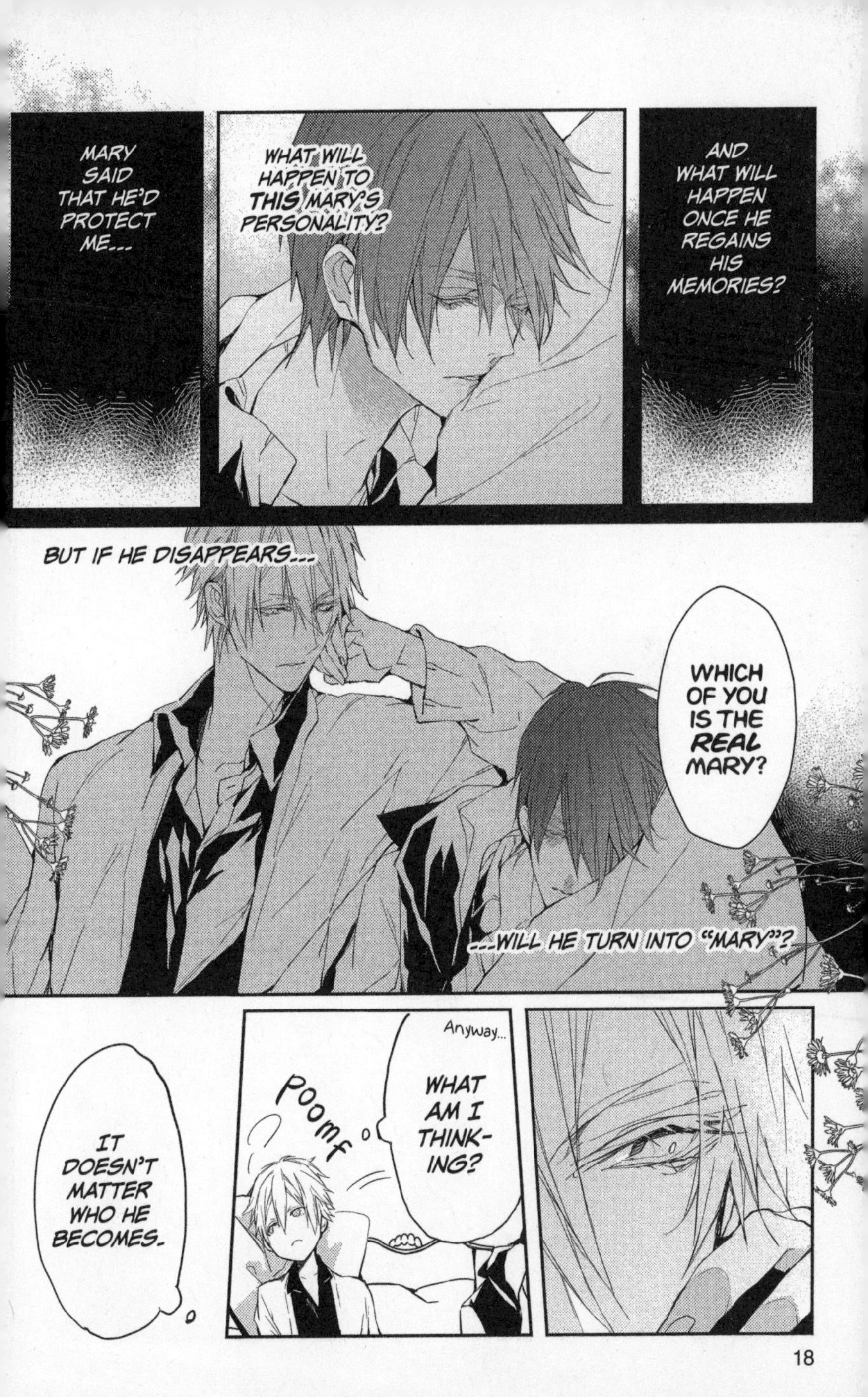
MARY SAID THAT HE'D PROTECT ME...
WHAT WILL HAPPEN TO THIS MARY'S PERSONALITY?
AND WHAT WILL HAPPEN ONCE HE REGAINS HIS MEMORIES?
BUT IF HE DISAPPEARS...
...WILL HE TURN INTO "MARY"?
WHICH OF YOU IS THE REAL MARY?
Poomf
Anyway...
WHAT AM I THINKING?
IT DOESN'T MATTER WHO HE BECOMES.

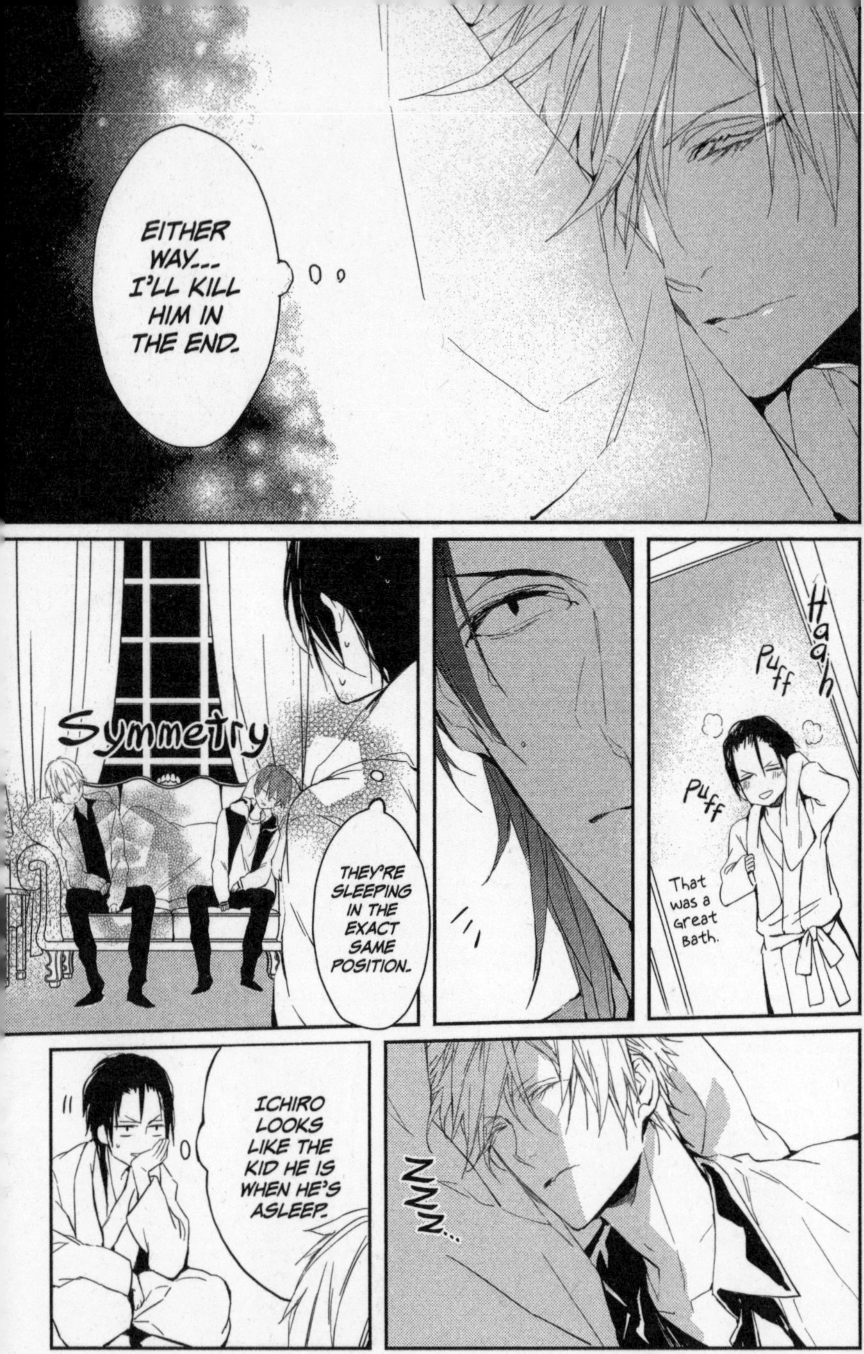
EITHER WAY... I'LL KILL HIM IN THE END.
Haah
Puff
Puff
That was a Great Bath.
THEY'RE SLEEPING IN THE EXACT SAME POSITION.
Symmetry
ZZZ...
ICHIRO LOOKS LIKE THE KID HE IS WHEN HE'S ASLEEP.

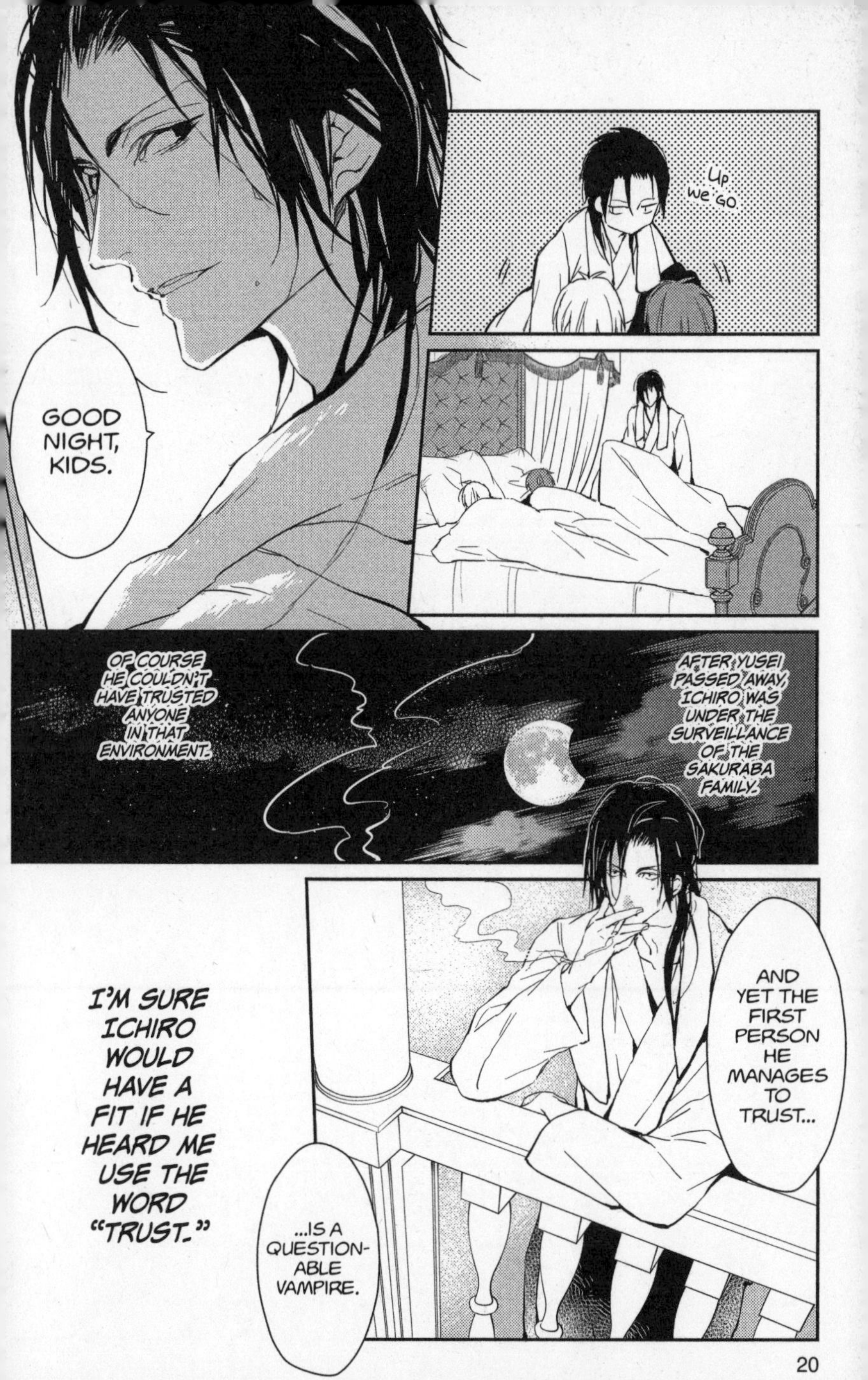
Up we go
GOOD NIGHT, KIDS.
AFTER YUSEI PASSED AWAY, ICHIRO WAS UNDER THE SURVEILLANCE OF THE SAKURABA FAMILY.
OF COURSE HE COULDN'T HAVE TRUSTED ANYONE IN THAT ENVIRONMENT.
AND YET THE FIRST PERSON HE FIRST MANAGES TO TRUST...
...IS A QUESTION-ABLE VAMPIRE.
I'M SURE ICHIRO WOULD HAVE A FIT IF HE HEARD ME USE THE WORD "TRUST."

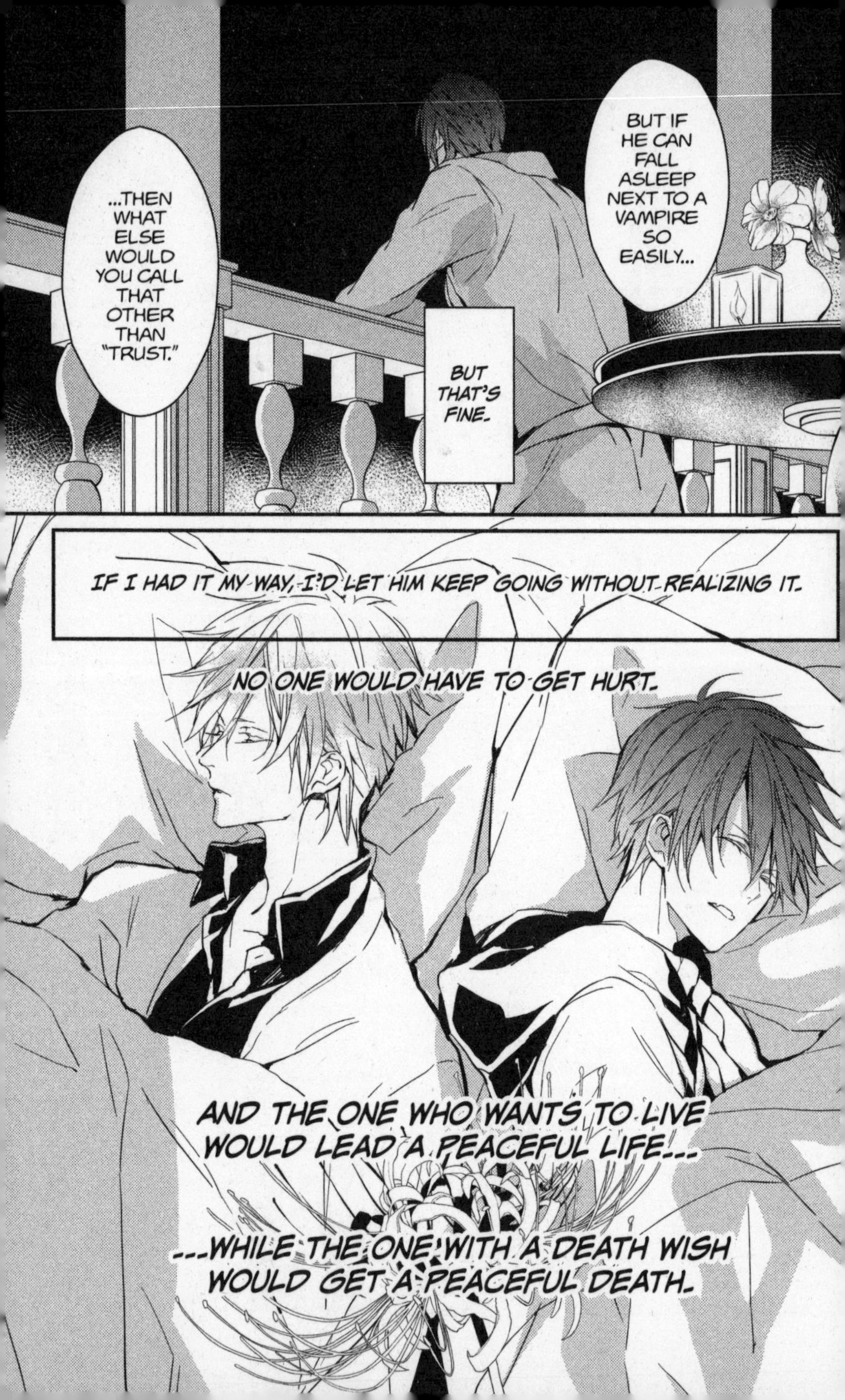
BUT IF HE CAN FALL ASLEEP NEXT TO A VAMPIRE SO EASILY...
...THEN WHAT ELSE WOULD YOU CALL THAT OTHER THAN "TRUST."
BUT THAT'S FINE.
IF I HAD IT MY WAY, I'D LET HIM KEEP GOING WITHOUT REALIZING IT.
NO ONE WOULD HAVE TO GET HURT.
AND THE ONE WHO WANTS TO LIVE WOULD LEAD A PEACEFUL LIFE...
...WHILE THE ONE WITH A DEATH WISH WOULD GET A PEACEFUL DEATH.

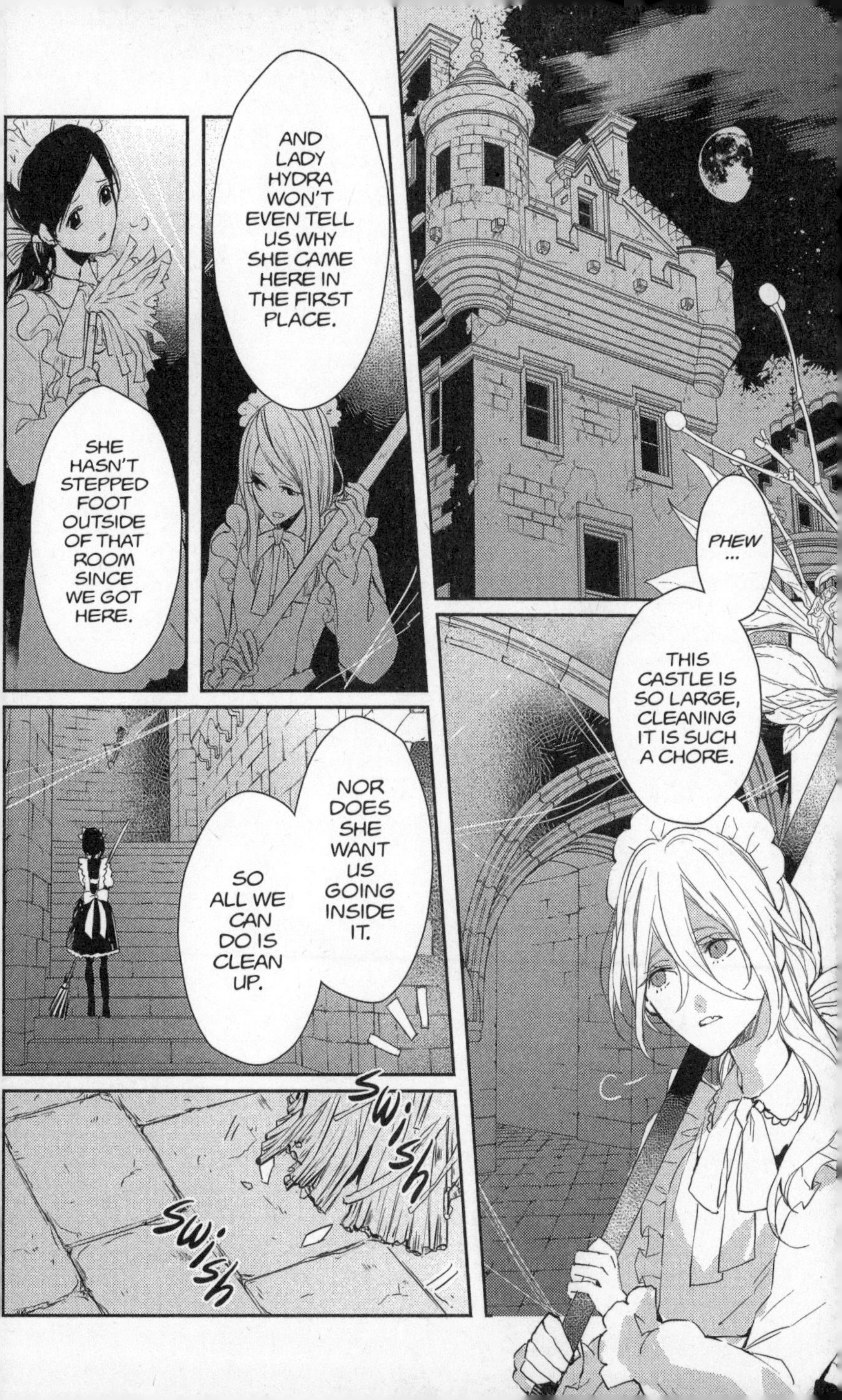
PHEW...
THIS CASTLE IS SO LARGE, CLEANING IT IS SUCH A CHORE.
AND LADY HYDRA WON'T EVEN TELL US WHY SHE CAME HERE IN THE FIRST PLACE.
SHE HASN'T STEPPED FOOT OUTSIDE OF THAT ROOM SINCE WE GOT HERE.
NOR DOES SHE WANT US GOING INSIDE IT.
SO ALL WE CAN DO IS CLEAN UP.
SWISH
SWISH

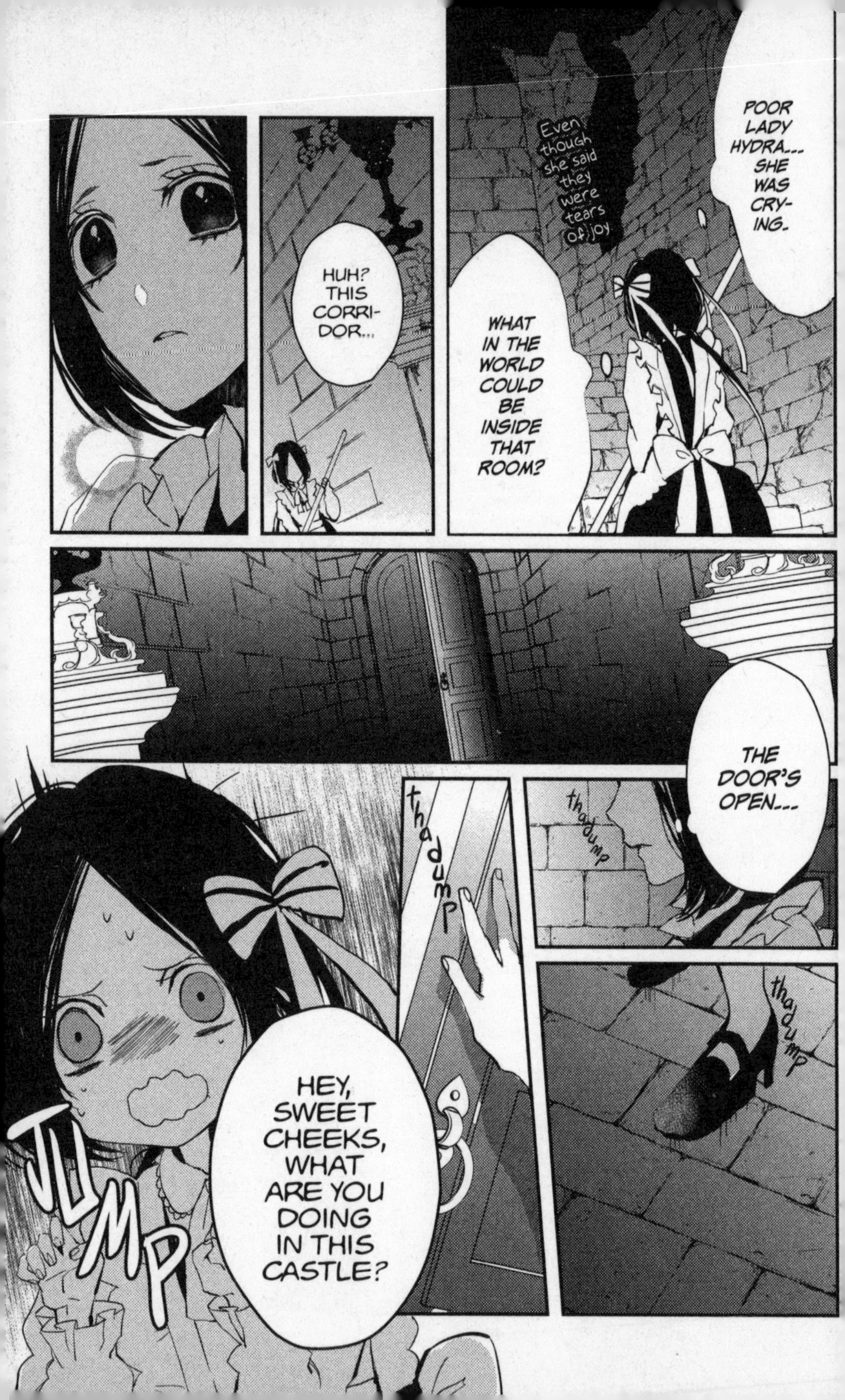
POOR LADY HYDRA... SHE WAS CRY-ING.
Even though she said they were tears of joy
WHAT IN THE WORLD COULD BE INSIDE THAT ROOM?
HUH? THIS CORRI-DOR...
THE DOOR'S OPEN...
thadump
thadump
thadump
JUMP
HEY, SWEET CHEEKS, WHAT ARE YOU DOING IN THIS CASTLE?

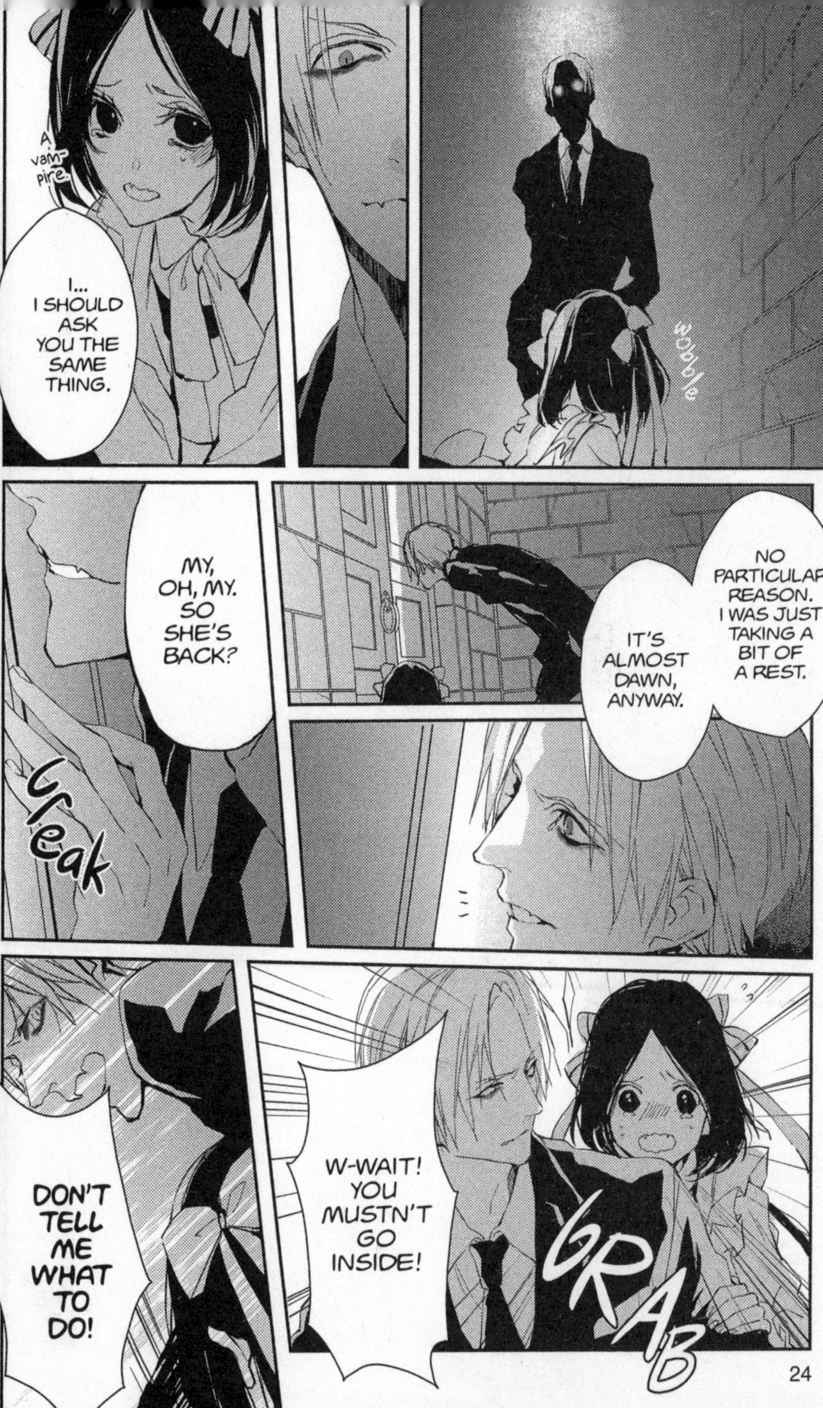
wobble
A vampire.
I... I SHOULD ASK YOU THE SAME THING.
NO PARTICULAR REASON. I WAS JUST TAKING A BIT OF A REST.
IT'S ALMOST DAWN, ANYWAY.
MY, OH, MY. SO SHE'S BACK?
creak
W-WAIT! YOU MUSTN'T GO INSIDE!
GRAB
DON'T TELL ME WHAT TO DO!

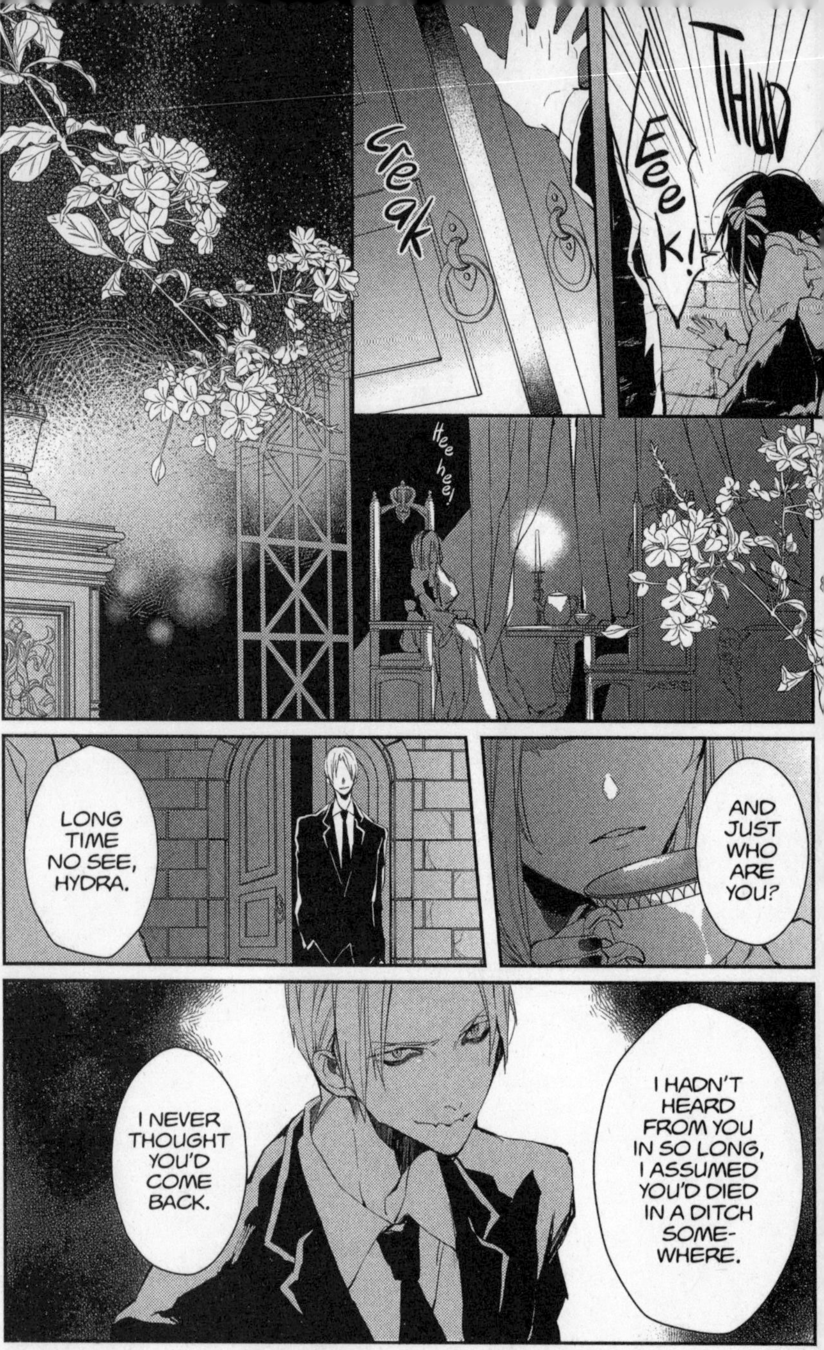
THUD
Eeek!
creak
Hee hee!
AND JUST WHO ARE YOU?
LONG TIME NO SEE, HYDRA.
I HADN'T HEARD FROM YOU IN SO LONG, I ASSUMED YOU'D DIED IN A DITCH SOME-WHERE.
I NEVER THOUGHT YOU'D COME BACK.

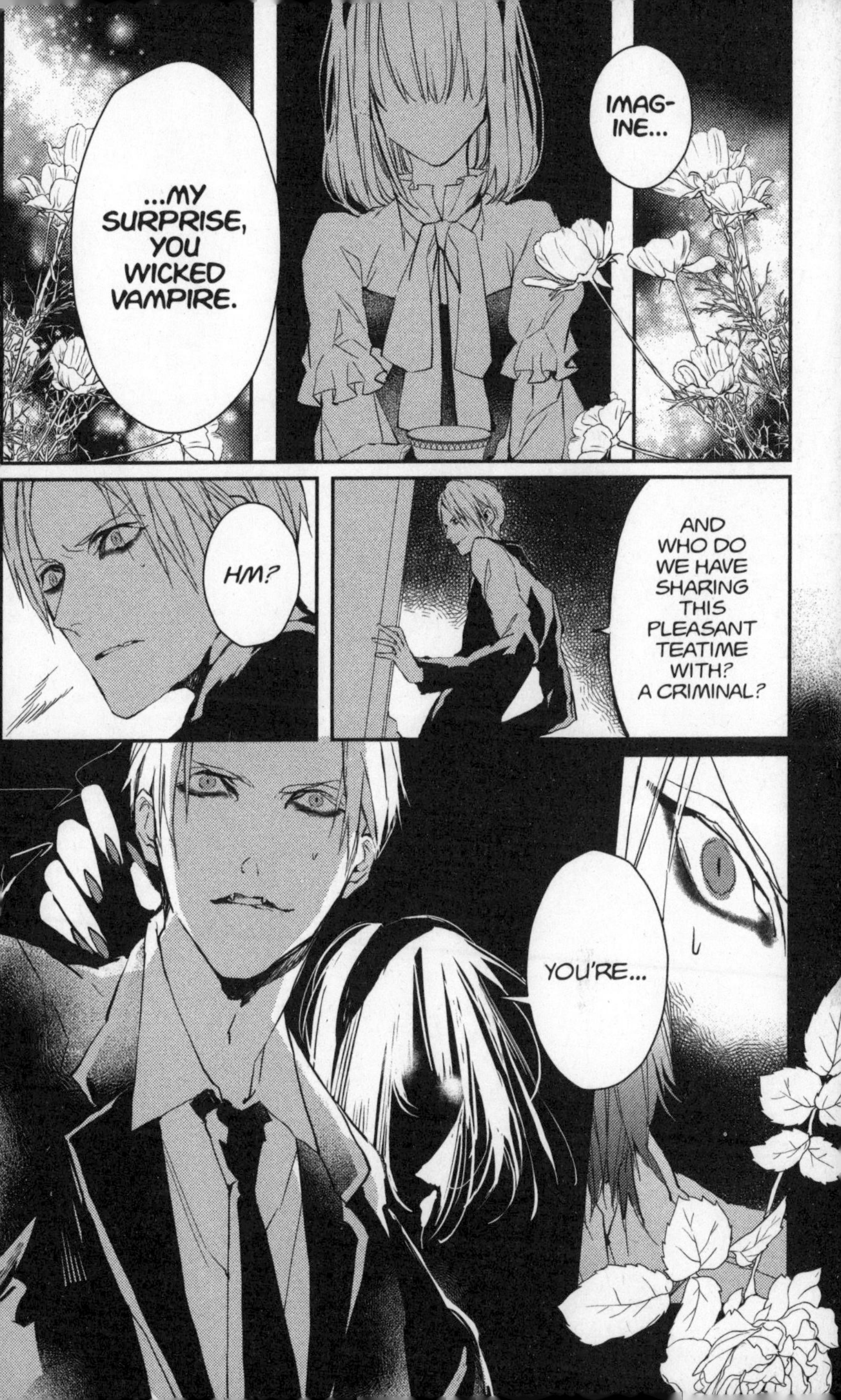
IMAGINE...
...MY SURPRISE, YOU WICKED VAMPIRE.
AND WHO DO WE HAVE SHARING THIS PLEASANT TEATIME WITH? A CRIMINAL?
HM?
YOU'RE...

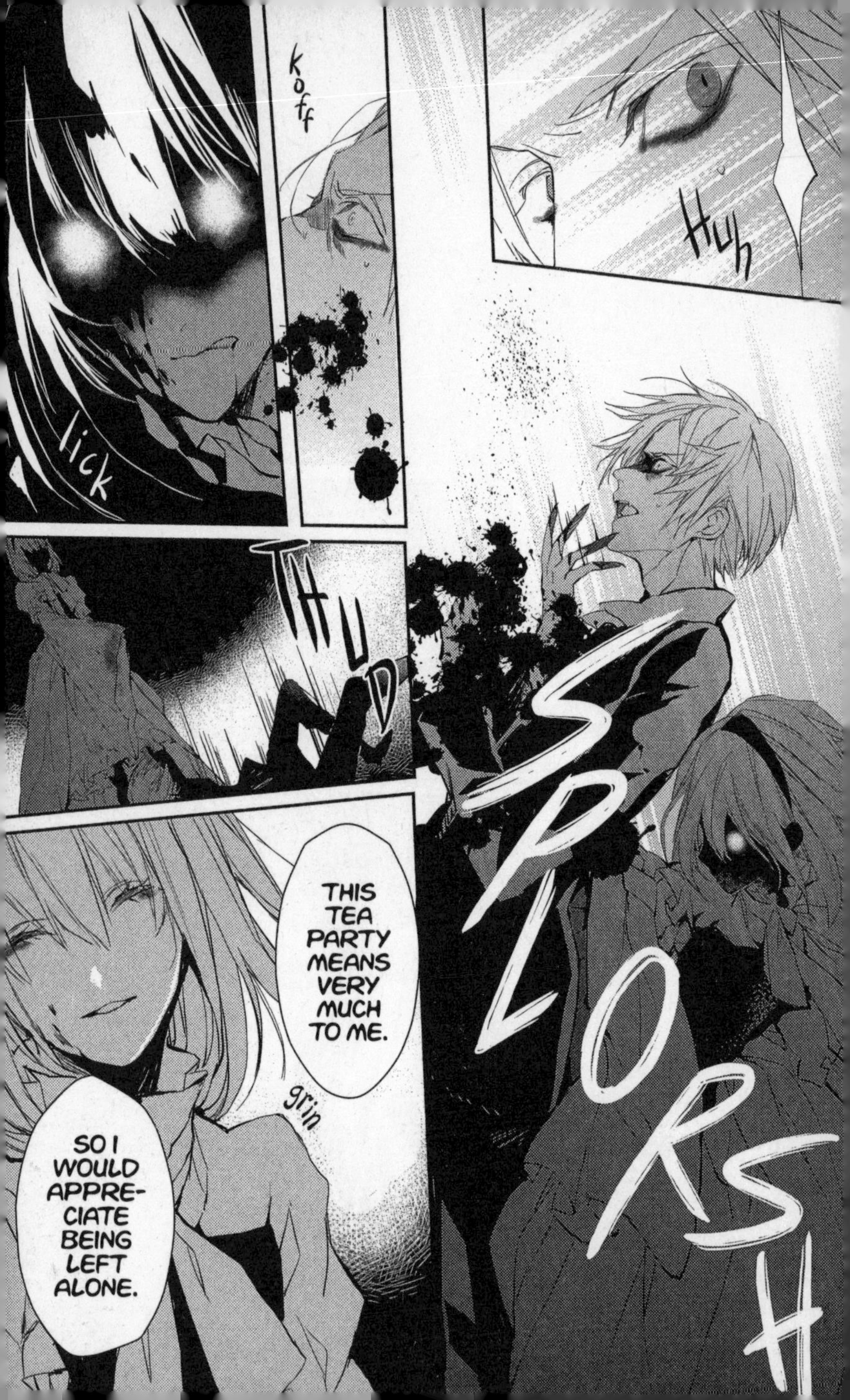
Huh
koff
lick
SPLORSH
THUD
THIS TEA PARTY MEANS VERY MUCH TO ME.
grin
SO I WOULD APPRECIATE BEING LEFT ALONE.

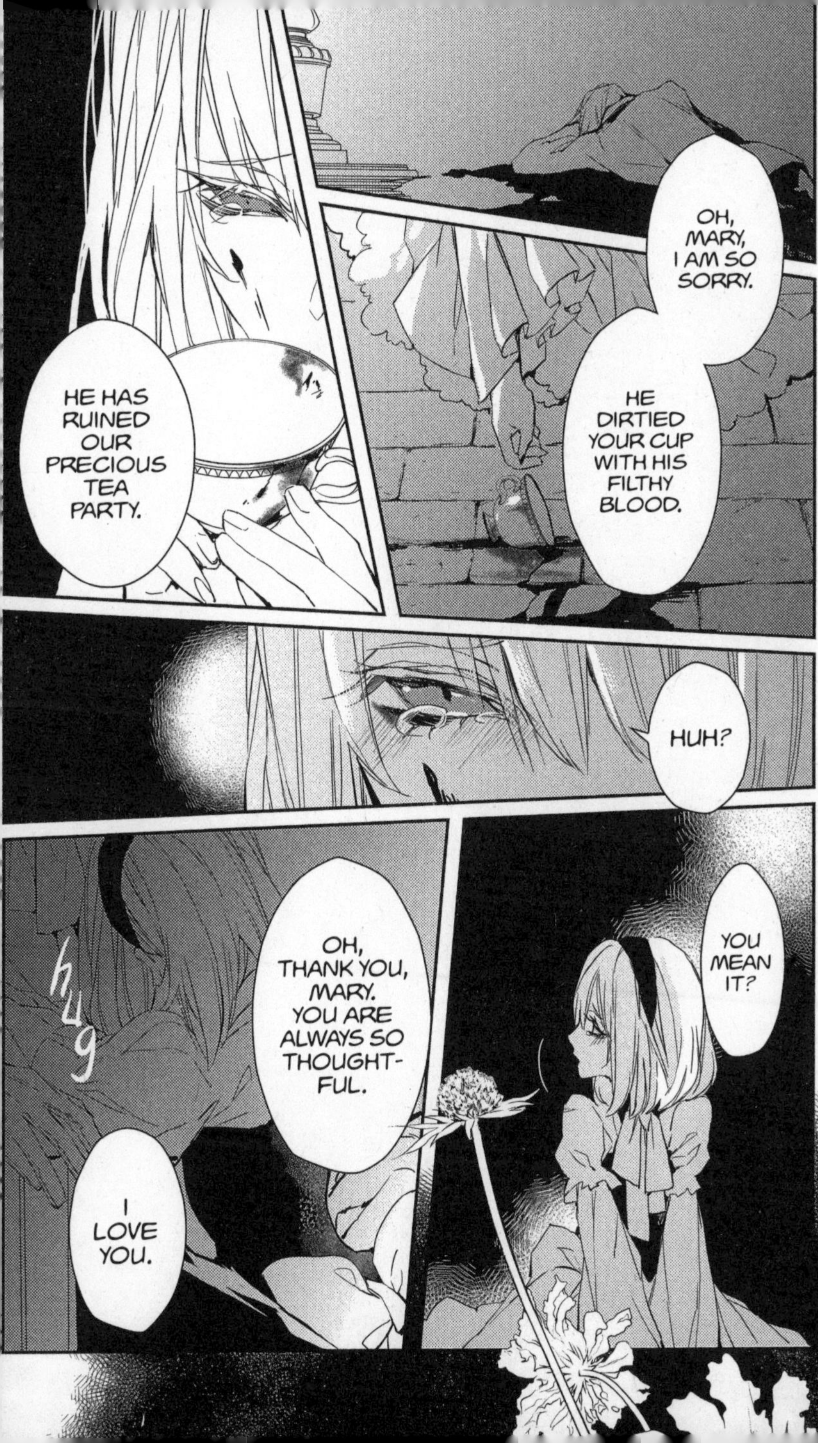
OH, MARY, I AM SO SORRY.
HE DIRTIED YOUR CUP WITH HIS FILTHY BLOOD.
HE HAS RUINED OUR PRECIOUS TEA PARTY.
HUH?
YOU MEAN IT?
OH, THANK YOU, MARY. YOU ARE ALWAYS SO THOUGHTFUL.
hug
I LOVE YOU.

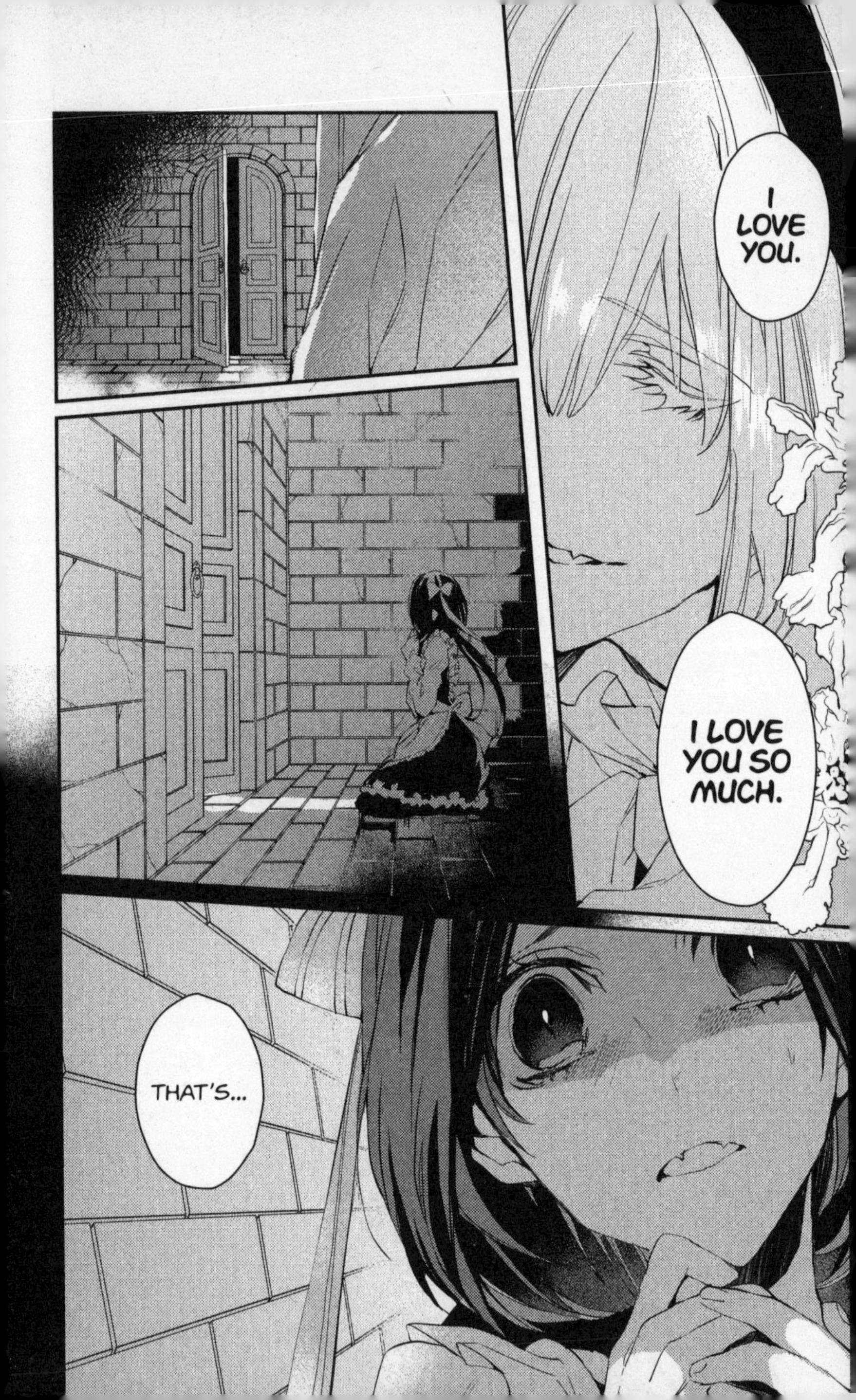
I LOVE YOU.
I LOVE YOU SO MUCH.
THAT'S...

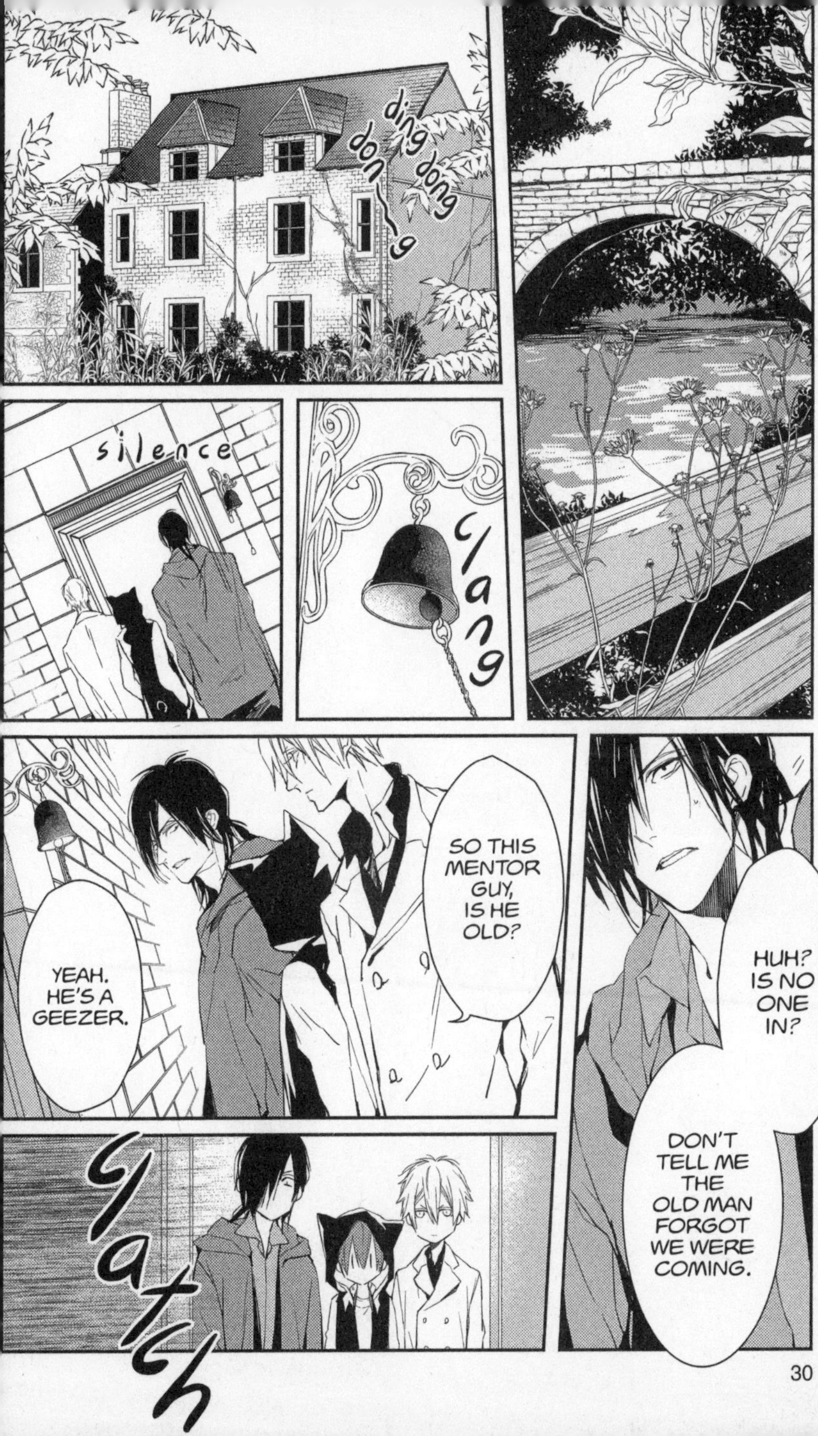
ding dong don—g
clang
silence
SO THIS MENTOR GUY, IS HE OLD?
YEAH. HE'S A GEEZER.
latch
HUH? IS NO ONE IN?
DON'T TELL ME THE OLD MAN FORGOT WE WERE COMING.

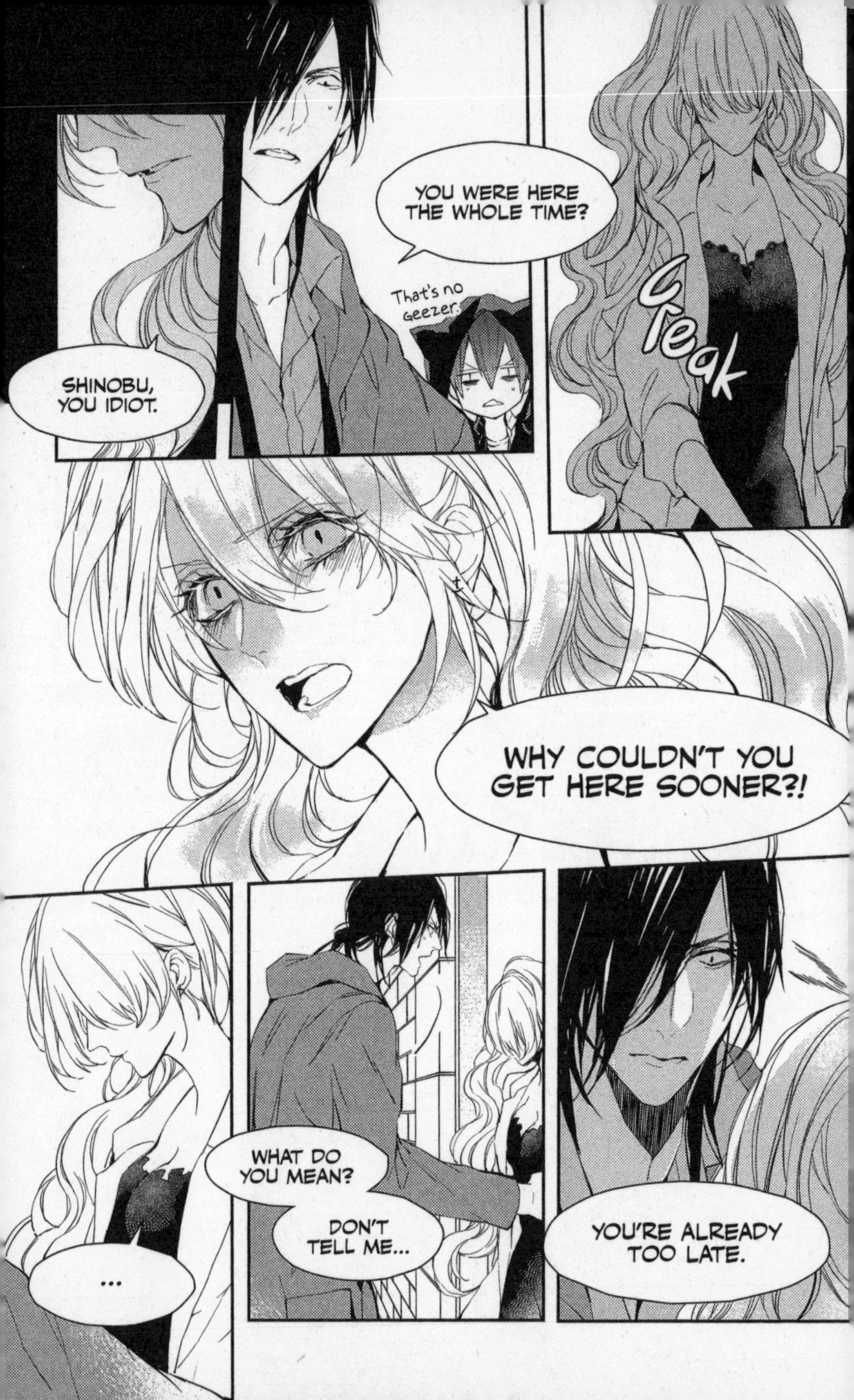
Creak
YOU WERE HERE THE WHOLE TIME?
That's no Geezer.
SHINOBU, YOU IDIOT.
WHY COULDN'T YOU GET HERE SOONER?!
YOU'RE ALREADY TOO LATE.
WHAT DO YOU MEAN?
DON'T TELL ME...
...

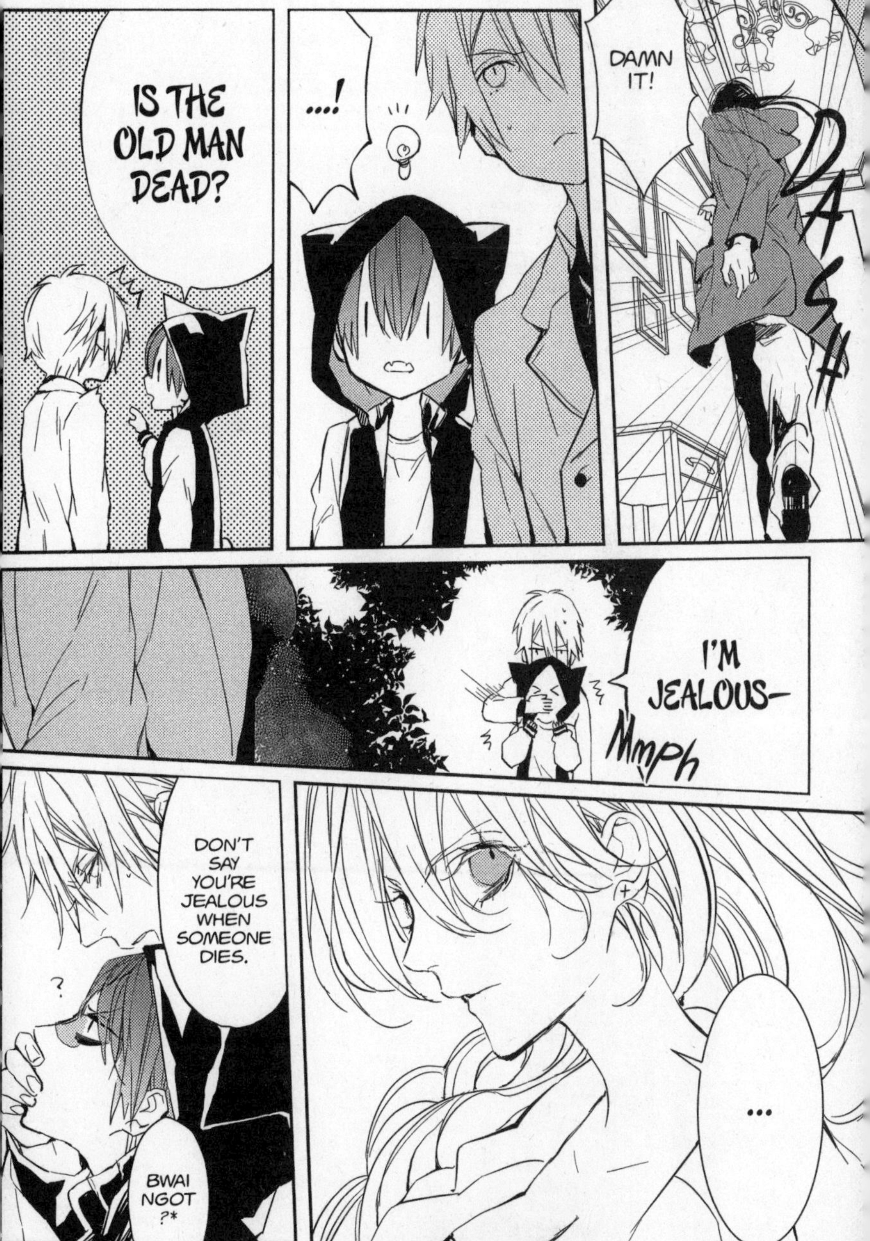
DAMN IT!
DASH
...!
IS THE OLD MAN DEAD?
I'M JEALOUS—
Mmph
...
DON'T SAY YOU'RE JEALOUS WHEN SOMEONE DIES.
BWAI NGOT ?*

*WHY NOT?

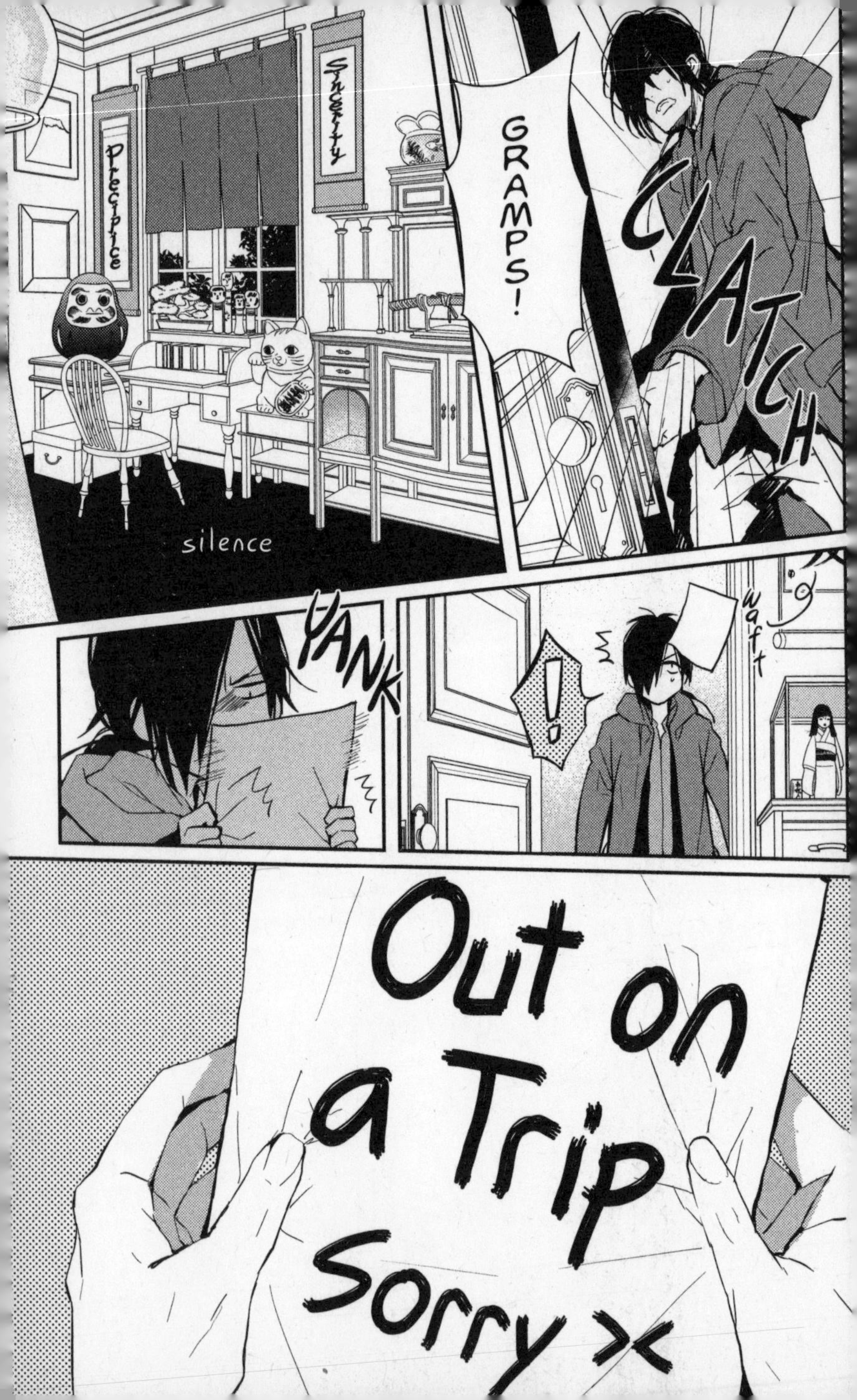
GRAMPS!
CLATCH
Sincerity
Precipice
silence
!
waft
YANK
Out on a Trip
Sorry ><

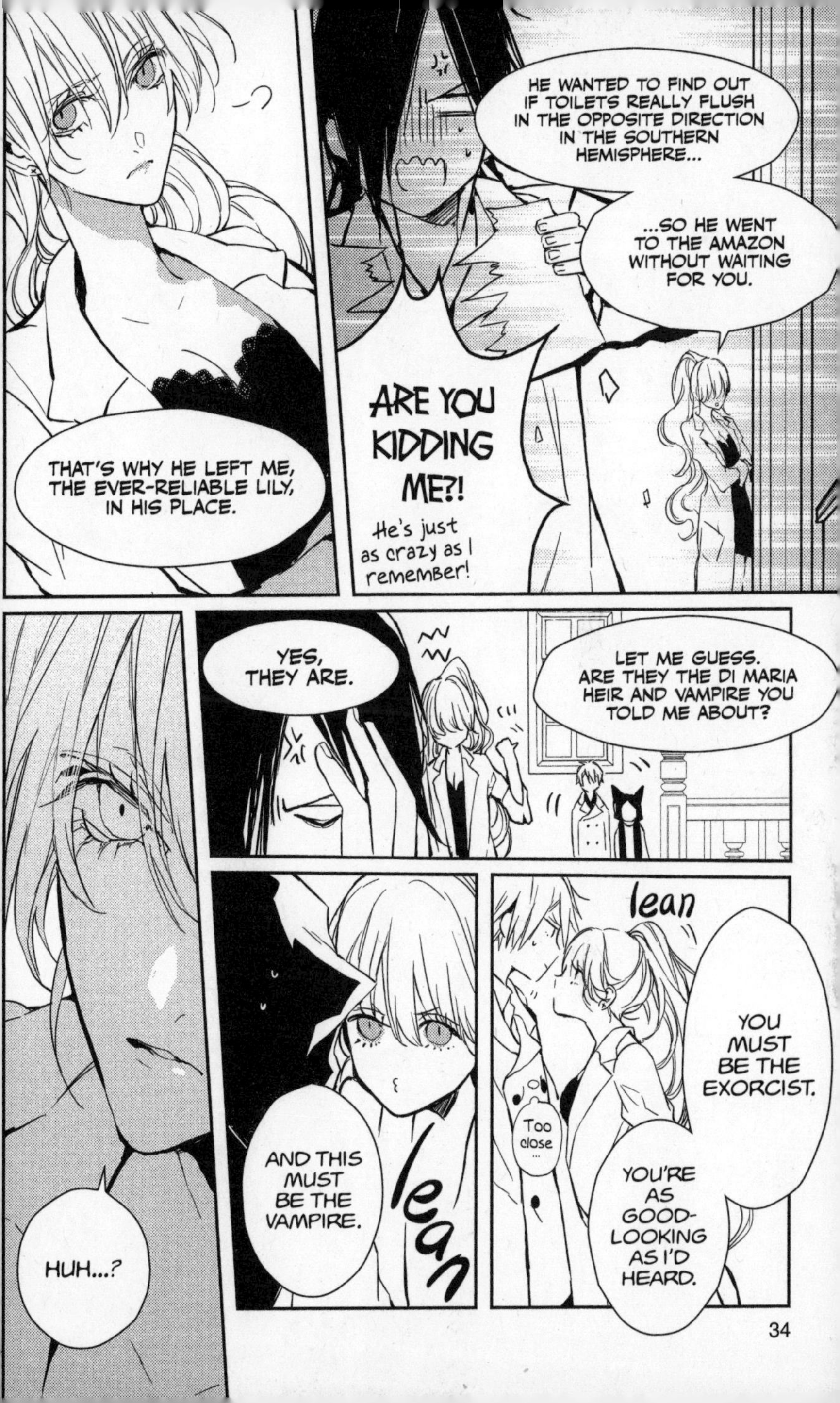
HE WANTED TO FIND OUT IF TOILETS REALLY FLUSH IN THE OPPOSITE DIRECTION IN THE SOUTHERN HEMISPHERE...
...SO HE WENT TO THE AMAZON WITHOUT WAITING FOR YOU.
ARE YOU KIDDING ME?!
He's just as crazy as I remember!
THAT'S WHY HE LEFT ME, THE EVER-RELIABLE LILY, IN HIS PLACE.
LET ME GUESS. ARE THEY THE DI MARIA HEIR AND VAMPIRE YOU TOLD ME ABOUT?
YES, THEY ARE.
lean
YOU MUST BE THE EXORCIST.
Too close...
YOU'RE AS GOOD-LOOKING AS I'D HEARD.
lean
AND THIS MUST BE THE VAMPIRE.
HUH...?

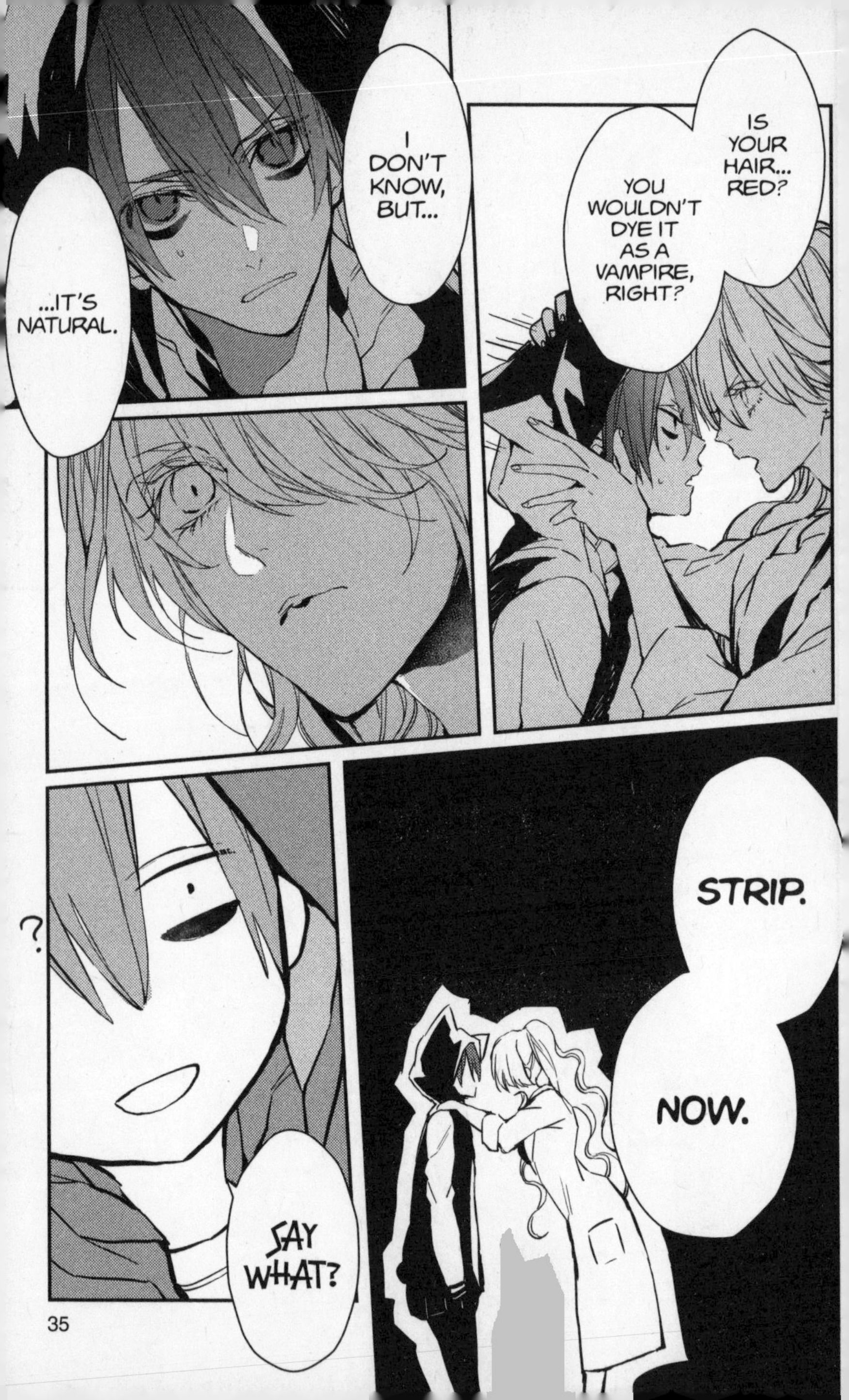
IS YOUR HAIR... RED?
YOU WOULDN'T DYE IT AS A VAMPIRE, RIGHT?
I DON'T KNOW, BUT...
...IT'S NATURAL.
STRIP.
NOW.
?
SAY WHAT?

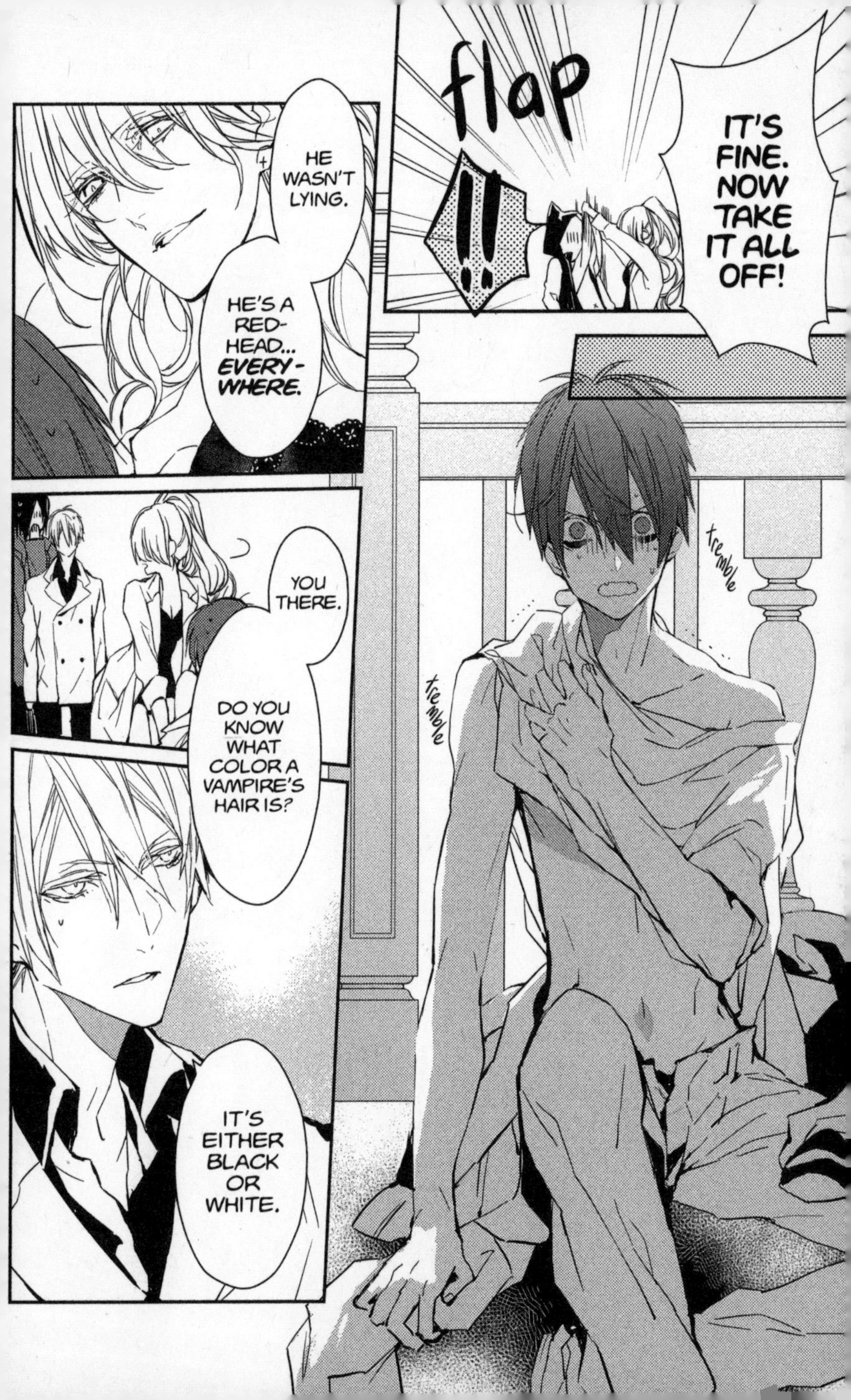
flap
!!
IT'S FINE. NOW TAKE IT ALL OFF!
tremble
tremble
HE WASN'T LYING.
HE'S A RED-HEAD... EVERY-WHERE.
YOU THERE.
DO YOU KNOW WHAT COLOR A VAMPIRE'S HAIR IS?
IT'S EITHER BLACK OR WHITE.

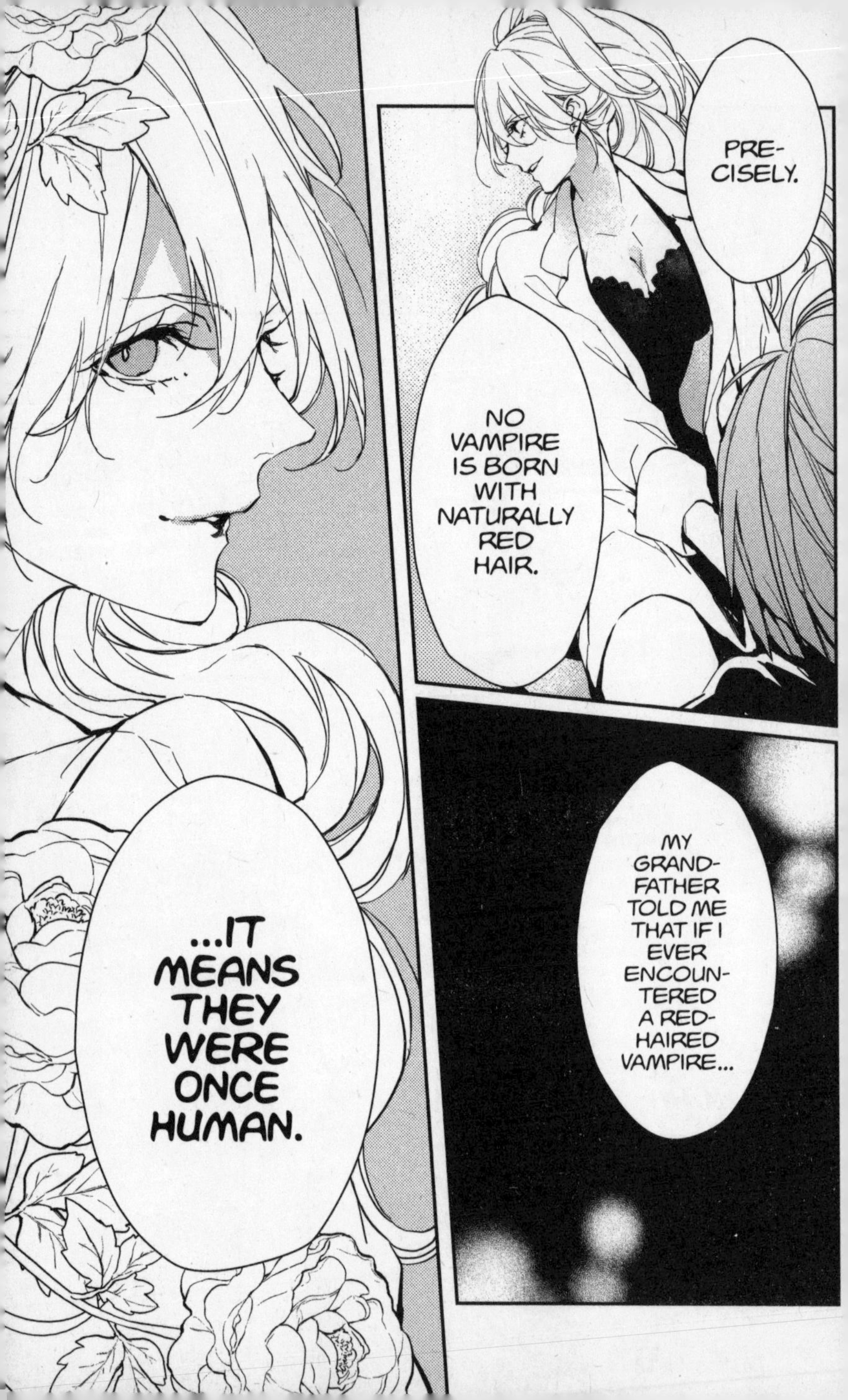
PRE-CISELY.
NO VAMPIRE IS BORN WITH NATURALLY RED HAIR.
MY GRAND-FATHER TOLD ME THAT IF I EVER ENCOUN-TERED A RED-HAIRED VAMPIRE...
...IT MEANS THEY WERE ONCE HUMAN.

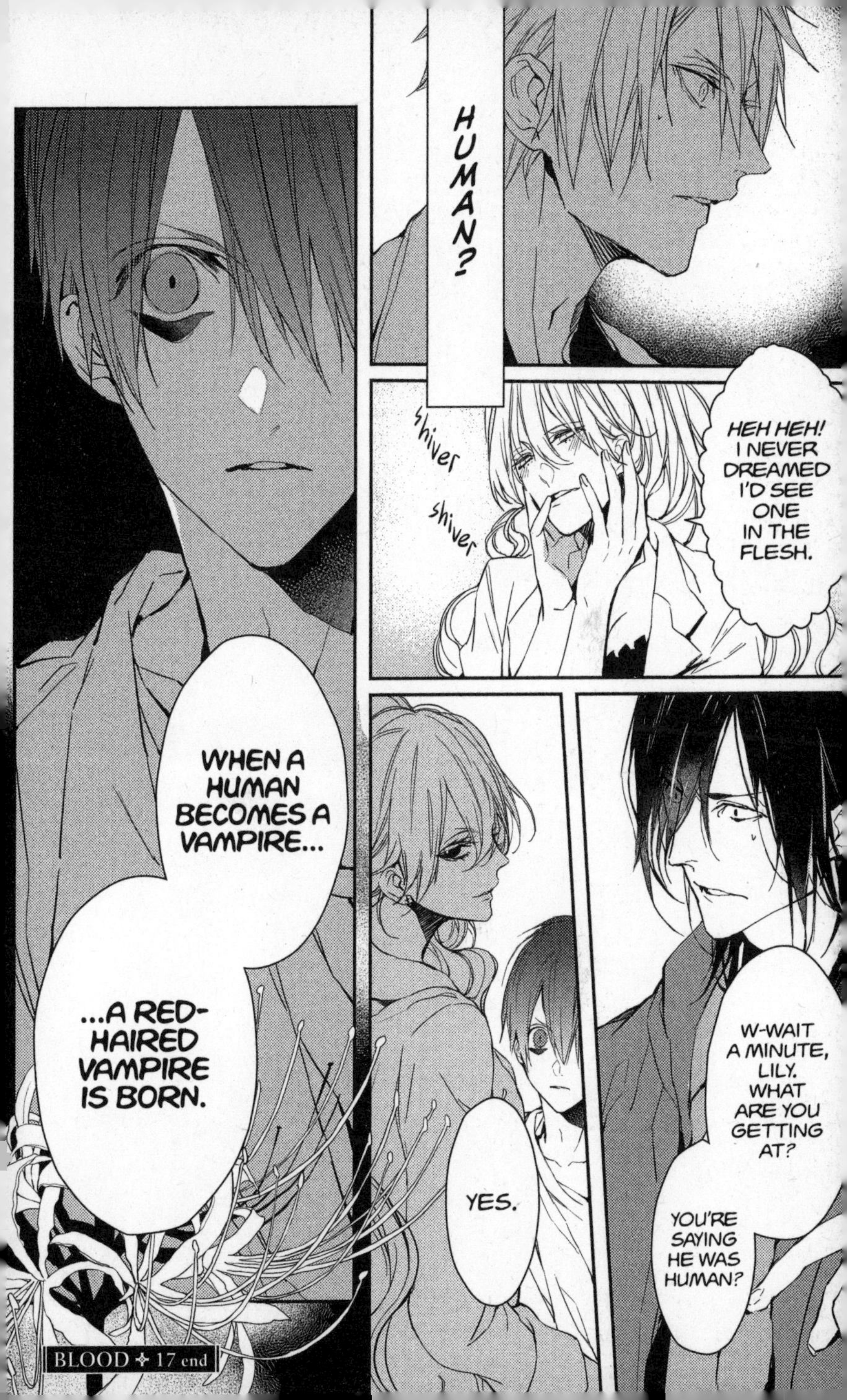
HUMAN?
shiver
shiver
HEH HEH! I NEVER DREAMED I'D SEE ONE IN THE FLESH.
W-WAIT A MINUTE, LILY. WHAT ARE YOU GETTING AT?
YOU'RE SAYING HE WAS HUMAN?
YES.
WHEN A HUMAN BECOMES A VAMPIRE...
...A RED-HAIRED VAMPIRE IS BORN.
BLOOD ✣ 17 end

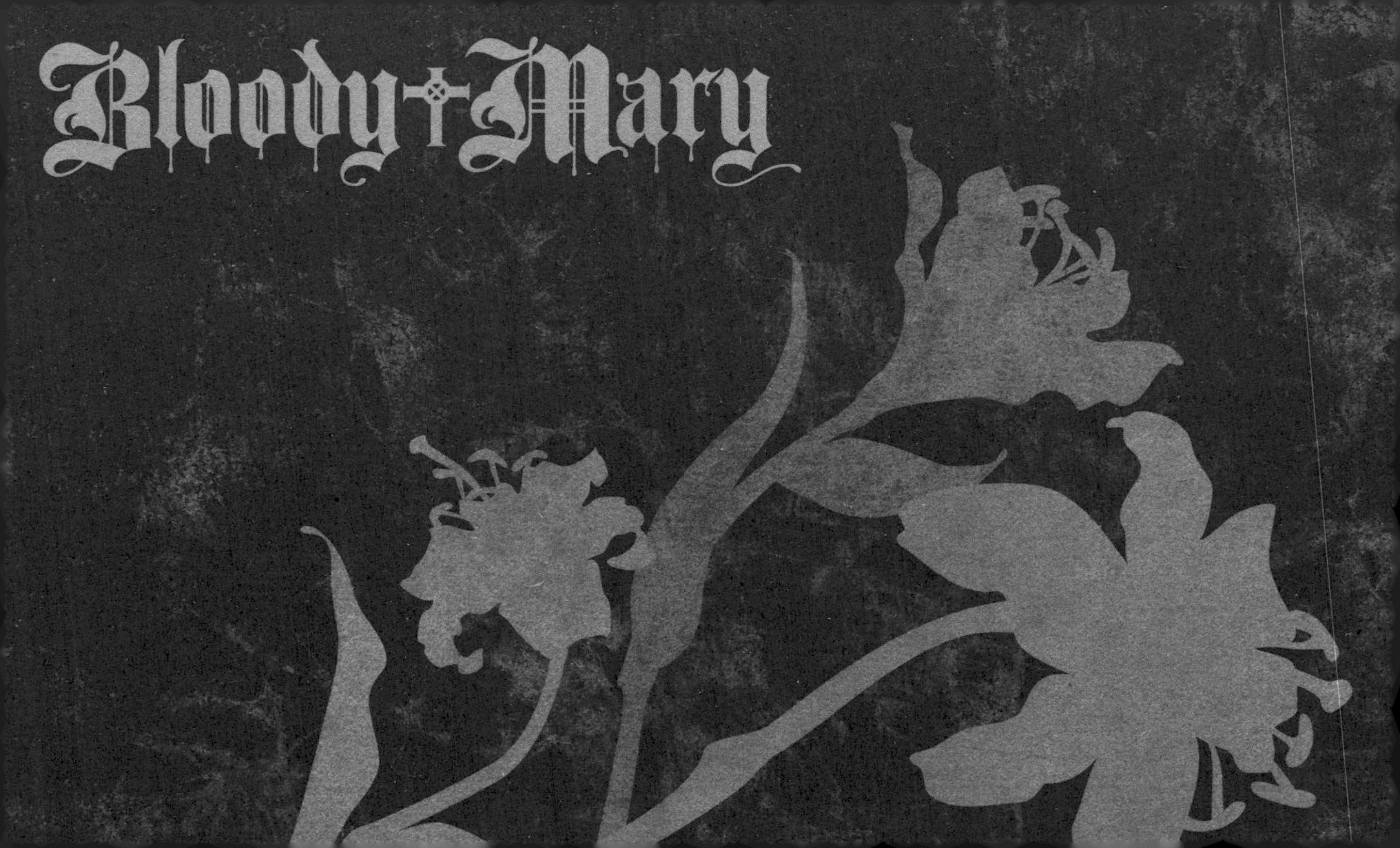
Bloody+Mary

Bloody✝Mary

WHAT'S THE MATTER, YOUNG MASTER?

IT'S ABOUT MARY ON THE OPPOSITE PAGE. HE'S WEARING A SUIT LIKE A TYPICAL VAMPIRE, BUT...

...I STILL THINK HE LOOKS BETTER IN THE *BUNNY-EARED HOODIE* YOU GOT HIM, HASE-GAWA.

...is pleased.

Hase-gawa...

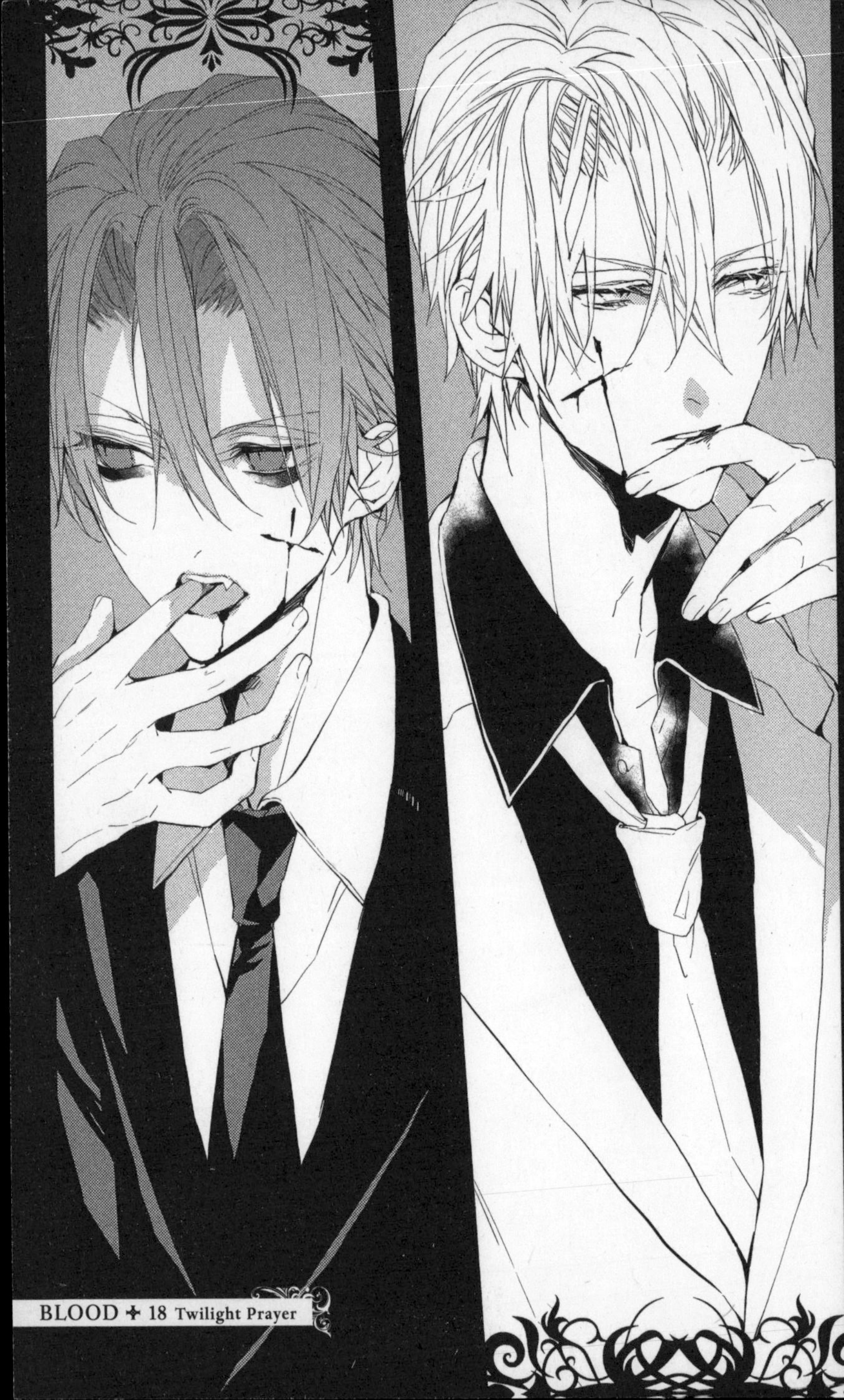
BLOOD ✣ 18 Twilight Prayer

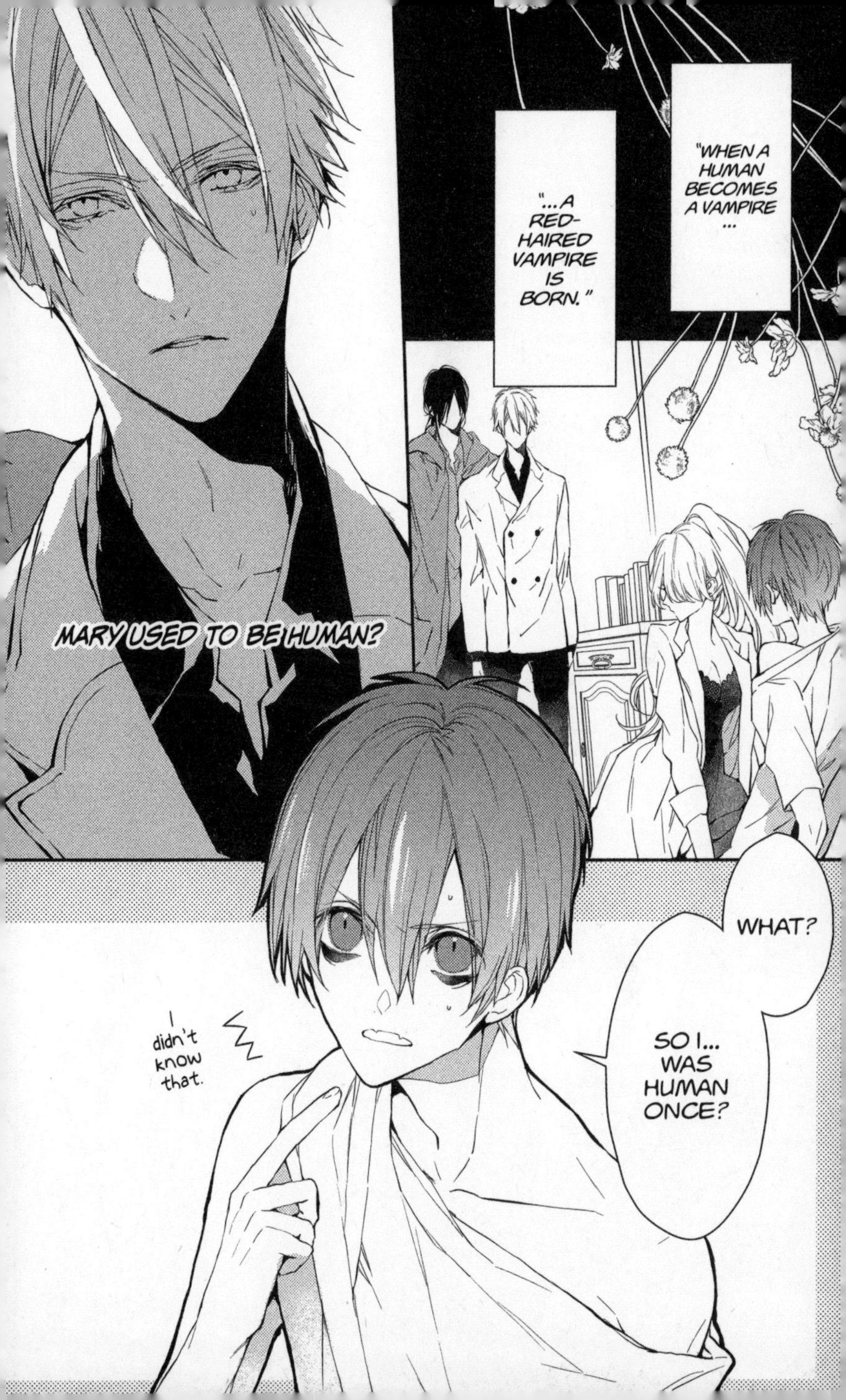
"WHEN A HUMAN BECOMES A VAMPIRE ...
"...A RED-HAIRED VAMPIRE IS BORN."
MARY USED TO BE HUMAN?
WHAT?
SO I... WAS HUMAN ONCE?
I didn't know that.

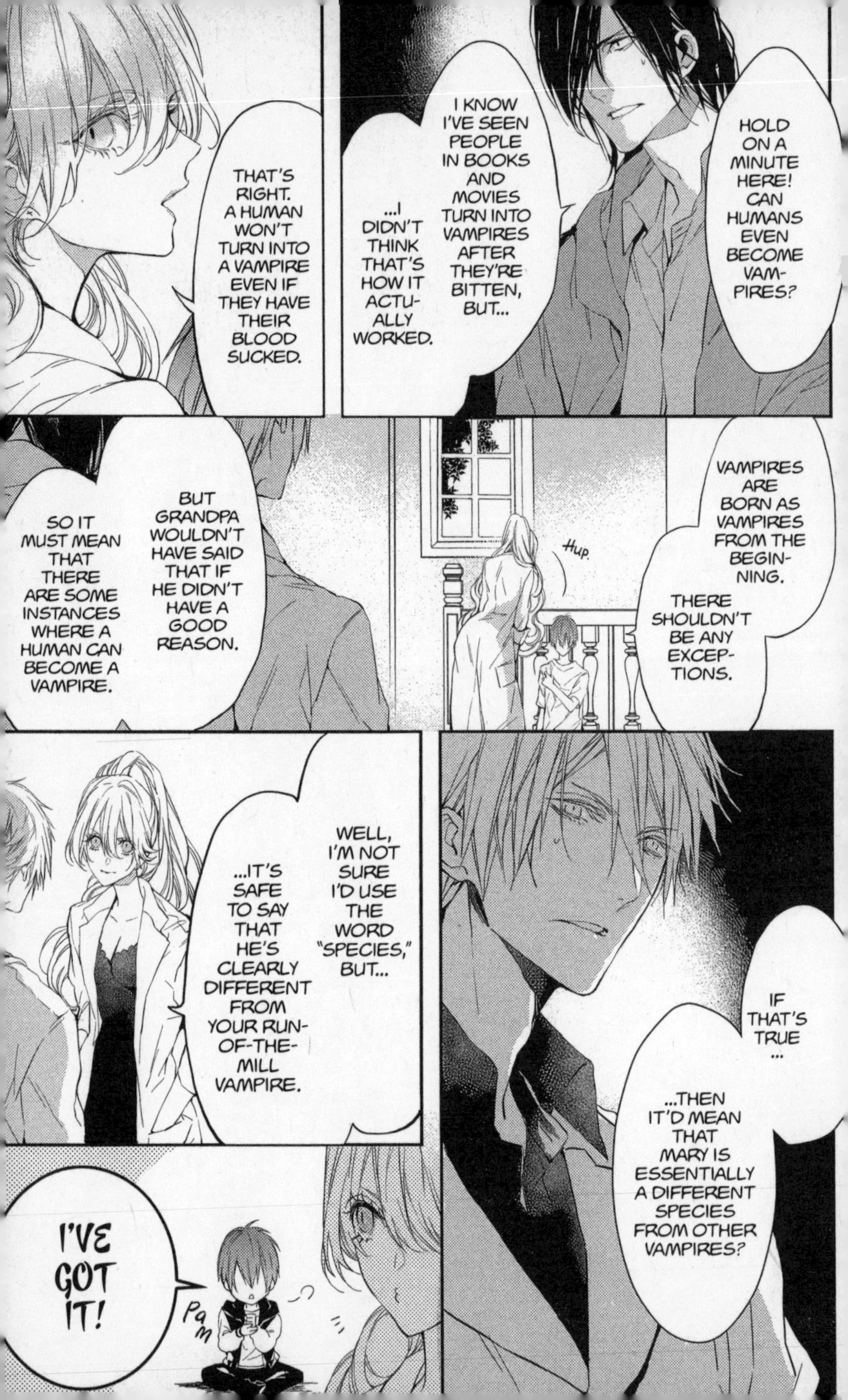
HOLD ON A MINUTE HERE! CAN HUMANS EVEN BECOME VAMPIRES?
I KNOW I'VE SEEN PEOPLE IN BOOKS AND MOVIES TURN INTO VAMPIRES AFTER THEY'RE BITTEN, BUT...
...I DIDN'T THINK THAT'S HOW IT ACTUALLY WORKED.
THAT'S RIGHT. A HUMAN WON'T TURN INTO A VAMPIRE EVEN IF THEY HAVE THEIR BLOOD SUCKED.
VAMPIRES ARE BORN AS VAMPIRES FROM THE BEGINNING.
THERE SHOULDN'T BE ANY EXCEPTIONS.
Hup.
BUT GRANDPA WOULDN'T HAVE SAID THAT IF HE DIDN'T HAVE A GOOD REASON.
SO IT MUST MEAN THAT THERE ARE SOME INSTANCES WHERE A HUMAN CAN BECOME A VAMPIRE.
IF THAT'S TRUE...
...THEN IT'D MEAN THAT MARY IS ESSENTIALLY A DIFFERENT SPECIES FROM OTHER VAMPIRES?
WELL, I'M NOT SURE I'D USE THE WORD "SPECIES," BUT...
...IT'S SAFE TO SAY THAT HE'S CLEARLY DIFFERENT FROM YOUR RUN-OF-THE-MILL VAMPIRE.
I'VE GOT IT!
Pam

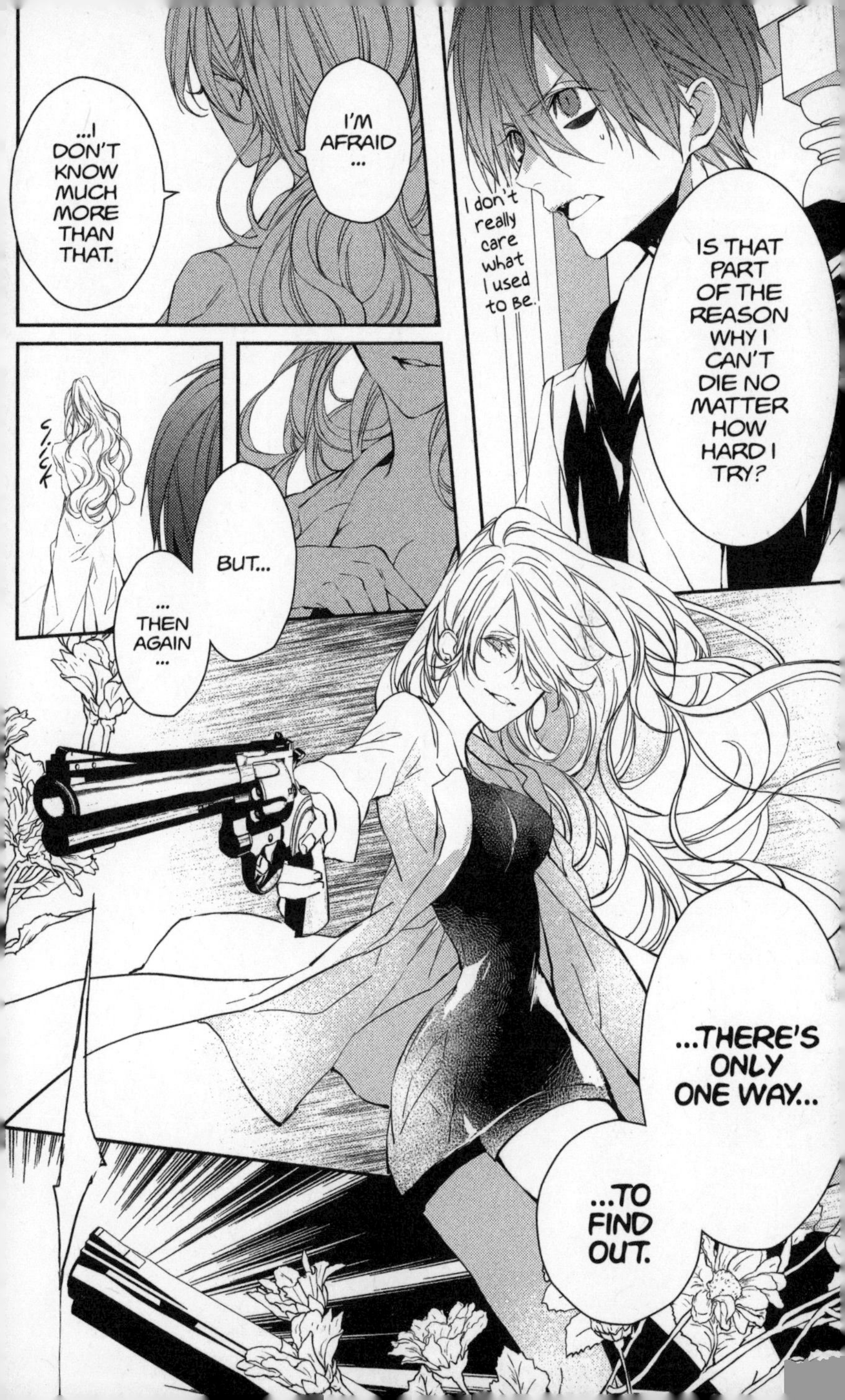
IS THAT PART OF THE REASON WHY I CAN'T DIE NO MATTER HOW HARD I TRY?
I don't really care what I used to be.
I'M AFRAID...
...I DON'T KNOW MUCH MORE THAN THAT.
BUT...
...THEN AGAIN...
CLICK
...THERE'S ONLY ONE WAY...
...TO FIND OUT.

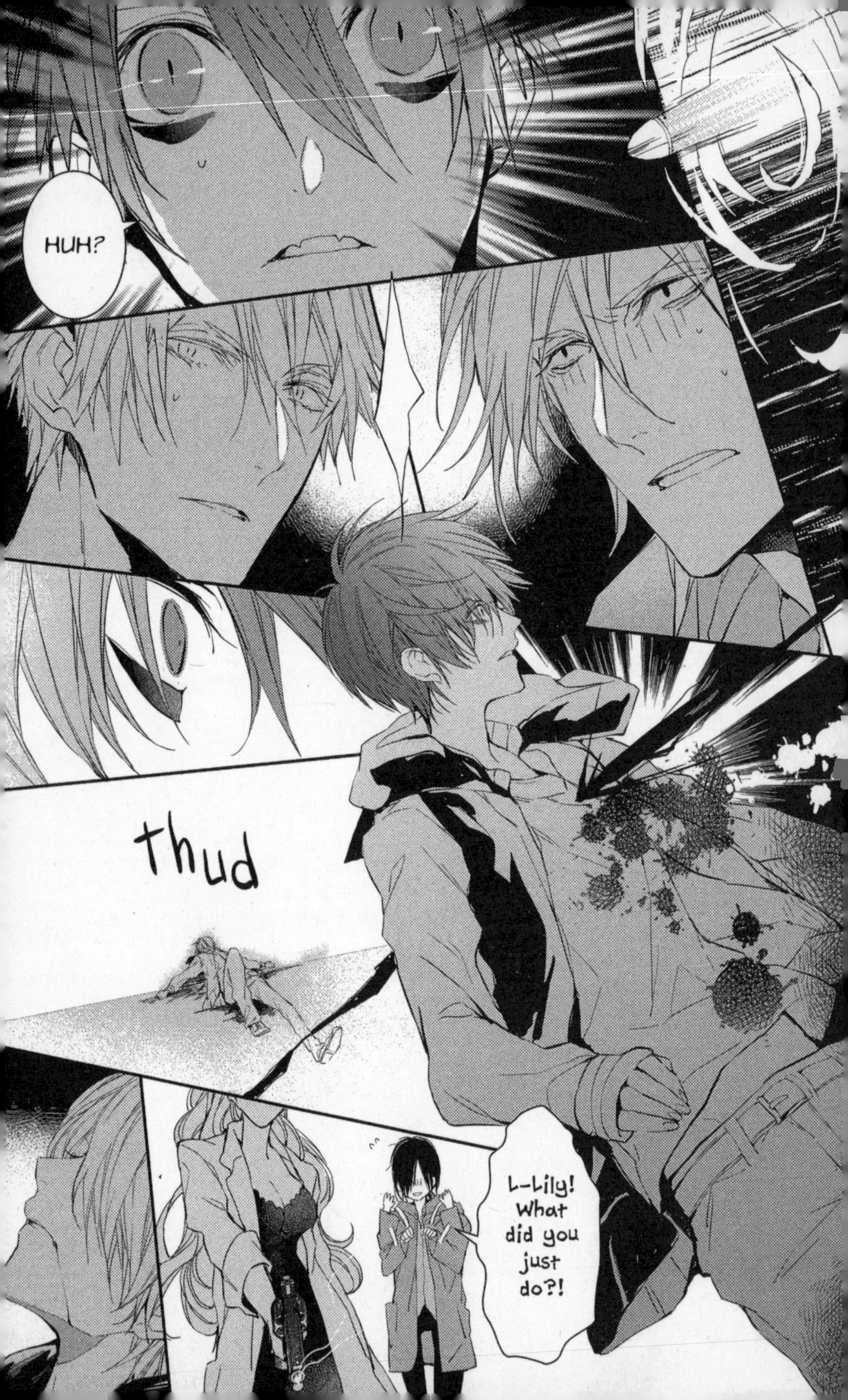
HUH?
thud
L-Lily! What did you just do?!

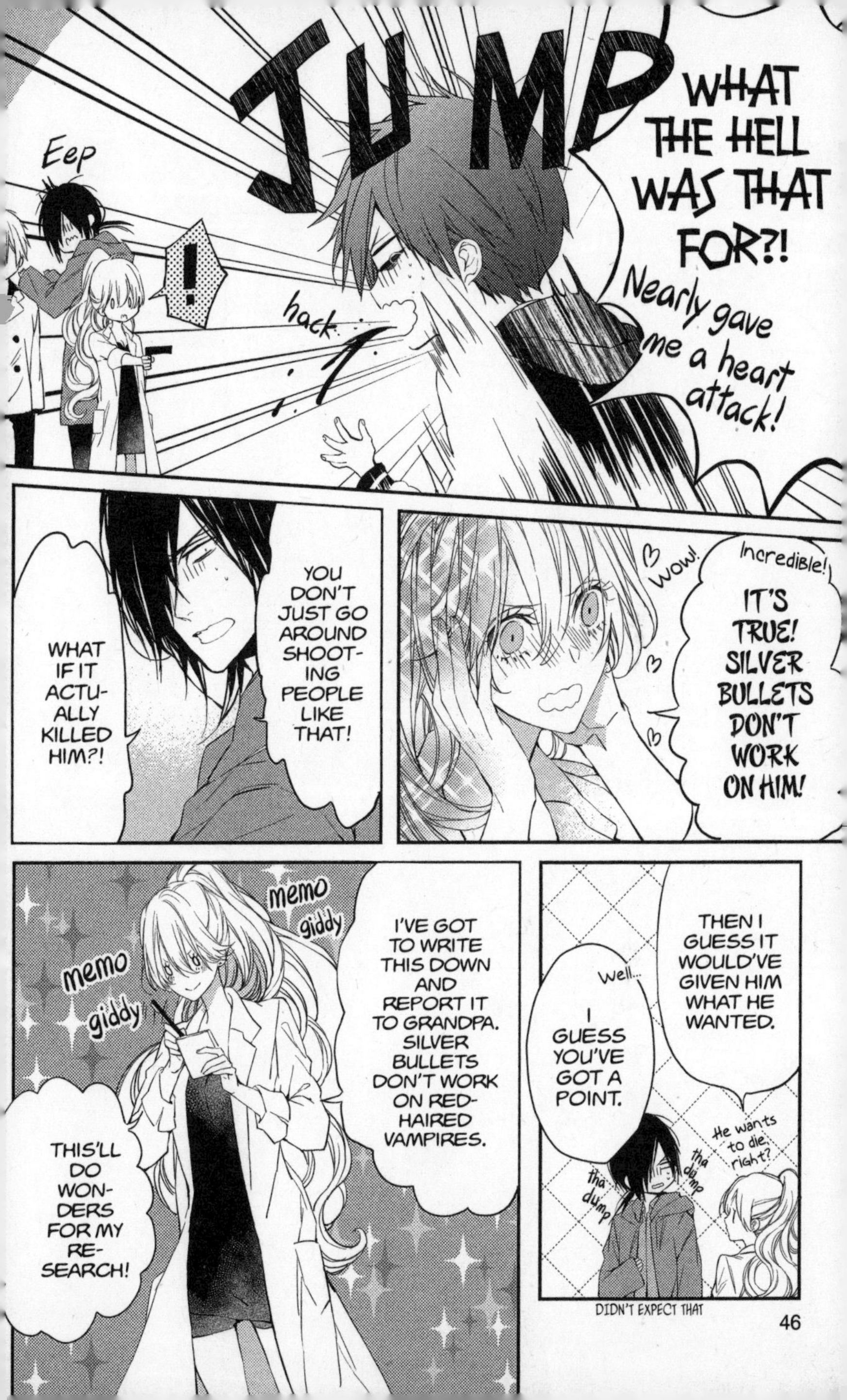
JUMP
WHAT THE HELL WAS THAT FOR?!
Nearly gave me a heart attack!
hack
!
Eep
Incredible!
Wow!
IT'S TRUE! SILVER BULLETS DON'T WORK ON HIM!
YOU DON'T JUST GO AROUND SHOOTING PEOPLE LIKE THAT!
WHAT IF IT ACTUALLY KILLED HIM?!
THEN I GUESS IT WOULD'VE GIVEN HIM WHAT HE WANTED.
He wants to die, right?
Well...
I GUESS YOU'VE GOT A POINT.
tha dump
tha dump
memo
giddy
memo
giddy
I'VE GOT TO WRITE THIS DOWN AND REPORT IT TO GRANDPA. SILVER BULLETS DON'T WORK ON RED-HAIRED VAMPIRES.
THIS'LL DO WONDERS FOR MY RESEARCH!

DIDN'T EXPECT THAT

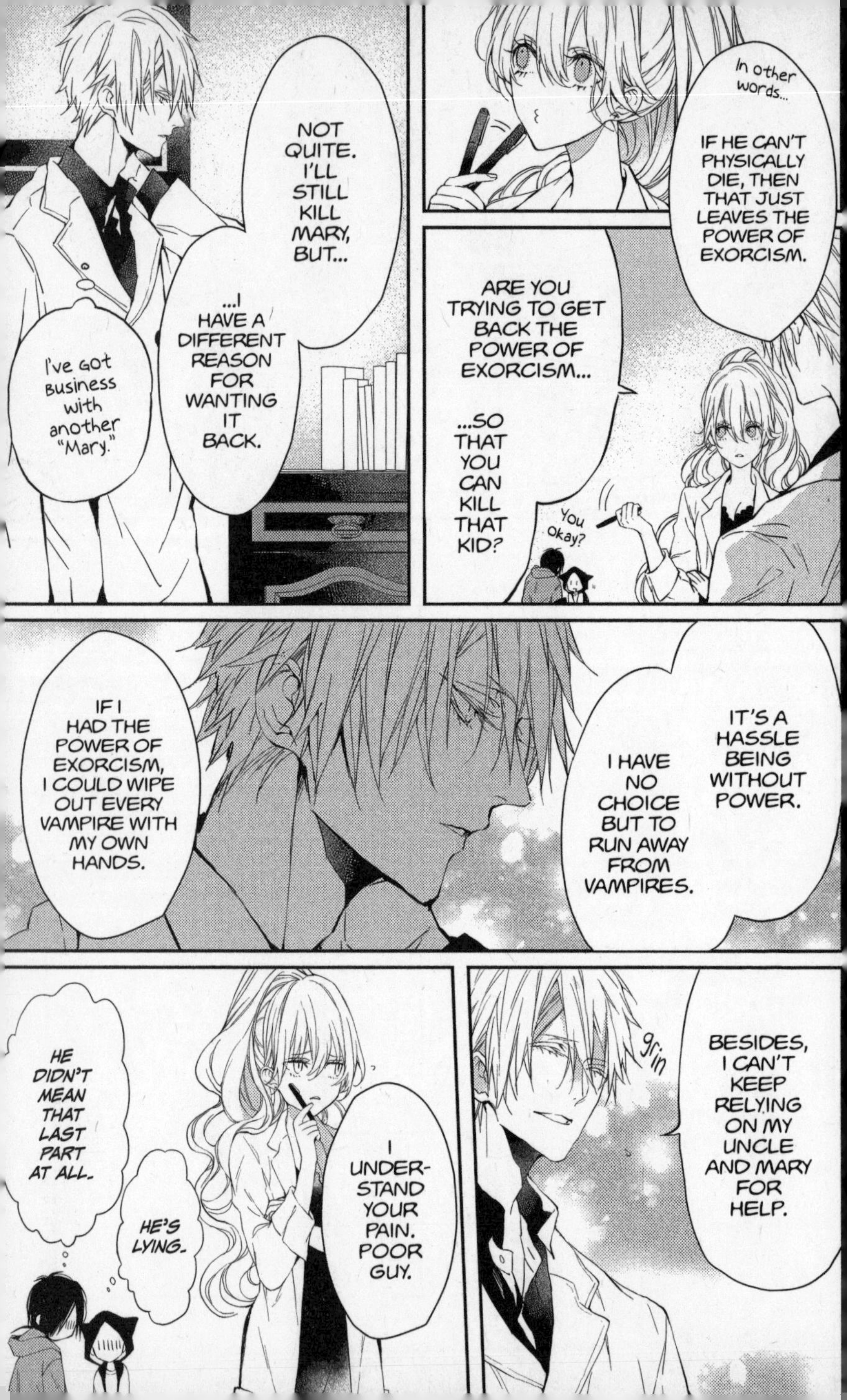
In other words...
IF HE CAN'T PHYSICALLY DIE, THEN THAT JUST LEAVES THE POWER OF EXORCISM.
ARE YOU TRYING TO GET BACK THE POWER OF EXORCISM...
...SO THAT YOU CAN KILL THAT KID?
You okay?
NOT QUITE. I'LL STILL KILL MARY, BUT...
...I HAVE A DIFFERENT REASON FOR WANTING IT BACK.
I've got business with another "Mary."
IT'S A HASSLE BEING WITHOUT POWER.
I HAVE NO CHOICE BUT TO RUN AWAY FROM VAMPIRES.
IF I HAD THE POWER OF EXORCISM, I COULD WIPE OUT EVERY VAMPIRE WITH MY OWN HANDS.
BESIDES, I CAN'T KEEP RELYING ON MY UNCLE AND MARY FOR HELP.
grin
I UNDER-STAND YOUR PAIN. POOR GUY.
HE'S LYING.
HE DIDN'T MEAN THAT LAST PART AT ALL.

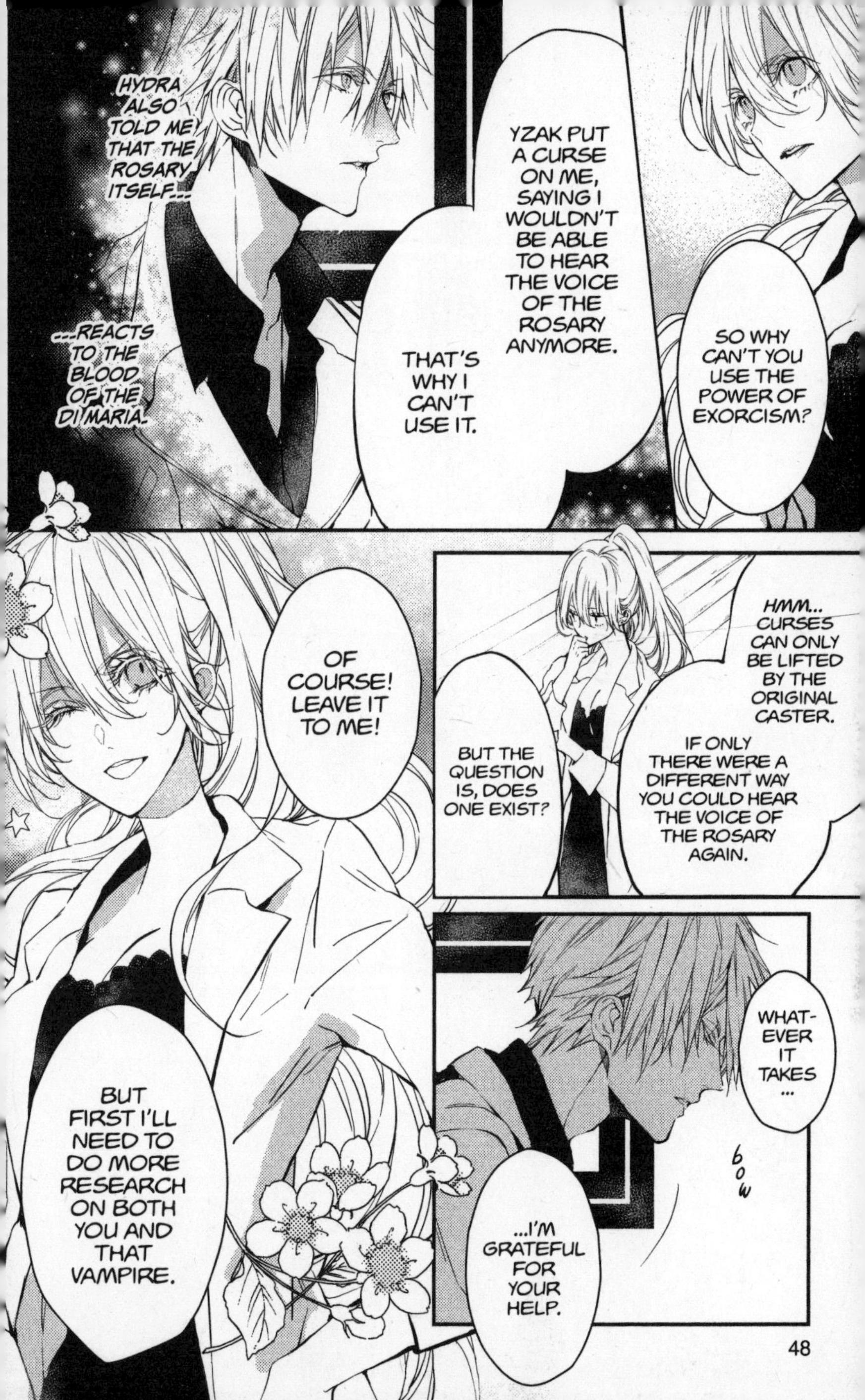
SO WHY CAN'T YOU USE THE POWER OF EXORCISM?
YZAK PUT A CURSE ON ME, SAYING I WOULDN'T BE ABLE TO HEAR THE VOICE OF THE ROSARY ANYMORE.
THAT'S WHY I CAN'T USE IT.
HYDRA ALSO TOLD ME THAT THE ROSARY ITSELF...
...REACTS TO THE BLOOD OF THE DI MARIA.
HMM... CURSES CAN ONLY BE LIFTED BY THE ORIGINAL CASTER.
IF ONLY THERE WERE A DIFFERENT WAY YOU COULD HEAR THE VOICE OF THE ROSARY AGAIN.
BUT THE QUESTION IS, DOES ONE EXIST?
WHATEVER IT TAKES...
bow
...I'M GRATEFUL FOR YOUR HELP.
OF COURSE! LEAVE IT TO ME!
BUT FIRST I'LL NEED TO DO MORE RESEARCH ON BOTH YOU AND THAT VAMPIRE.

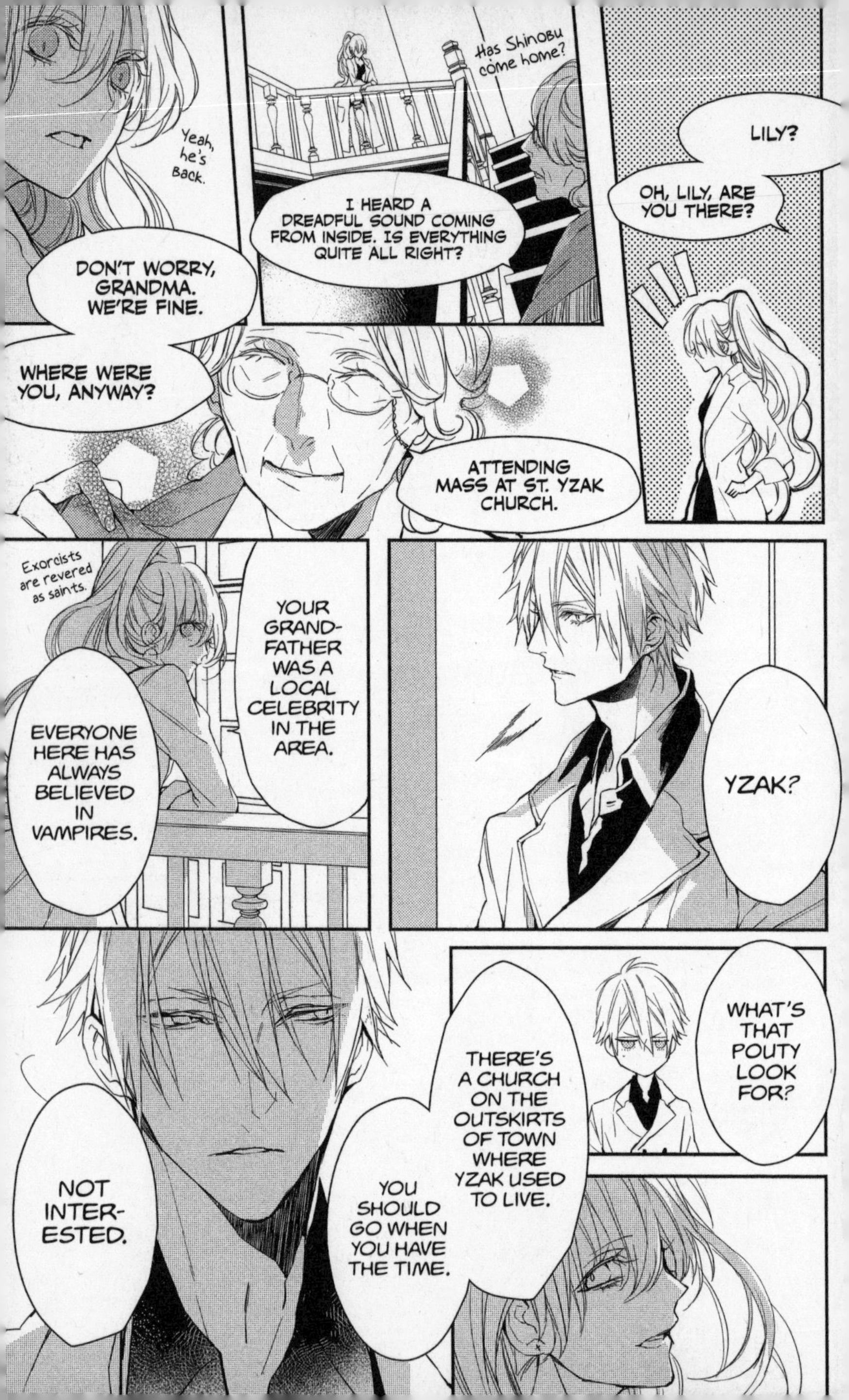
LILY?
OH, LILY, ARE YOU THERE?
Has Shinobu come home?
I HEARD A DREADFUL SOUND COMING FROM INSIDE. IS EVERYTHING QUITE ALL RIGHT?
Yeah, he's Back.
DON'T WORRY, GRANDMA. WE'RE FINE.
WHERE WERE YOU, ANYWAY?
ATTENDING MASS AT ST. YZAK CHURCH.
YZAK?
YOUR GRAND-FATHER WAS A LOCAL CELEBRITY IN THE AREA.
EVERYONE HERE HAS ALWAYS BELIEVED IN VAMPIRES.
Exorcists are revered as saints.
WHAT'S THAT POUTY LOOK FOR?
THERE'S A CHURCH ON THE OUTSKIRTS OF TOWN WHERE YZAK USED TO LIVE.
YOU SHOULD GO WHEN YOU HAVE THE TIME.
NOT INTER-ESTED.

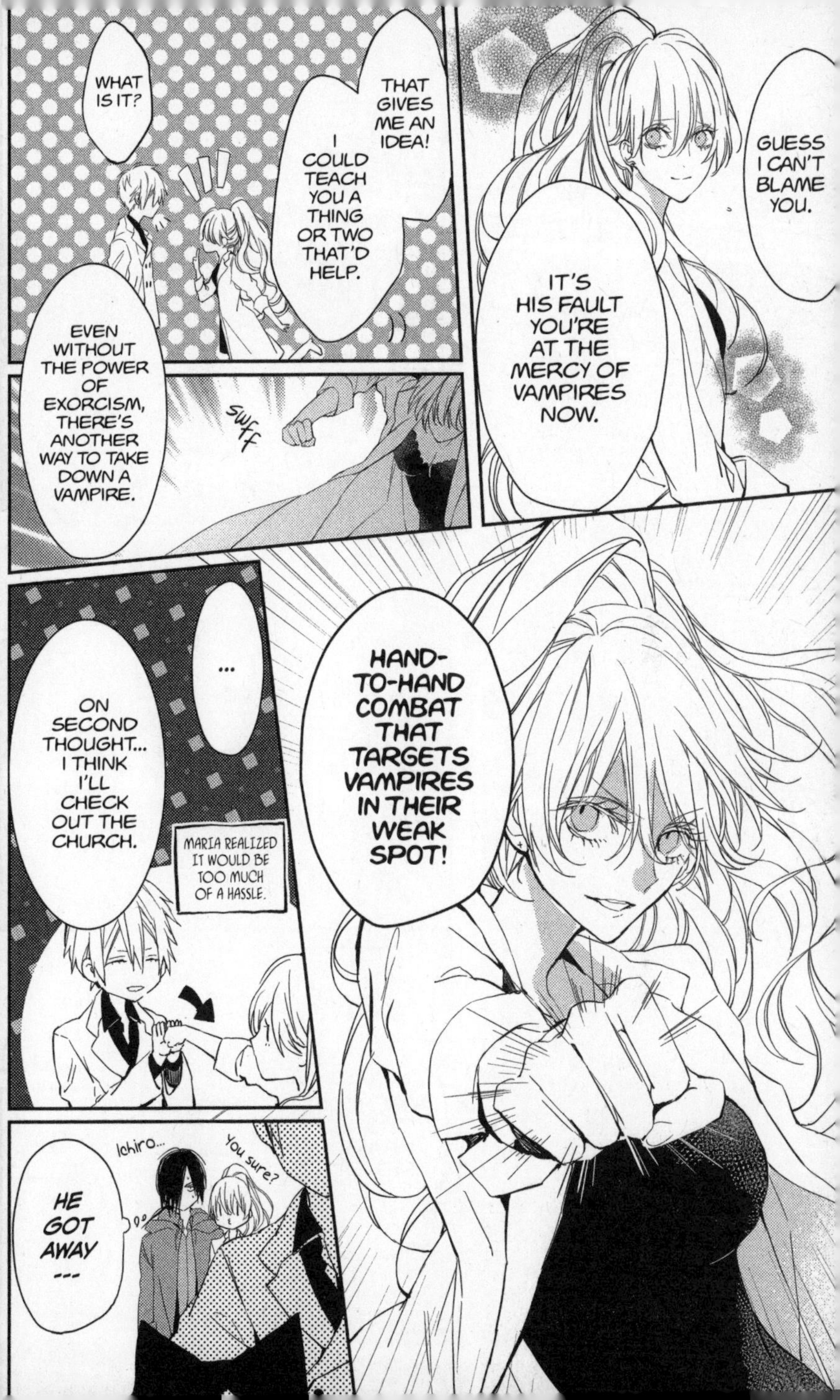
GUESS I CAN'T BLAME YOU.
IT'S HIS FAULT YOU'RE AT THE MERCY OF VAMPIRES NOW.
THAT GIVES ME AN IDEA!
I COULD TEACH YOU A THING OR TWO THAT'D HELP.
WHAT IS IT?
EVEN WITHOUT THE POWER OF EXORCISM, THERE'S ANOTHER WAY TO TAKE DOWN A VAMPIRE.
swff
HAND-TO-HAND COMBAT THAT TARGETS VAMPIRES IN THEIR WEAK SPOT!
...
ON SECOND THOUGHT... I THINK I'LL CHECK OUT THE CHURCH.
MARIA REALIZED IT WOULD BE TOO MUCH OF A HASSLE.
You sure?
Ichiro...
HE GOT AWAY ---

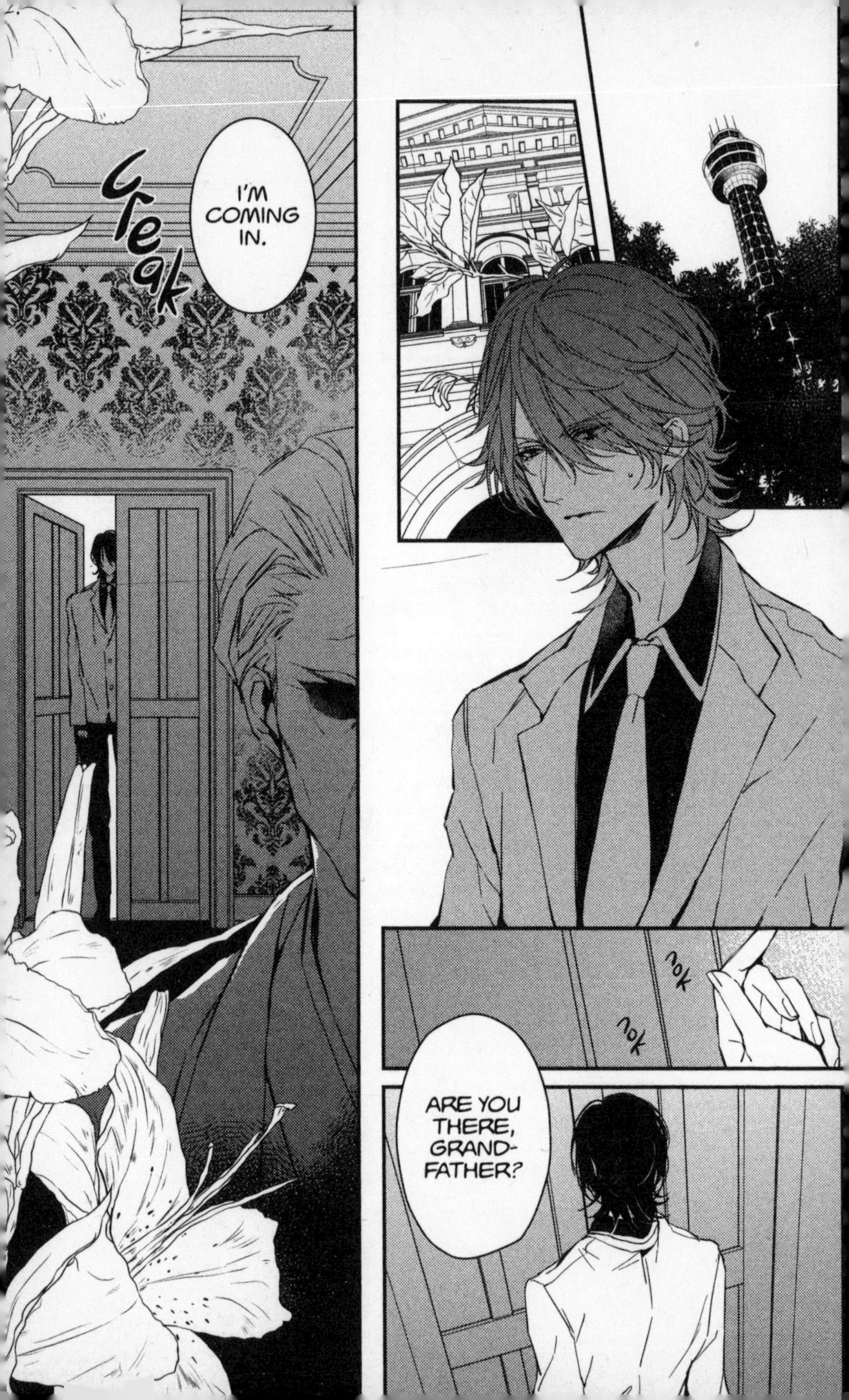
nok
nok
ARE YOU THERE, GRAND-FATHER?
creak
I'M COMING IN.

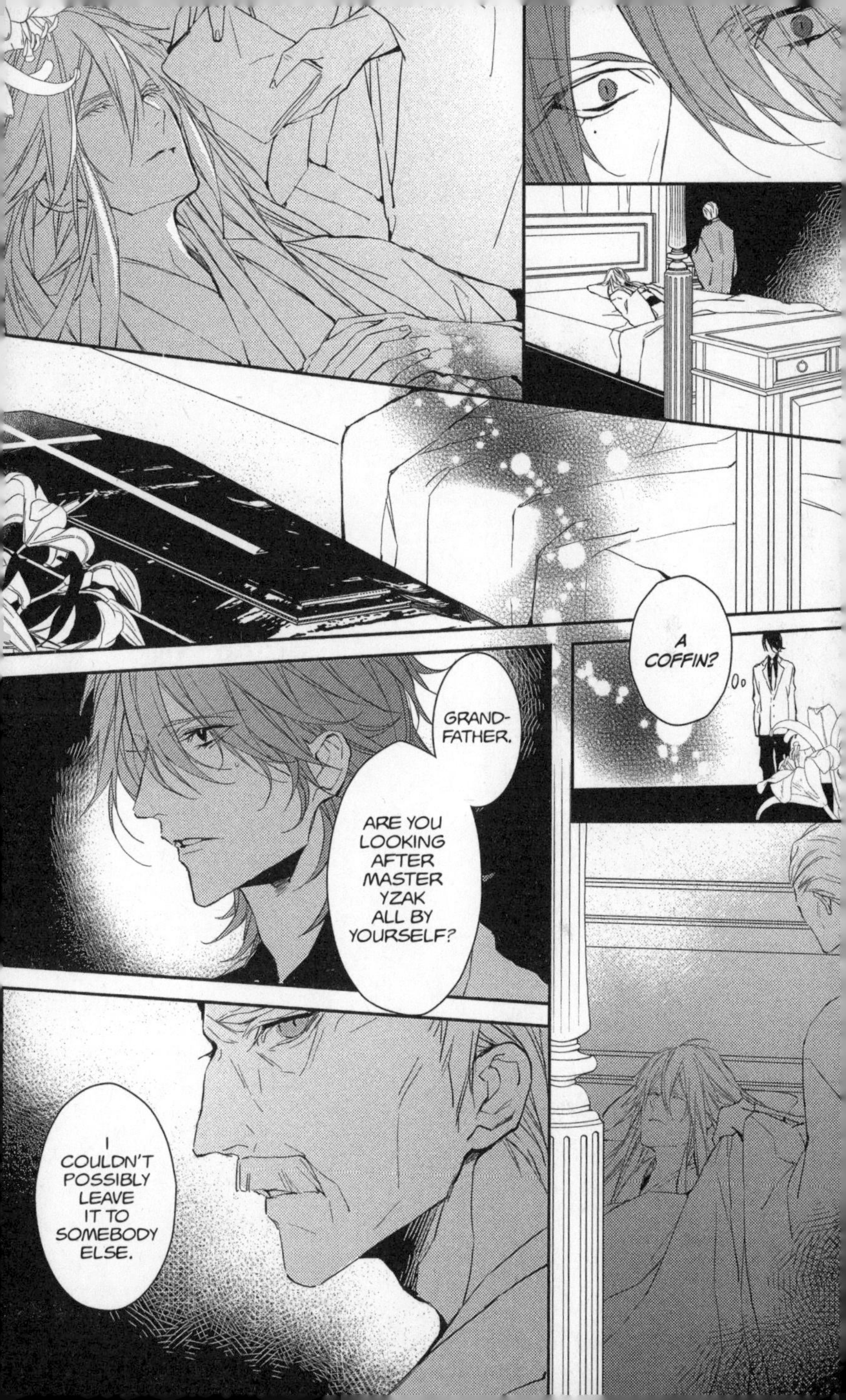
A COFFIN?
GRAND-FATHER.
ARE YOU LOOKING AFTER MASTER YZAK ALL BY YOURSELF?
I COULDN'T POSSIBLY LEAVE IT TO SOMEBODY ELSE.

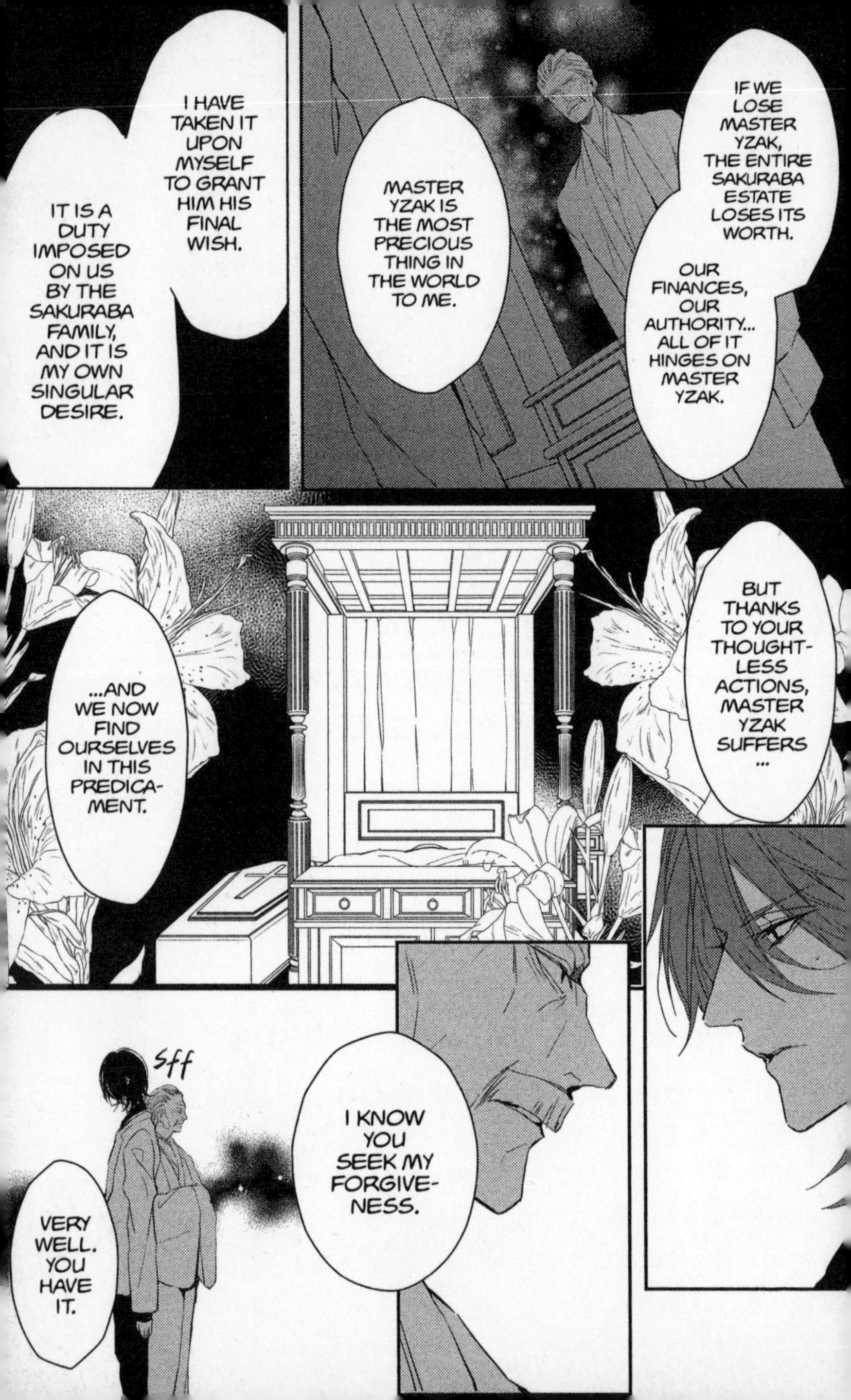
IF WE LOSE MASTER YZAK, THE ENTIRE SAKURABA ESTATE LOSES ITS WORTH.
OUR FINANCES, OUR AUTHORITY... ALL OF IT HINGES ON MASTER YZAK.
MASTER YZAK IS THE MOST PRECIOUS THING IN THE WORLD TO ME.
I HAVE TAKEN IT UPON MYSELF TO GRANT HIM HIS FINAL WISH.
IT IS A DUTY IMPOSED ON US BY THE SAKURABA FAMILY, AND IT IS MY OWN SINGULAR DESIRE.
BUT THANKS TO YOUR THOUGHT-LESS ACTIONS, MASTER YZAK SUFFERS...
...AND WE NOW FIND OURSELVES IN THIS PREDICA-MENT.
I KNOW YOU SEEK MY FORGIVE-NESS.
SFF
VERY WELL. YOU HAVE IT.

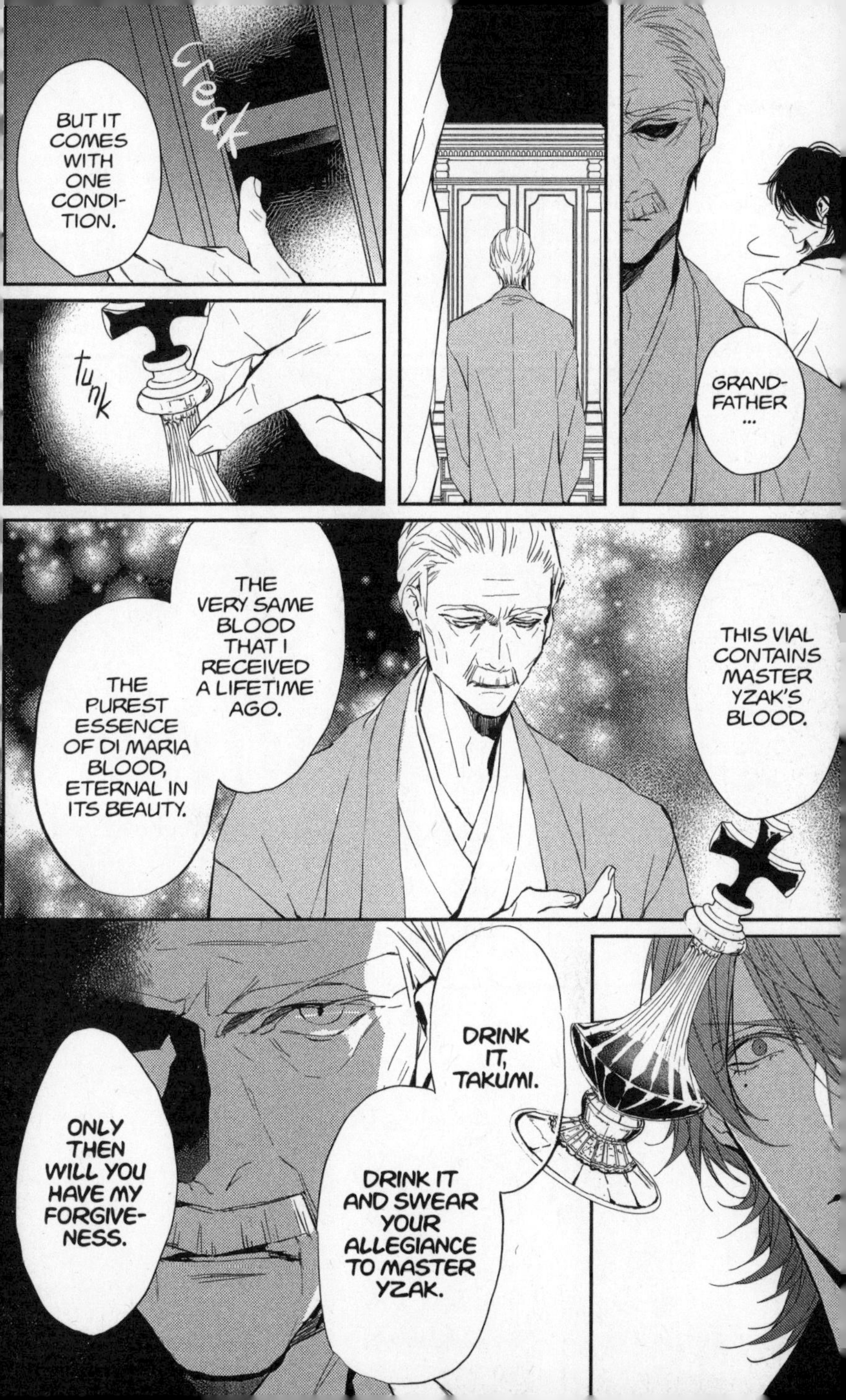
GRAND-FATHER...
BUT IT COMES WITH ONE CONDITION.
creak
tunk
THIS VIAL CONTAINS MASTER YZAK'S BLOOD.
THE VERY SAME BLOOD THAT I RECEIVED A LIFETIME AGO.
THE PUREST ESSENCE OF DI MARIA BLOOD, ETERNAL IN ITS BEAUTY.
DRINK IT, TAKUMI.
DRINK IT AND SWEAR YOUR ALLEGIANCE TO MASTER YZAK.
ONLY THEN WILL YOU HAVE MY FORGIVENESS.

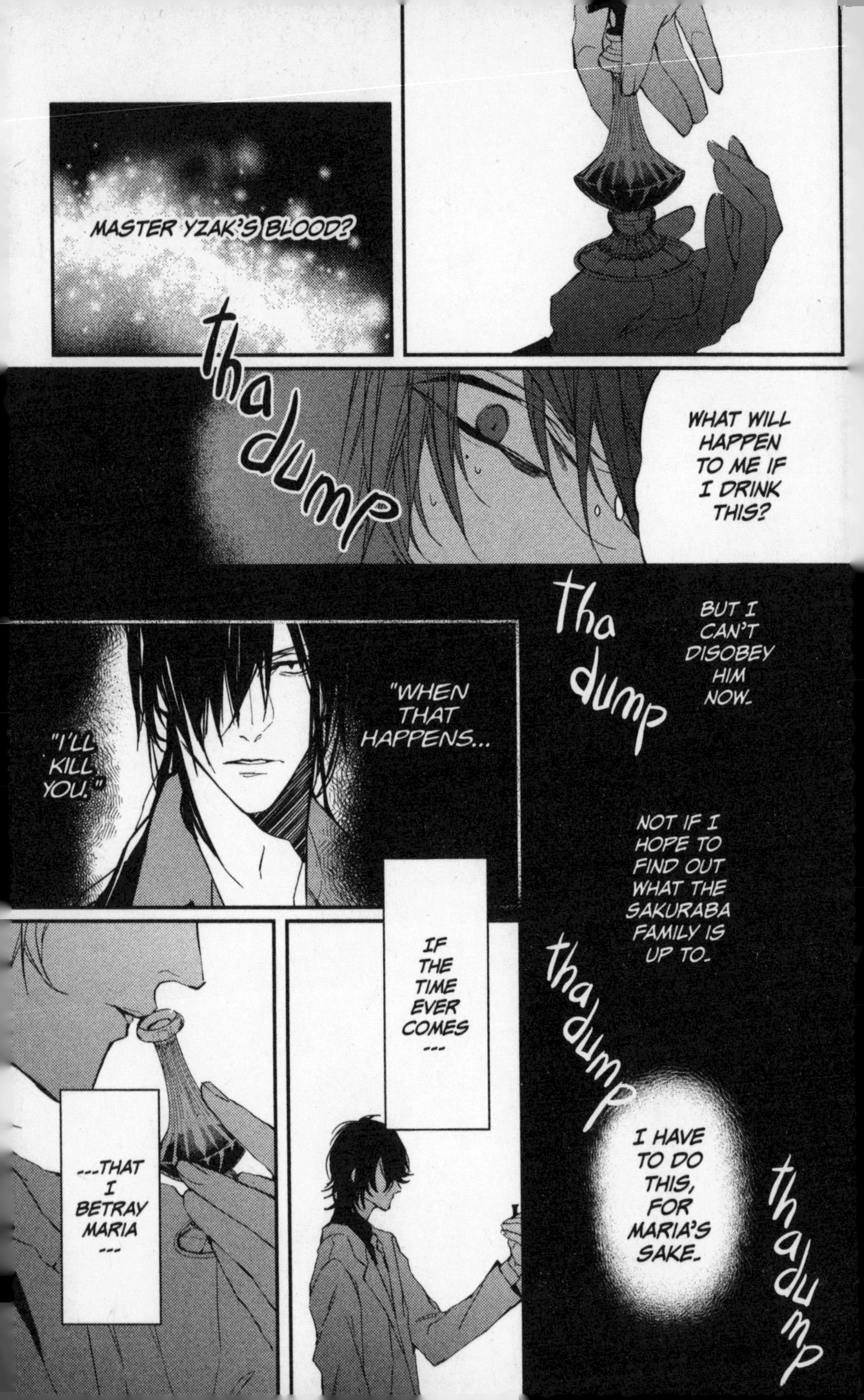
MASTER YZAK'S BLOOD?
tha dump
WHAT WILL HAPPEN TO ME IF I DRINK THIS?
tha dump
BUT I CAN'T DISOBEY HIM NOW.
NOT IF I HOPE TO FIND OUT WHAT THE SAKURABA FAMILY IS UP TO.
tha dump
I HAVE TO DO THIS, FOR MARIA'S SAKE.
tha dump
"WHEN THAT HAPPENS...
"I'LL KILL YOU."
IF THE TIME EVER COMES ---
---THAT I BETRAY MARIA ---

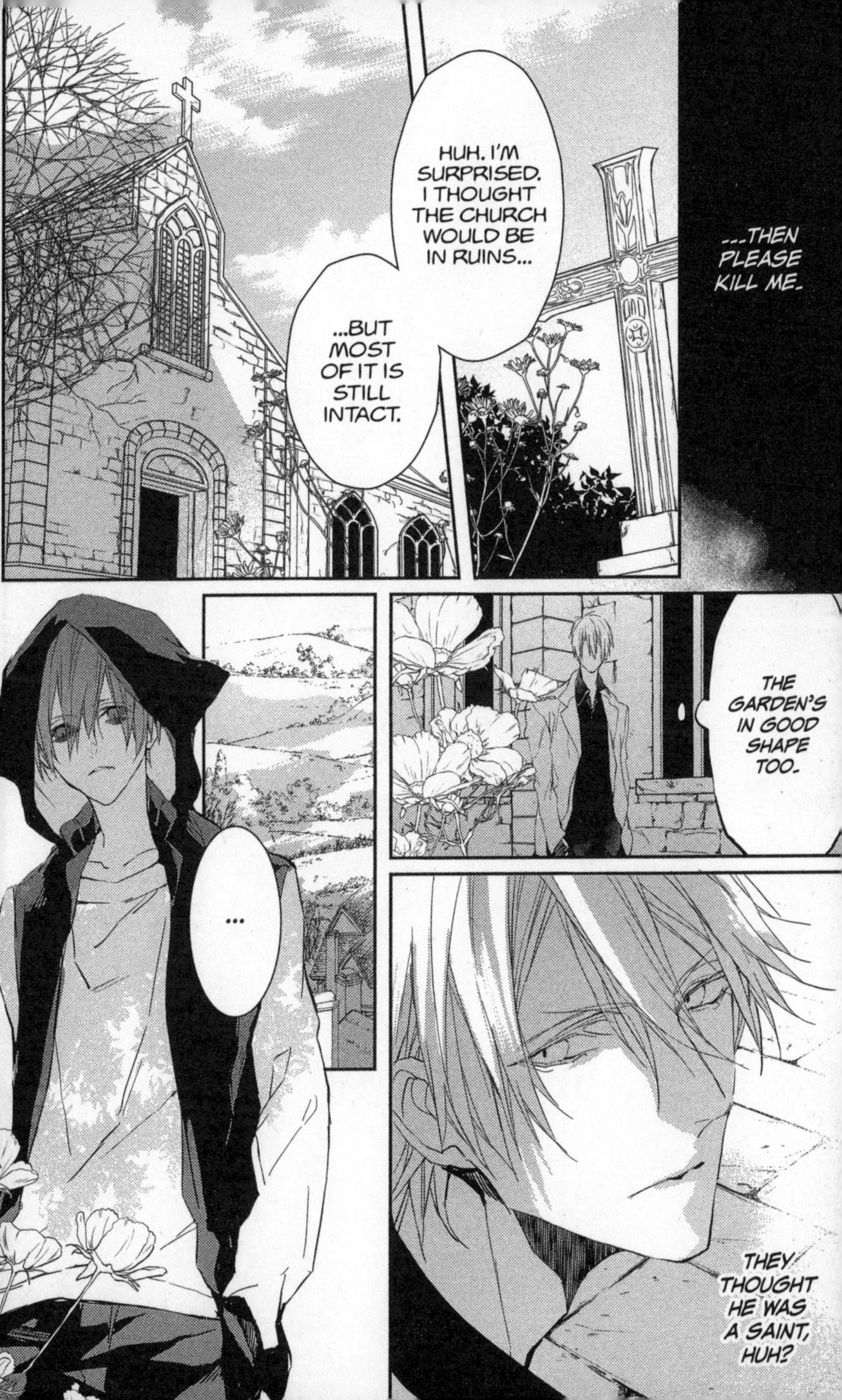

---THEN PLEASE KILL ME.
HUH. I'M SURPRISED. I THOUGHT THE CHURCH WOULD BE IN RUINS...
...BUT MOST OF IT IS STILL INTACT.
THE GARDEN'S IN GOOD SHAPE TOO.
THEY THOUGHT HE WAS A SAINT, HUH?
...

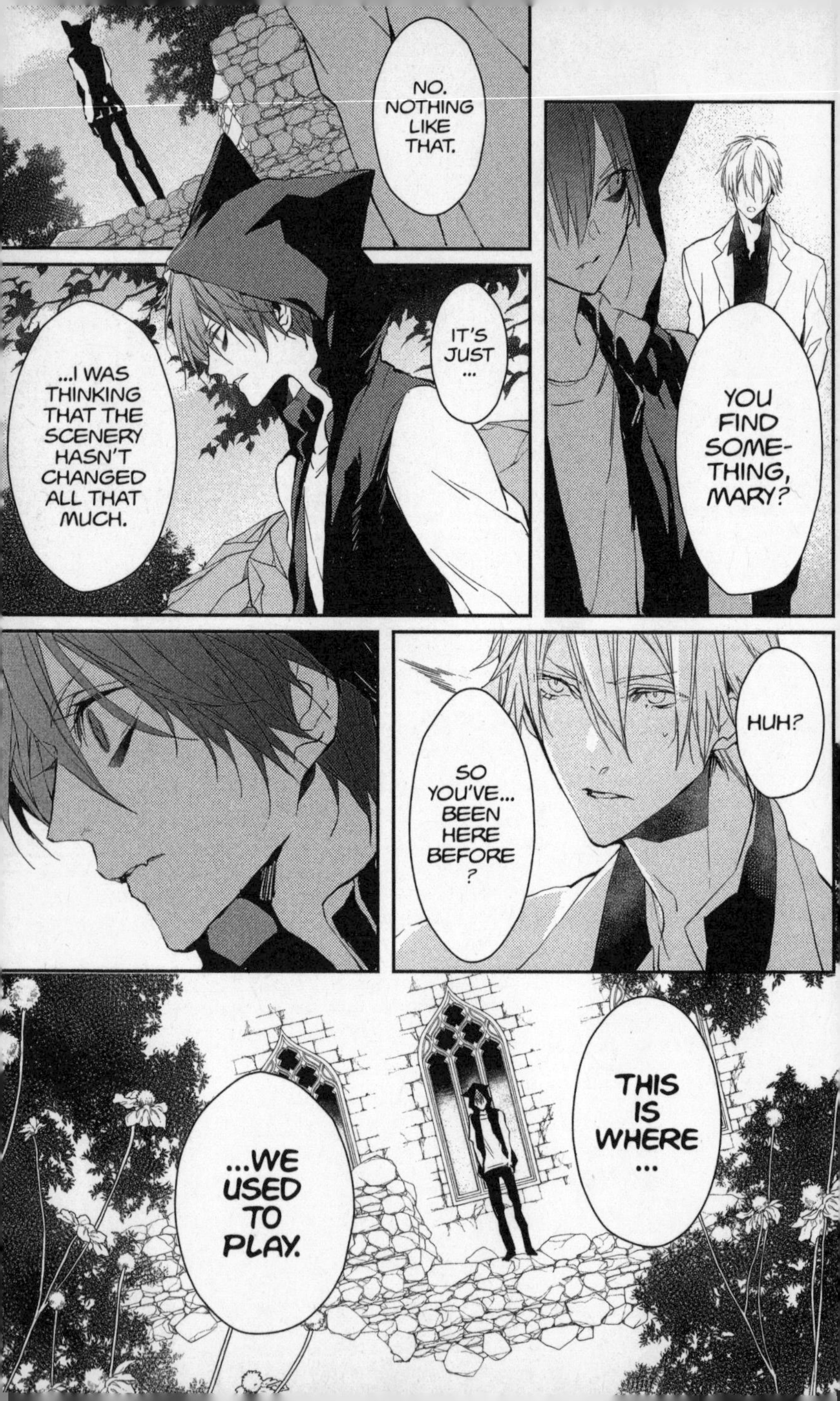
YOU FIND SOMETHING, MARY?
NO. NOTHING LIKE THAT.
IT'S JUST ...
...I WAS THINKING THAT THE SCENERY HASN'T CHANGED ALL THAT MUCH.
HUH?
SO YOU'VE... BEEN HERE BEFORE?
THIS IS WHERE ...
...WE USED TO PLAY.

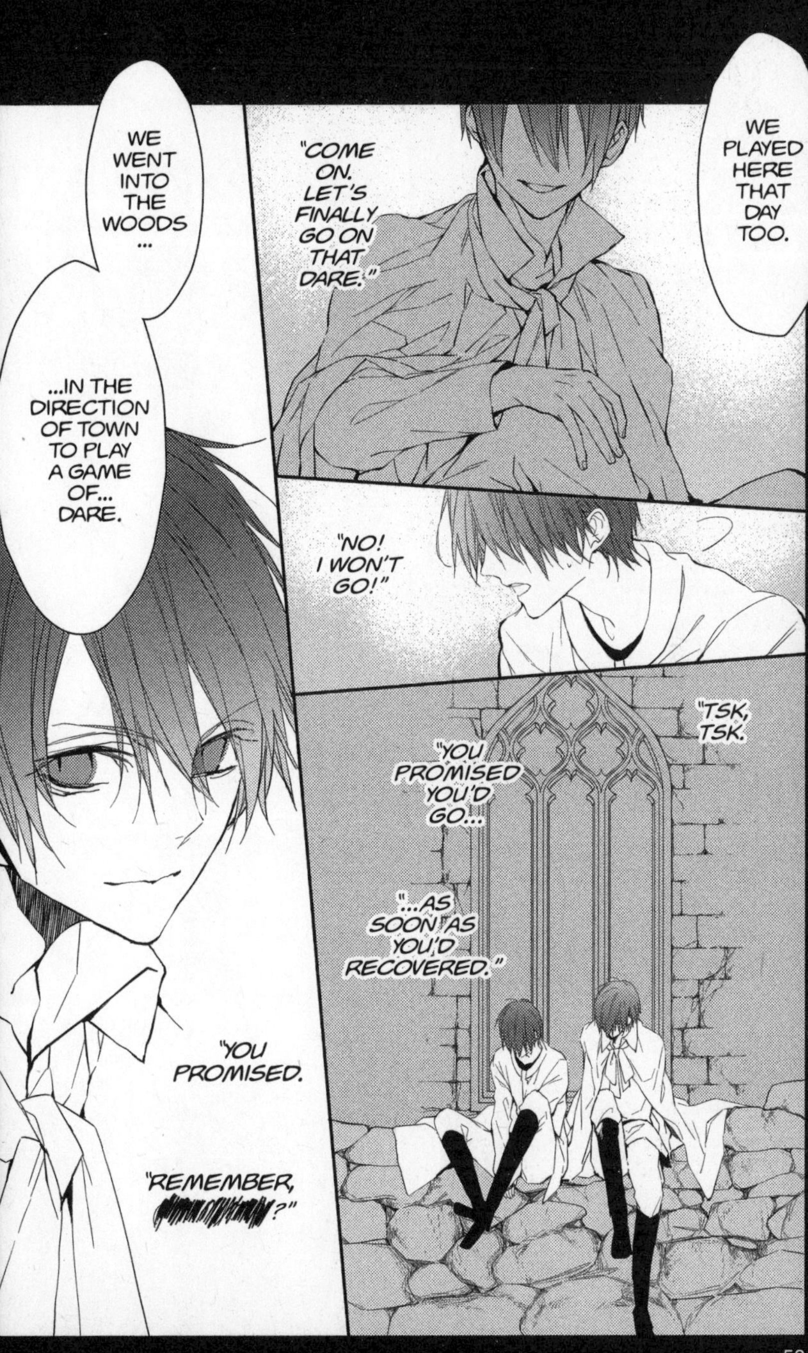
WE PLAYED HERE THAT DAY TOO.
WE WENT INTO THE WOODS...
...IN THE DIRECTION OF TOWN TO PLAY A GAME OF... DARE.
"COME ON. LET'S FINALLY GO ON THAT DARE."
"NO! I WON'T GO!"
"TSK, TSK.
"YOU PROMISED YOU'D GO...
"...AS SOON AS YOU'D RECOVERED."
"YOU PROMISED.
"REMEMBER, [redacted]?"

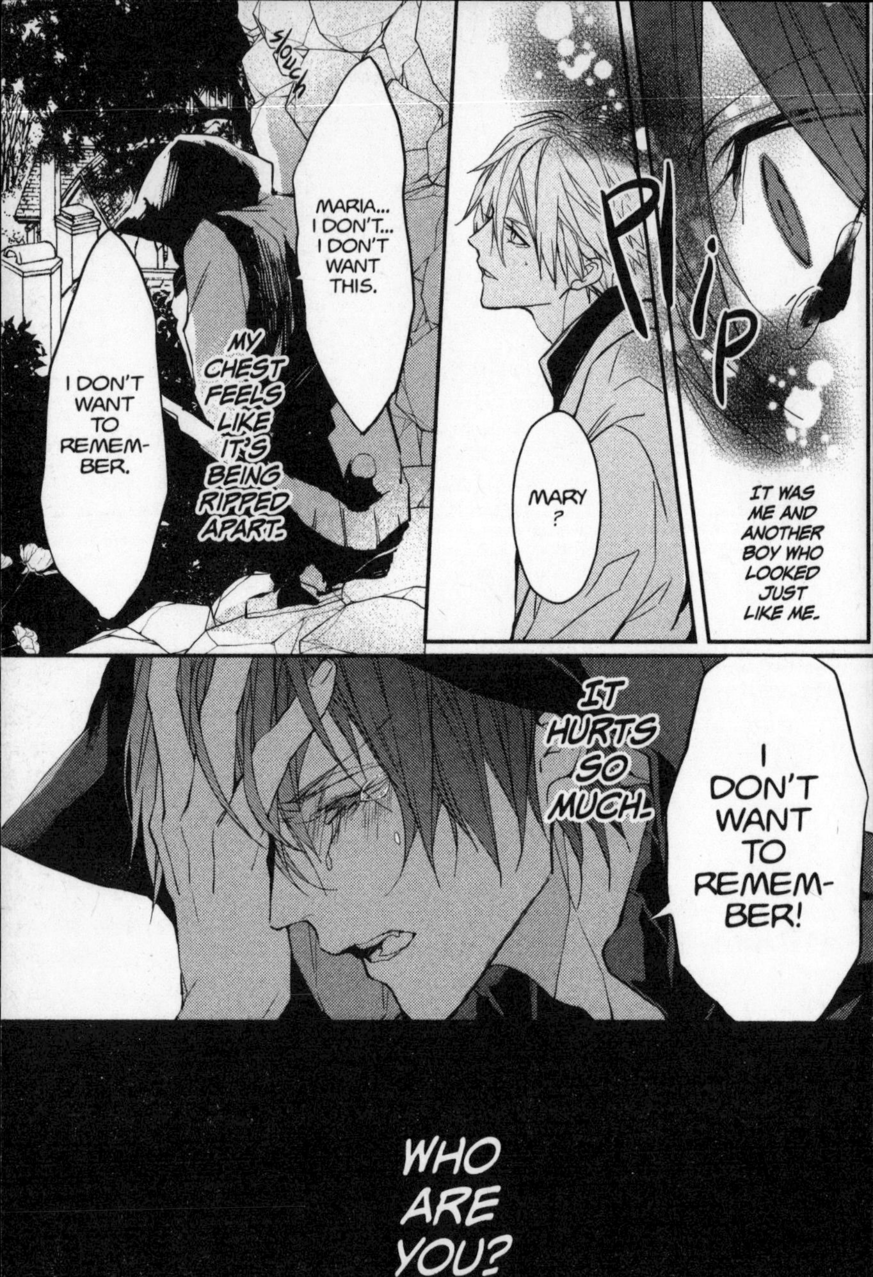
PLIP
IT WAS ME AND ANOTHER BOY WHO LOOKED JUST LIKE ME.
MARY?
slouch
MARIA... I DON'T... I DON'T WANT THIS.
MY CHEST FEELS LIKE IT'S BEING RIPPED APART.
I DON'T WANT TO REMEMBER.
I DON'T WANT TO REMEMBER!
IT HURTS SO MUCH.
WHO ARE YOU?

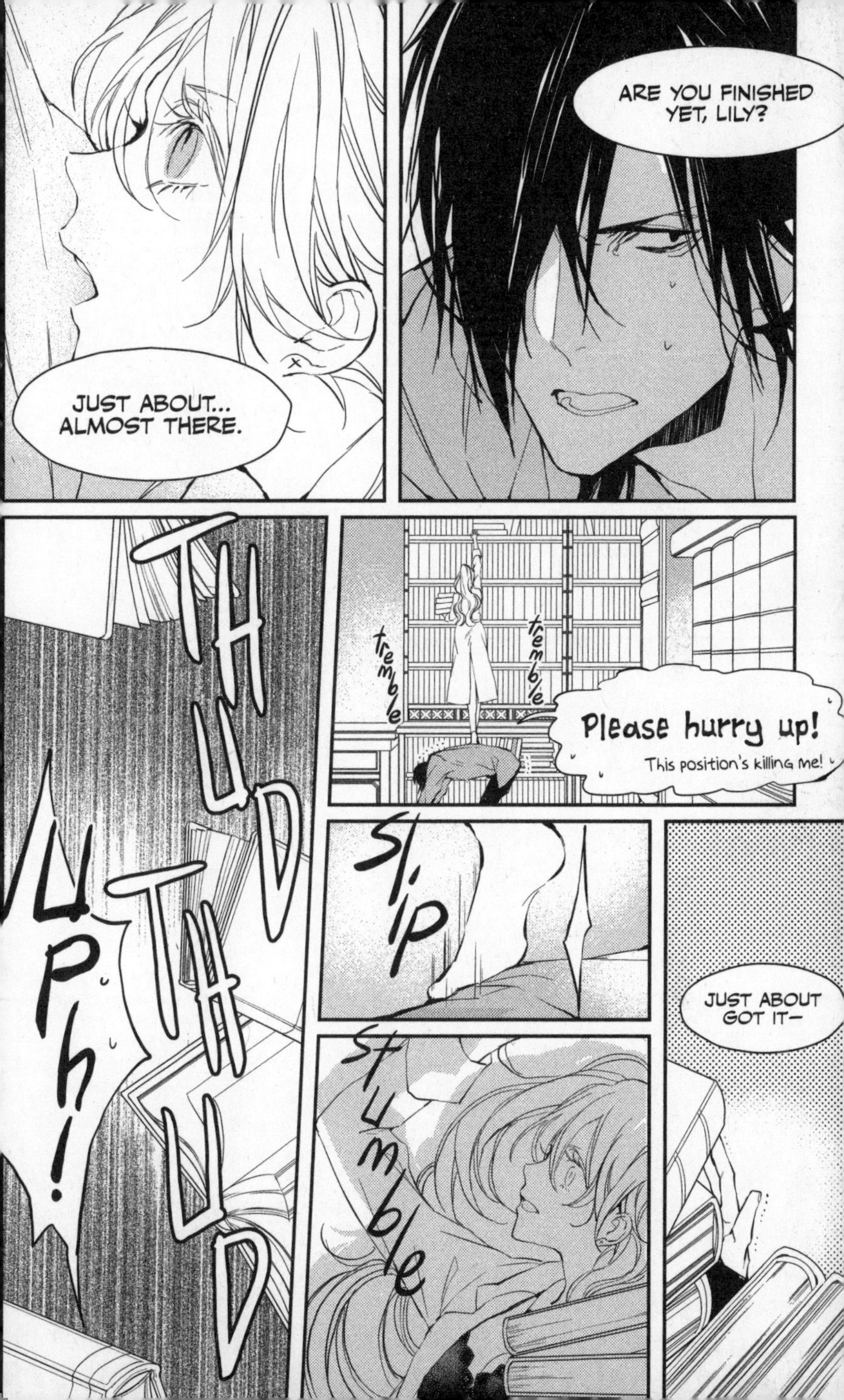
ARE YOU FINISHED YET, LILY?
JUST ABOUT... ALMOST THERE.
tremble
tremble
Please hurry up!
This position's killing me!
JUST ABOUT GOT IT—
slip
stumble
THUD
THUD
UPH!!

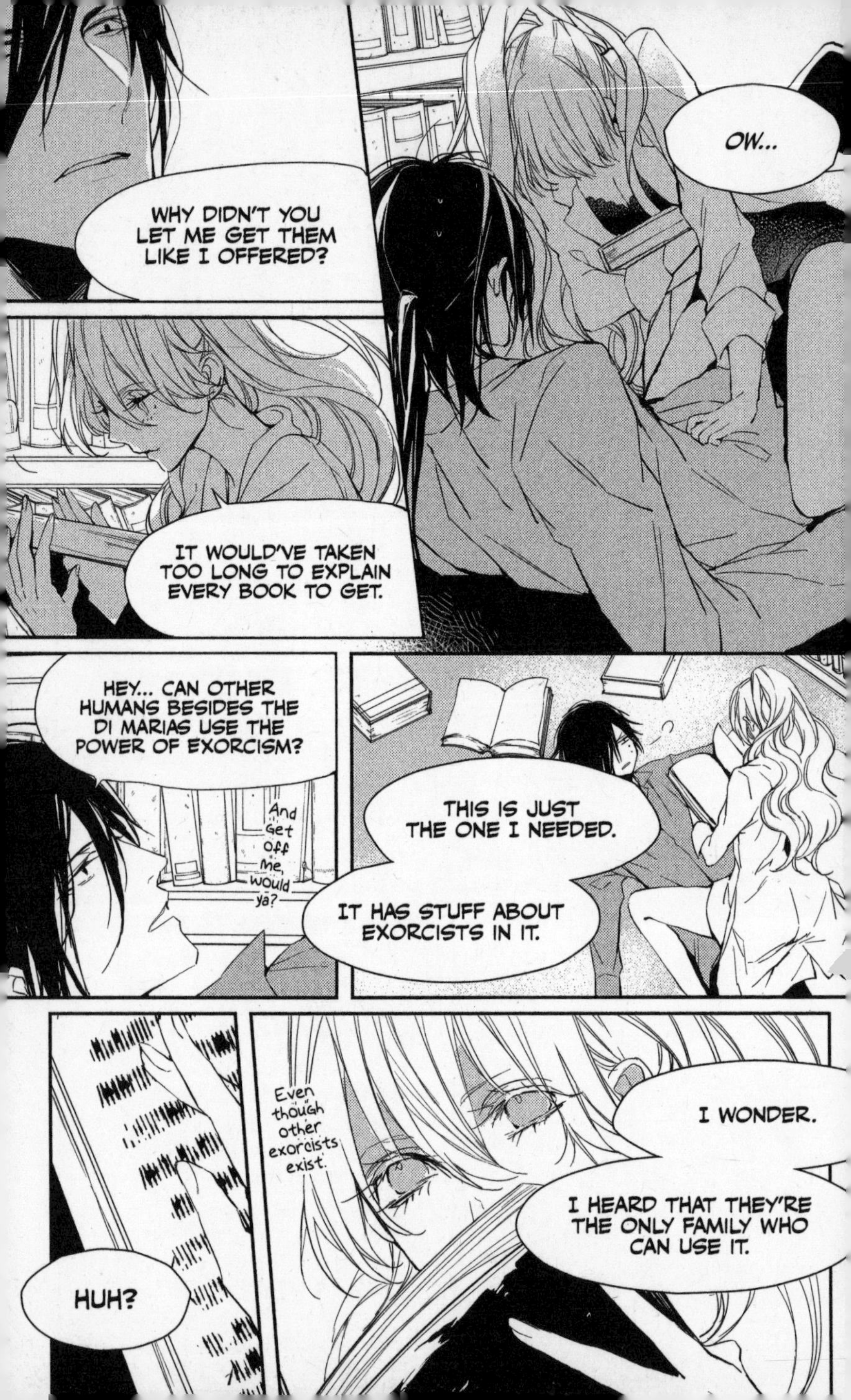
OW...
WHY DIDN'T YOU LET ME GET THEM LIKE I OFFERED?
IT WOULD'VE TAKEN TOO LONG TO EXPLAIN EVERY BOOK TO GET.
THIS IS JUST THE ONE I NEEDED.
IT HAS STUFF ABOUT EXORCISTS IN IT.
HEY... CAN OTHER HUMANS BESIDES THE DI MARIAS USE THE POWER OF EXORCISM?
And get off me, would ya?
I WONDER.
I HEARD THAT THEY'RE THE ONLY FAMILY WHO CAN USE IT.
Even though other exorcists exist.
HUH?

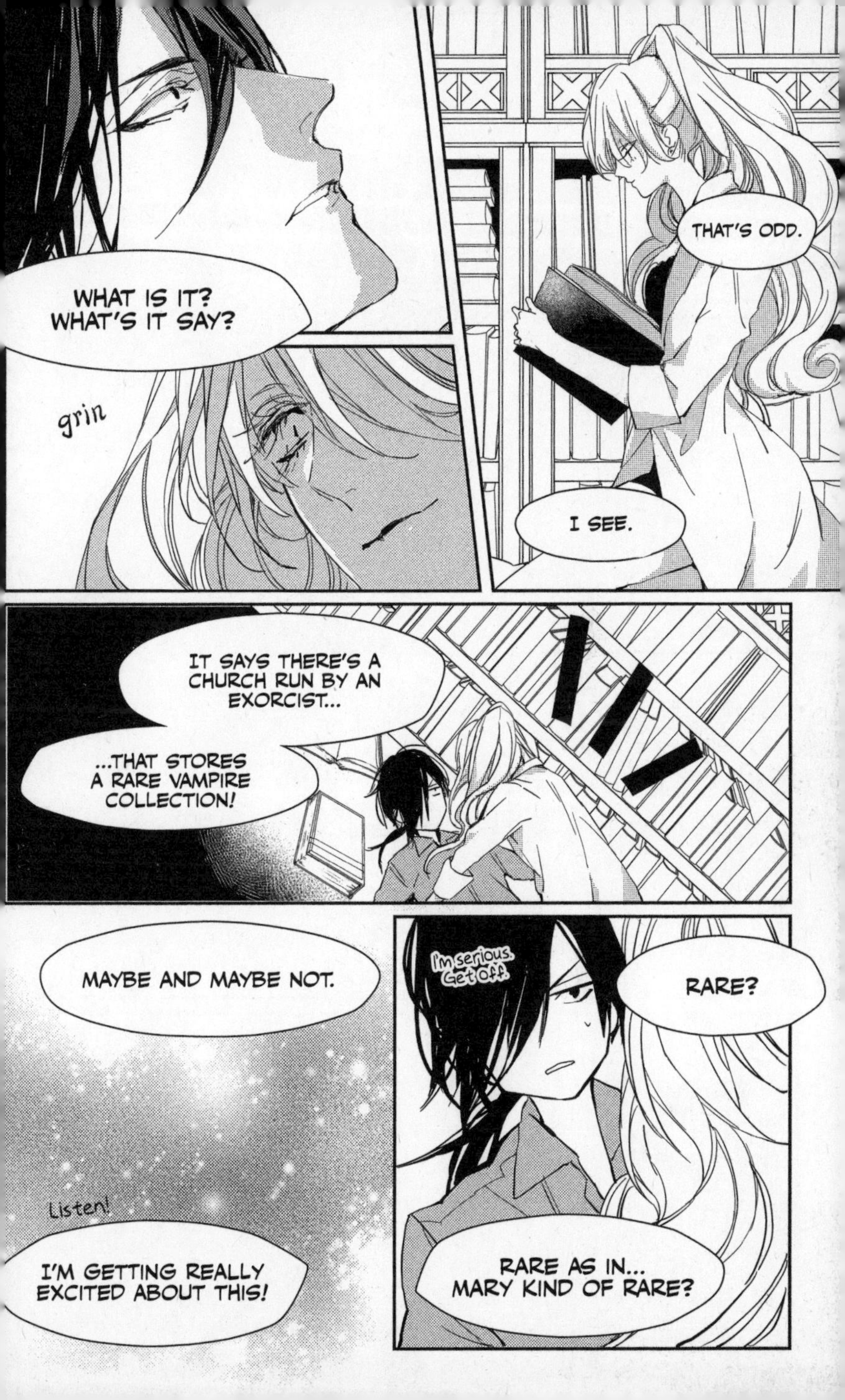
THAT'S ODD.
I SEE.
WHAT IS IT? WHAT'S IT SAY?
grin
IT SAYS THERE'S A CHURCH RUN BY AN EXORCIST...
...THAT STORES A RARE VAMPIRE COLLECTION!
RARE?
I'm serious. Get off.
RARE AS IN... MARY KIND OF RARE?
MAYBE AND MAYBE NOT.
Listen!
I'M GETTING REALLY EXCITED ABOUT THIS!

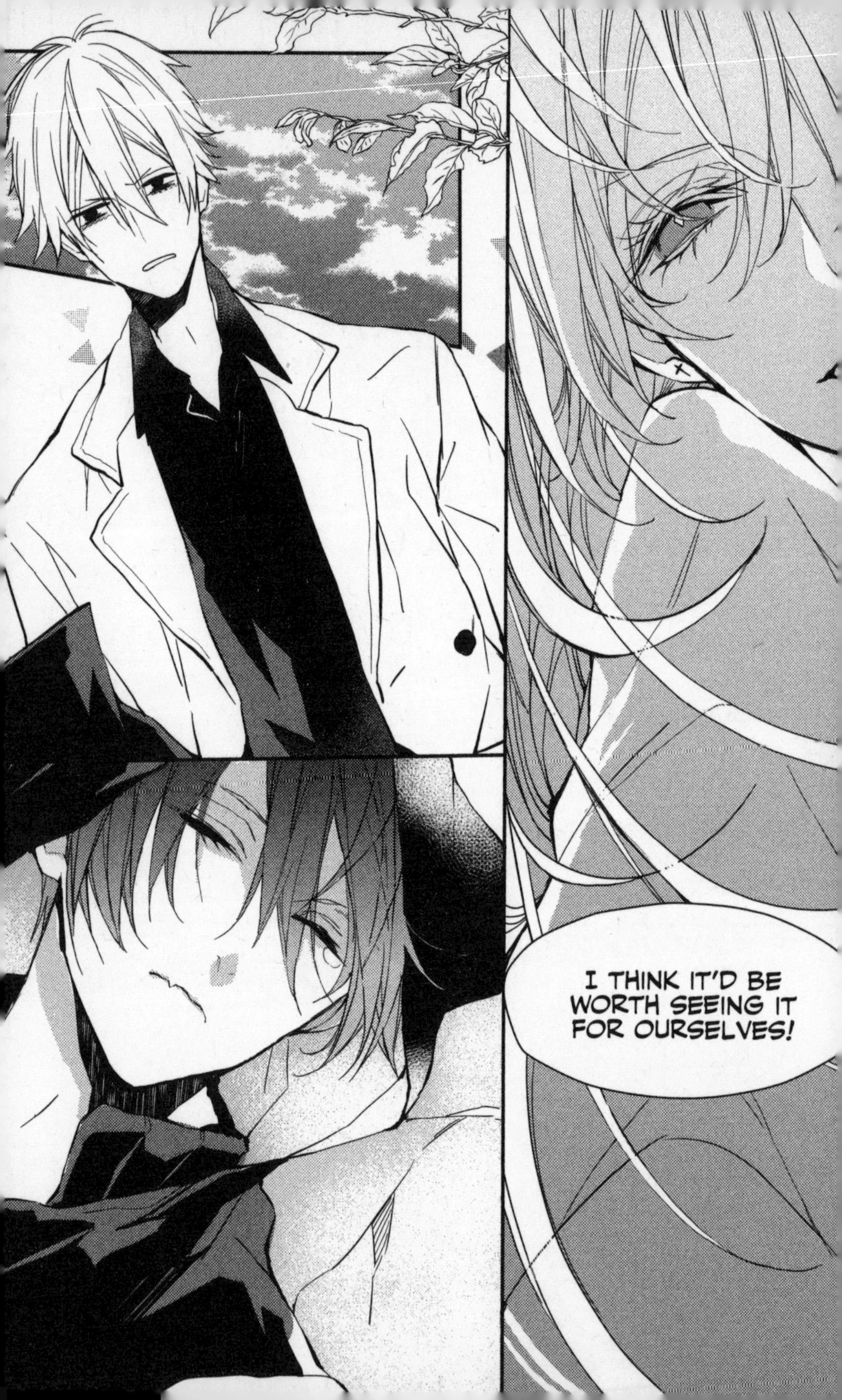
I THINK IT'D BE WORTH SEEING IT FOR OURSELVES!

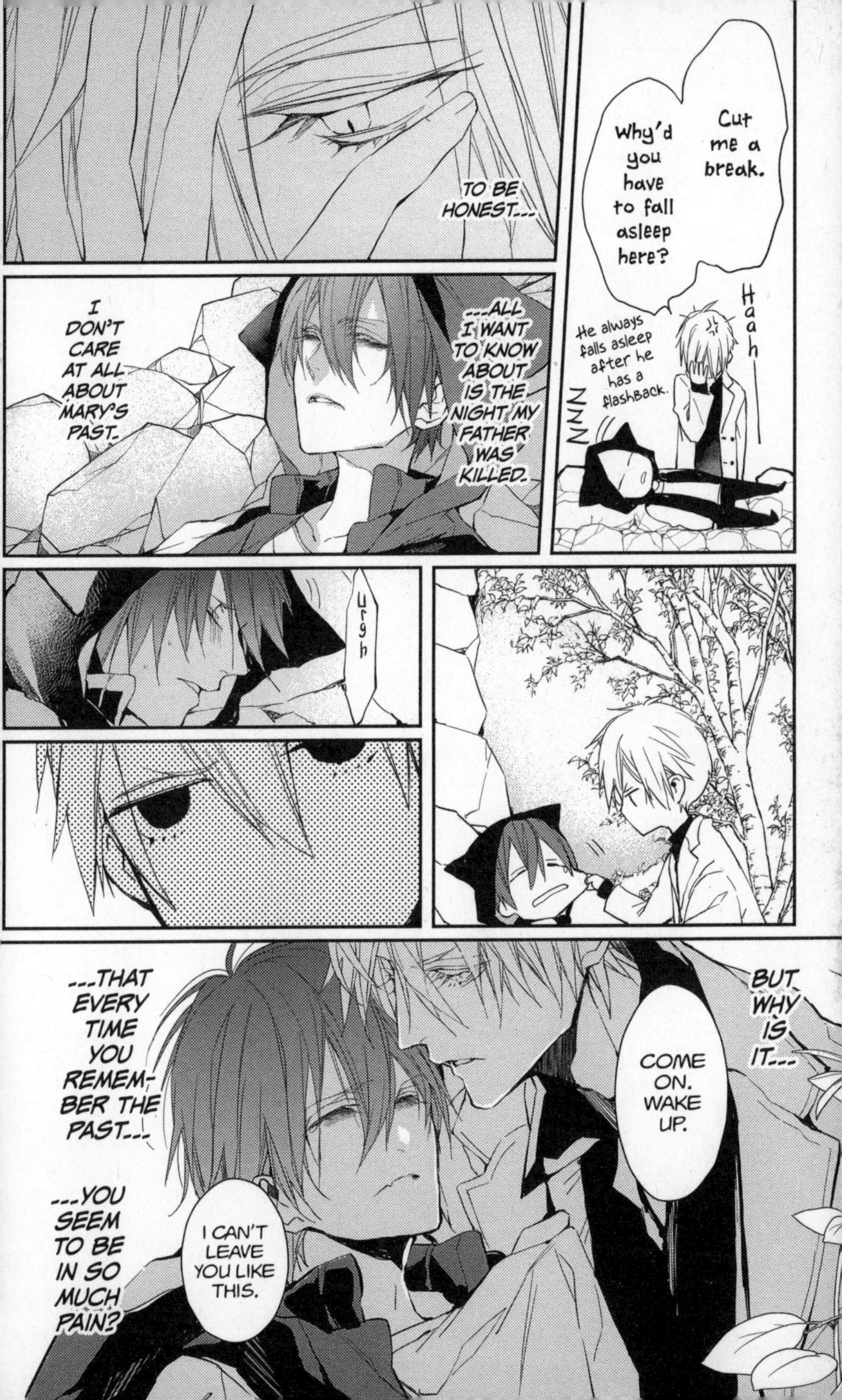

Cut me a break.
Why'd you have to fall asleep here?
Haah
He always falls asleep after he has a flashback.
NNN
TO BE HONEST...
...ALL I WANT TO KNOW ABOUT IS THE NIGHT MY FATHER WAS KILLED.
I DON'T CARE AT ALL ABOUT MARY'S PAST.
Urgh
BUT WHY IS IT...
COME ON. WAKE UP.
...THAT EVERY TIME YOU REMEMBER THE PAST...
I CAN'T LEAVE YOU LIKE THIS.
...YOU SEEM TO BE IN SO MUCH PAIN?

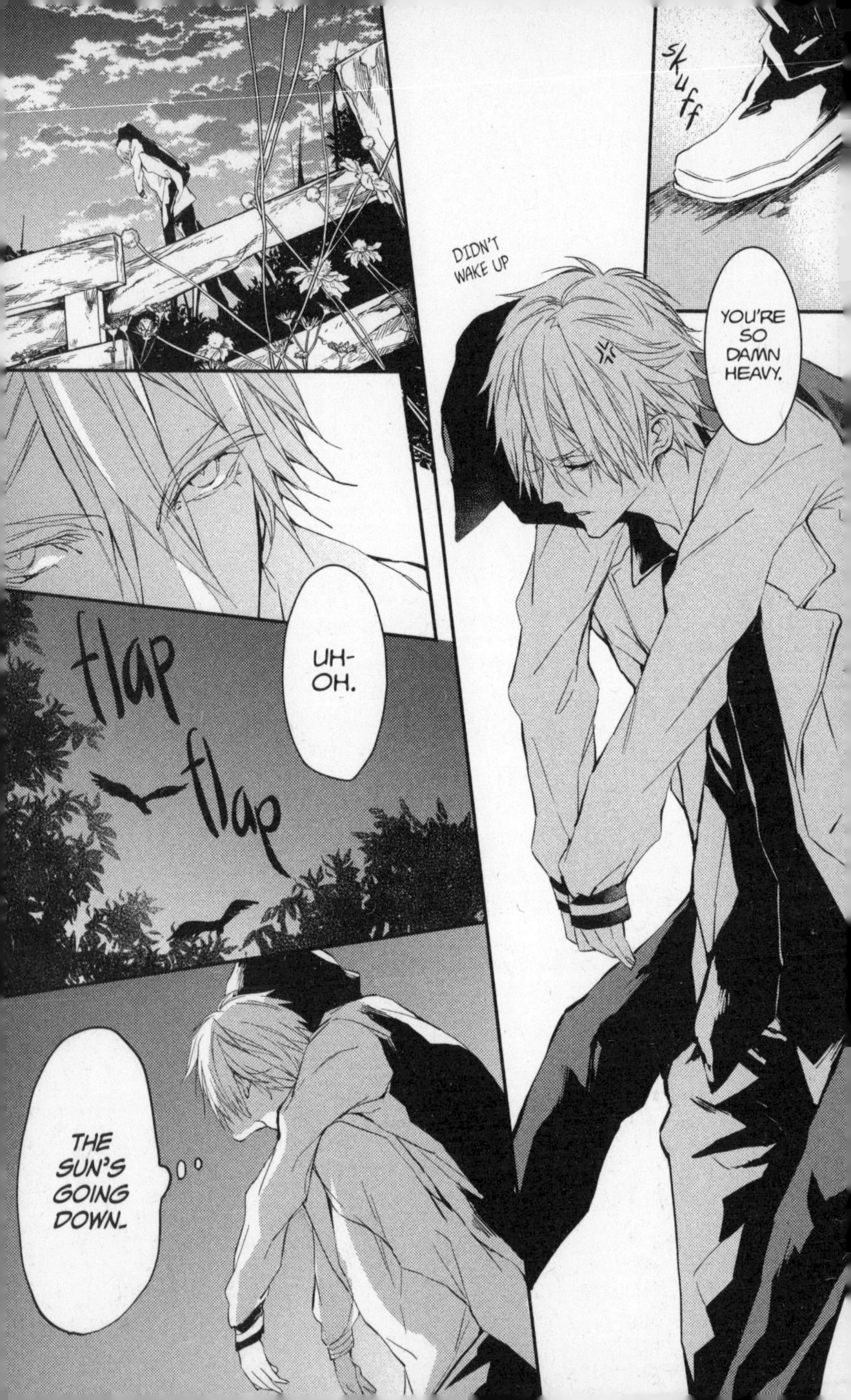
skuff
DIDN'T WAKE UP
YOU'RE SO DAMN HEAVY.
UH-OH.
flap flap
THE SUN'S GOING DOWN...

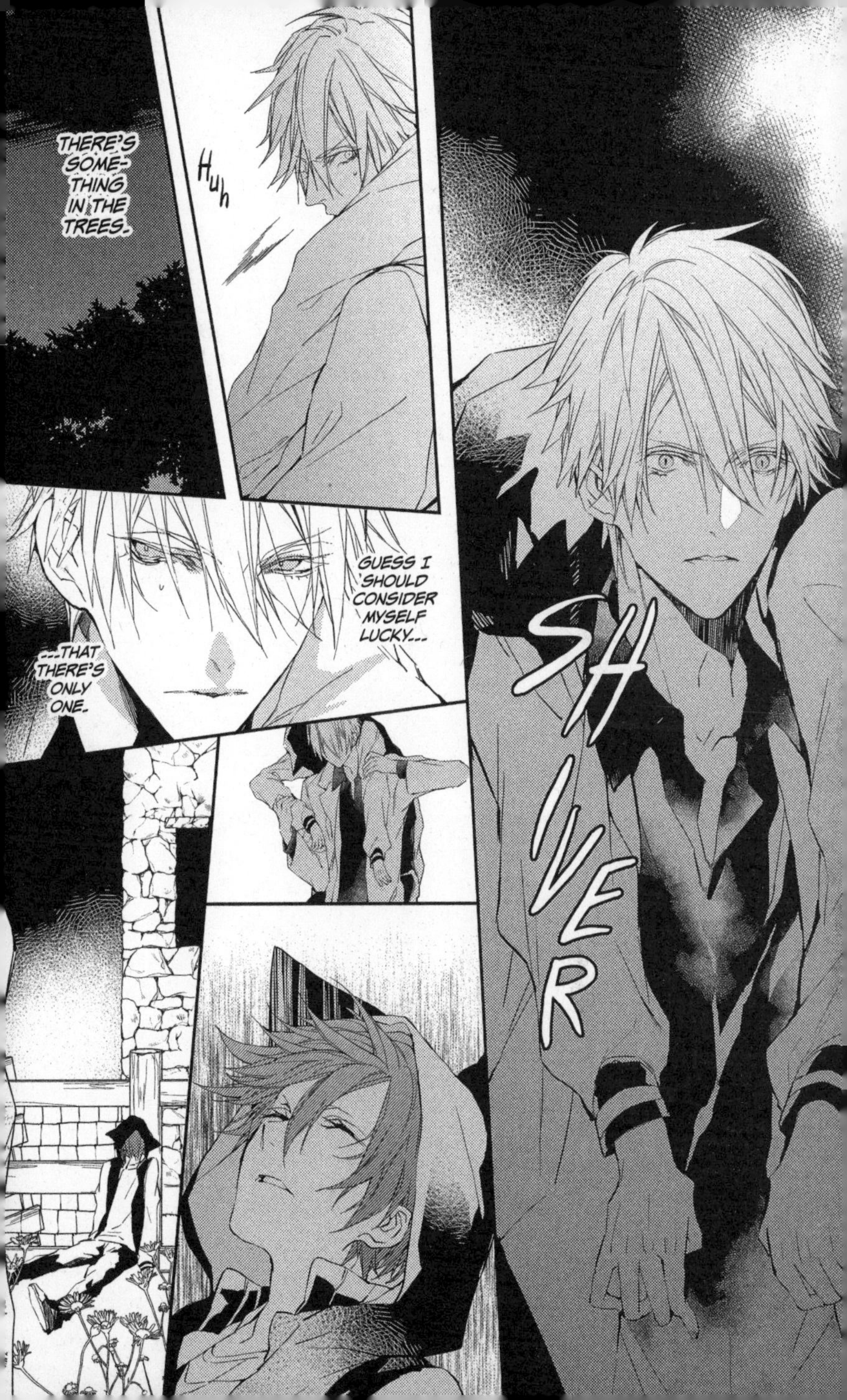
SHIVER
Huh
THERE'S SOME-THING IN THE TREES.
GUESS I SHOULD CONSIDER MYSELF LUCKY...
...THAT THERE'S ONLY ONE.

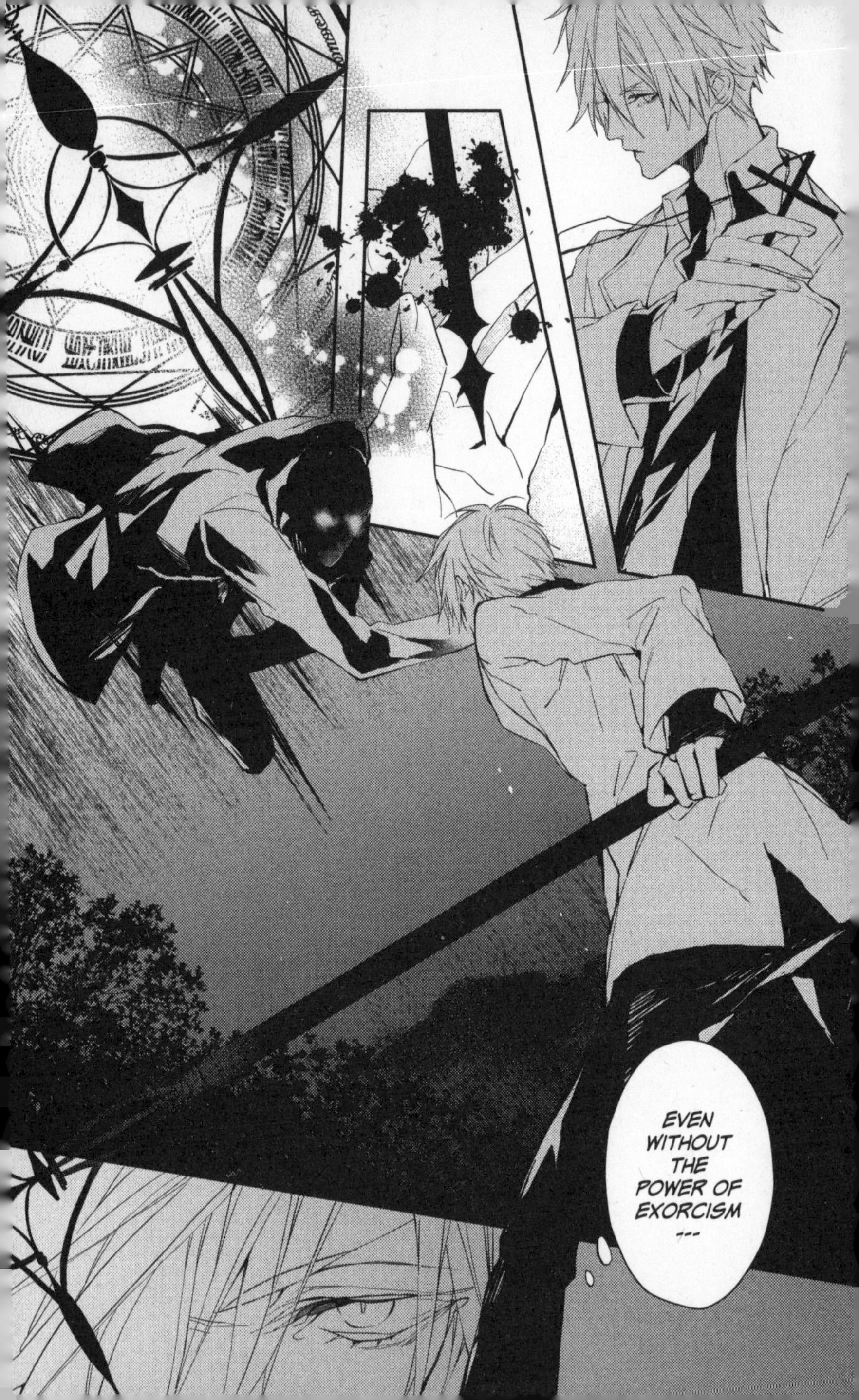
EVEN WITHOUT THE POWER OF EXORCISM...

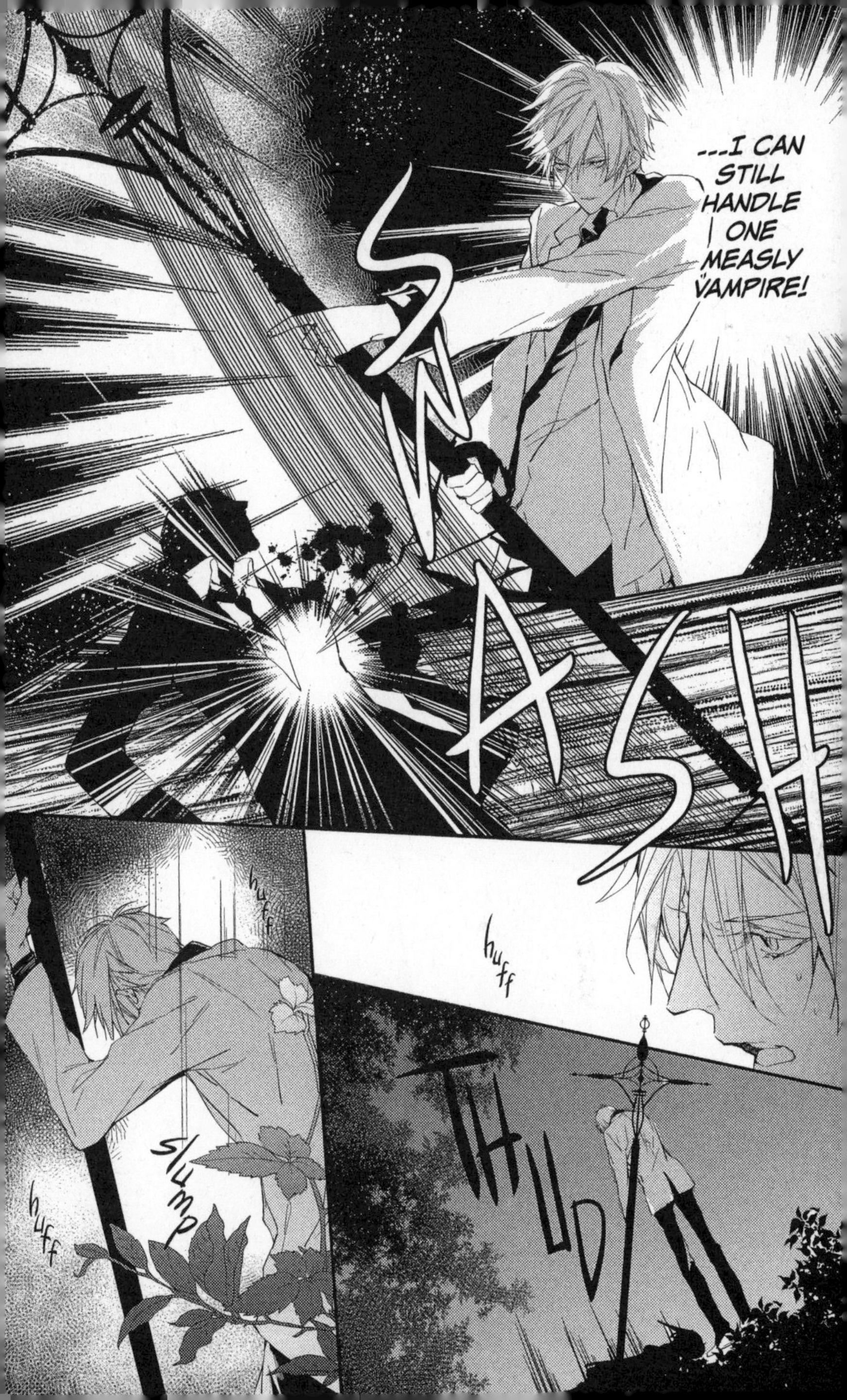
---I CAN STILL HANDLE ONE MEASLY VAMPIRE!
SWASH
huff
THUD
huff
slump
huff

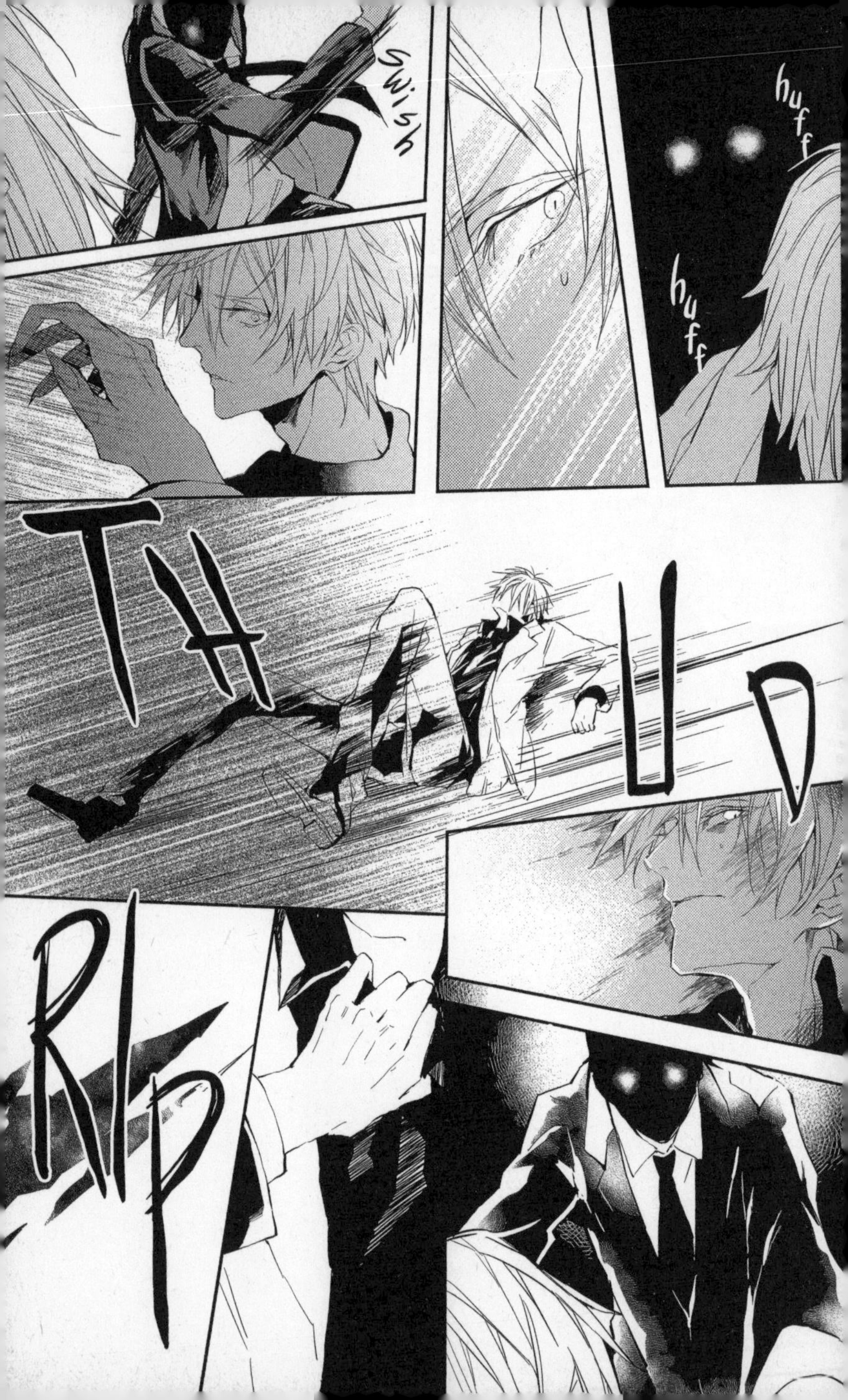
huff
huff
huff
huff
SWISH
THUD
RIP

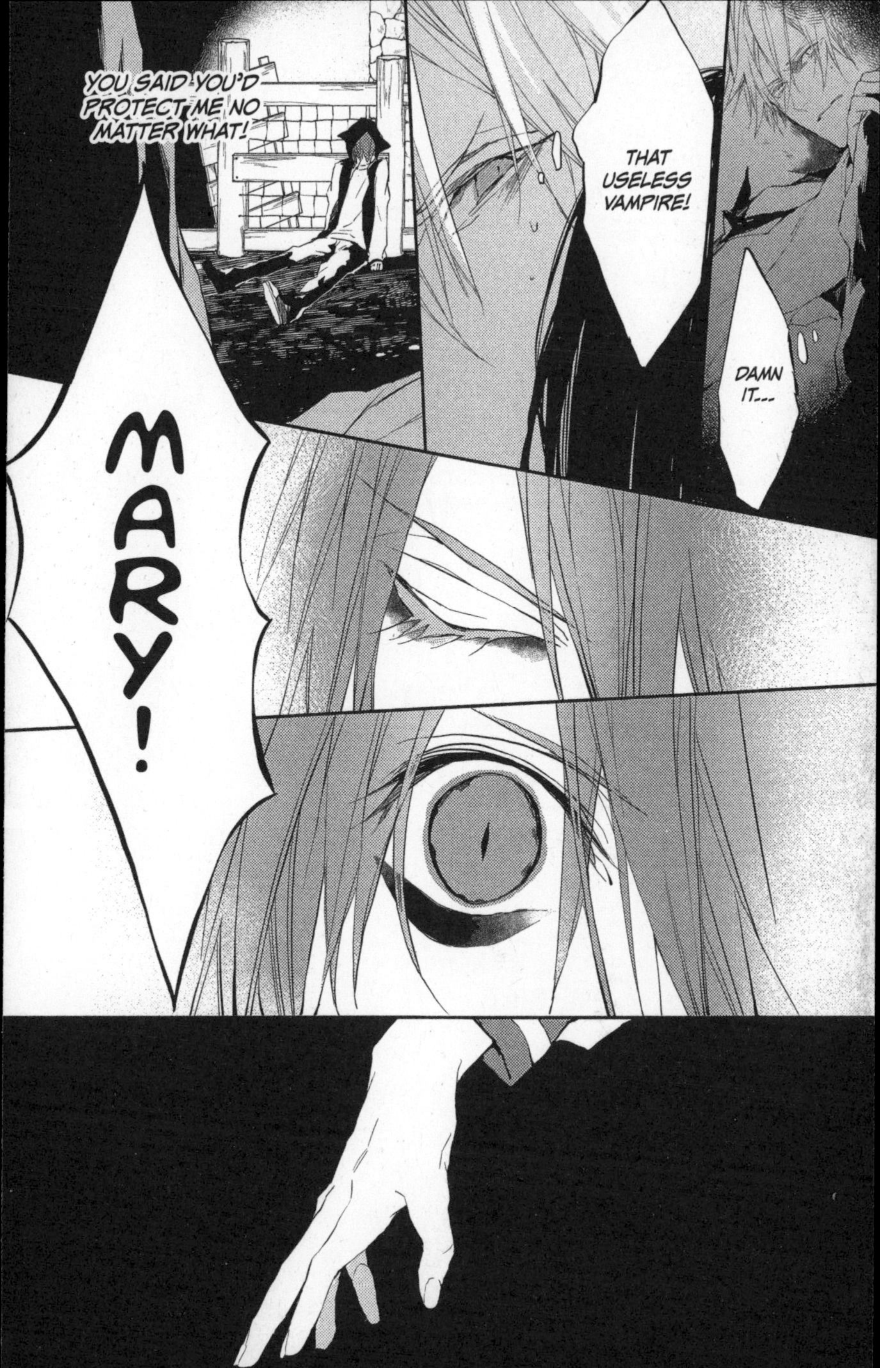
DAMN IT...
THAT USELESS VAMPIRE!
YOU SAID YOU'D PROTECT ME NO MATTER WHAT!
MARY!

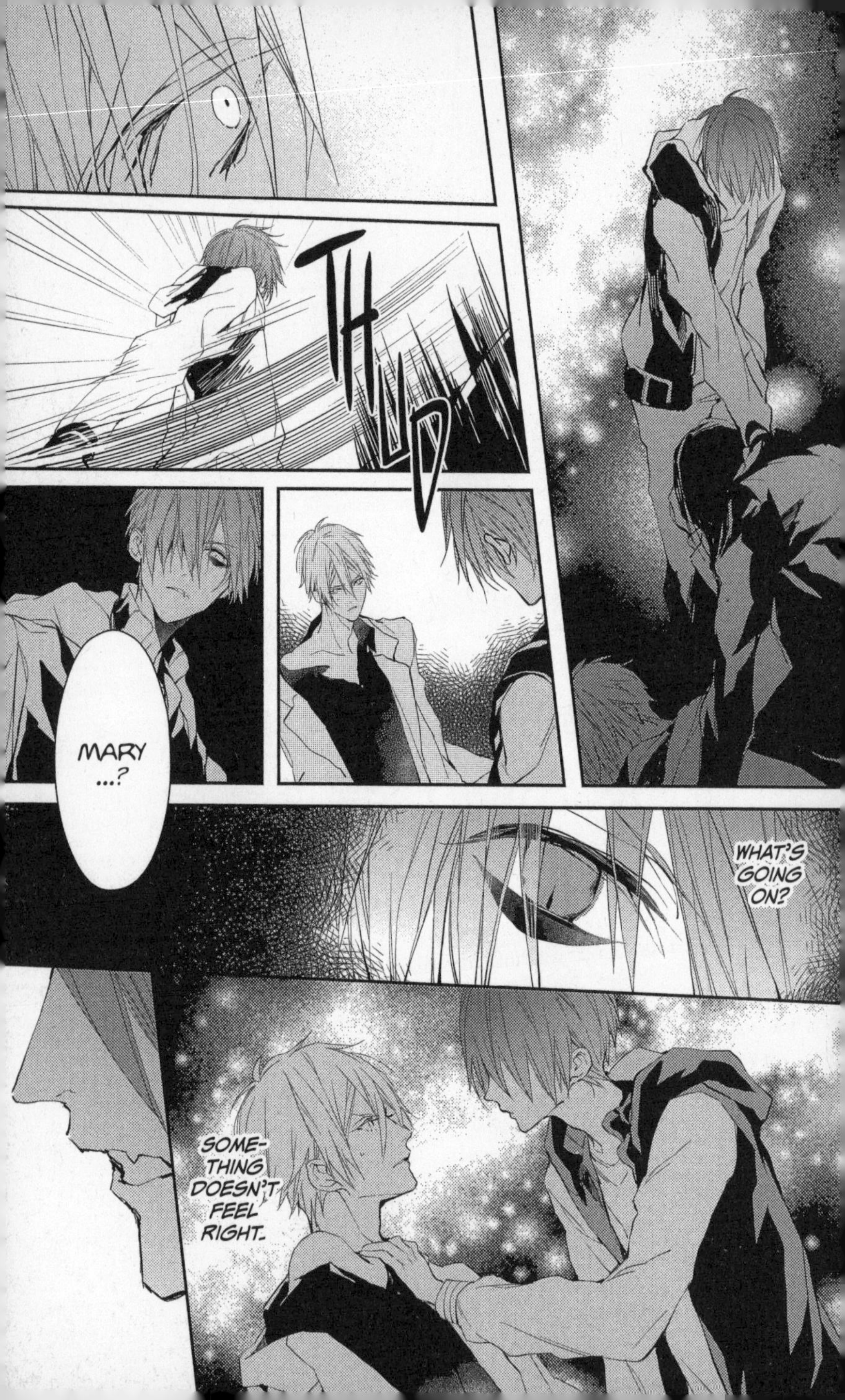
THUD
MARY ...?
WHAT'S GOING ON?
SOME-THING DOESN'T FEEL RIGHT.

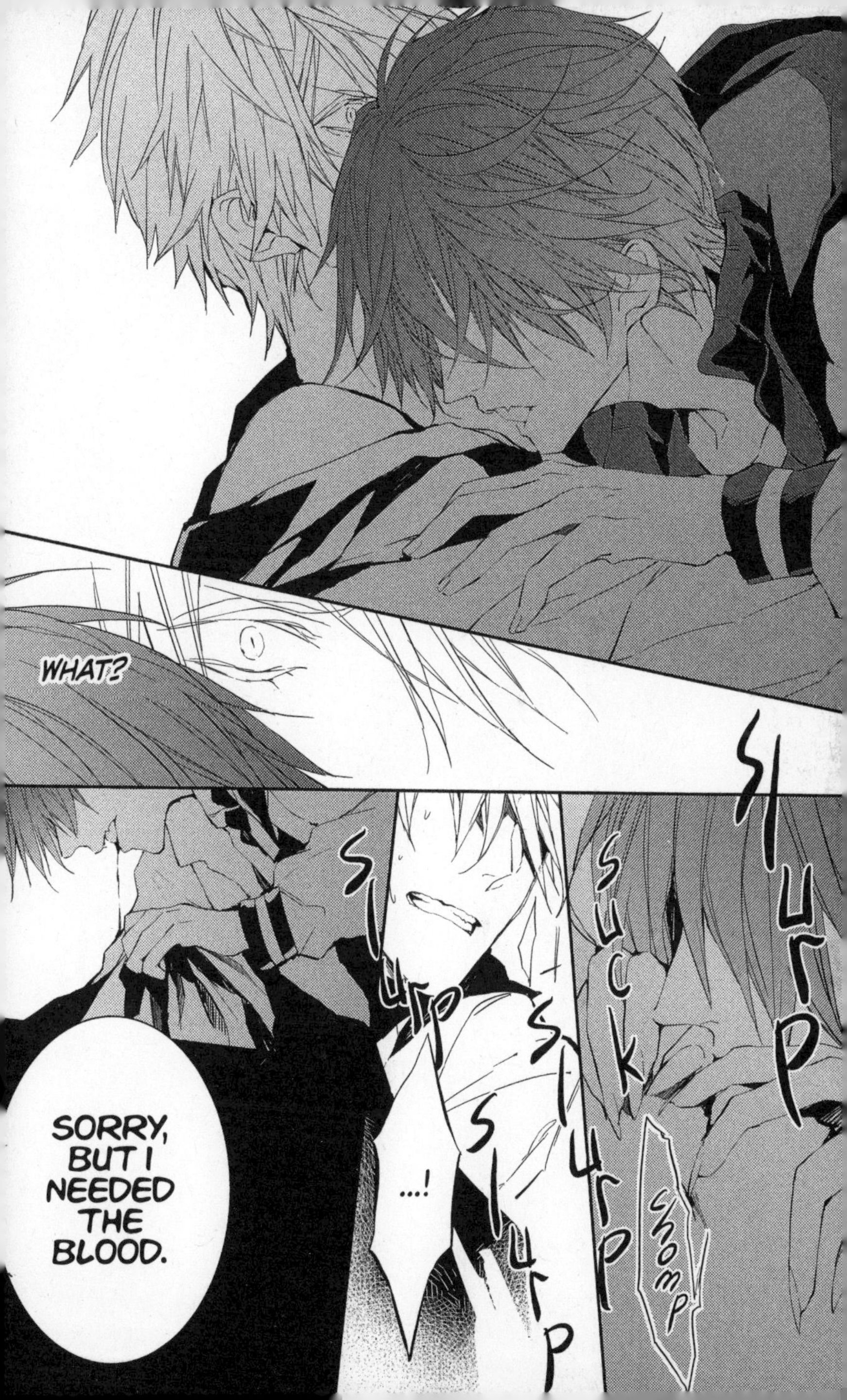
WHAT?
slurp
chomp
suck
slurp
slurp
slurp
...!
SORRY, BUT I NEEDED THE BLOOD.

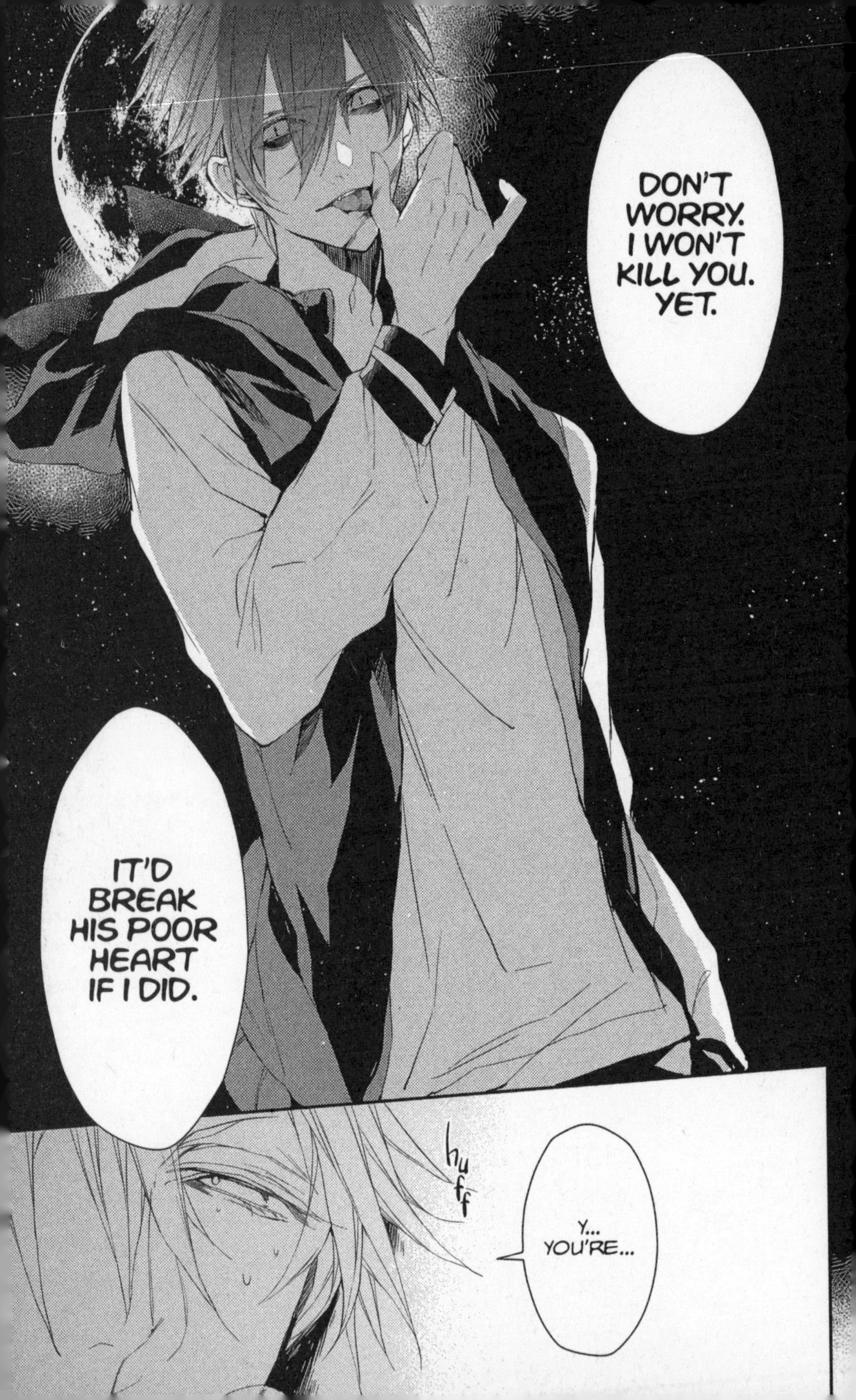
DON'T WORRY. I WON'T KILL YOU. YET.
IT'D BREAK HIS POOR HEART IF I DID.
huff
Y... YOU'RE...

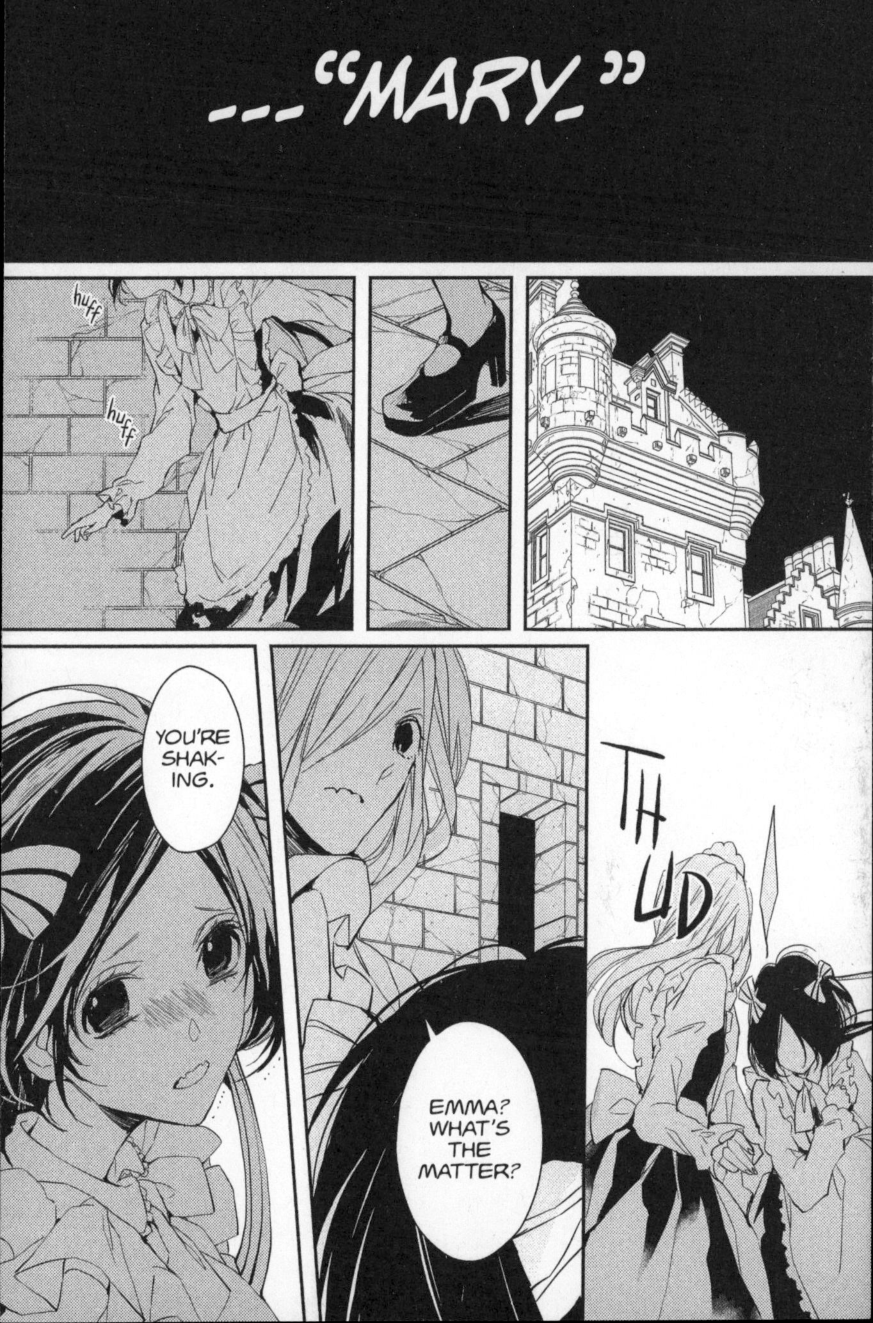
---"MARY."
huff
huff
THUD
EMMA? WHAT'S THE MATTER?
YOU'RE SHAKING.

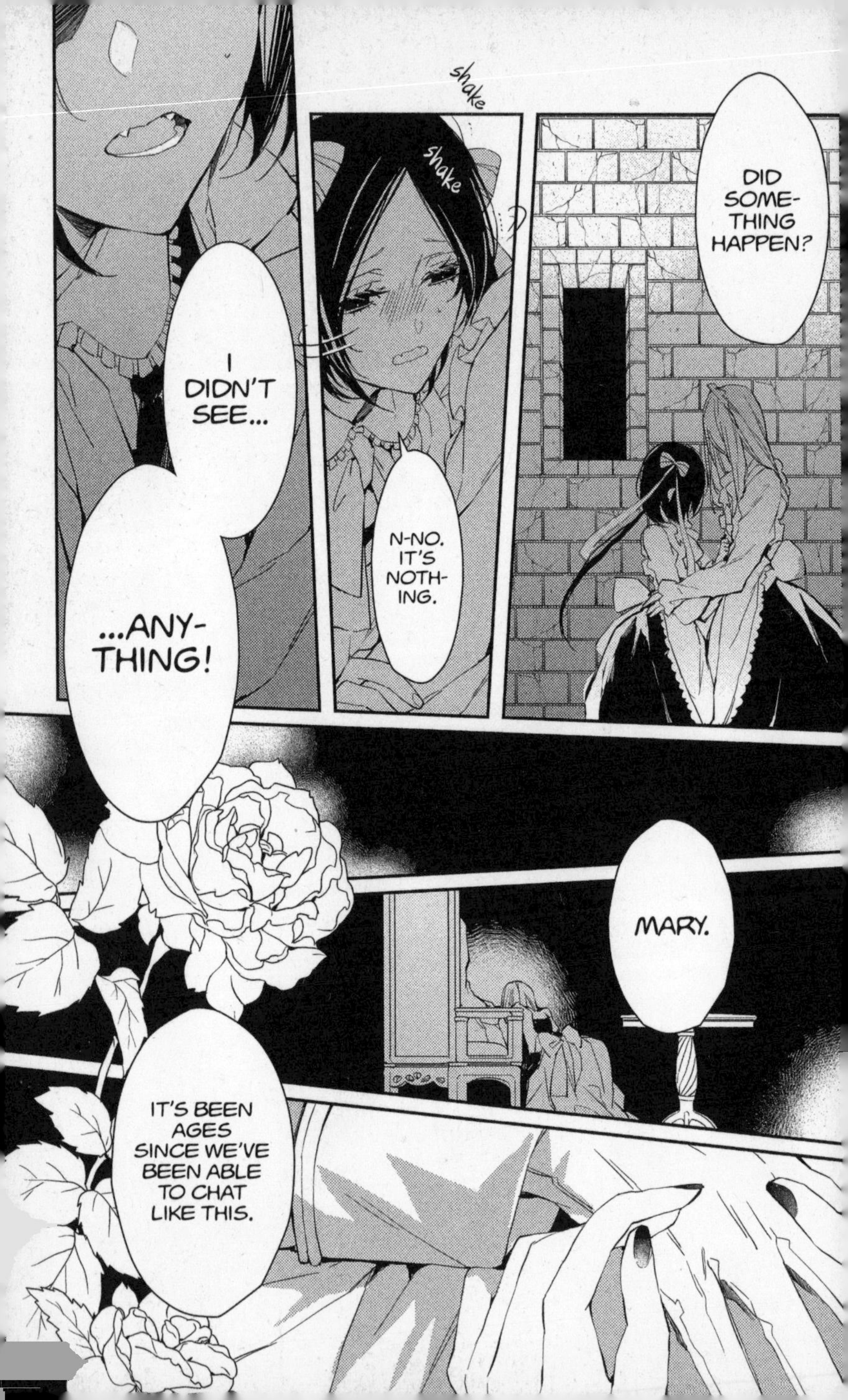
DID SOMETHING HAPPEN?
shake
shake
N-NO. IT'S NOTHING.
I DIDN'T SEE...
...ANYTHING!
MARY.
IT'S BEEN AGES SINCE WE'VE BEEN ABLE TO CHAT LIKE THIS.

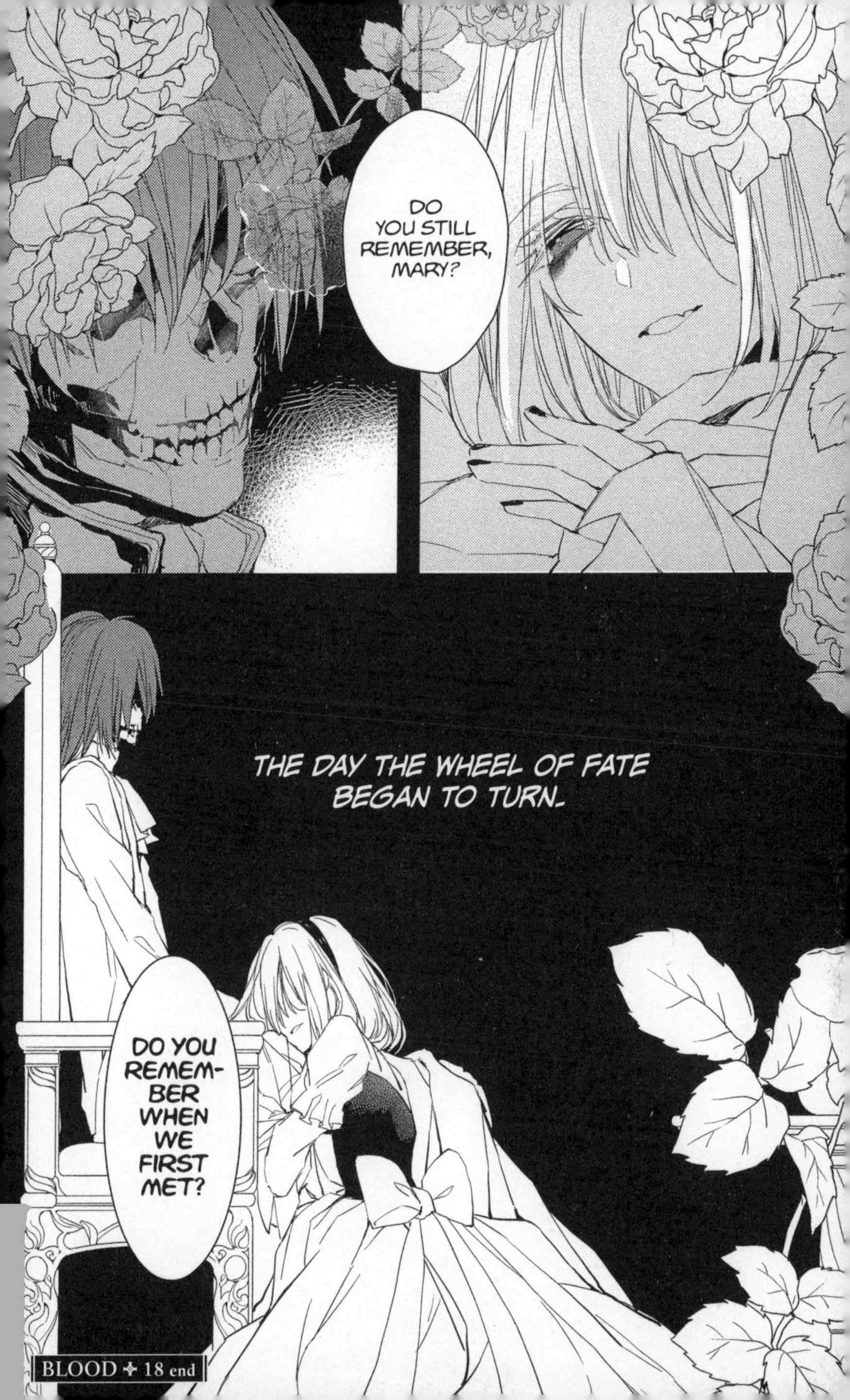
DO YOU STILL REMEMBER, MARY?
THE DAY THE WHEEL OF FATE BEGAN TO TURN.
DO YOU REMEMBER WHEN WE FIRST MET?
BLOOD ✦ 18 end

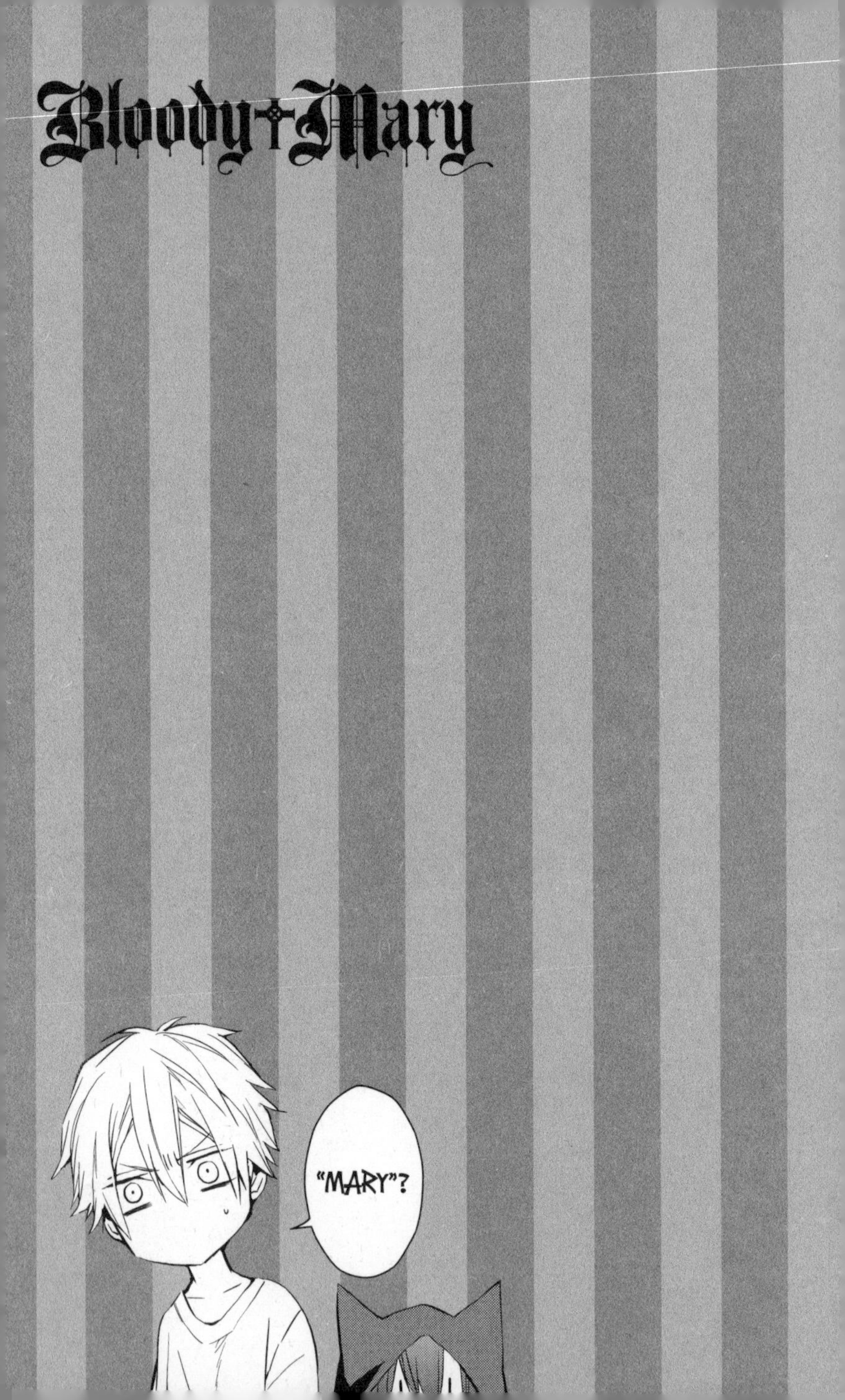
Bloody+Mary
"MARY"?

Bloody+Mary

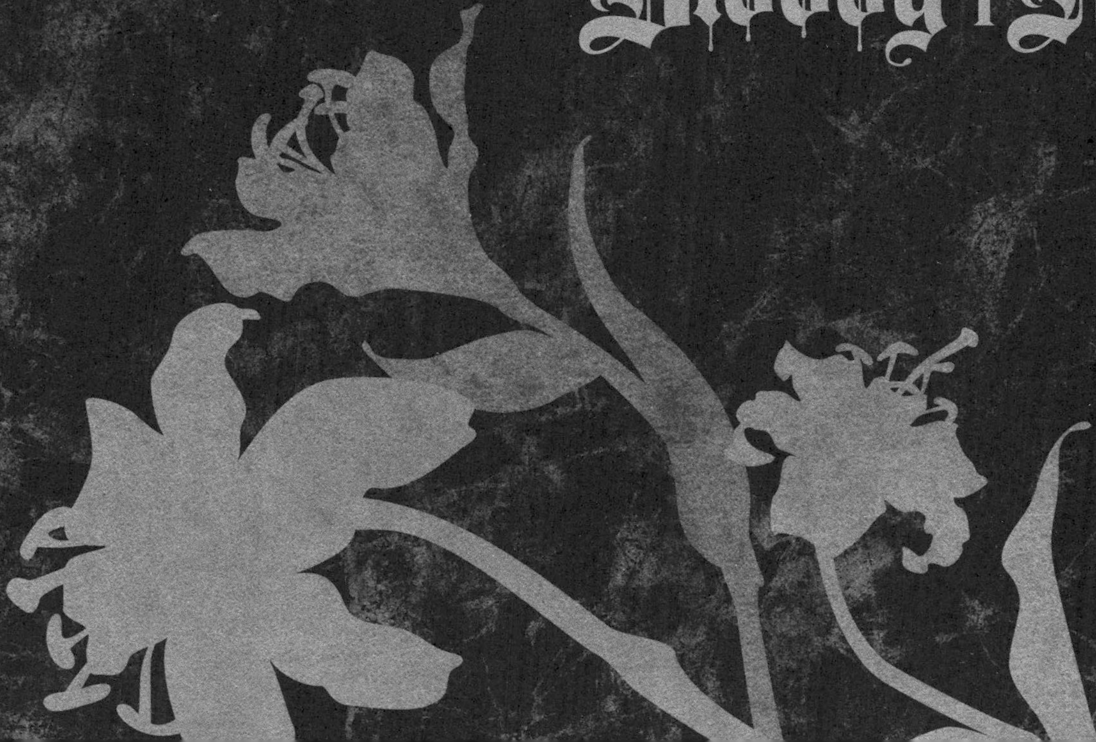

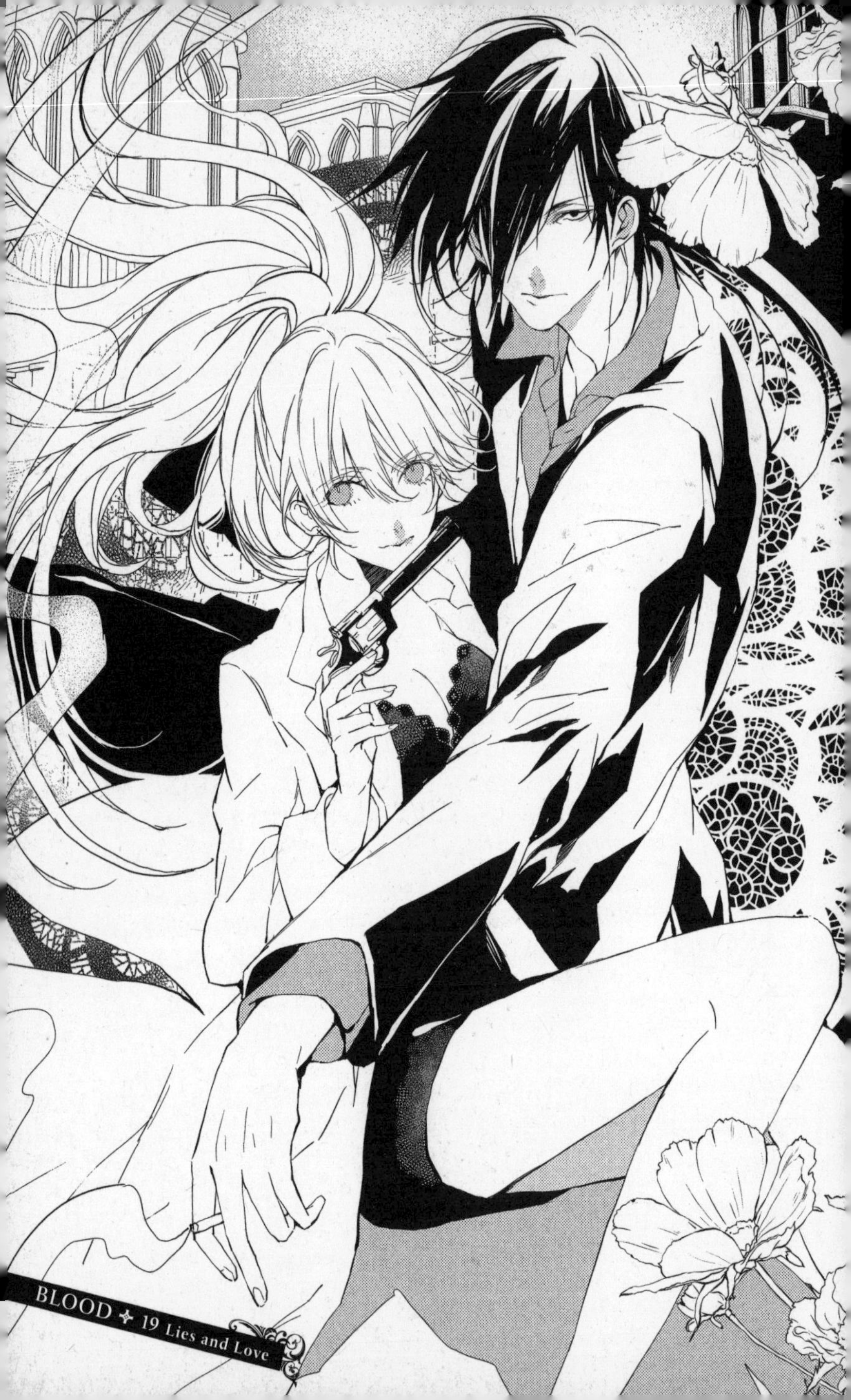
BLOOD ✦ 19 Lies and Love

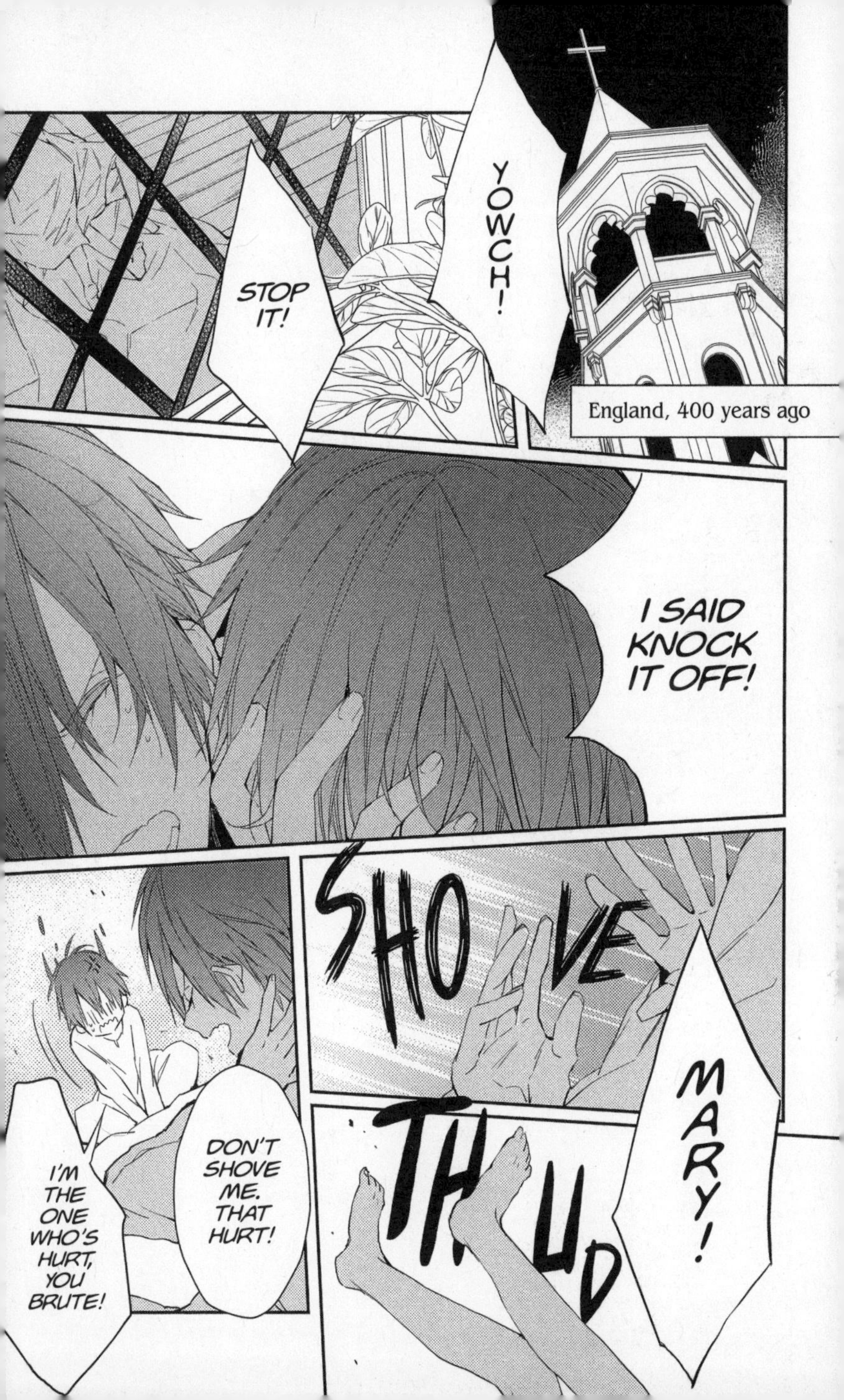
England, 400 years ago
YOWCH!
STOP IT!
I SAID KNOCK IT OFF!
SHOVE
MARY!
THUD
DON'T SHOVE ME. THAT HURT!
I'M THE ONE WHO'S HURT, YOU BRUTE!

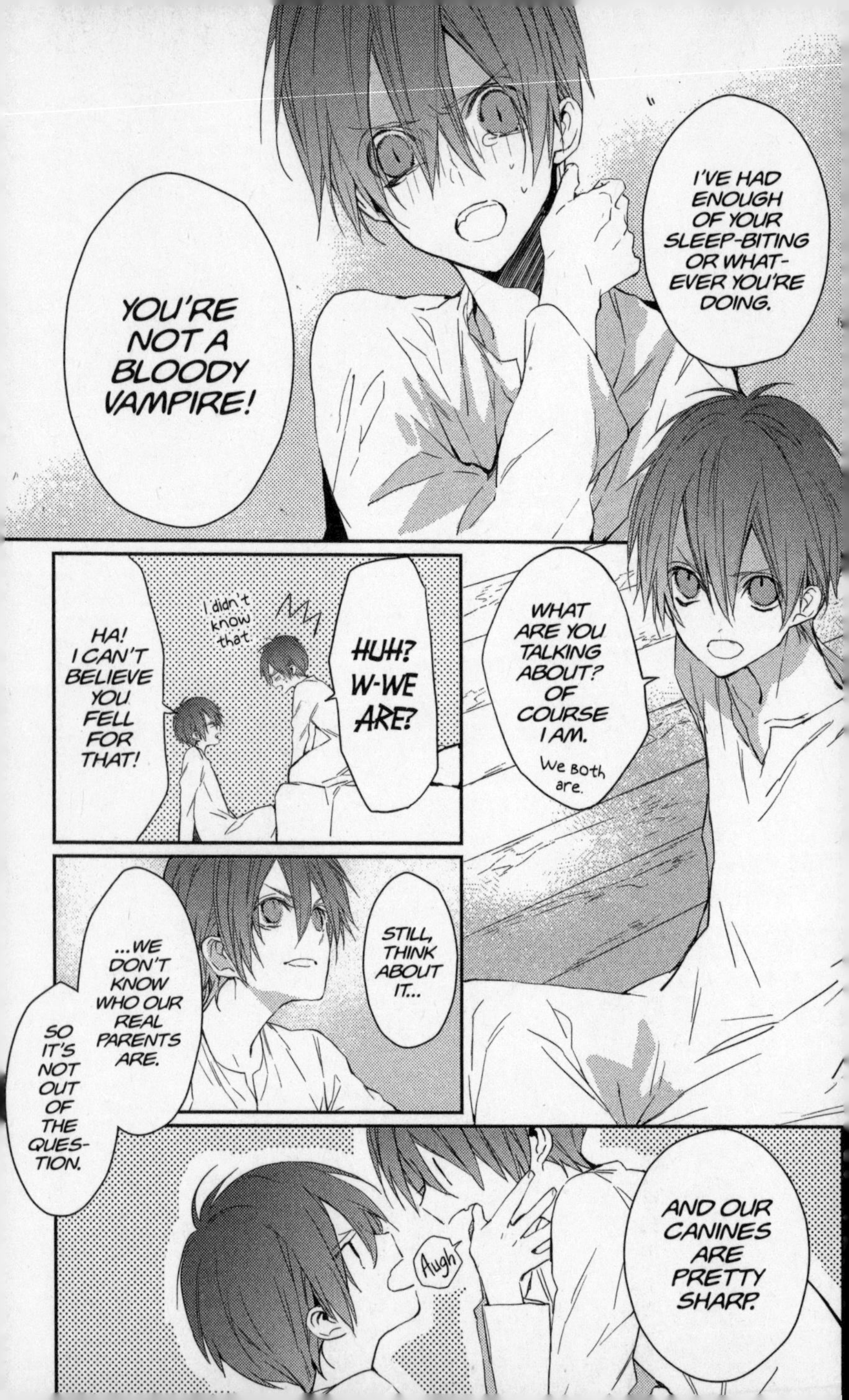
I'VE HAD ENOUGH OF YOUR SLEEP-BITING OR WHAT-EVER YOU'RE DOING.
YOU'RE NOT A BLOODY VAMPIRE!
WHAT ARE YOU TALKING ABOUT? OF COURSE I AM.
We both are.
HUH? W-WE ARE?
I didn't know that.
HA! I CAN'T BELIEVE YOU FELL FOR THAT!
STILL, THINK ABOUT IT...
...WE DON'T KNOW WHO OUR REAL PARENTS ARE.
SO IT'S NOT OUT OF THE QUES-TION.
AND OUR CANINES ARE PRETTY SHARP.
Augh

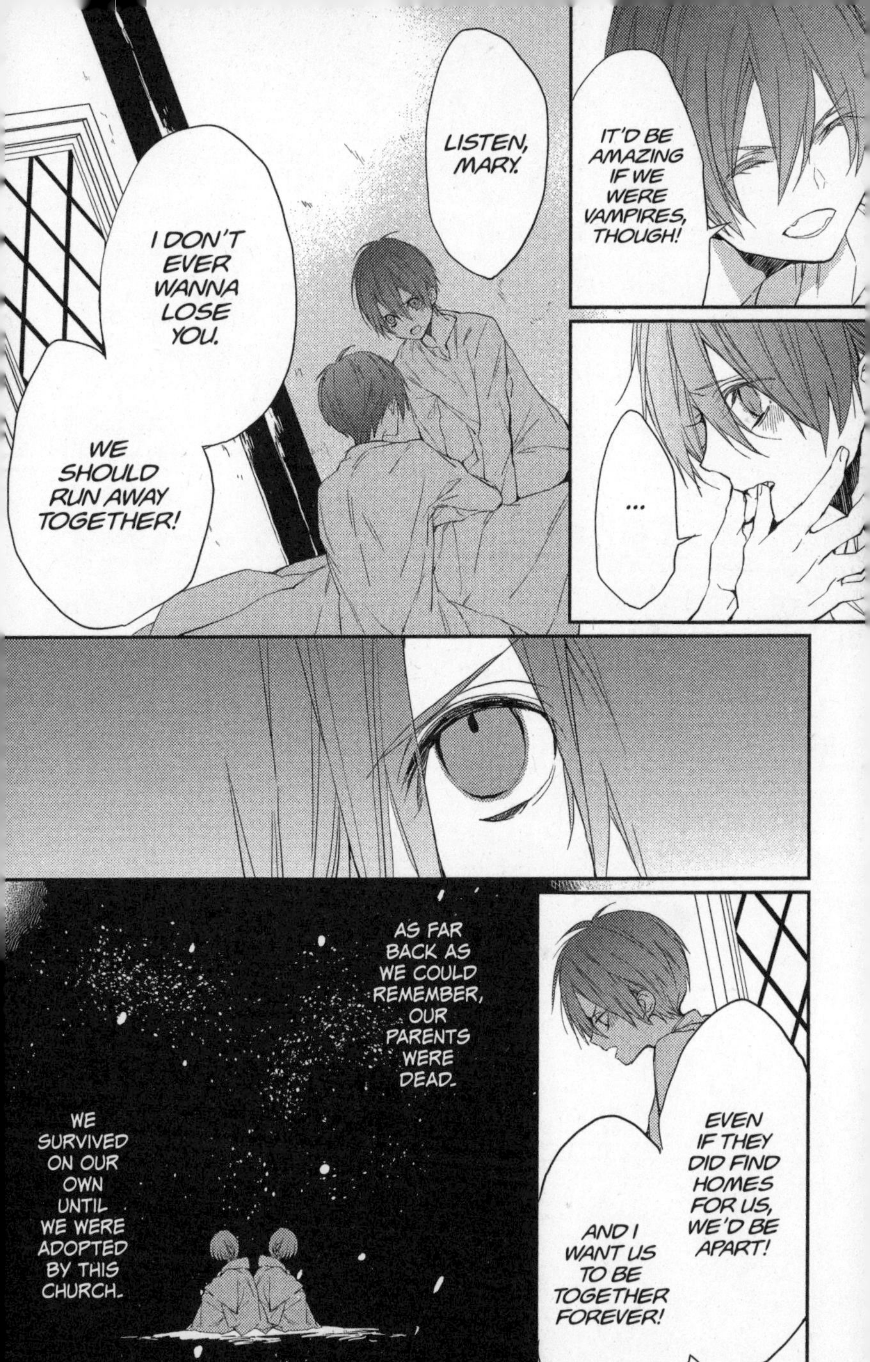

IT'D BE AMAZING IF WE WERE VAMPIRES, THOUGH!
...
LISTEN, MARY.
I DON'T EVER WANNA LOSE YOU.
WE SHOULD RUN AWAY TOGETHER!
EVEN IF THEY DID FIND HOMES FOR US, WE'D BE APART!
AND I WANT US TO BE TOGETHER FOREVER!
AS FAR BACK AS WE COULD REMEMBER, OUR PARENTS WERE DEAD.
WE SURVIVED ON OUR OWN UNTIL WE WERE ADOPTED BY THIS CHURCH.

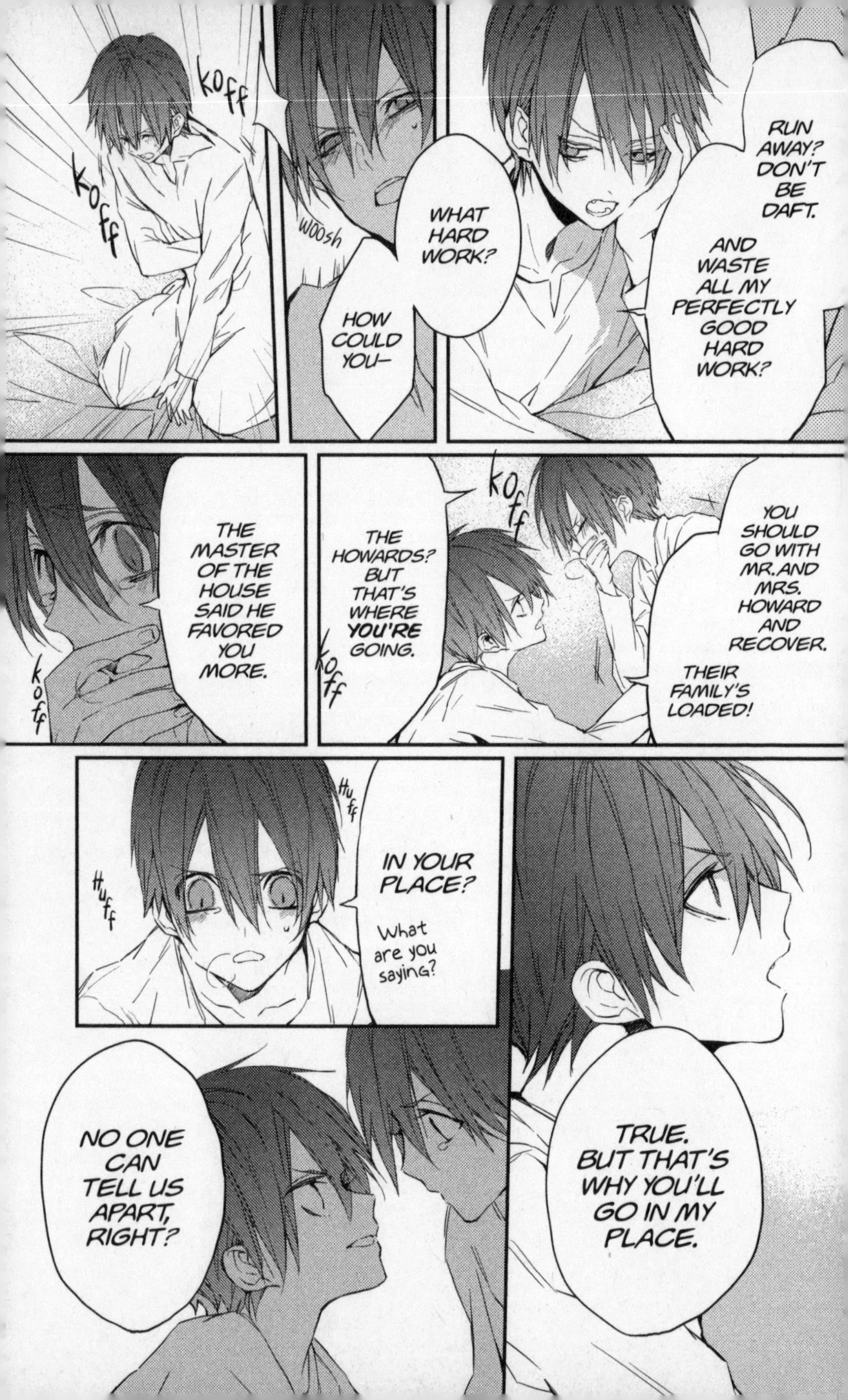
RUN AWAY? DON'T BE DAFT.
AND WASTE ALL MY PERFECTLY GOOD HARD WORK?
WHAT HARD WORK?
HOW COULD YOU—
WOOSH
KOFF
KOFF
YOU SHOULD GO WITH MR. AND MRS. HOWARD AND RECOVER.
THEIR FAMILY'S LOADED!
KOFF
THE HOWARDS? BUT THAT'S WHERE **YOU'RE** GOING.
KOFF
THE MASTER OF THE HOUSE SAID HE FAVORED YOU MORE.
KOFF
TRUE. BUT THAT'S WHY YOU'LL GO IN MY PLACE.
HUFF
IN YOUR PLACE?
What are you saying?
HUFF
NO ONE CAN TELL US APART, RIGHT?

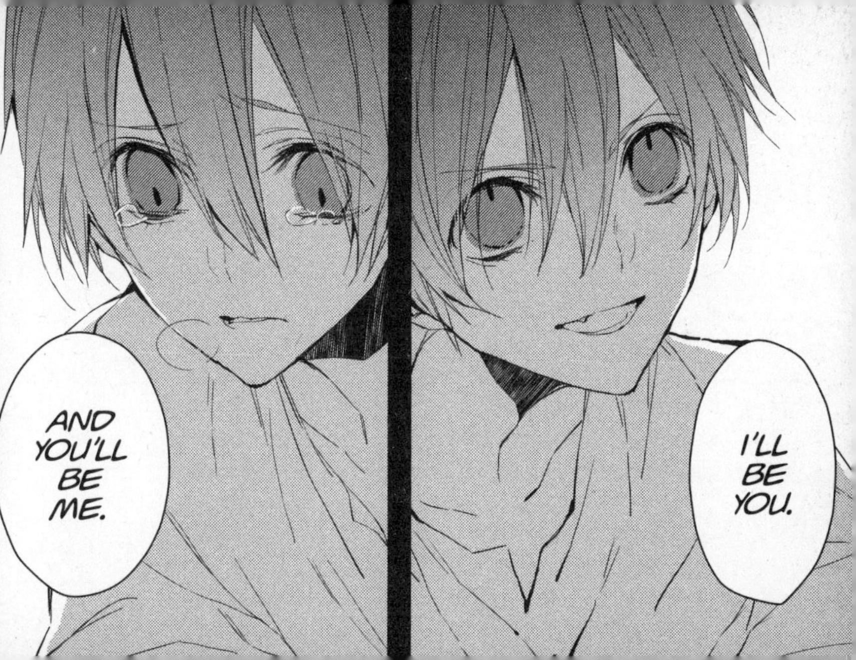
I'LL BE YOU.
AND YOU'LL BE ME.

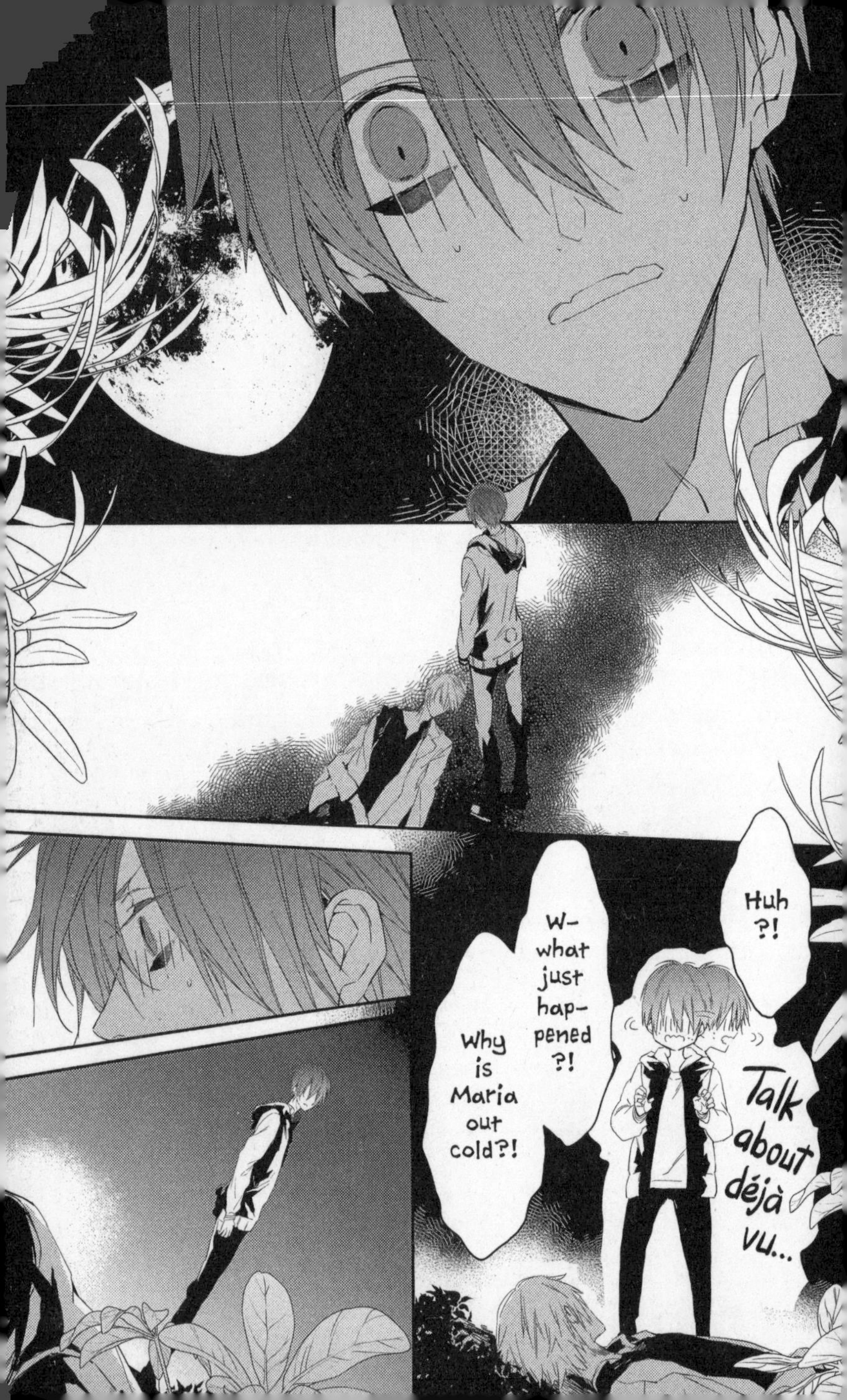
Huh?!
W-what just hap-pened?!
Why is Maria out cold?!
Talk about déjà vu...

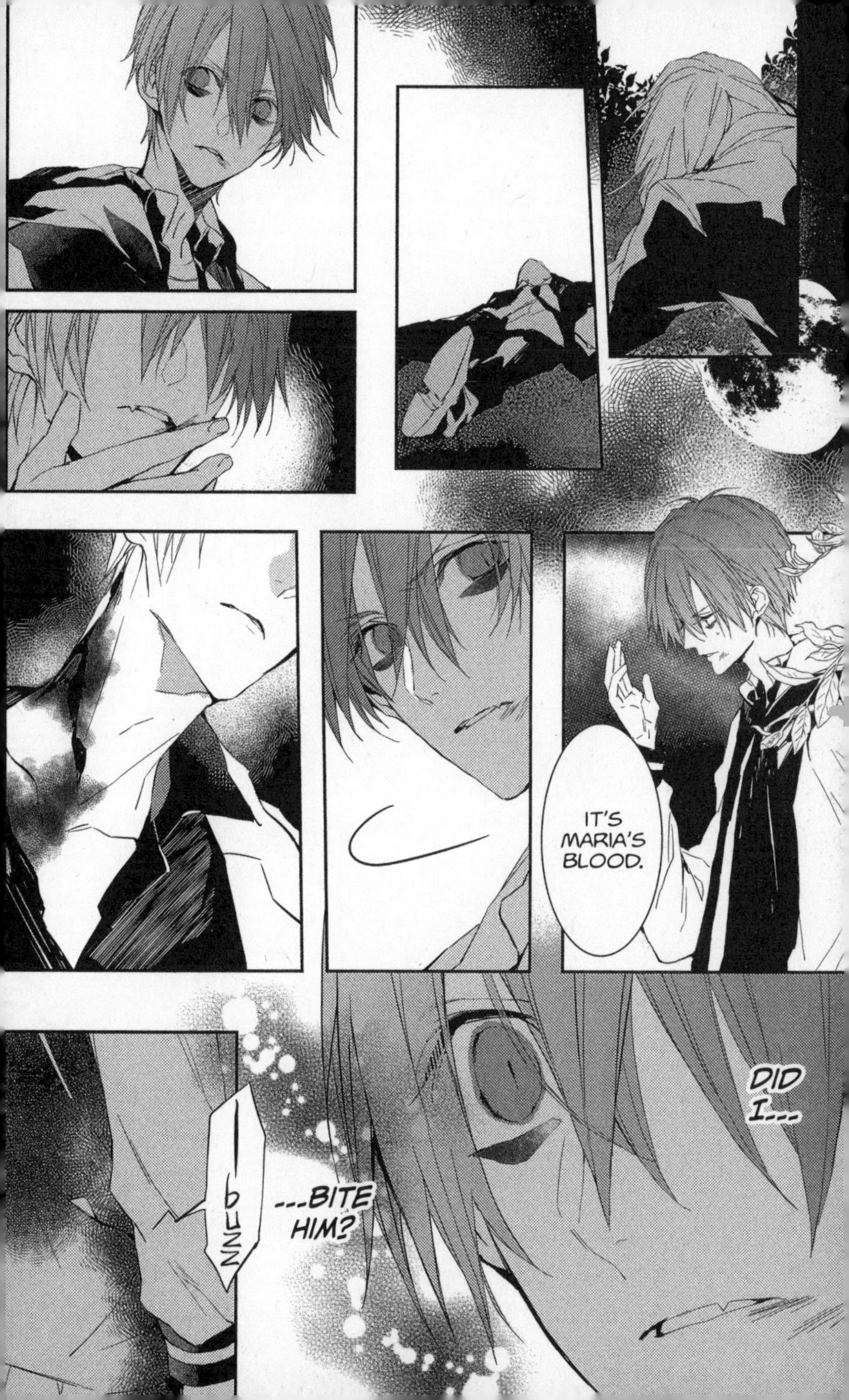
IT'S MARIA'S BLOOD.
DID I...
...BITE HIM?
BUZZ

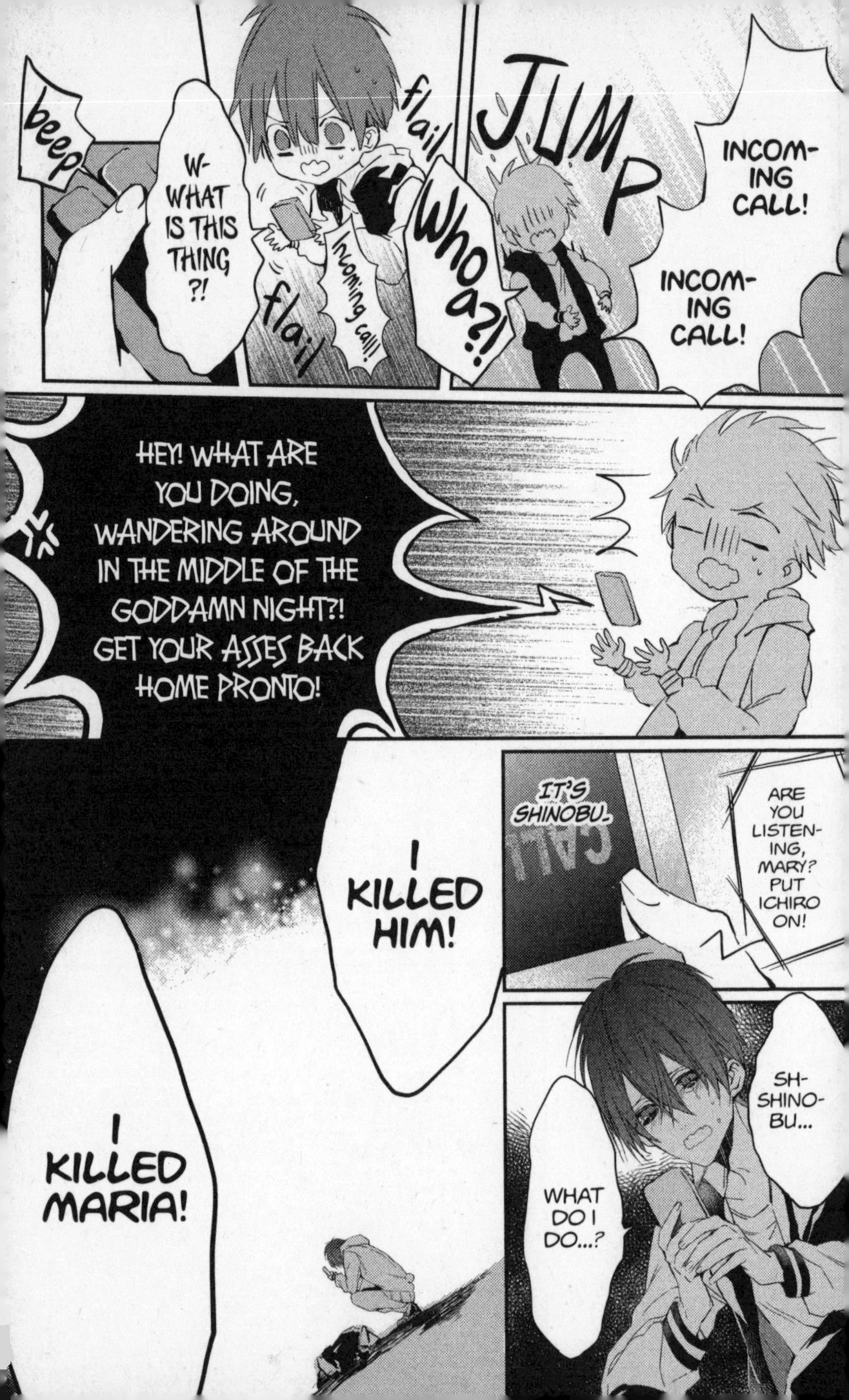
INCOMING CALL!
JUMP
INCOMING CALL!
Whoa?!
flail
W-WHAT IS THIS THING?!
incoming call!
flail
beep
HEY! WHAT ARE YOU DOING, WANDERING AROUND IN THE MIDDLE OF THE GODDAMN NIGHT?! GET YOUR ASSES BACK HOME PRONTO!
ARE YOU LISTENING, MARY? PUT ICHIRO ON!
IT'S SHINOBU.
SH-SHINOBU...
WHAT DO I DO...?
I KILLED HIM!
I KILLED MARIA!

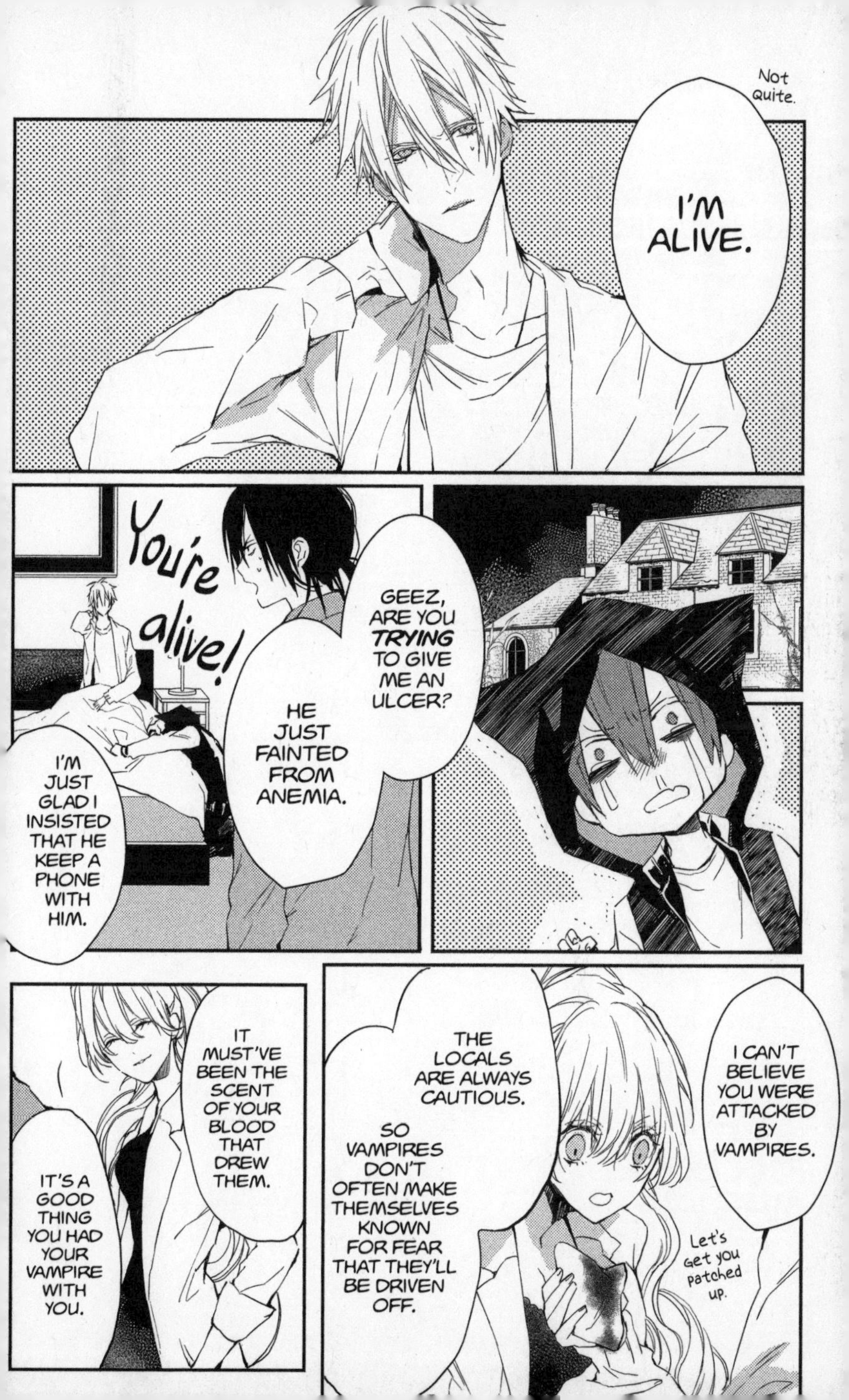
Not Quite.
I'M ALIVE.
GEEZ, ARE YOU TRYING TO GIVE ME AN ULCER?
You're alive!
HE JUST FAINTED FROM ANEMIA.
I'M JUST GLAD I INSISTED THAT HE KEEP A PHONE WITH HIM.
I CAN'T BELIEVE YOU WERE ATTACKED BY VAMPIRES.
THE LOCALS ARE ALWAYS CAUTIOUS.
SO VAMPIRES DON'T OFTEN MAKE THEMSELVES KNOWN FOR FEAR THAT THEY'LL BE DRIVEN OFF.
Let's get you patched up.
IT MUST'VE BEEN THE SCENT OF YOUR BLOOD THAT DREW THEM.
IT'S A GOOD THING YOU HAD YOUR VAMPIRE WITH YOU.

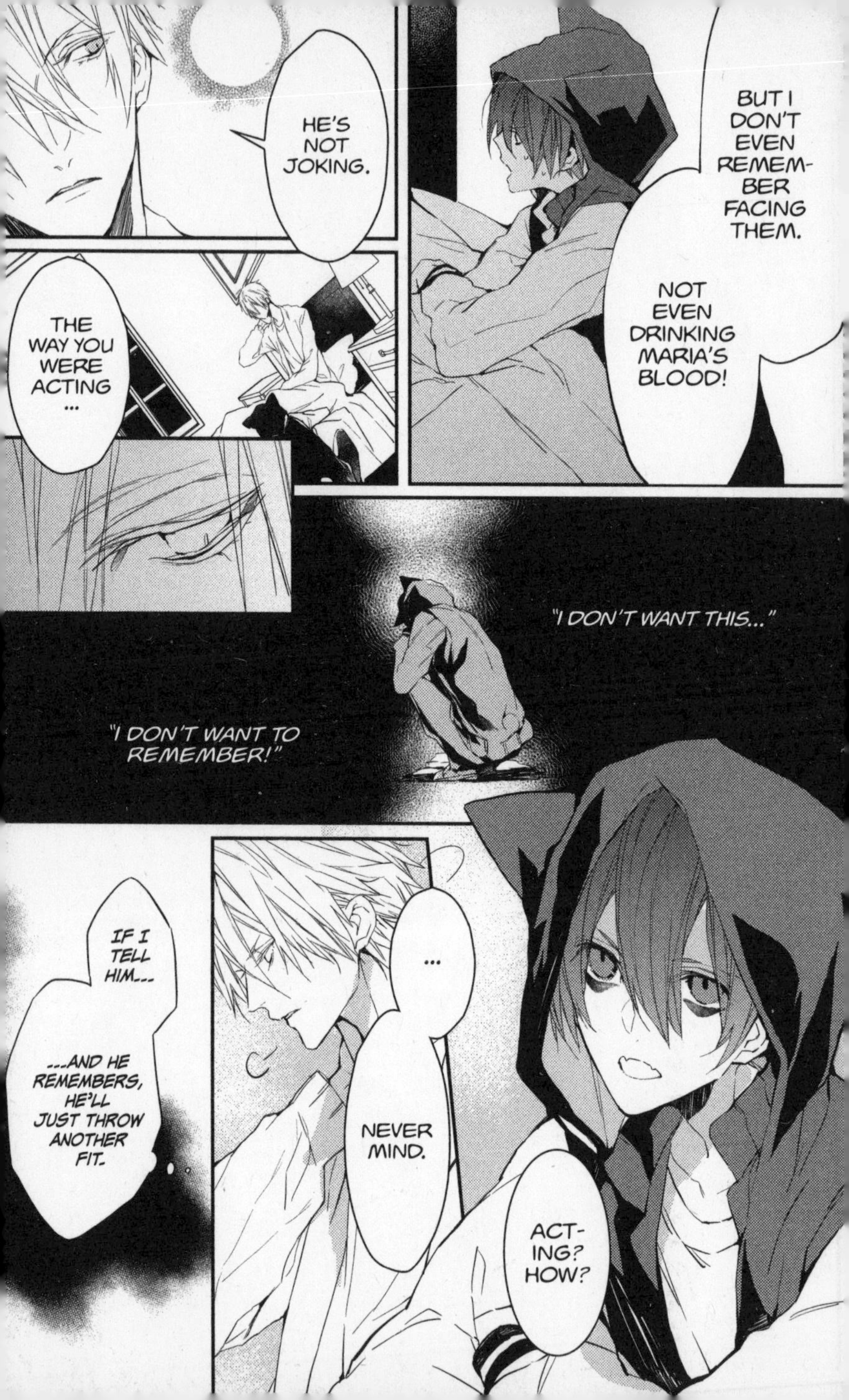
BUT I DON'T EVEN REMEMBER FACING THEM.
NOT EVEN DRINKING MARIA'S BLOOD!
HE'S NOT JOKING.
THE WAY YOU WERE ACTING ...
"I DON'T WANT THIS..."
"I DON'T WANT TO REMEMBER!"
ACT-ING? HOW?
...
IF I TELL HIM...
...AND HE REMEMBERS, HE'LL JUST THROW ANOTHER FIT.
NEVER MIND.

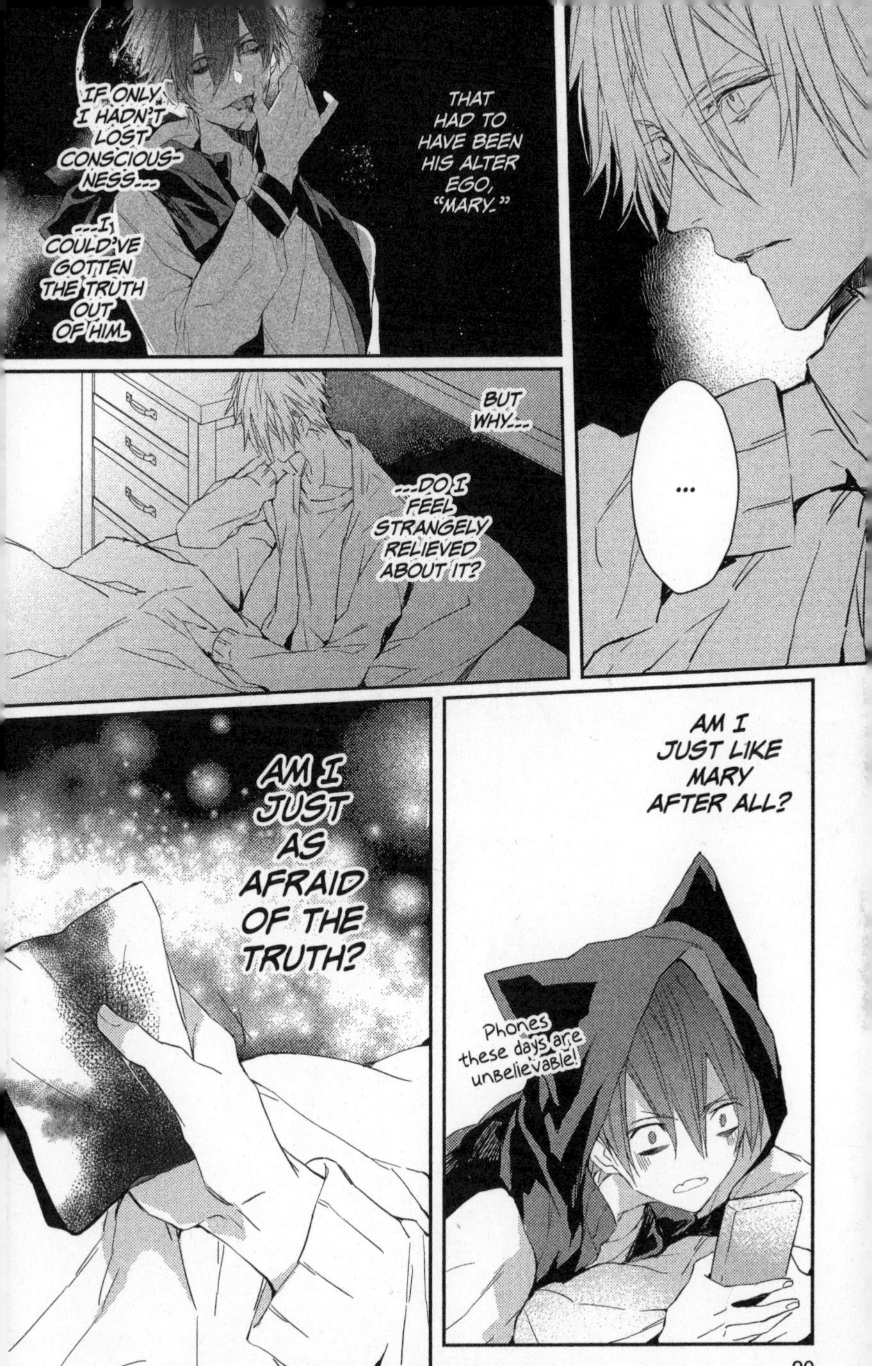
...
THAT HAD TO HAVE BEEN HIS ALTER EGO, "MARY."
IF ONLY I HADN'T LOST CONSCIOUS-NESS...
...I COULD'VE GOTTEN THE TRUTH OUT OF HIM.
BUT WHY...
...DO I FEEL STRANGELY RELIEVED ABOUT IT?
AM I JUST LIKE MARY AFTER ALL?
Phones these days are unbelievable!
AM I JUST AS AFRAID OF THE TRUTH?

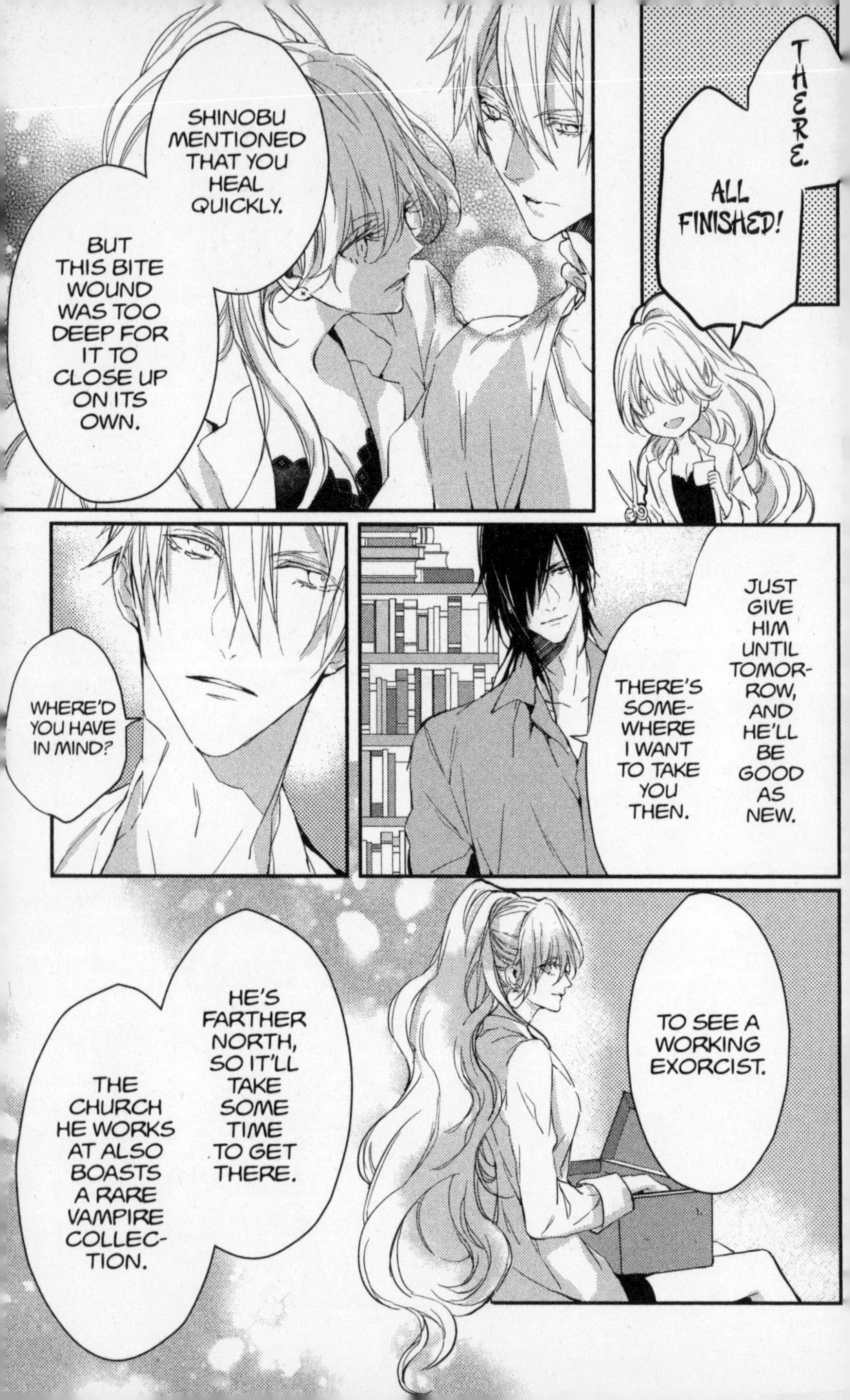
THERE.
ALL FINISHED!
SHINOBU MENTIONED THAT YOU HEAL QUICKLY.
BUT THIS BITE WOUND WAS TOO DEEP FOR IT TO CLOSE UP ON ITS OWN.
JUST GIVE HIM UNTIL TOMORROW, AND HE'LL BE GOOD AS NEW.
THERE'S SOMEWHERE I WANT TO TAKE YOU THEN.
WHERE'D YOU HAVE IN MIND?
TO SEE A WORKING EXORCIST.
HE'S FARTHER NORTH, SO IT'LL TAKE SOME TIME TO GET THERE.
THE CHURCH HE WORKS AT ALSO BOASTS A RARE VAMPIRE COLLECTION.

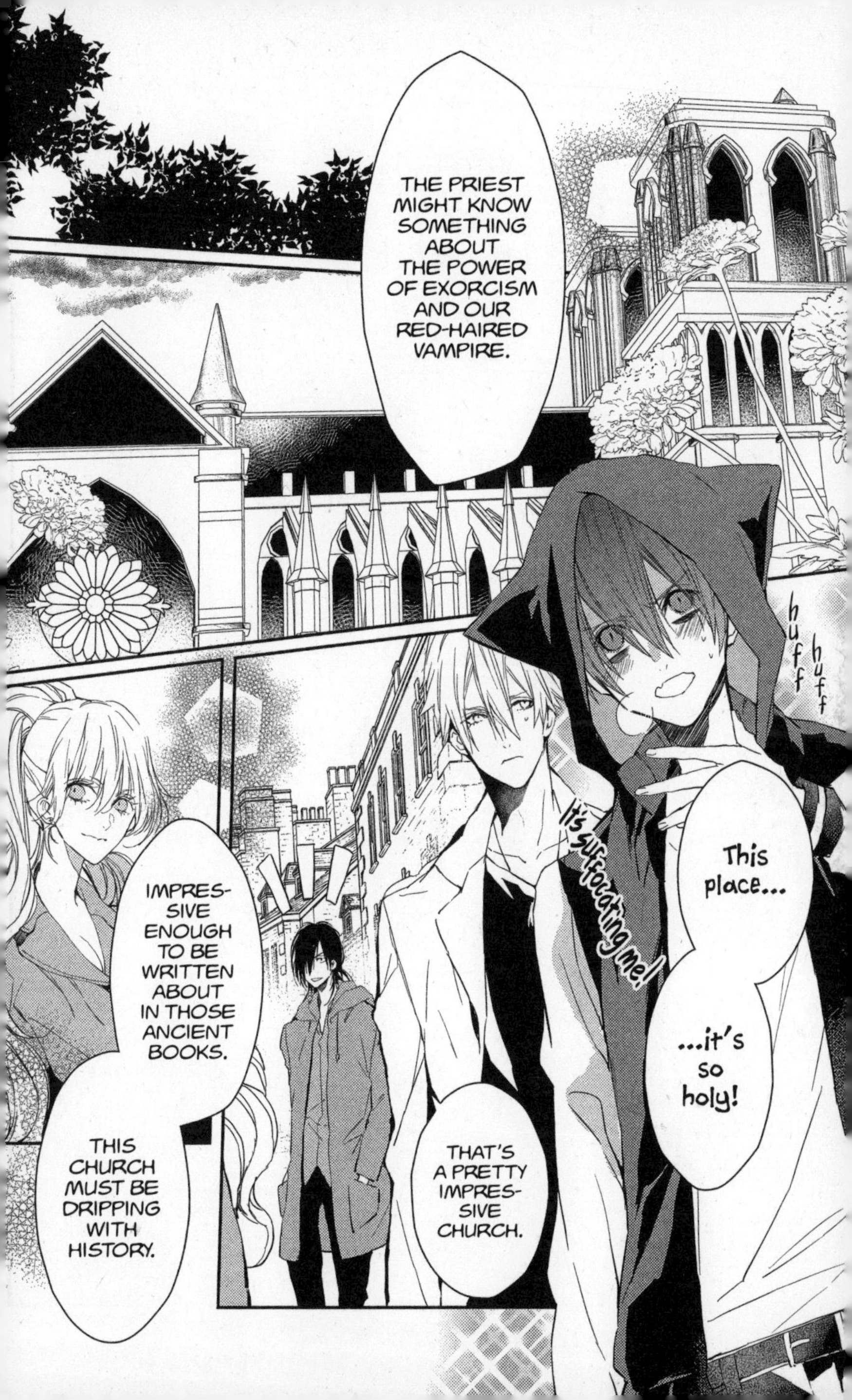
THE PRIEST MIGHT KNOW SOMETHING ABOUT THE POWER OF EXORCISM AND OUR RED-HAIRED VAMPIRE.
huff huff
This place...
...it's so holy!
It's suffocating me!
THAT'S A PRETTY IMPRES-SIVE CHURCH.
IMPRES-SIVE ENOUGH TO BE WRITTEN ABOUT IN THOSE ANCIENT BOOKS.
THIS CHURCH MUST BE DRIPPING WITH HISTORY.

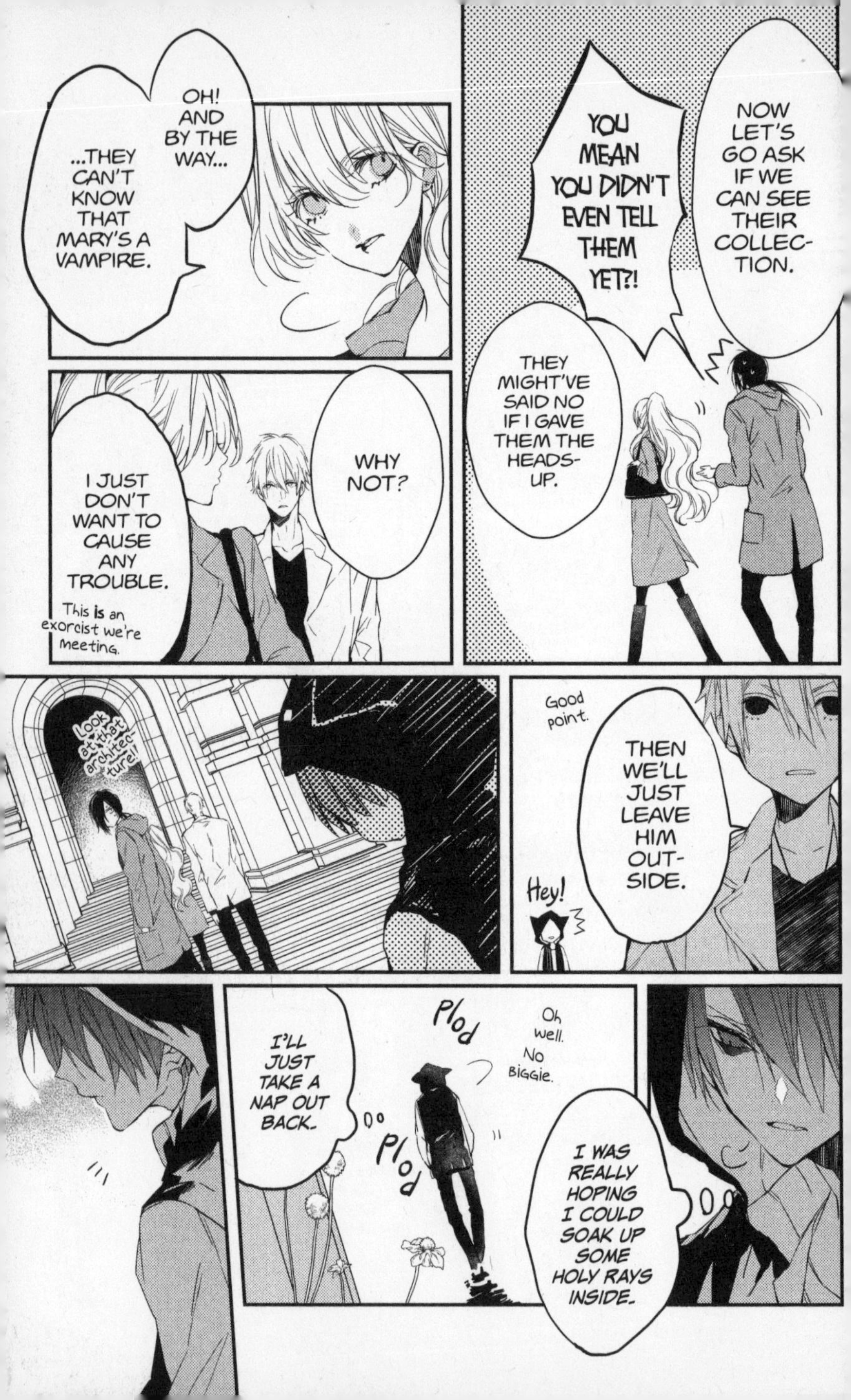

NOW LET'S GO ASK IF WE CAN SEE THEIR COLLEC-TION.
YOU MEAN YOU DIDN'T EVEN TELL THEM YET?!
THEY MIGHT'VE SAID NO IF I GAVE THEM THE HEADS-UP.
OH! AND BY THE WAY...
...THEY CAN'T KNOW THAT MARY'S A VAMPIRE.
WHY NOT?
I JUST DON'T WANT TO CAUSE ANY TROUBLE.
This is an exorcist we're meeting.
Good point.
THEN WE'LL JUST LEAVE HIM OUT-SIDE.
Hey!
Look at that architec-ture!!
I WAS REALLY HOPING I COULD SOAK UP SOME HOLY RAYS INSIDE.
Plod
Oh well. No biggie.
I'LL JUST TAKE A NAP OUT BACK.
Plod

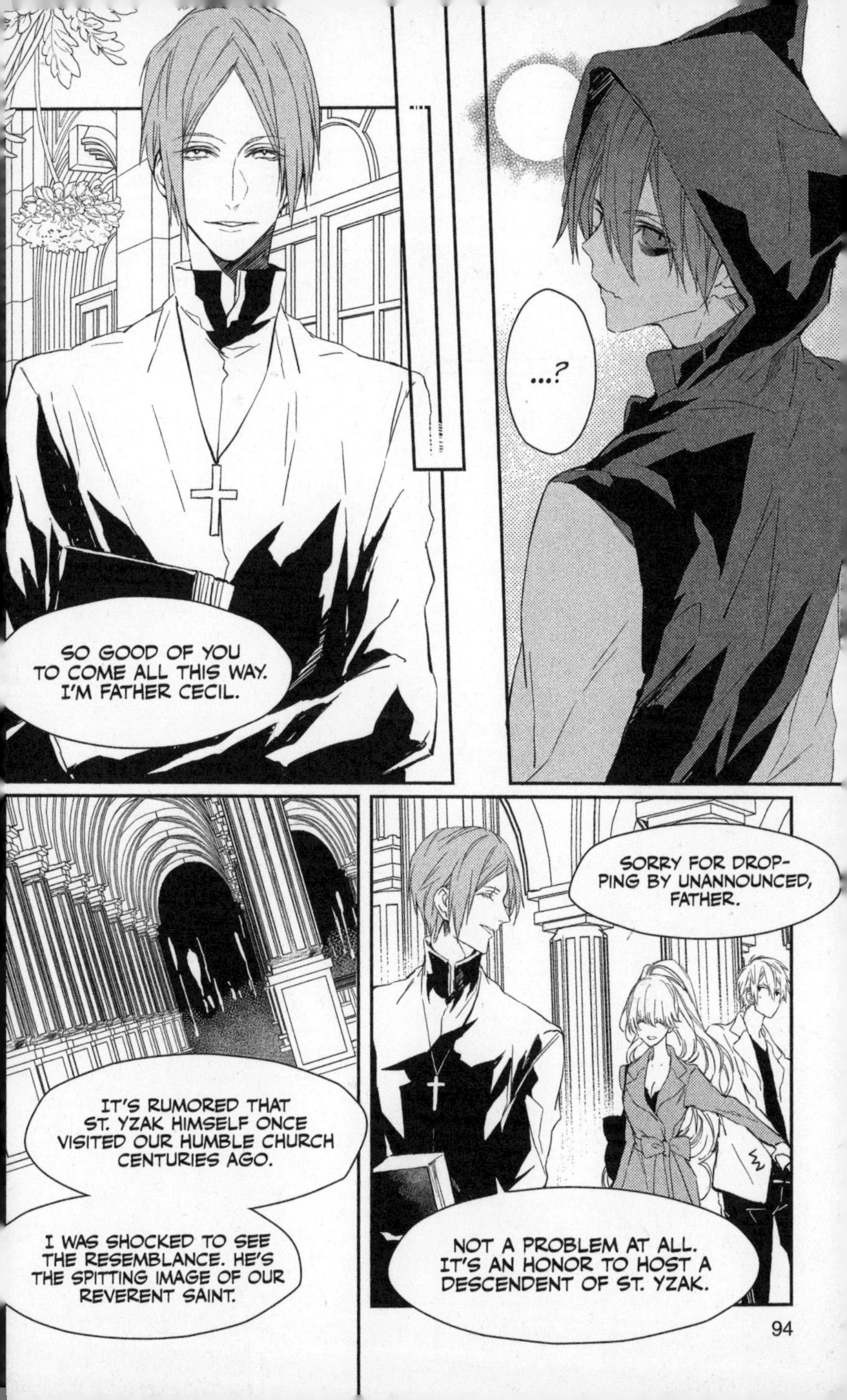

...?
SO GOOD OF YOU TO COME ALL THIS WAY. I'M FATHER CECIL.
SORRY FOR DROP-PING BY UNANNOUNCED, FATHER.
NOT A PROBLEM AT ALL. IT'S AN HONOR TO HOST A DESCENDENT OF ST. YZAK.
IT'S RUMORED THAT ST. YZAK HIMSELF ONCE VISITED OUR HUMBLE CHURCH CENTURIES AGO.
I WAS SHOCKED TO SEE THE RESEMBLANCE. HE'S THE SPITTING IMAGE OF OUR REVERENT SAINT.

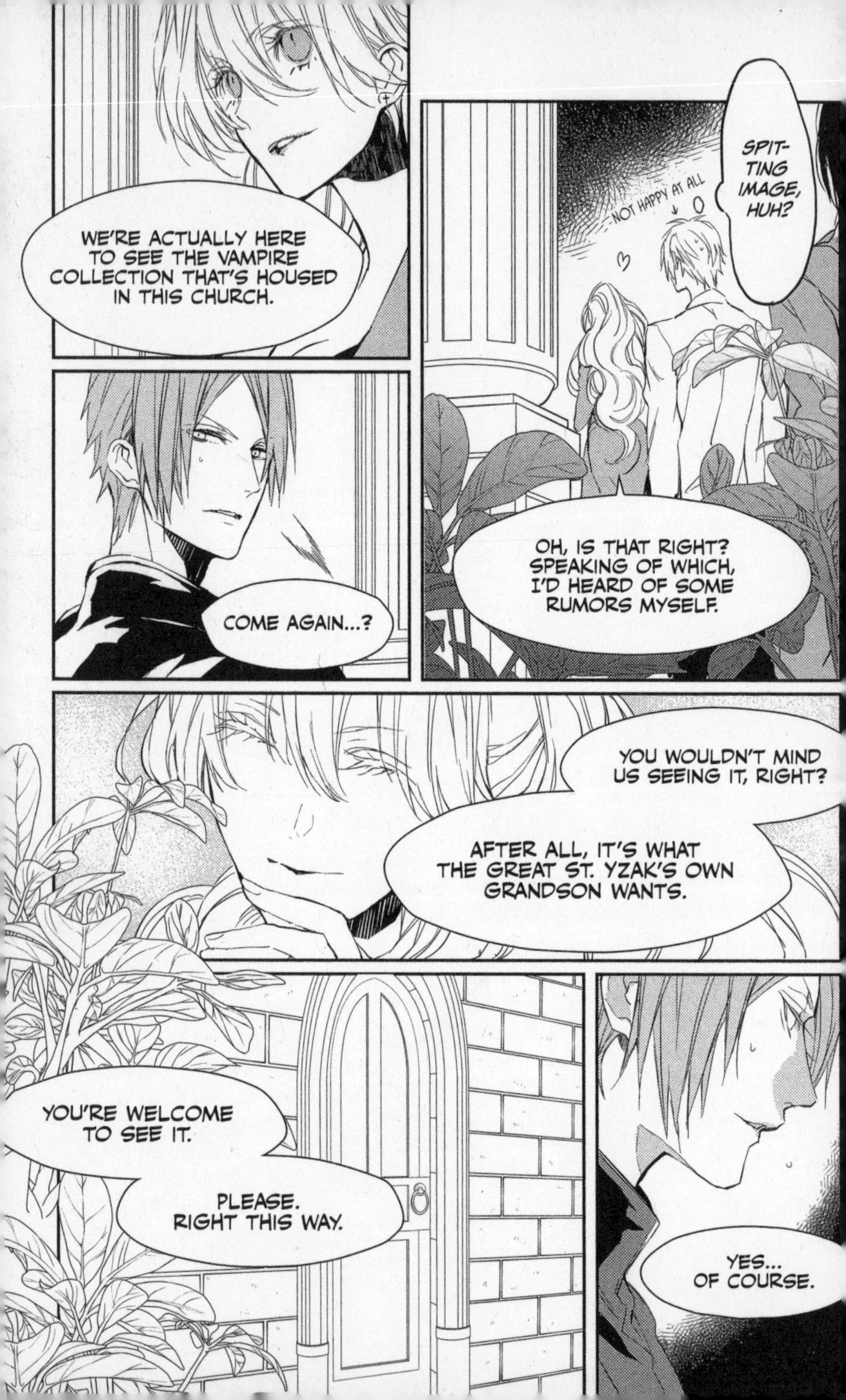
SPIT-
TING
IMAGE,
HUH?
NOT HAPPY AT ALL
OH, IS THAT RIGHT? SPEAKING OF WHICH, I'D HEARD OF SOME RUMORS MYSELF.
WE'RE ACTUALLY HERE TO SEE THE VAMPIRE COLLECTION THAT'S HOUSED IN THIS CHURCH.
COME AGAIN...?
YOU WOULDN'T MIND US SEEING IT, RIGHT?
AFTER ALL, IT'S WHAT THE GREAT ST. YZAK'S OWN GRANDSON WANTS.
YES... OF COURSE.
YOU'RE WELCOME TO SEE IT.
PLEASE. RIGHT THIS WAY.

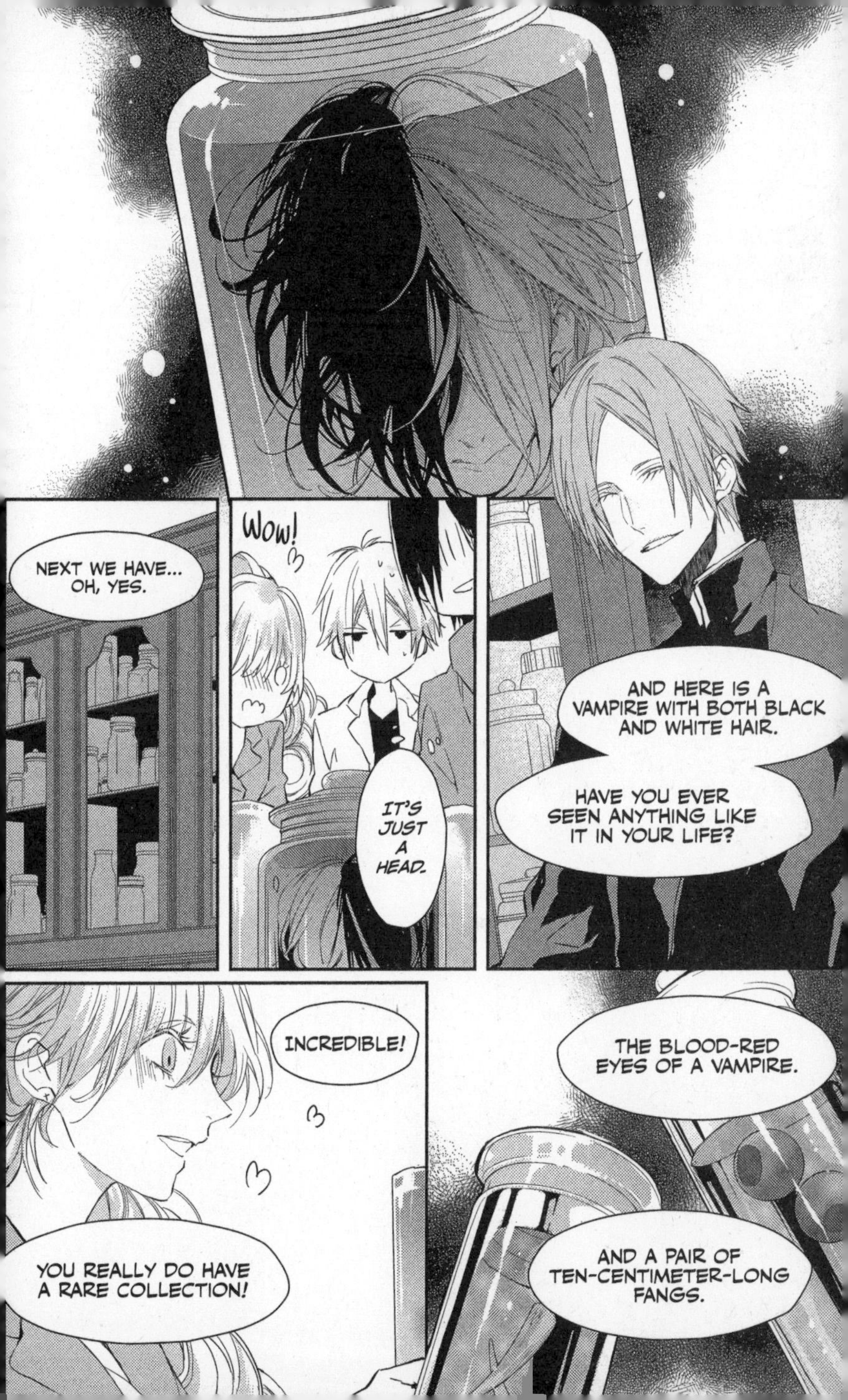
AND HERE IS A VAMPIRE WITH BOTH BLACK AND WHITE HAIR.
HAVE YOU EVER SEEN ANYTHING LIKE IT IN YOUR LIFE?
WOW!
IT'S JUST A HEAD.
NEXT WE HAVE... OH, YES.
THE BLOOD-RED EYES OF A VAMPIRE.
AND A PAIR OF TEN-CENTIMETER-LONG FANGS.
INCREDIBLE!
YOU REALLY DO HAVE A RARE COLLECTION!

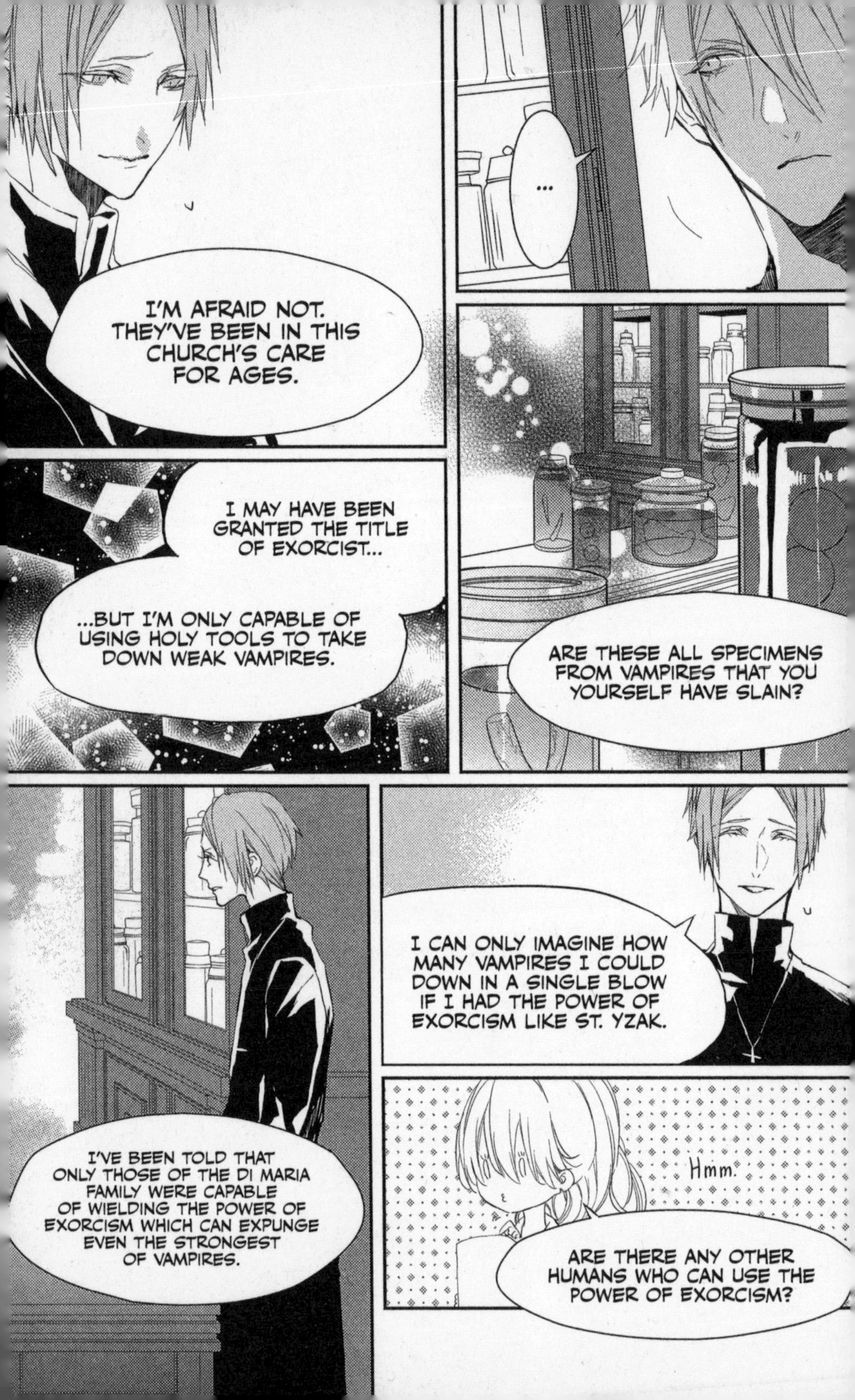
...
I'M AFRAID NOT. THEY'VE BEEN IN THIS CHURCH'S CARE FOR AGES.
ARE THESE ALL SPECIMENS FROM VAMPIRES THAT YOU YOURSELF HAVE SLAIN?
I MAY HAVE BEEN GRANTED THE TITLE OF EXORCIST...
...BUT I'M ONLY CAPABLE OF USING HOLY TOOLS TO TAKE DOWN WEAK VAMPIRES.
I CAN ONLY IMAGINE HOW MANY VAMPIRES I COULD DOWN IN A SINGLE BLOW IF I HAD THE POWER OF EXORCISM LIKE ST. YZAK.
Hmm.
ARE THERE ANY OTHER HUMANS WHO CAN USE THE POWER OF EXORCISM?
I'VE BEEN TOLD THAT ONLY THOSE OF THE DI MARIA FAMILY WERE CAPABLE OF WIELDING THE POWER OF EXORCISM WHICH CAN EXPUNGE EVEN THE STRONGEST OF VAMPIRES.

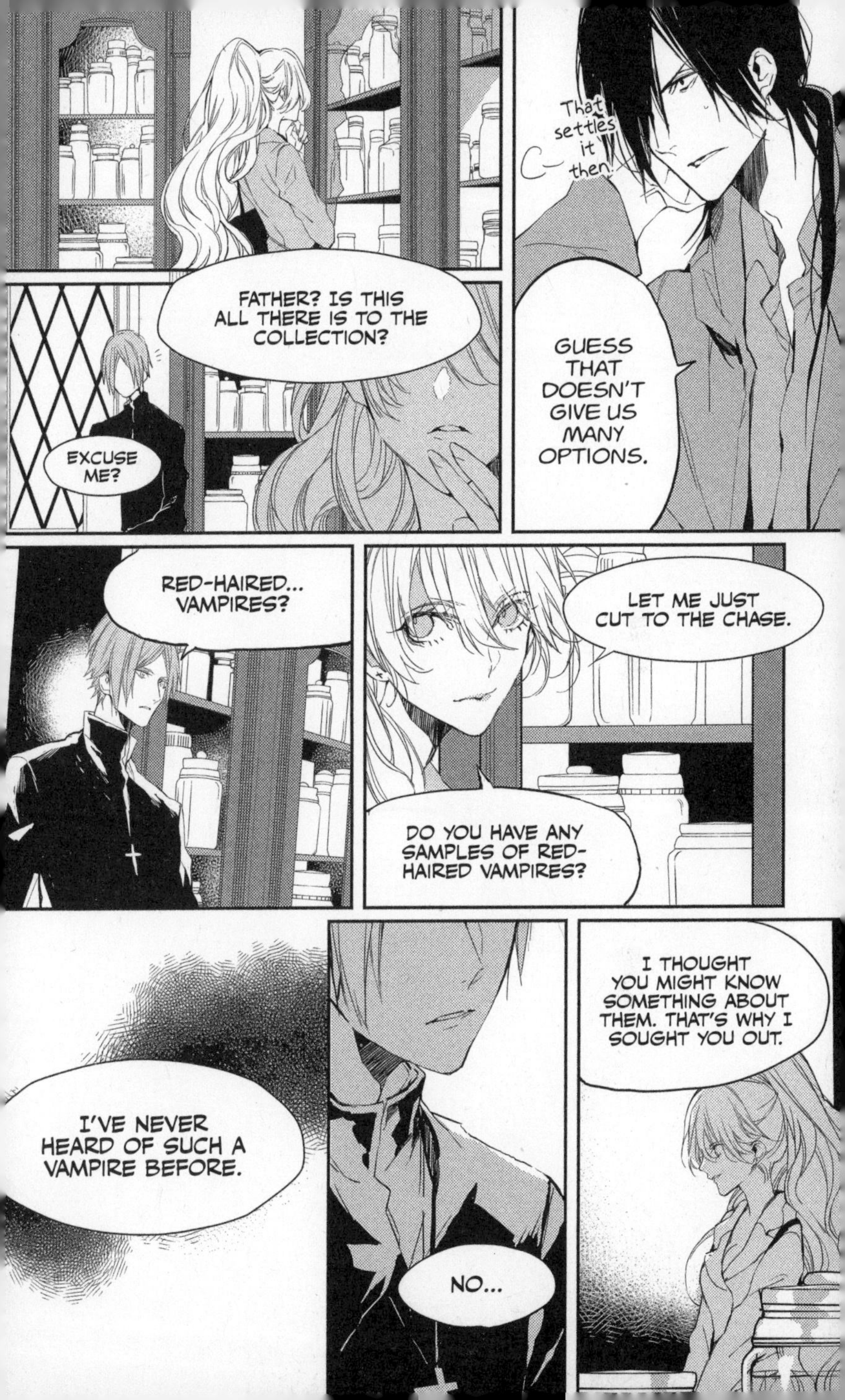
That settles it then.
GUESS THAT DOESN'T GIVE US MANY OPTIONS.
FATHER? IS THIS ALL THERE IS TO THE COLLECTION?
EXCUSE ME?
LET ME JUST CUT TO THE CHASE.
DO YOU HAVE ANY SAMPLES OF RED-HAIRED VAMPIRES?
RED-HAIRED... VAMPIRES?
I THOUGHT YOU MIGHT KNOW SOMETHING ABOUT THEM. THAT'S WHY I SOUGHT YOU OUT.
NO...
I'VE NEVER HEARD OF SUCH A VAMPIRE BEFORE.

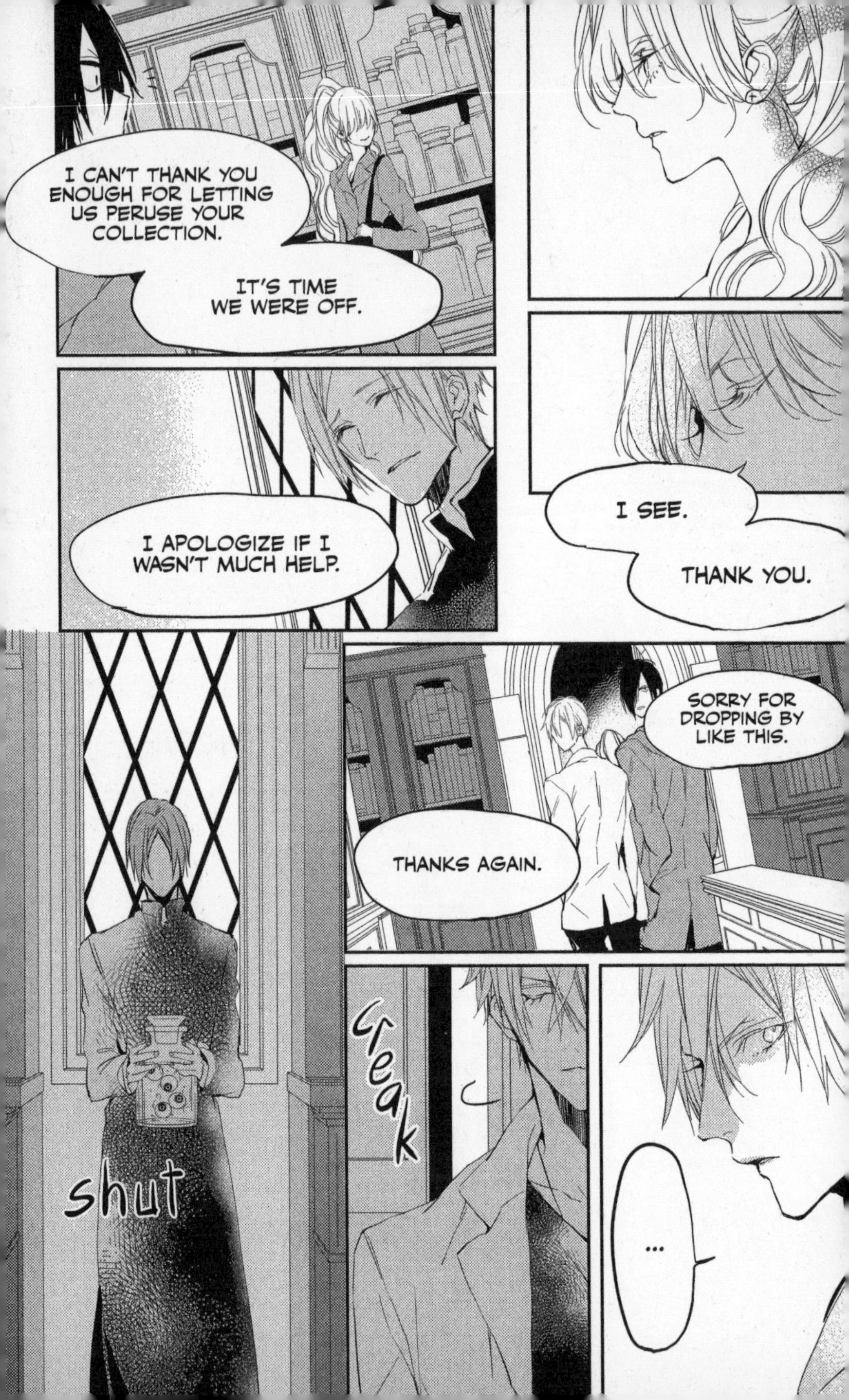
I CAN'T THANK YOU ENOUGH FOR LETTING US PERUSE YOUR COLLECTION.
IT'S TIME WE WERE OFF.
I SEE.
THANK YOU.
I APOLOGIZE IF I WASN'T MUCH HELP.
SORRY FOR DROPPING BY LIKE THIS.
THANKS AGAIN.
...
creak
shut

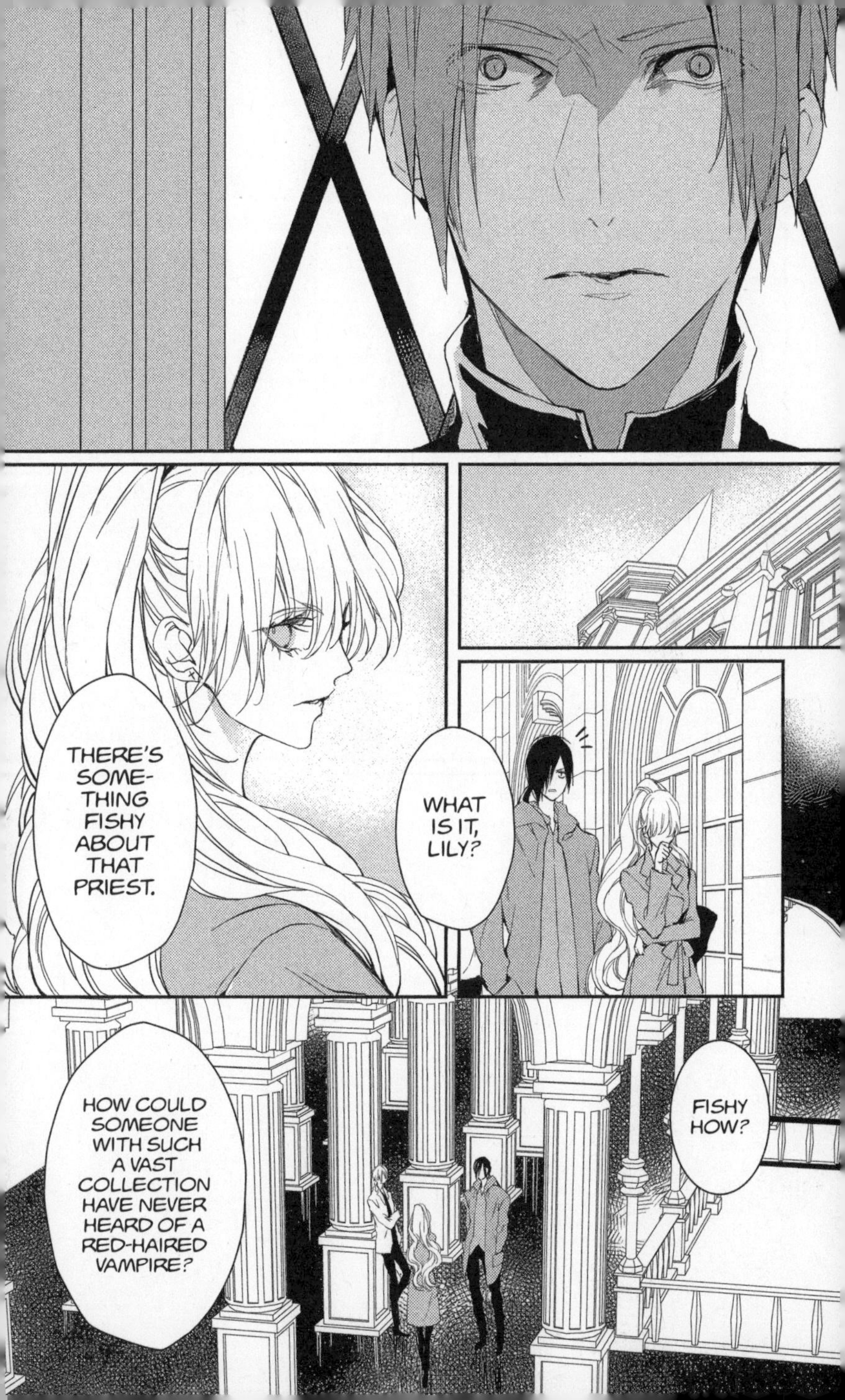
WHAT IS IT, LILY?
THERE'S SOMETHING FISHY ABOUT THAT PRIEST.
FISHY HOW?
HOW COULD SOMEONE WITH SUCH A VAST COLLECTION HAVE NEVER HEARD OF A RED-HAIRED VAMPIRE?

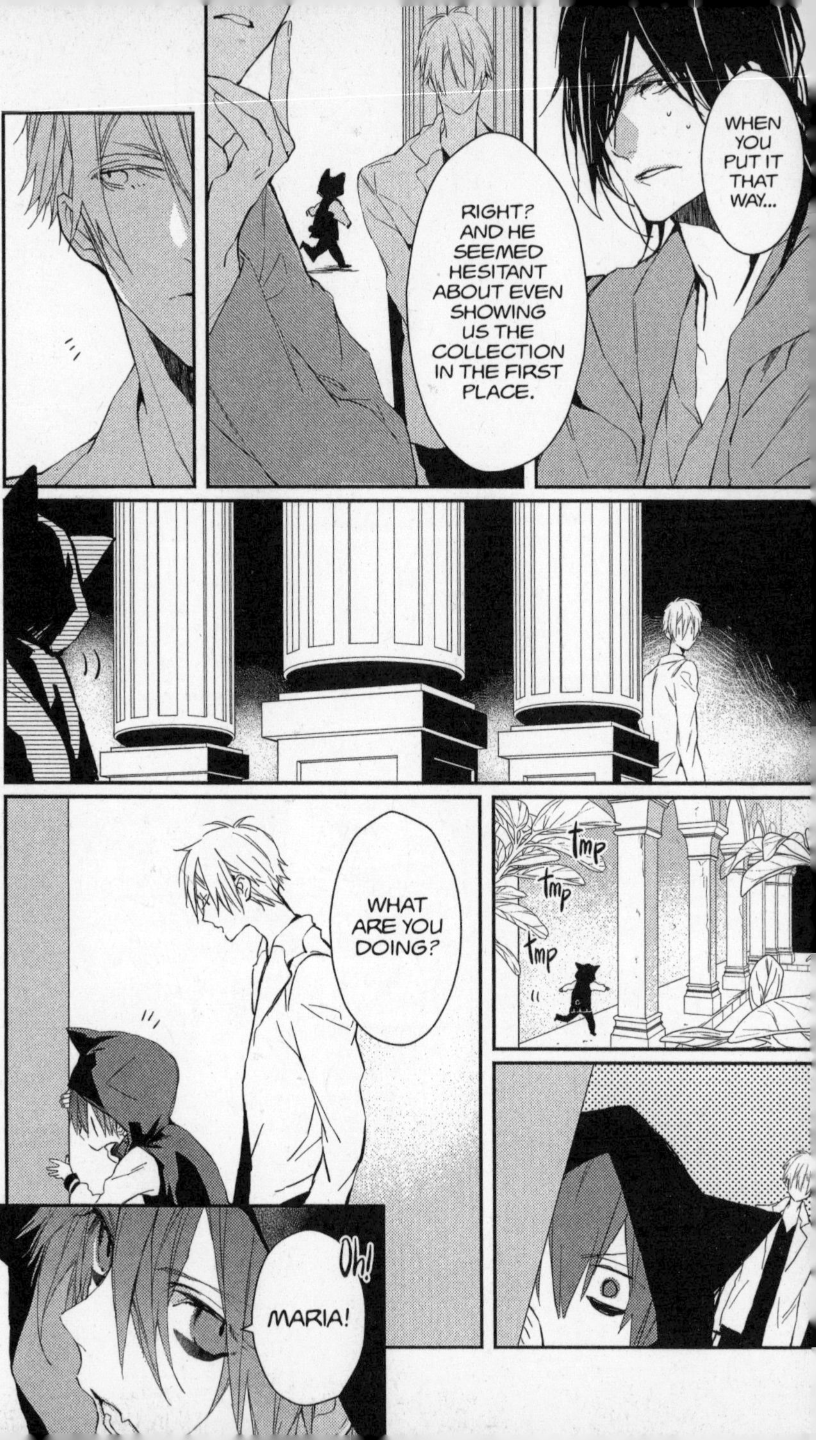

WHEN YOU PUT IT THAT WAY...
RIGHT? AND HE SEEMED HESITANT ABOUT EVEN SHOWING US THE COLLECTION IN THE FIRST PLACE.
tmp
tmp
tmp
WHAT ARE YOU DOING?
Oh!
MARIA!

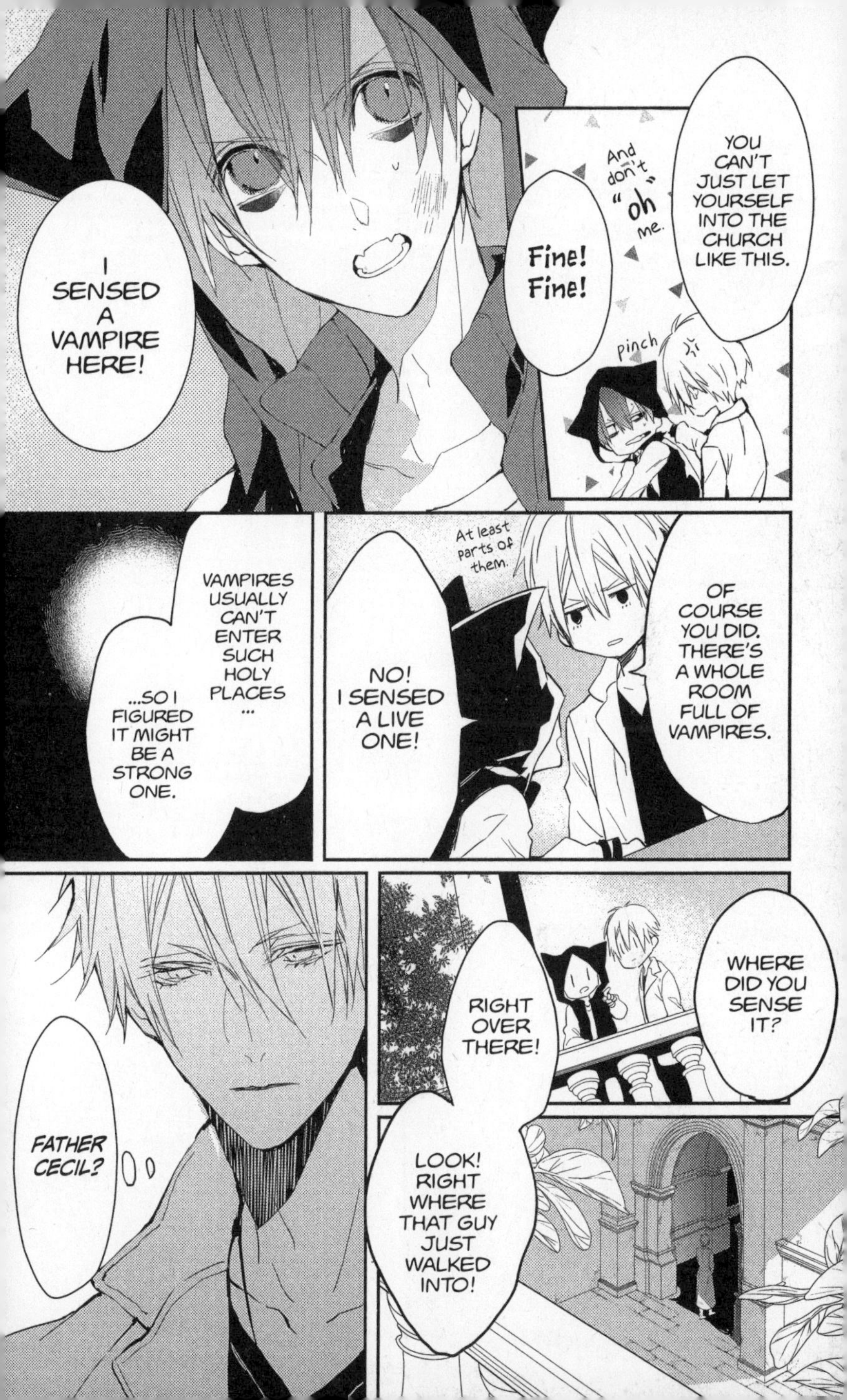
I SENSED A VAMPIRE HERE!
YOU CAN'T JUST LET YOURSELF INTO THE CHURCH LIKE THIS.
And don't "oh" me.
Fine! Fine!
pinch
OF COURSE YOU DID. THERE'S A WHOLE ROOM FULL OF VAMPIRES.
At least parts of them.
NO! I SENSED A LIVE ONE!
VAMPIRES USUALLY CAN'T ENTER SUCH HOLY PLACES ...
...SO I FIGURED IT MIGHT BE A STRONG ONE.
WHERE DID YOU SENSE IT?
RIGHT OVER THERE!
LOOK! RIGHT WHERE THAT GUY JUST WALKED INTO!
FATHER CECIL?

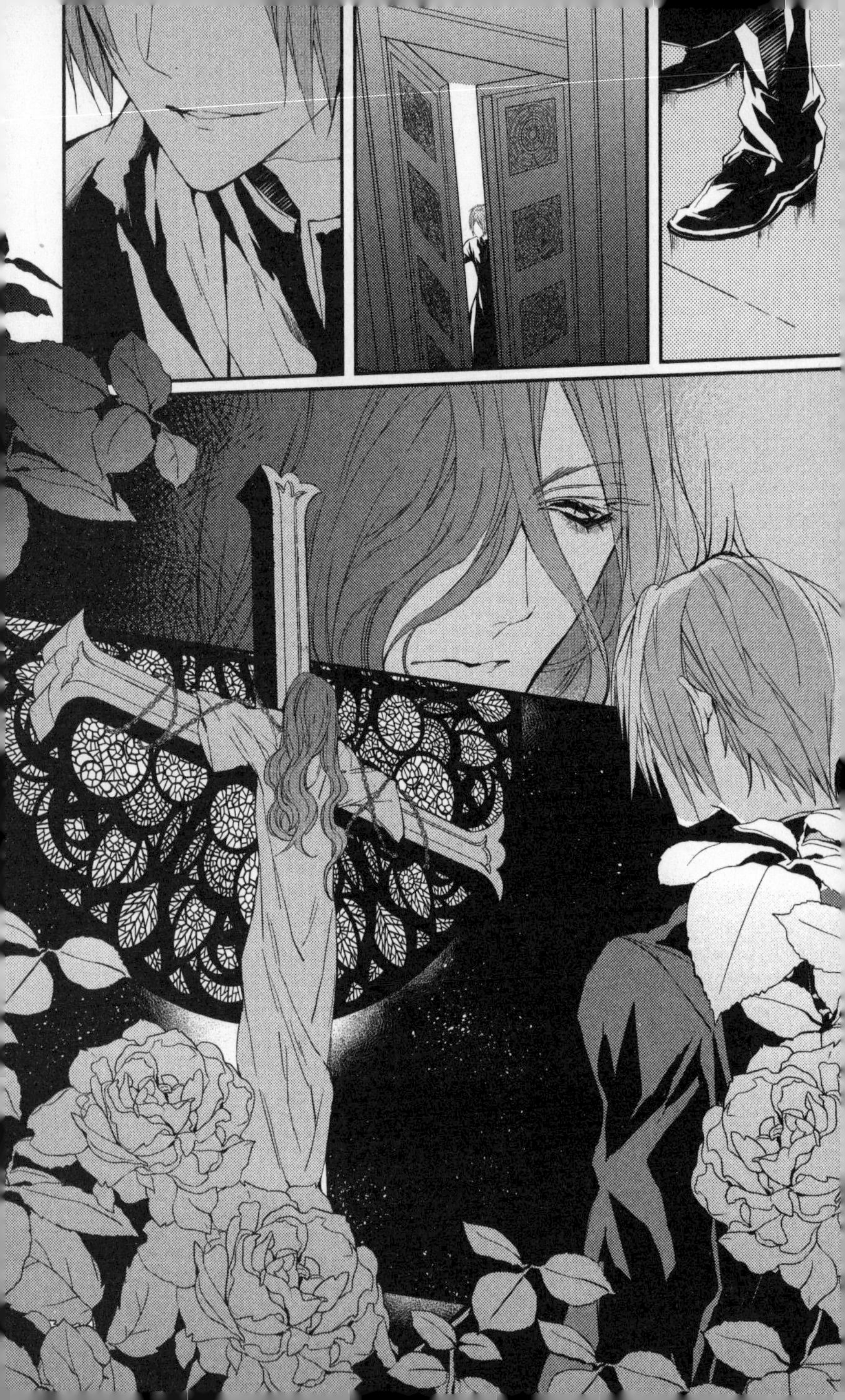

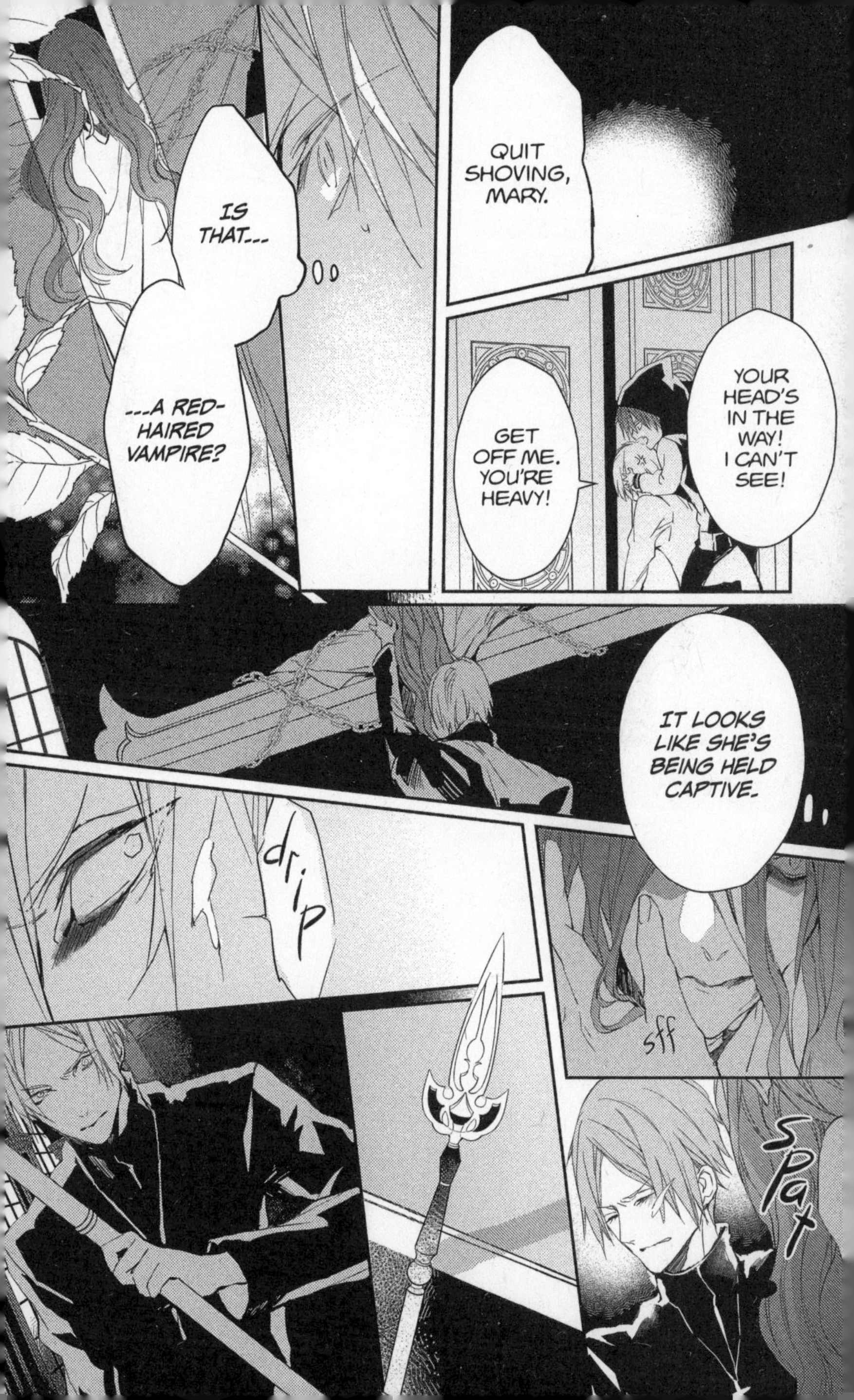
QUIT SHOVING, MARY.
YOUR HEAD'S IN THE WAY! I CAN'T SEE!
GET OFF ME. YOU'RE HEAVY!
IS THAT...
...A RED-HAIRED VAMPIRE?
IT LOOKS LIKE SHE'S BEING HELD CAPTIVE.
sff
drip
spat

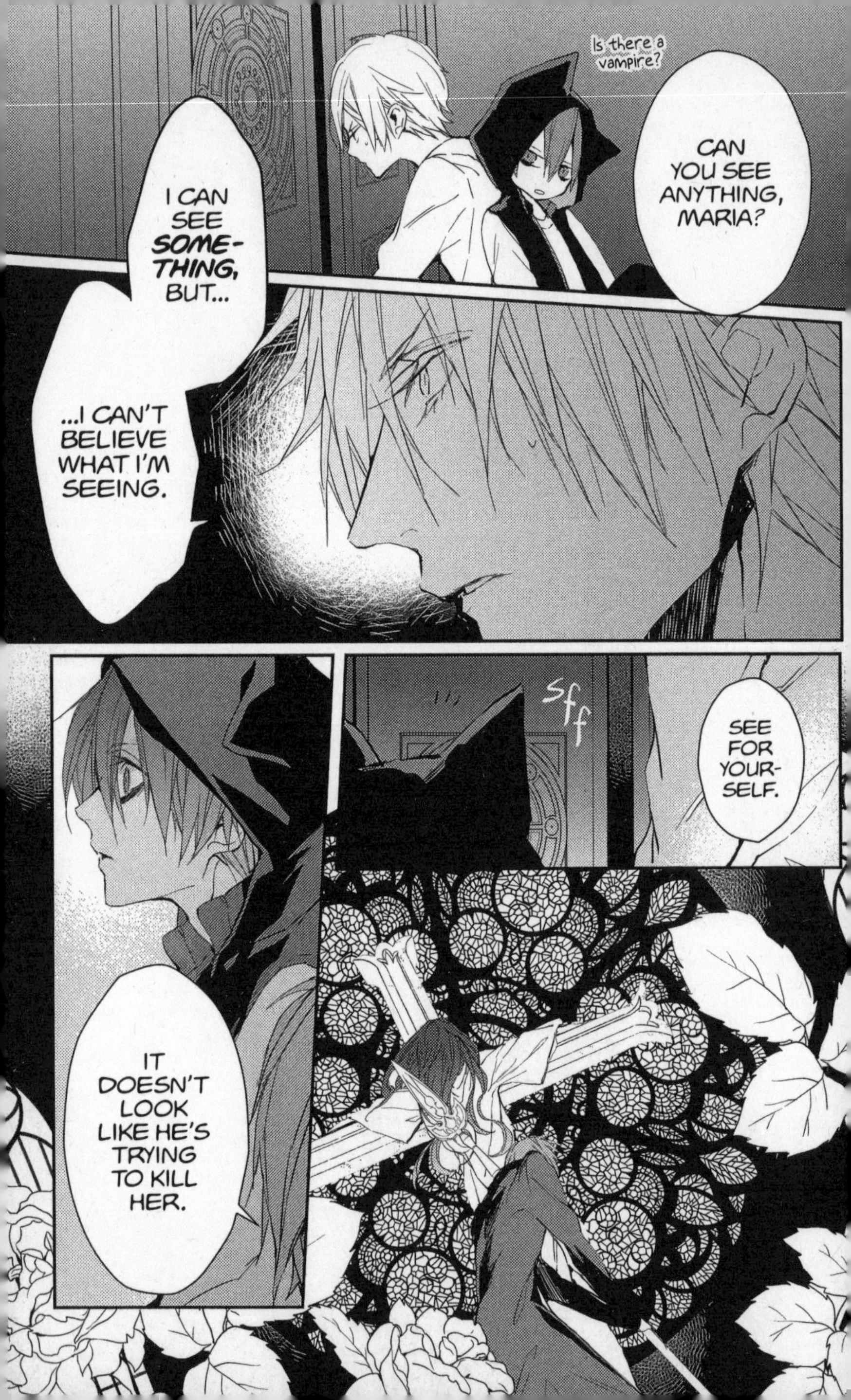
Is there a vampire?
CAN YOU SEE ANYTHING, MARIA?
I CAN SEE SOME-THING, BUT...
...I CAN'T BELIEVE WHAT I'M SEEING.
sff
SEE FOR YOUR-SELF.
IT DOESN'T LOOK LIKE HE'S TRYING TO KILL HER.

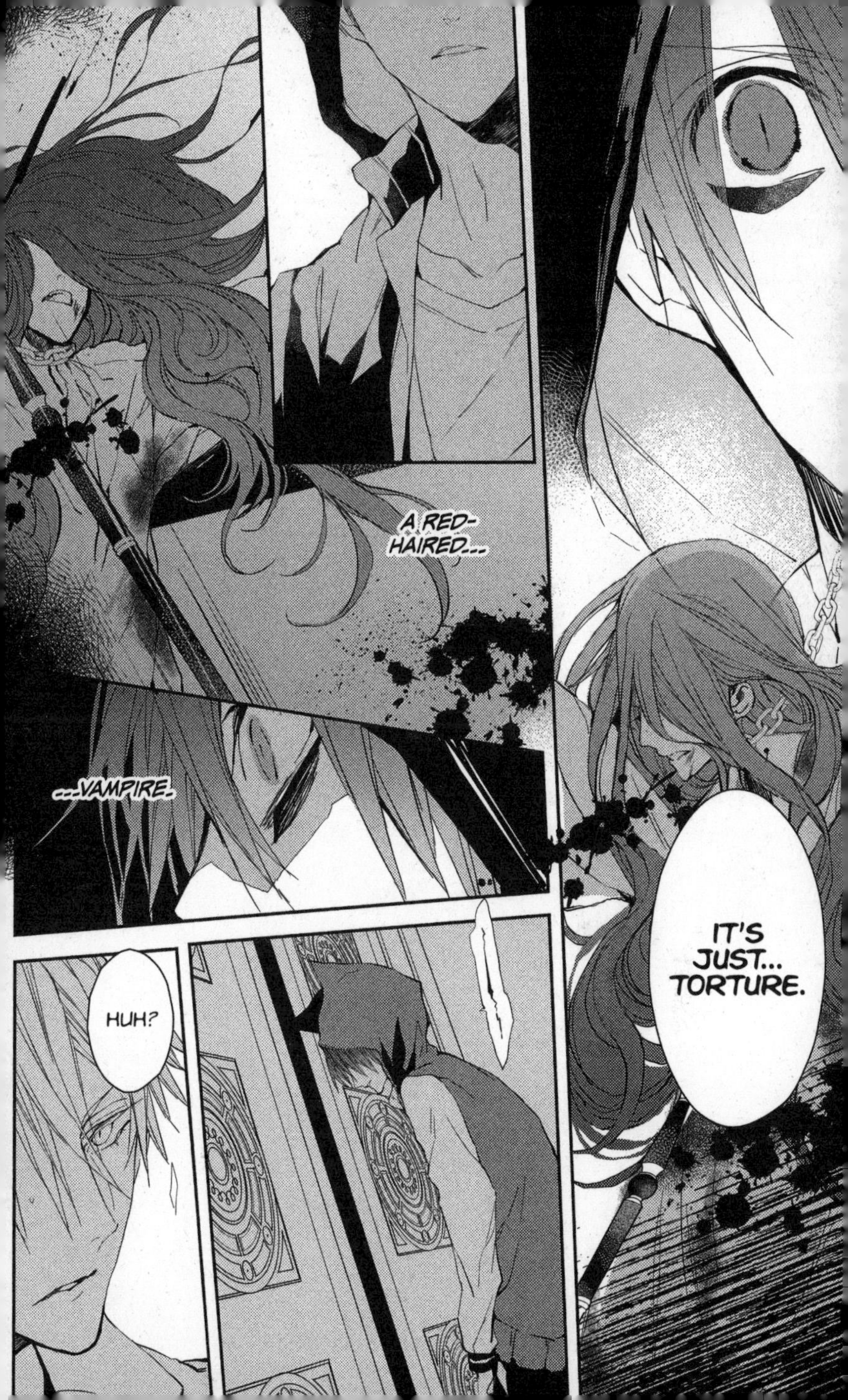
A RED-HAIRED...
...VAMPIRE.
IT'S JUST... TORTURE.
HUH?

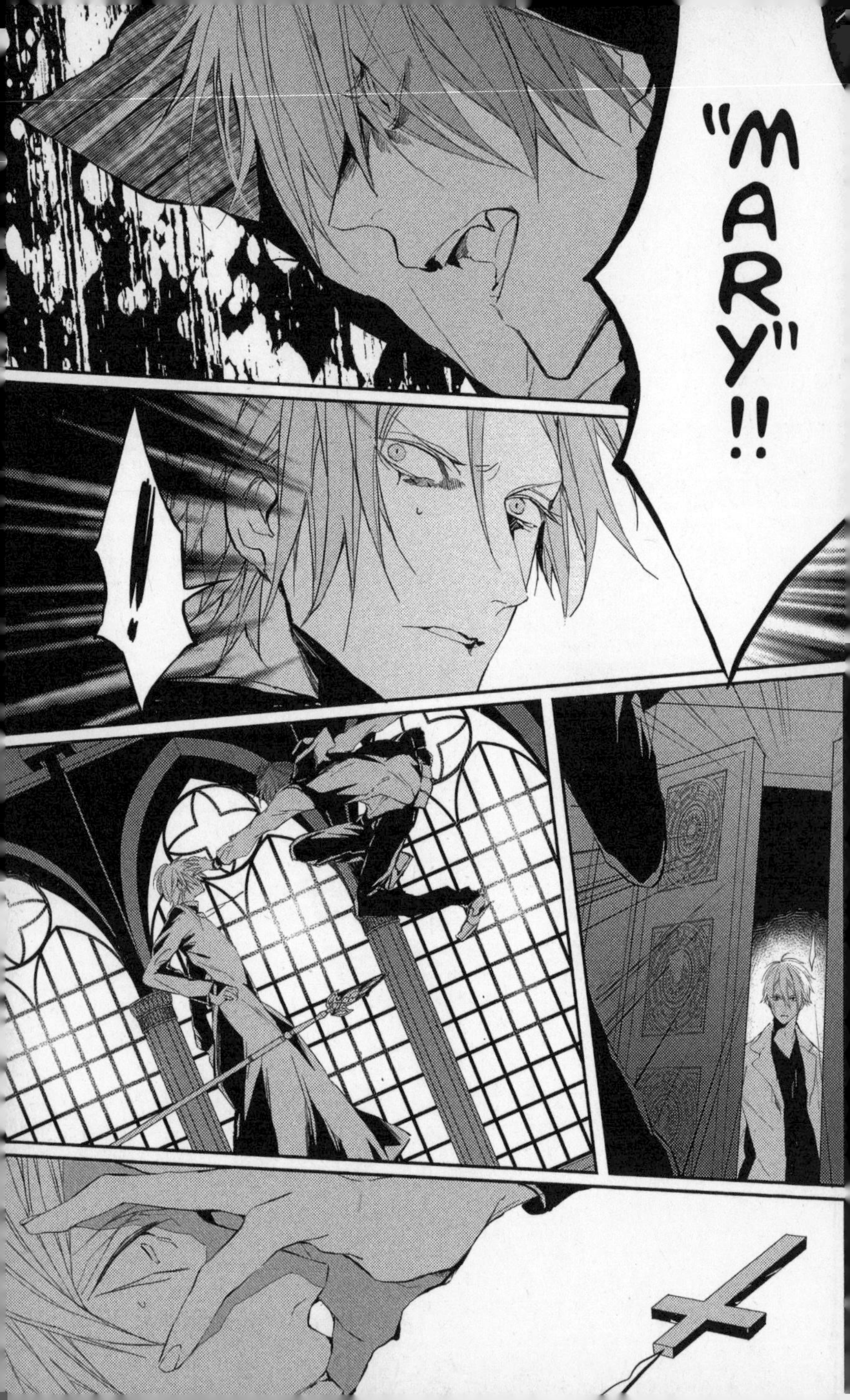
"MARY"!!
!

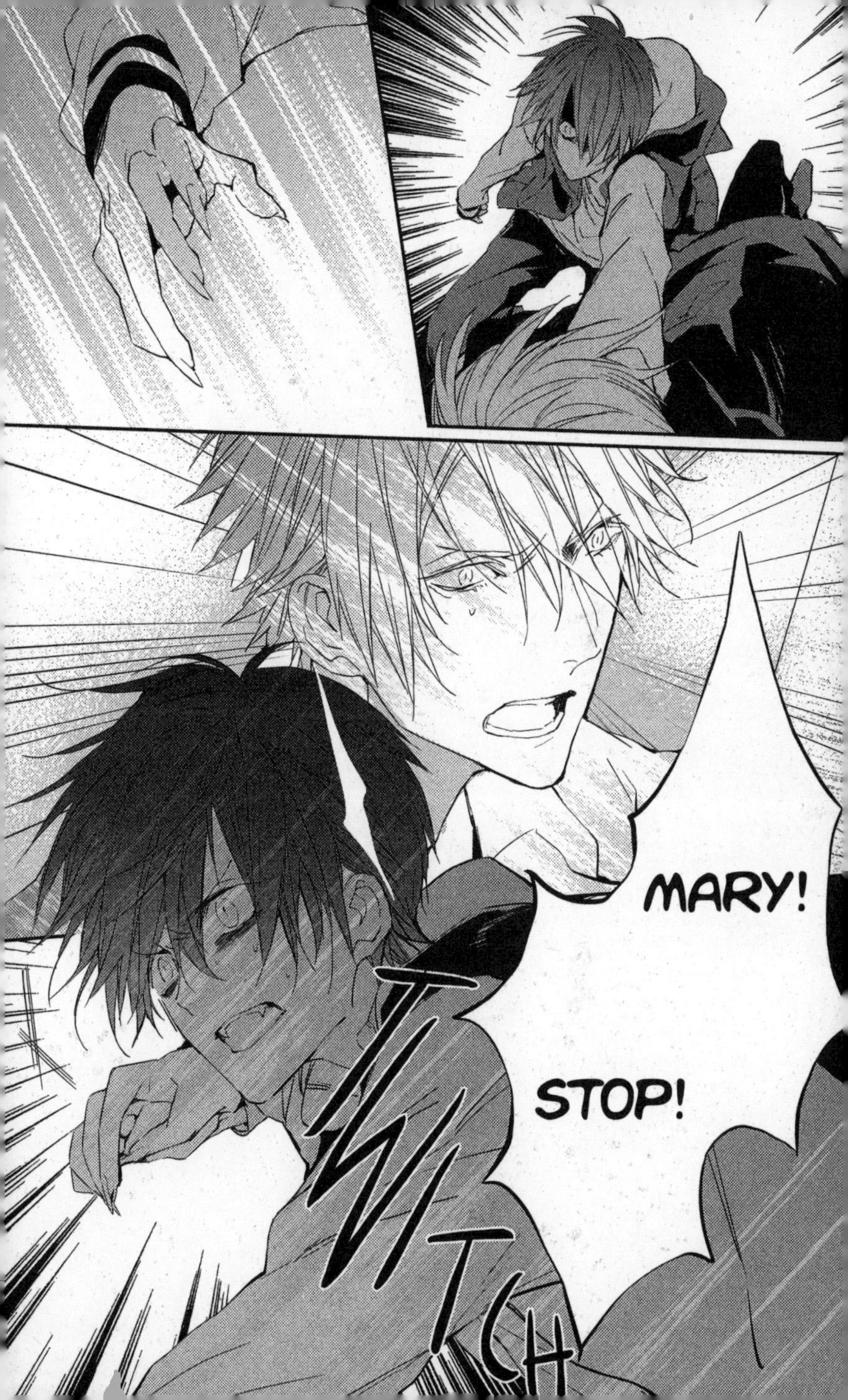
MARY!
STOP!
TWITCH

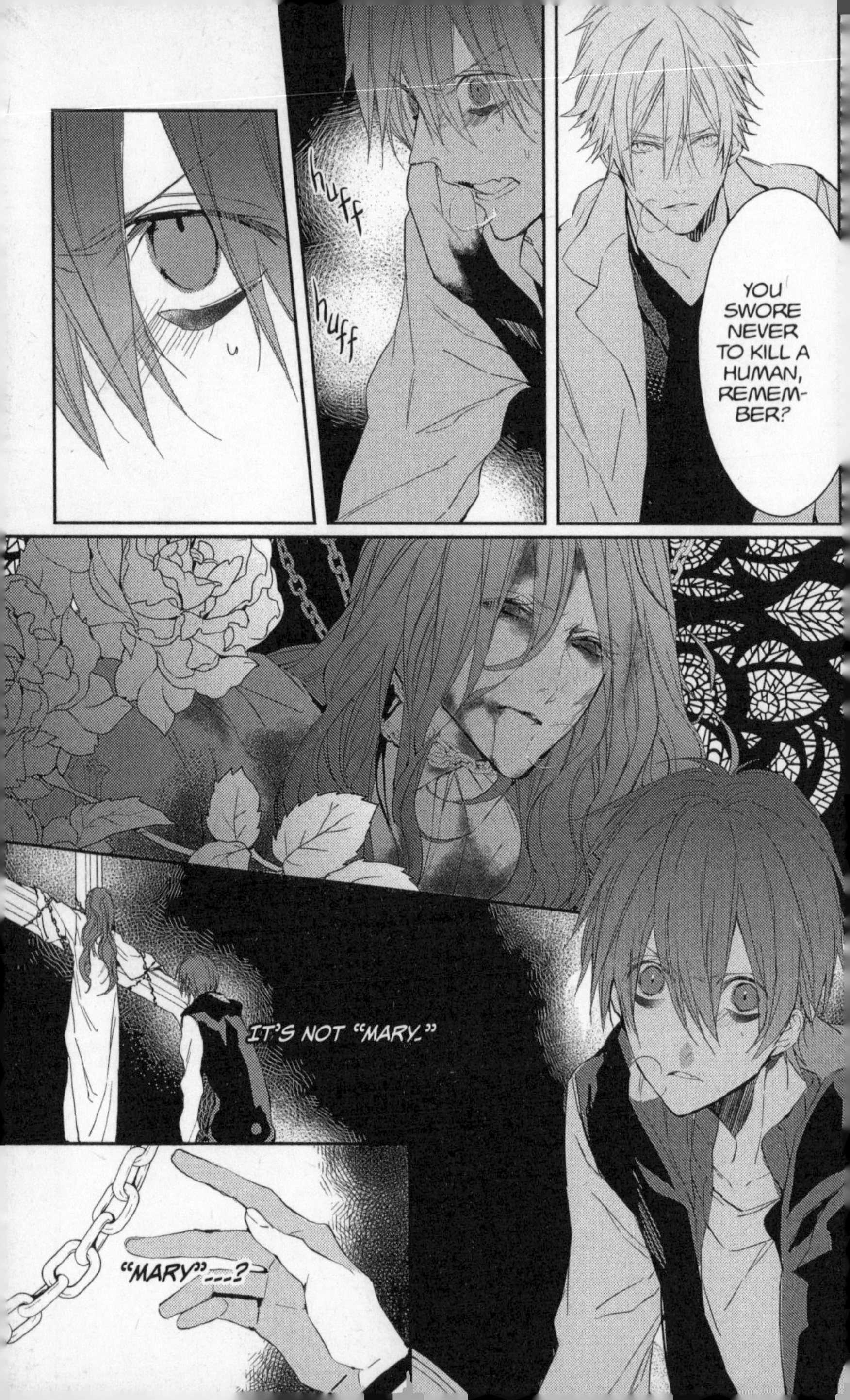
YOU SWORE NEVER TO KILL A HUMAN, REMEMBER?
huff
huff
IT'S NOT "MARY."
"MARY"...?

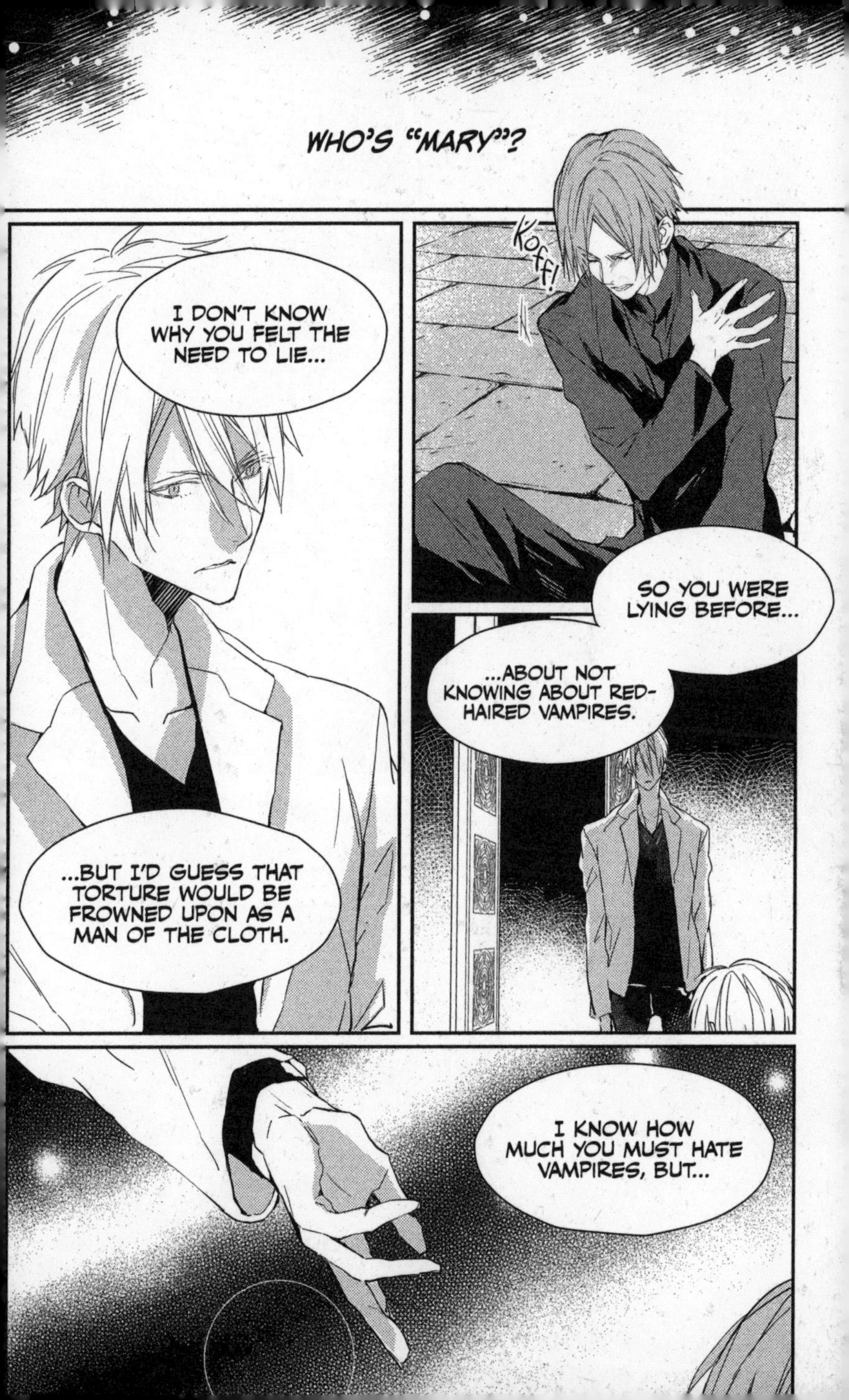
WHO'S "MARY"?
KOFF!
SO YOU WERE LYING BEFORE...
...ABOUT NOT KNOWING ABOUT RED-HAIRED VAMPIRES.
I DON'T KNOW WHY YOU FELT THE NEED TO LIE...
...BUT I'D GUESS THAT TORTURE WOULD BE FROWNED UPON AS A MAN OF THE CLOTH.
I KNOW HOW MUCH YOU MUST HATE VAMPIRES, BUT...

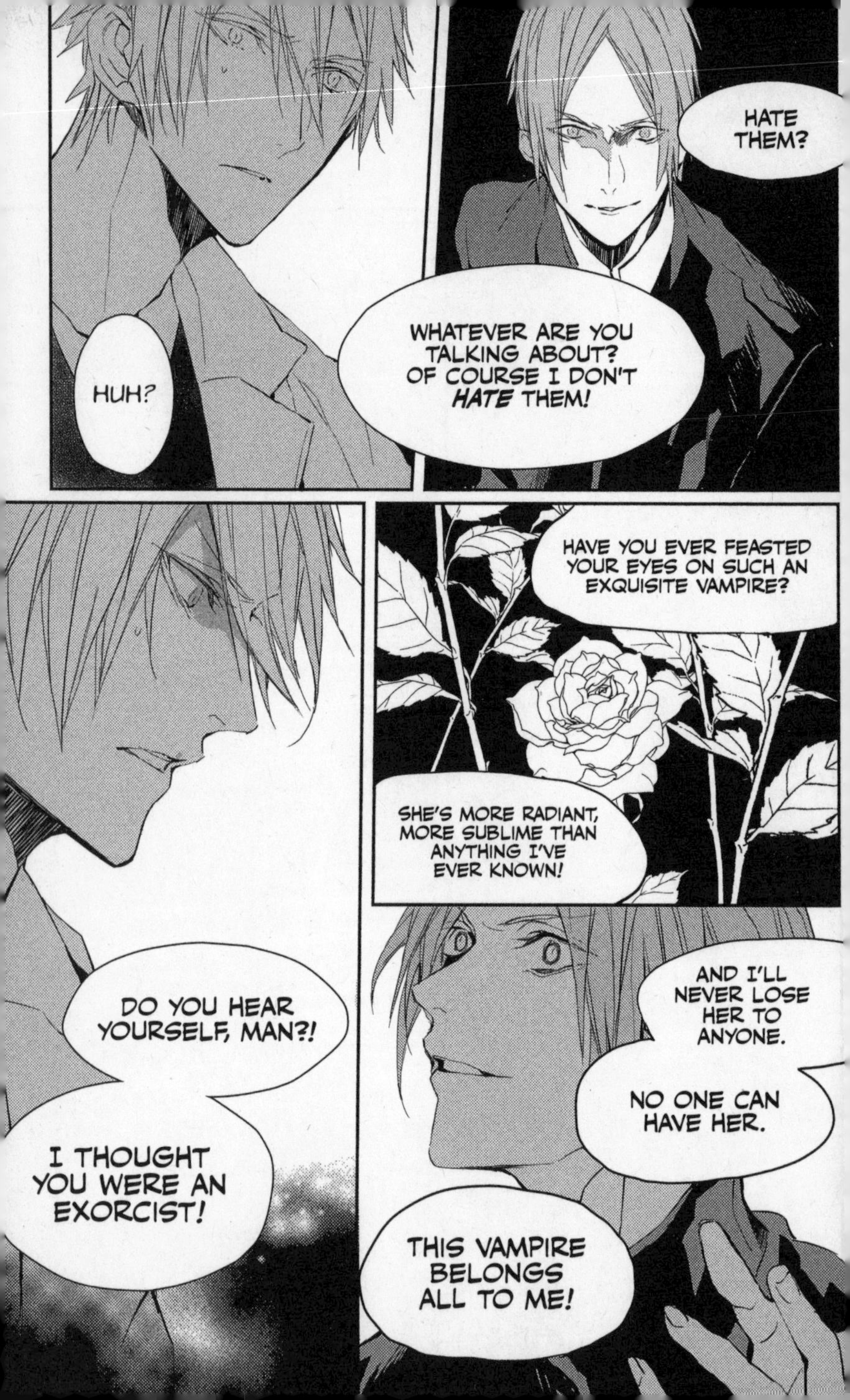
HATE THEM?
WHATEVER ARE YOU TALKING ABOUT? OF COURSE I DON'T *HATE* THEM!
HUH?
HAVE YOU EVER FEASTED YOUR EYES ON SUCH AN EXQUISITE VAMPIRE?
SHE'S MORE RADIANT, MORE SUBLIME THAN ANYTHING I'VE EVER KNOWN!
AND I'LL NEVER LOSE HER TO ANYONE.
NO ONE CAN HAVE HER.
THIS VAMPIRE BELONGS ALL TO ME!
DO YOU HEAR YOURSELF, MAN?!
I THOUGHT YOU WERE AN EXORCIST!

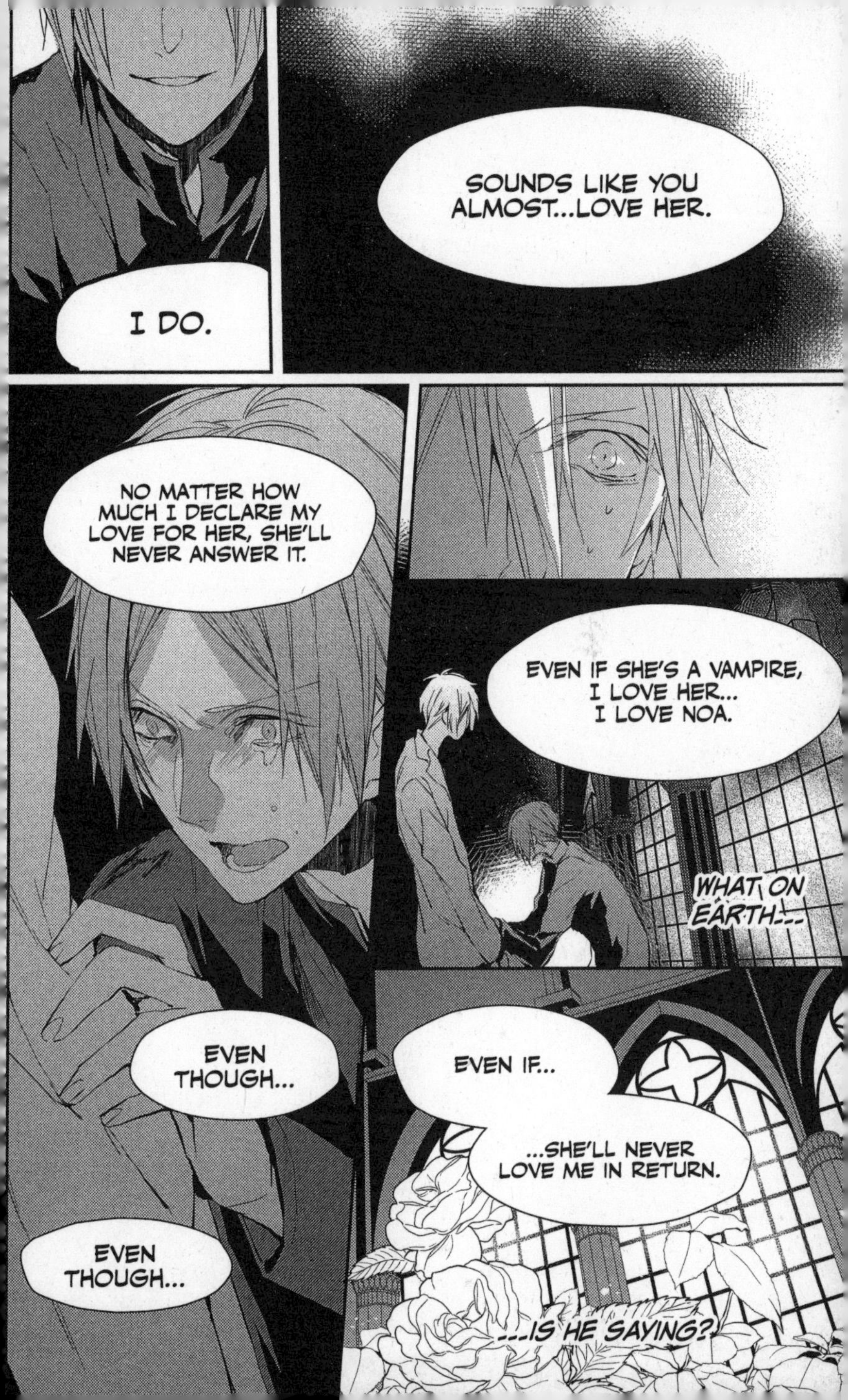
SOUNDS LIKE YOU ALMOST...LOVE HER.
I DO.
EVEN IF SHE'S A VAMPIRE, I LOVE HER... I LOVE NOA.
WHAT ON EARTH---
EVEN IF...
...SHE'LL NEVER LOVE ME IN RETURN.
---IS HE SAYING?
NO MATTER HOW MUCH I DECLARE MY LOVE FOR HER, SHE'LL NEVER ANSWER IT.
EVEN THOUGH...
EVEN THOUGH...

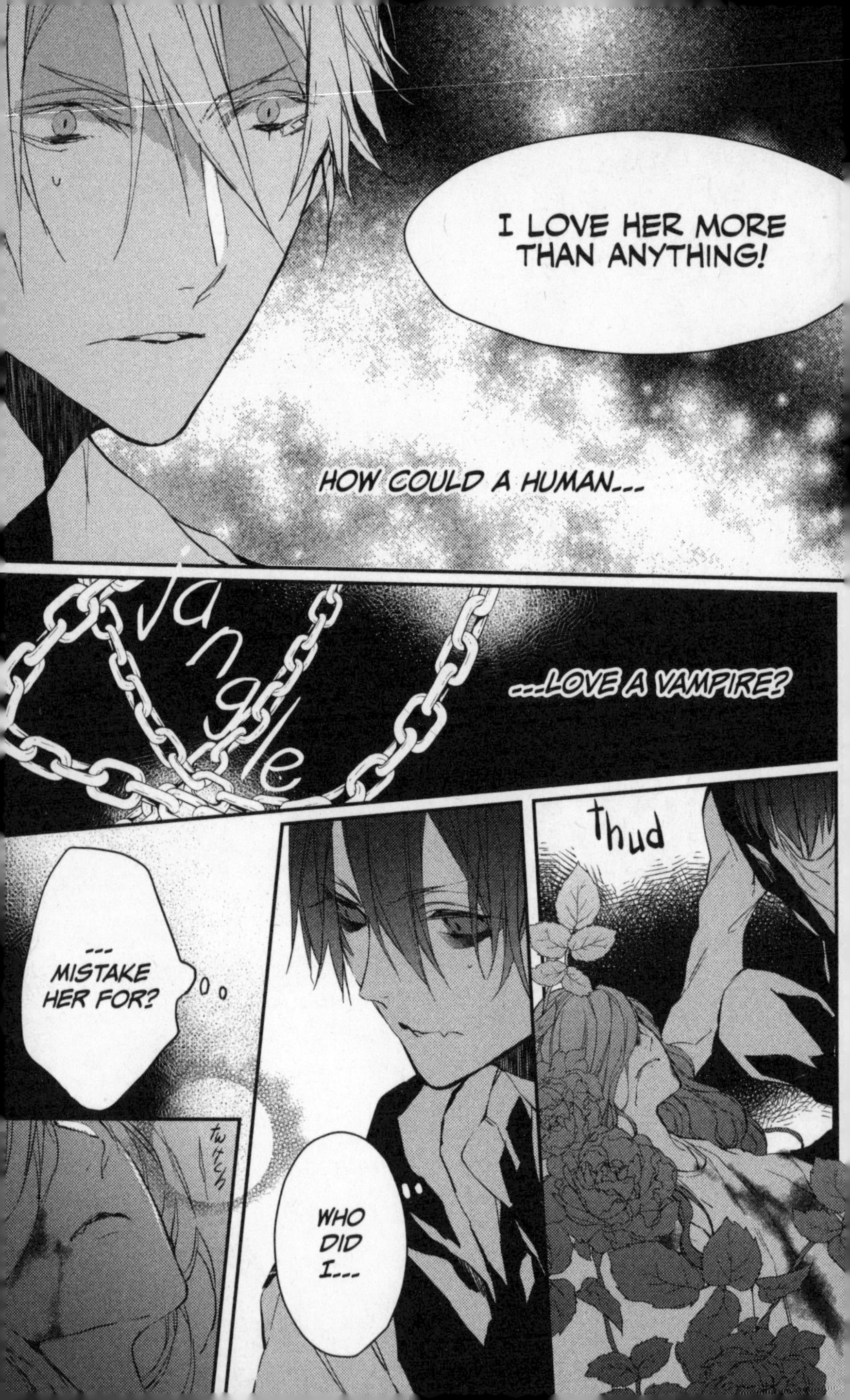
I LOVE HER MORE THAN ANYTHING!
HOW COULD A HUMAN...
Jangle
...LOVE A VAMPIRE?
thud
WHO DID I...
... MISTAKE HER FOR?
twitch

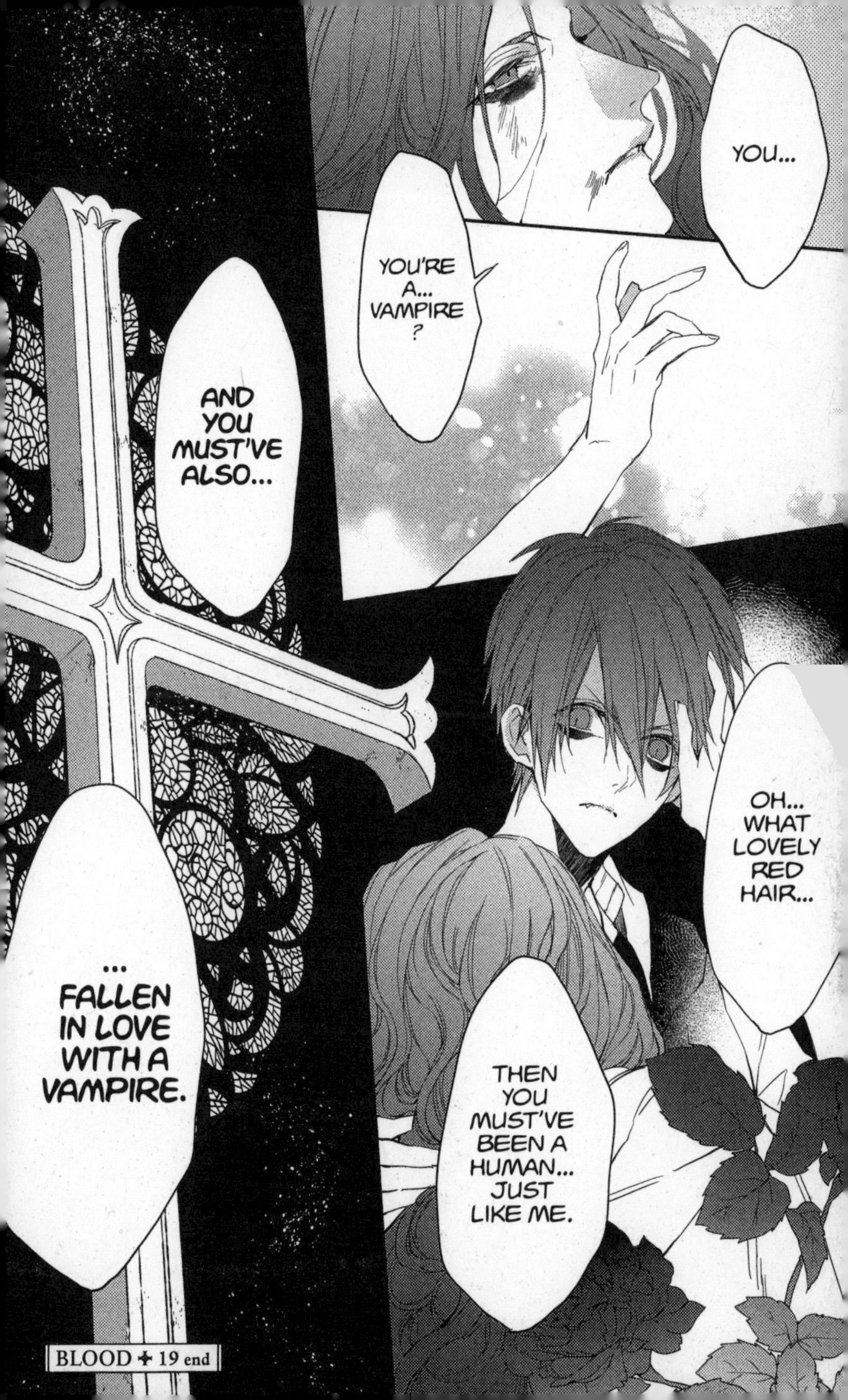
YOU...
YOU'RE A... VAMPIRE?
OH... WHAT LOVELY RED HAIR...
THEN YOU MUST'VE BEEN A HUMAN... JUST LIKE ME.
AND YOU MUST'VE ALSO...
...FALLEN IN LOVE WITH A VAMPIRE.
BLOOD ✚ 19 end

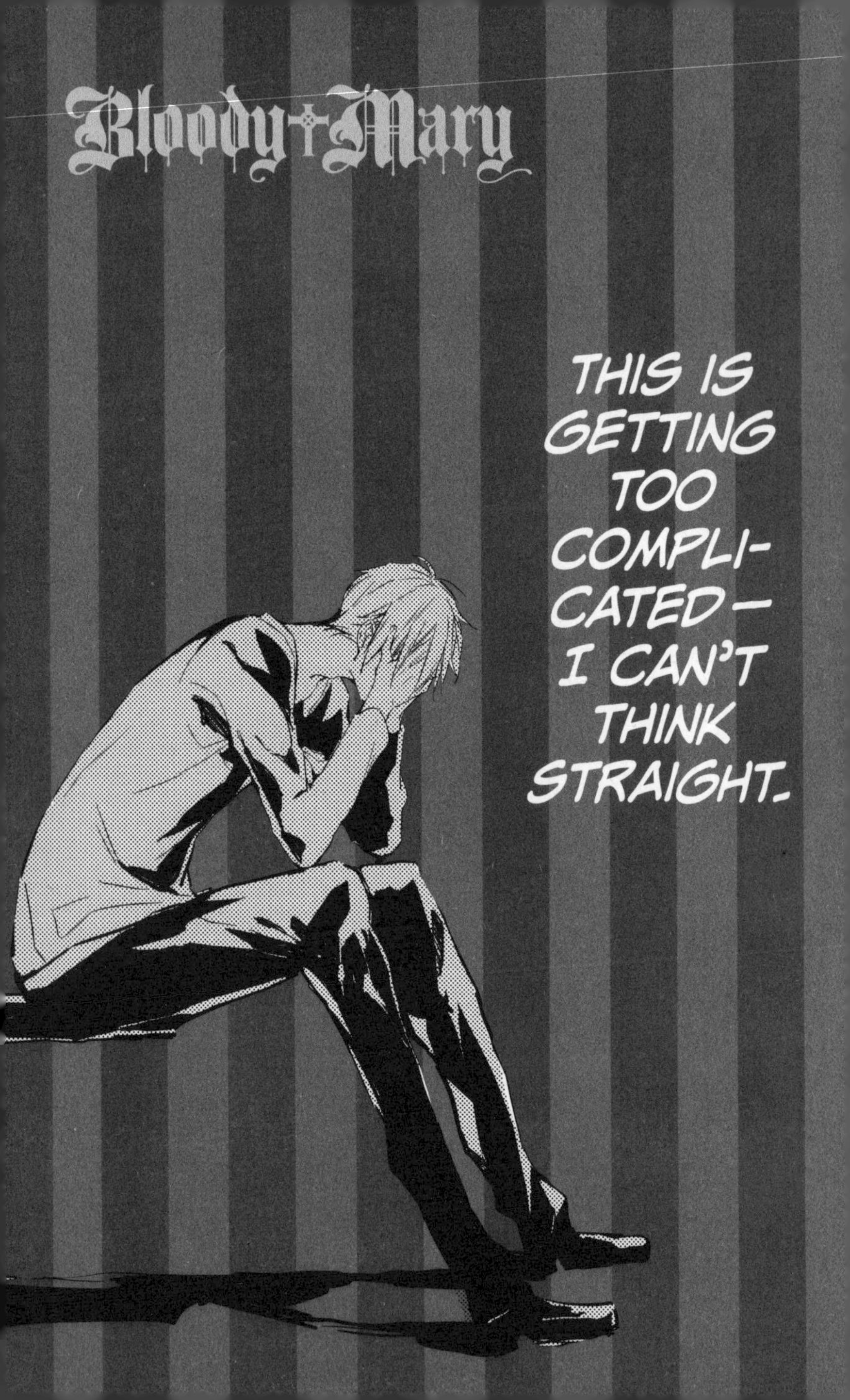
Bloody+Mary
THIS IS GETTING TOO COMPLI-CATED—I CAN'T THINK STRAIGHT.

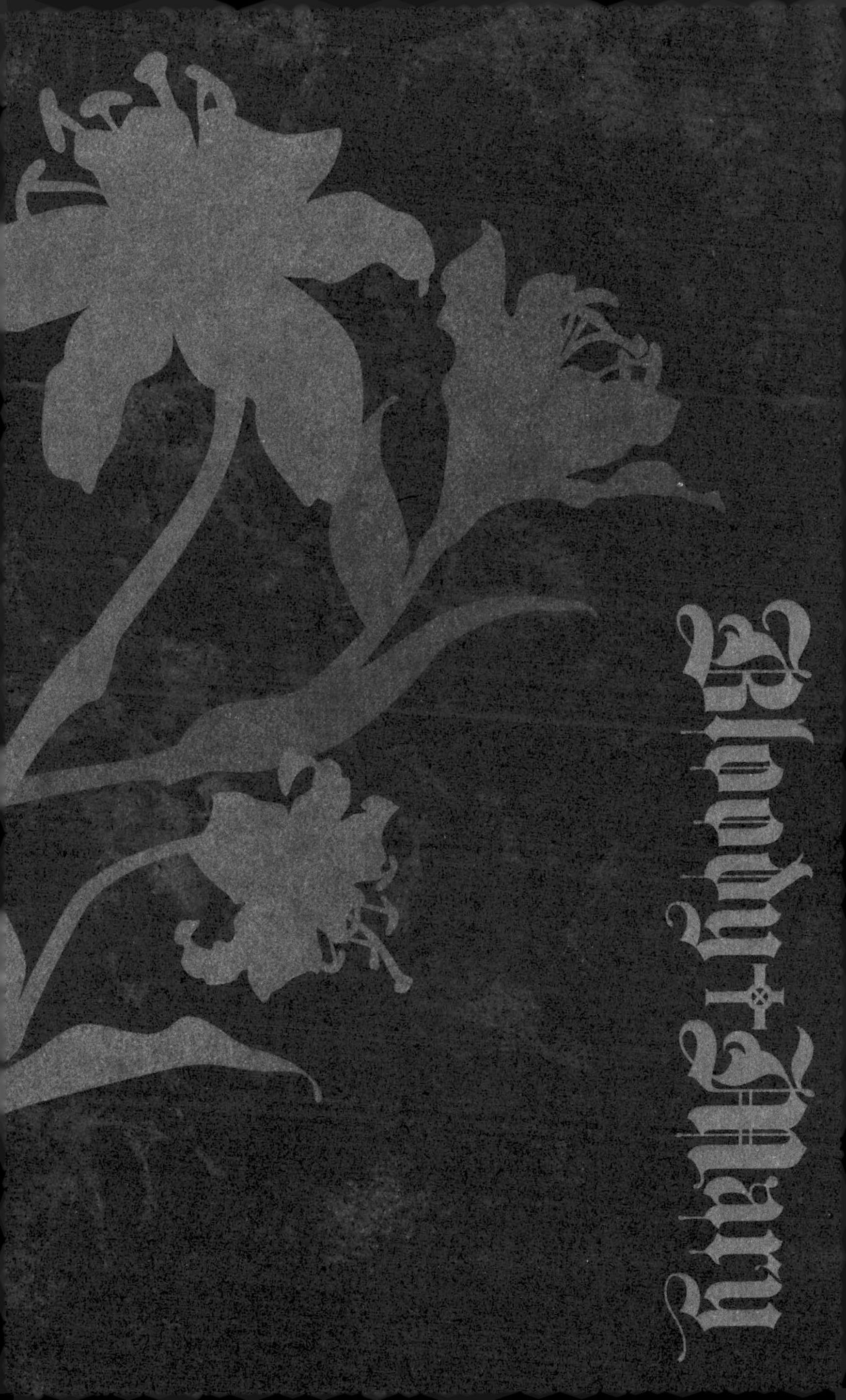
Bloody+Mary

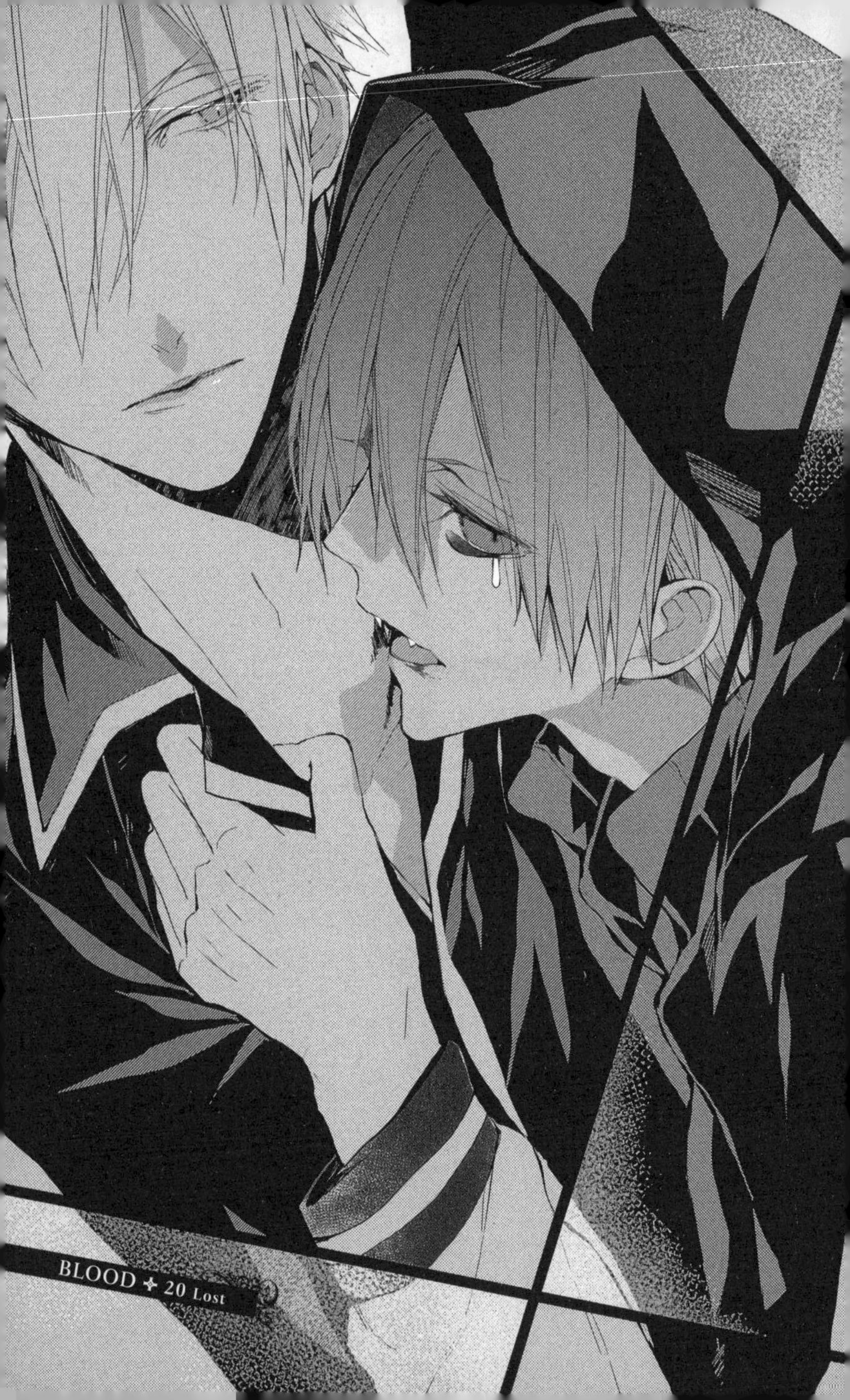
BLOOD ✣ 20 Lost

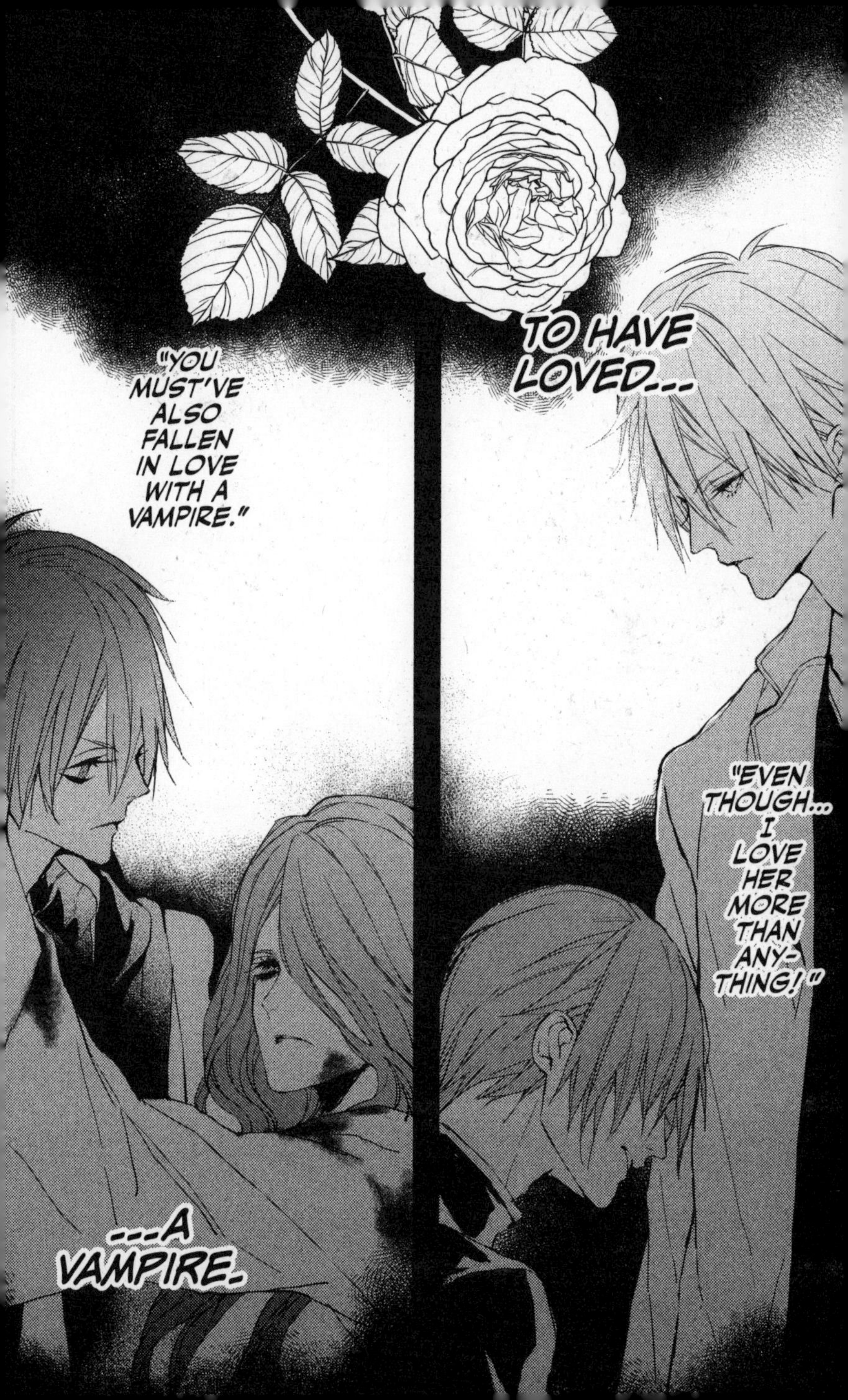
TO HAVE LOVED...
"EVEN THOUGH... I LOVE HER MORE THAN ANY-THING!"
"YOU MUST'VE ALSO FALLEN IN LOVE WITH A VAMPIRE."
...A VAMPIRE.

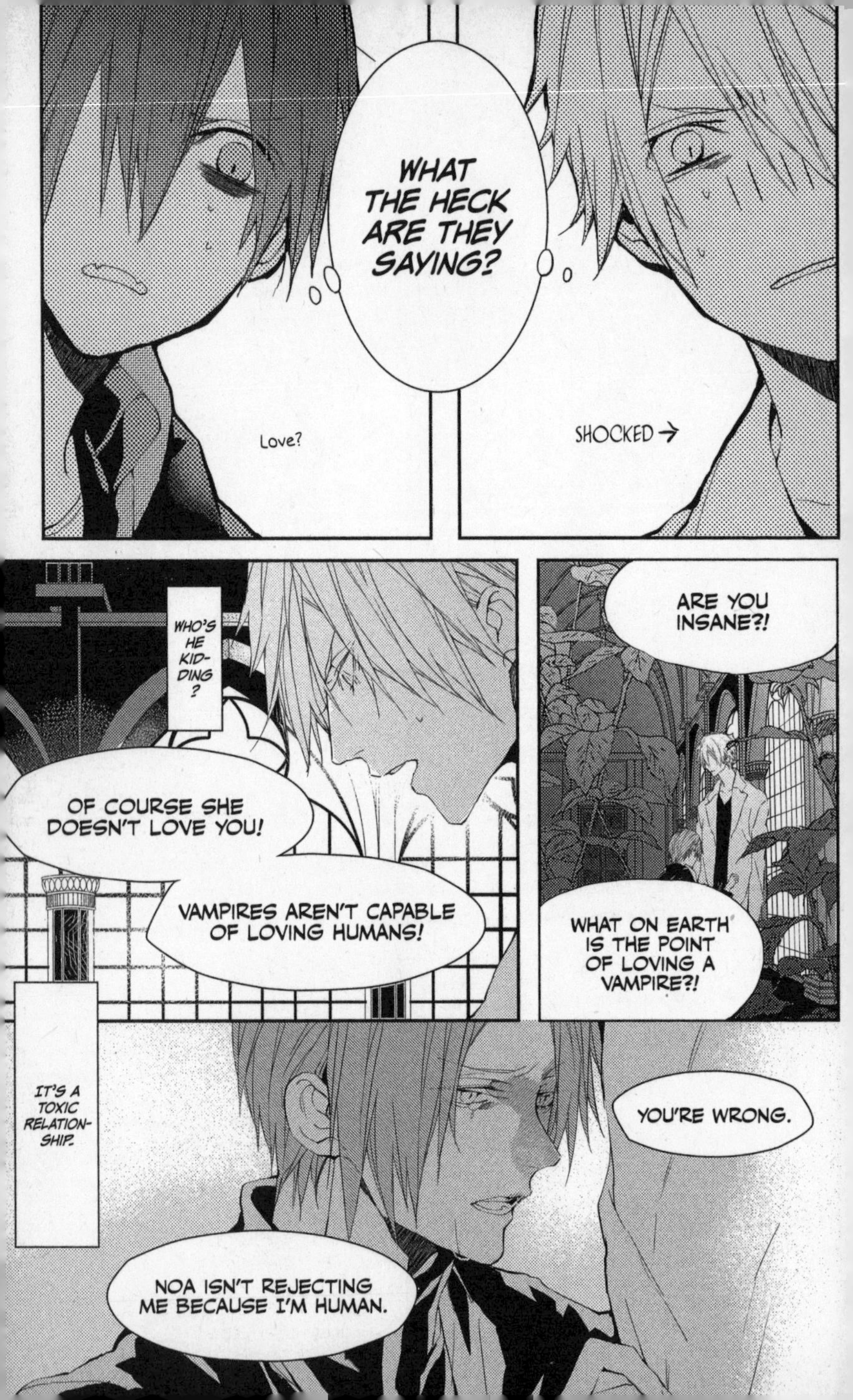
WHAT THE HECK ARE THEY SAYING?
SHOCKED →
Love?
ARE YOU INSANE?!
WHAT ON EARTH IS THE POINT OF LOVING A VAMPIRE?!
WHO'S HE KID-DING?
OF COURSE SHE DOESN'T LOVE YOU!
VAMPIRES AREN'T CAPABLE OF LOVING HUMANS!
YOU'RE WRONG.
IT'S A TOXIC RELATION-SHIP.
NOA ISN'T REJECTING ME BECAUSE I'M HUMAN.

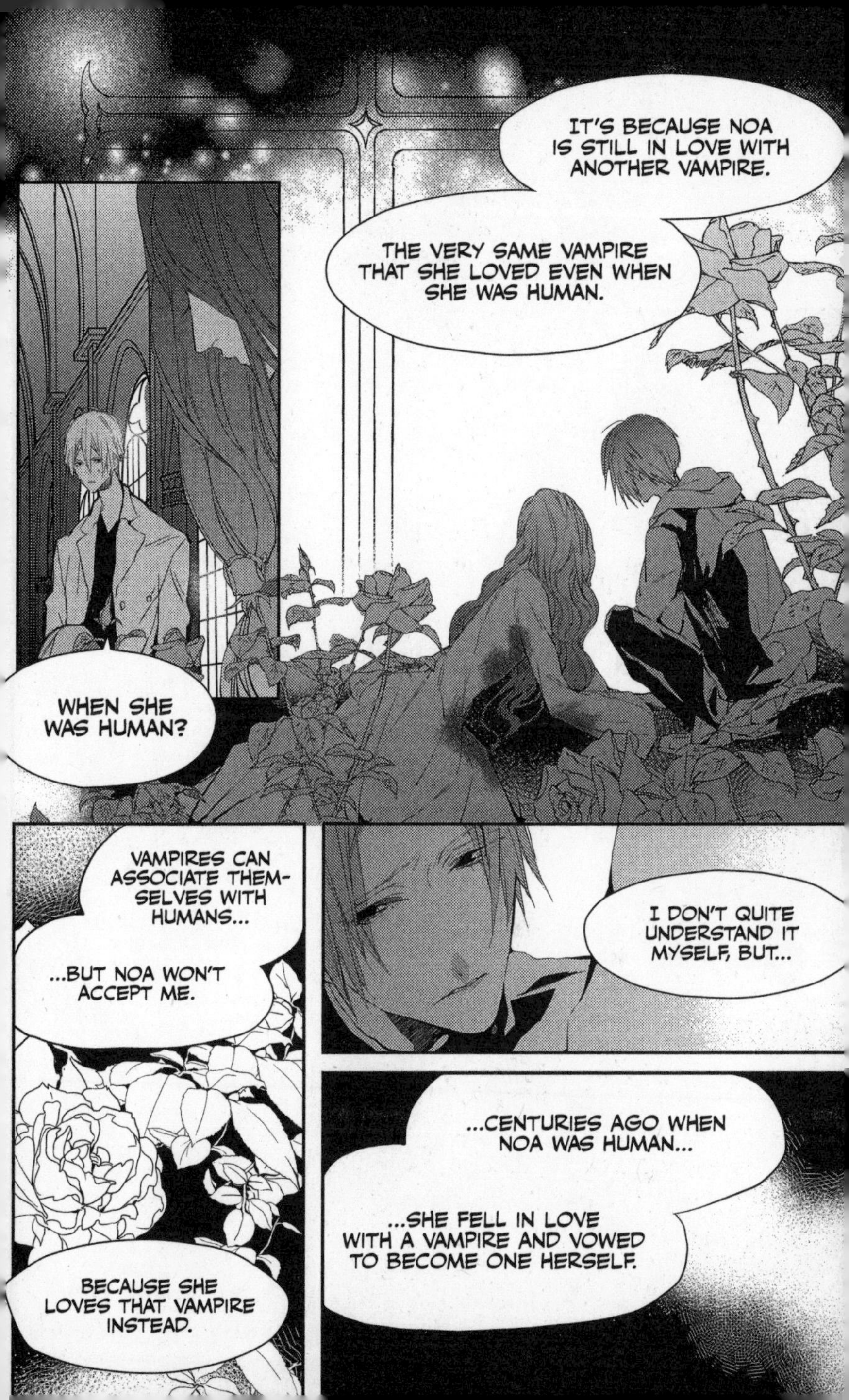
IT'S BECAUSE NOA IS STILL IN LOVE WITH ANOTHER VAMPIRE.
THE VERY SAME VAMPIRE THAT SHE LOVED EVEN WHEN SHE WAS HUMAN.
WHEN SHE WAS HUMAN?
I DON'T QUITE UNDERSTAND IT MYSELF, BUT...
...CENTURIES AGO WHEN NOA WAS HUMAN...
...SHE FELL IN LOVE WITH A VAMPIRE AND VOWED TO BECOME ONE HERSELF.
VAMPIRES CAN ASSOCIATE THEM-SELVES WITH HUMANS...
...BUT NOA WON'T ACCEPT ME.
BECAUSE SHE LOVES THAT VAMPIRE INSTEAD.

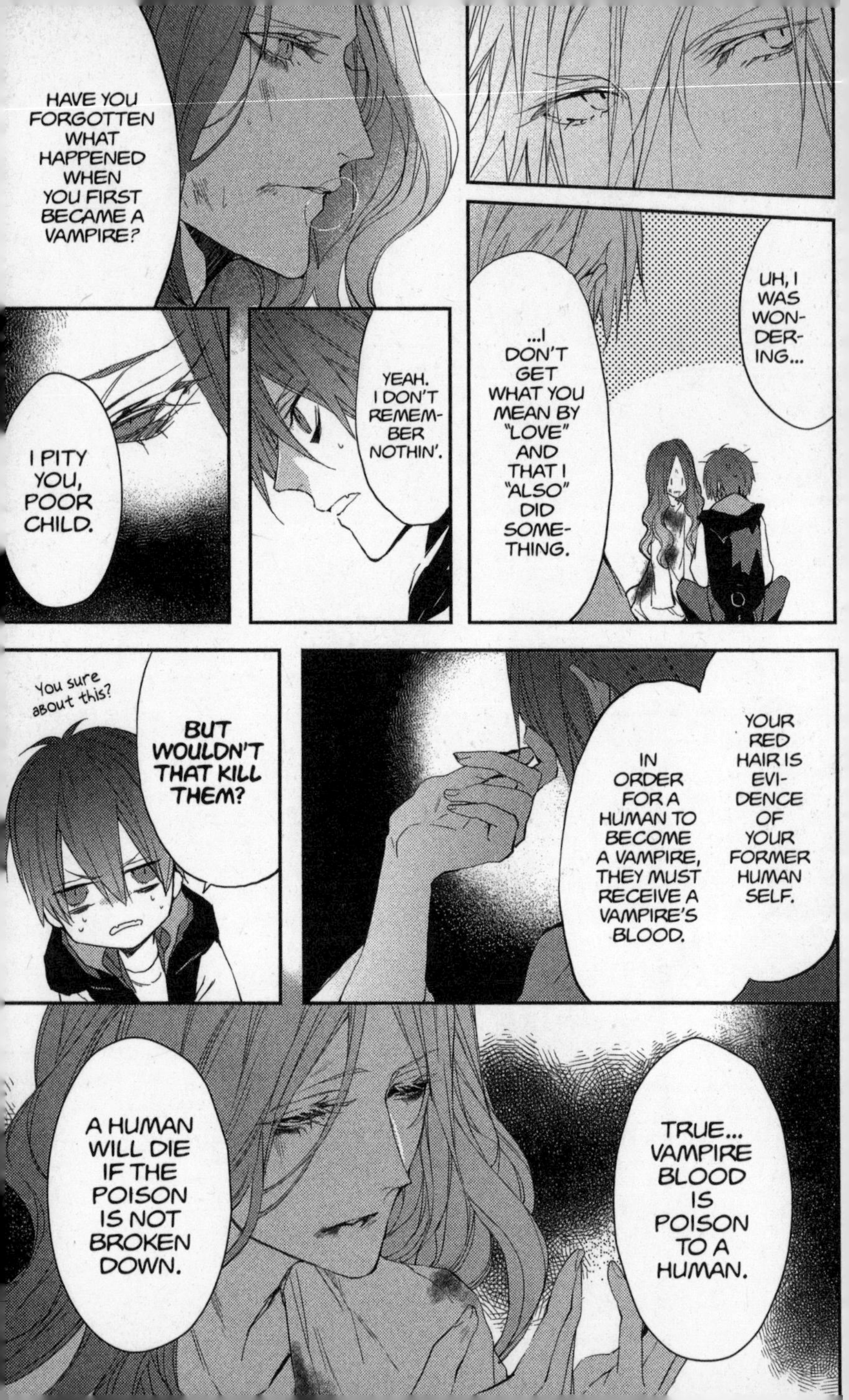
UH, I WAS WONDERING...
...I DON'T GET WHAT YOU MEAN BY "LOVE" AND THAT I "ALSO" DID SOMETHING.
HAVE YOU FORGOTTEN WHAT HAPPENED WHEN YOU FIRST BECAME A VAMPIRE?
YEAH. I DON'T REMEMBER NOTHIN'.
I PITY YOU, POOR CHILD.
YOUR RED HAIR IS EVIDENCE OF YOUR FORMER HUMAN SELF.
IN ORDER FOR A HUMAN TO BECOME A VAMPIRE, THEY MUST RECEIVE A VAMPIRE'S BLOOD.
BUT WOULDN'T THAT KILL THEM?
You sure about this?
TRUE... VAMPIRE BLOOD IS POISON TO A HUMAN.
A HUMAN WILL DIE IF THE POISON IS NOT BROKEN DOWN.

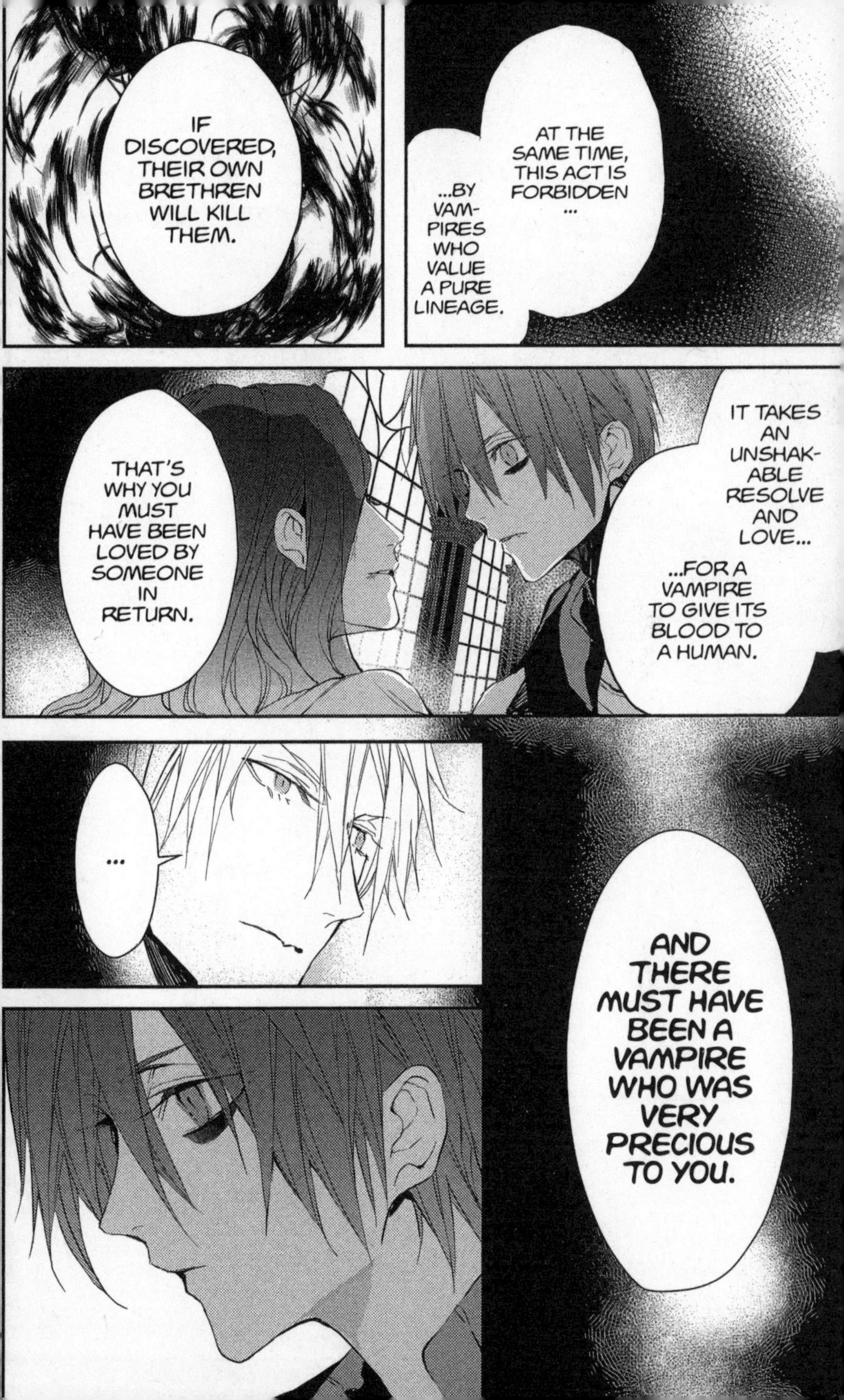
AT THE SAME TIME, THIS ACT IS FORBIDDEN...
...BY VAMPIRES WHO VALUE A PURE LINEAGE.
IF DISCOVERED, THEIR OWN BRETHREN WILL KILL THEM.
IT TAKES AN UNSHAKABLE RESOLVE AND LOVE...
...FOR A VAMPIRE TO GIVE ITS BLOOD TO A HUMAN.
THAT'S WHY YOU MUST HAVE BEEN LOVED BY SOMEONE IN RETURN.
AND THERE MUST HAVE BEEN A VAMPIRE WHO WAS VERY PRECIOUS TO YOU.
...

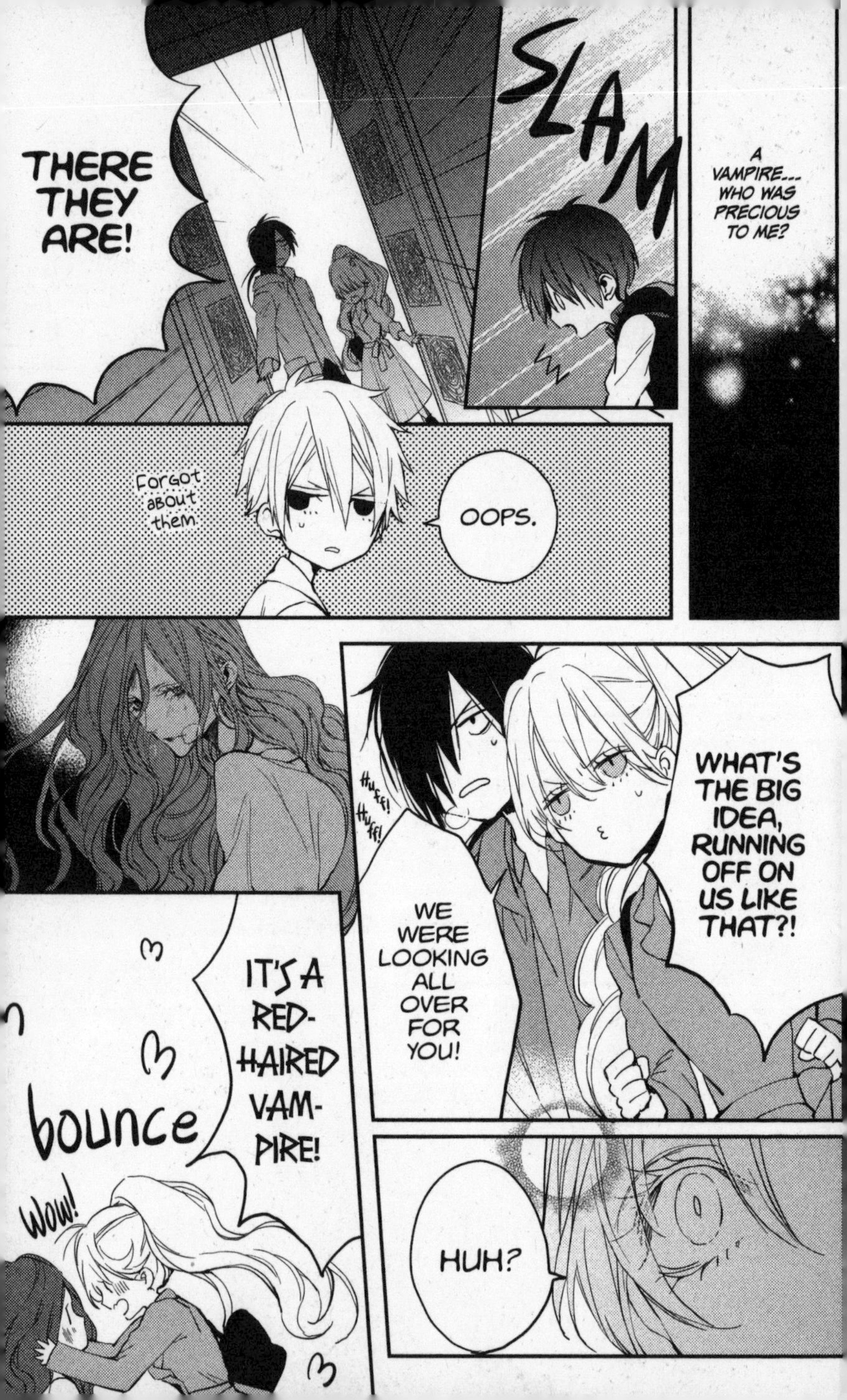
A VAMPIRE... WHO WAS PRECIOUS TO ME?
SLAM
THERE THEY ARE!
OOPS.
Forgot about them.
WHAT'S THE BIG IDEA, RUNNING OFF ON US LIKE THAT?!
Huff! Huff!
WE WERE LOOKING ALL OVER FOR YOU!
HUH?
IT'S A RED-HAIRED VAMPIRE!
bounce
Wow!

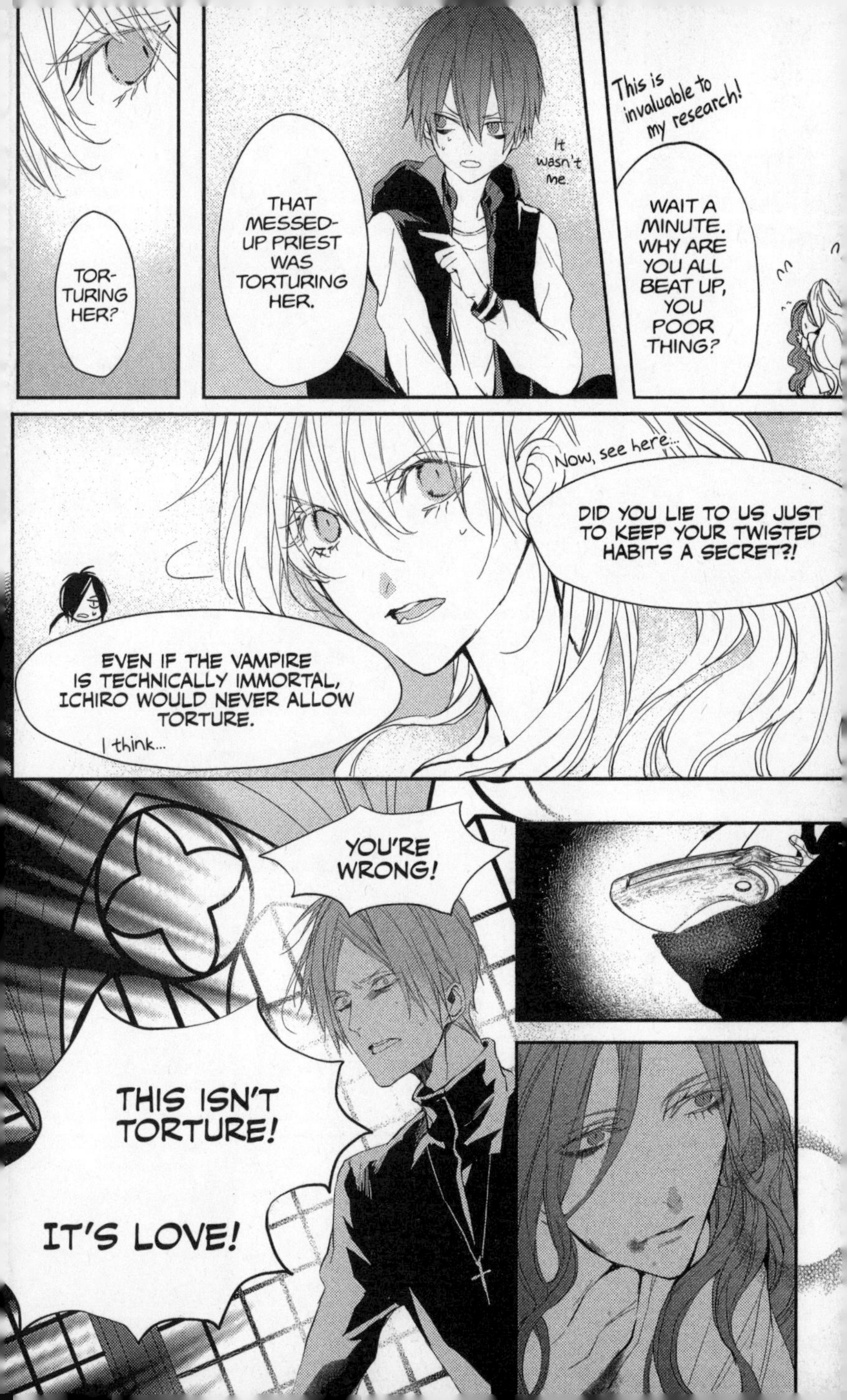
This is invaluable to my research!
WAIT A MINUTE. WHY ARE YOU ALL BEAT UP, YOU POOR THING?
It wasn't me.
THAT MESSED-UP PRIEST WAS TORTURING HER.
TORTURING HER?
Now, see here...
DID YOU LIE TO US JUST TO KEEP YOUR TWISTED HABITS A SECRET?!
EVEN IF THE VAMPIRE IS TECHNICALLY IMMORTAL, ICHIRO WOULD NEVER ALLOW TORTURE.
I think...
YOU'RE WRONG!
THIS ISN'T TORTURE!
IT'S LOVE!

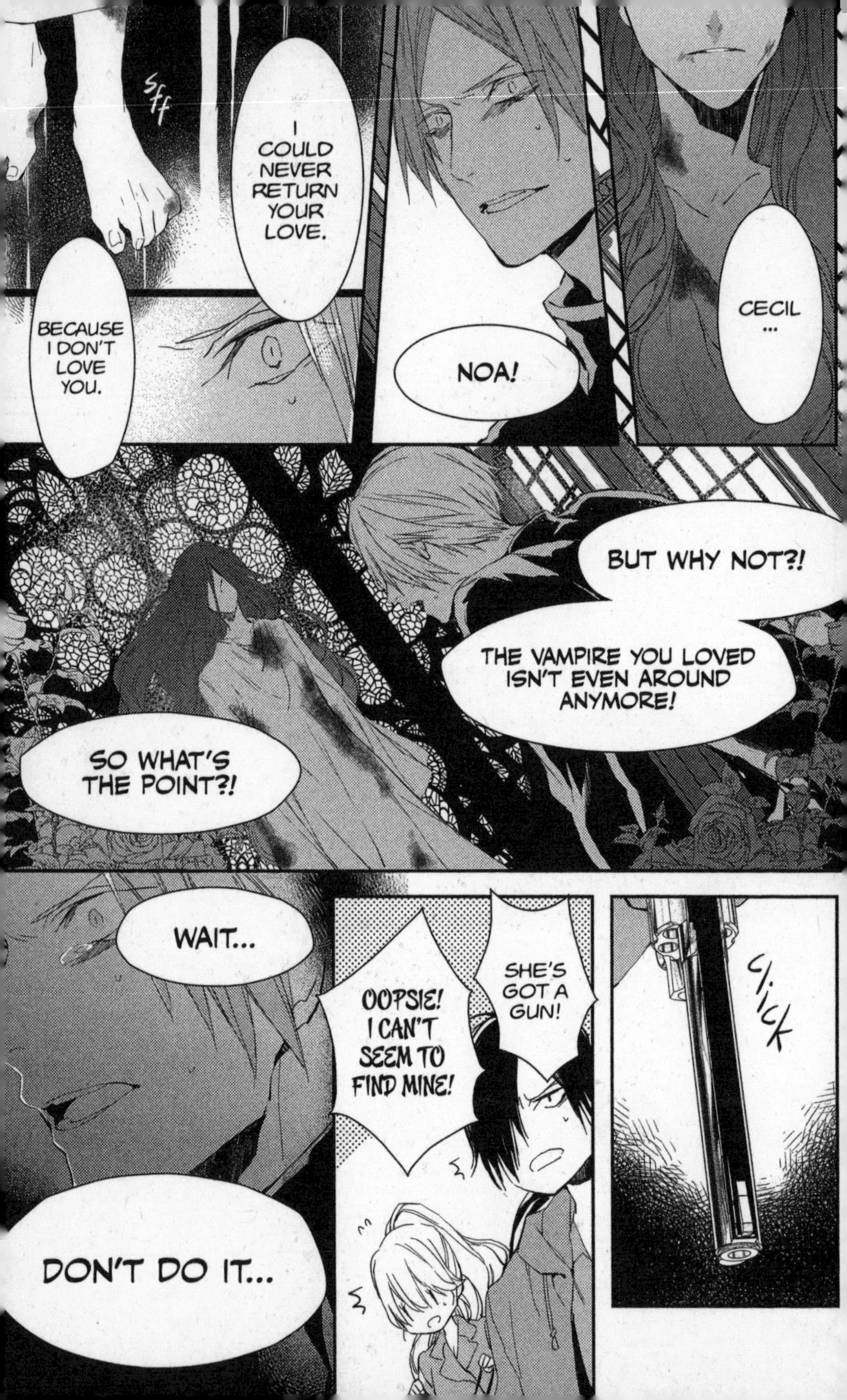
CECIL...
NOA!
sff
I COULD NEVER RETURN YOUR LOVE.
BECAUSE I DON'T LOVE YOU.
BUT WHY NOT?!
THE VAMPIRE YOU LOVED ISN'T EVEN AROUND ANYMORE!
SO WHAT'S THE POINT?!
click
SHE'S GOT A GUN!
OOPSIE! I CAN'T SEEM TO FIND MINE!
WAIT...
DON'T DO IT...

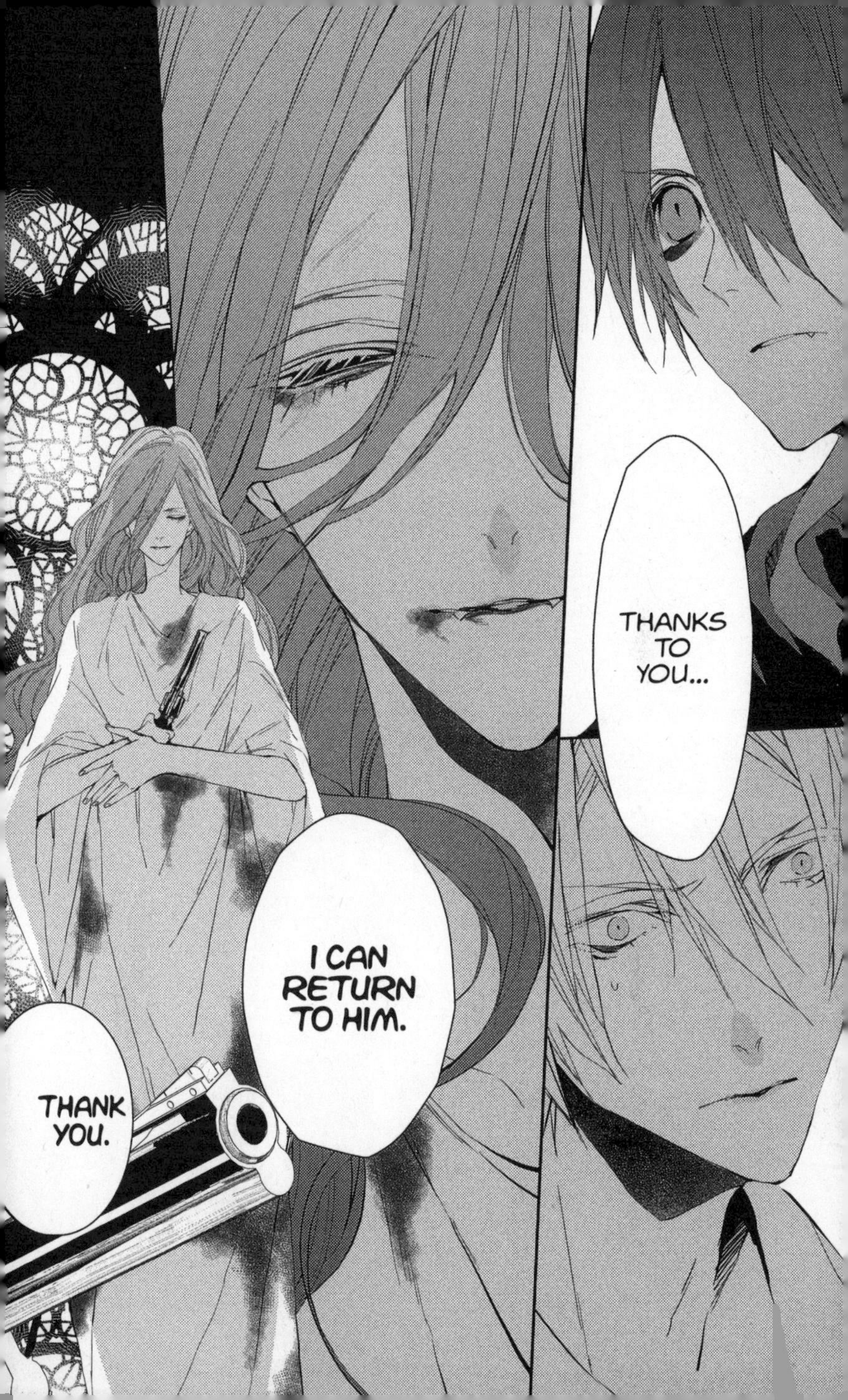
THANKS TO YOU...
I CAN RETURN TO HIM.
THANK YOU.

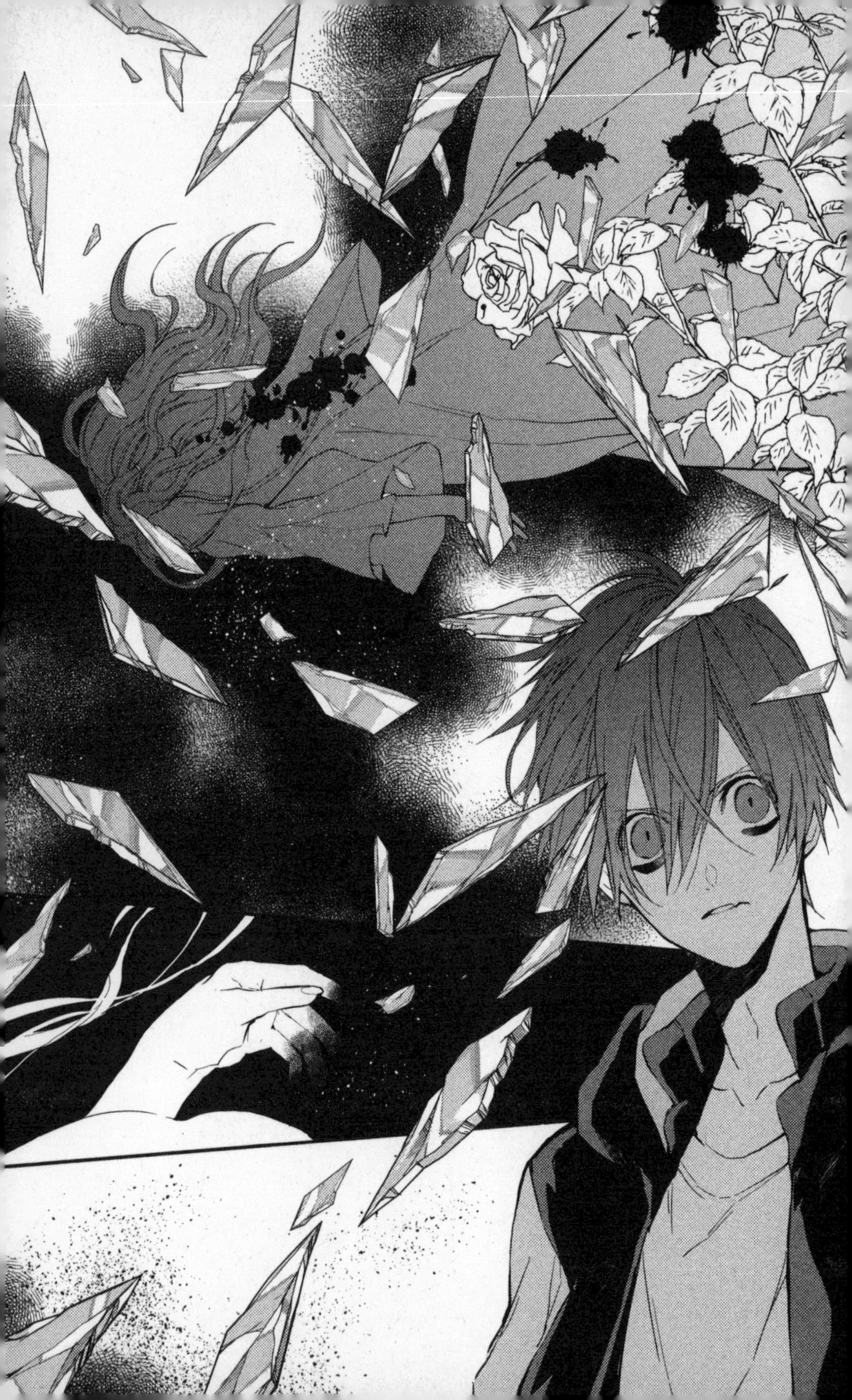

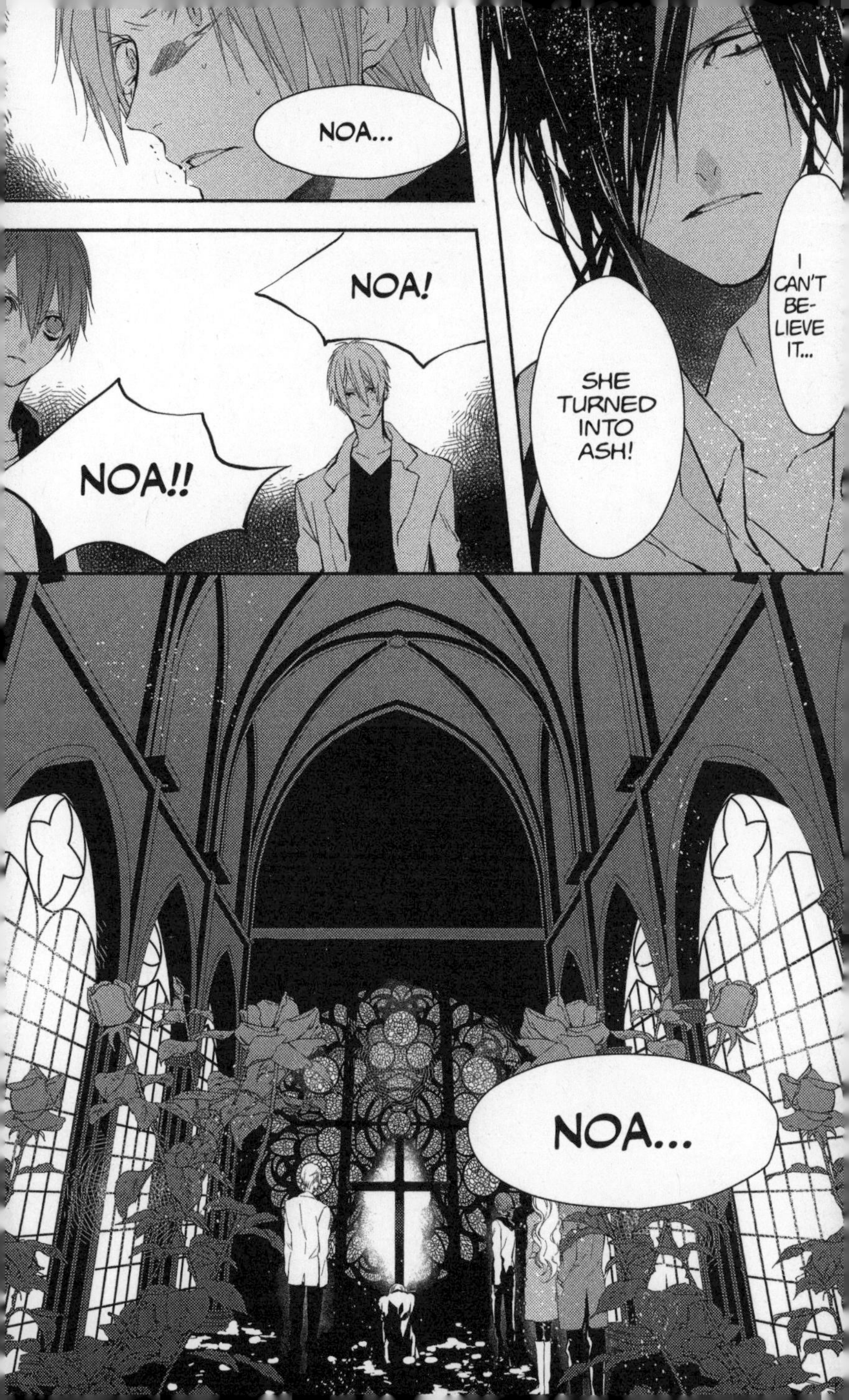
I CAN'T BE-LIEVE IT...
SHE TURNED INTO ASH!
NOA...
NOA!
NOA!!
NOA...

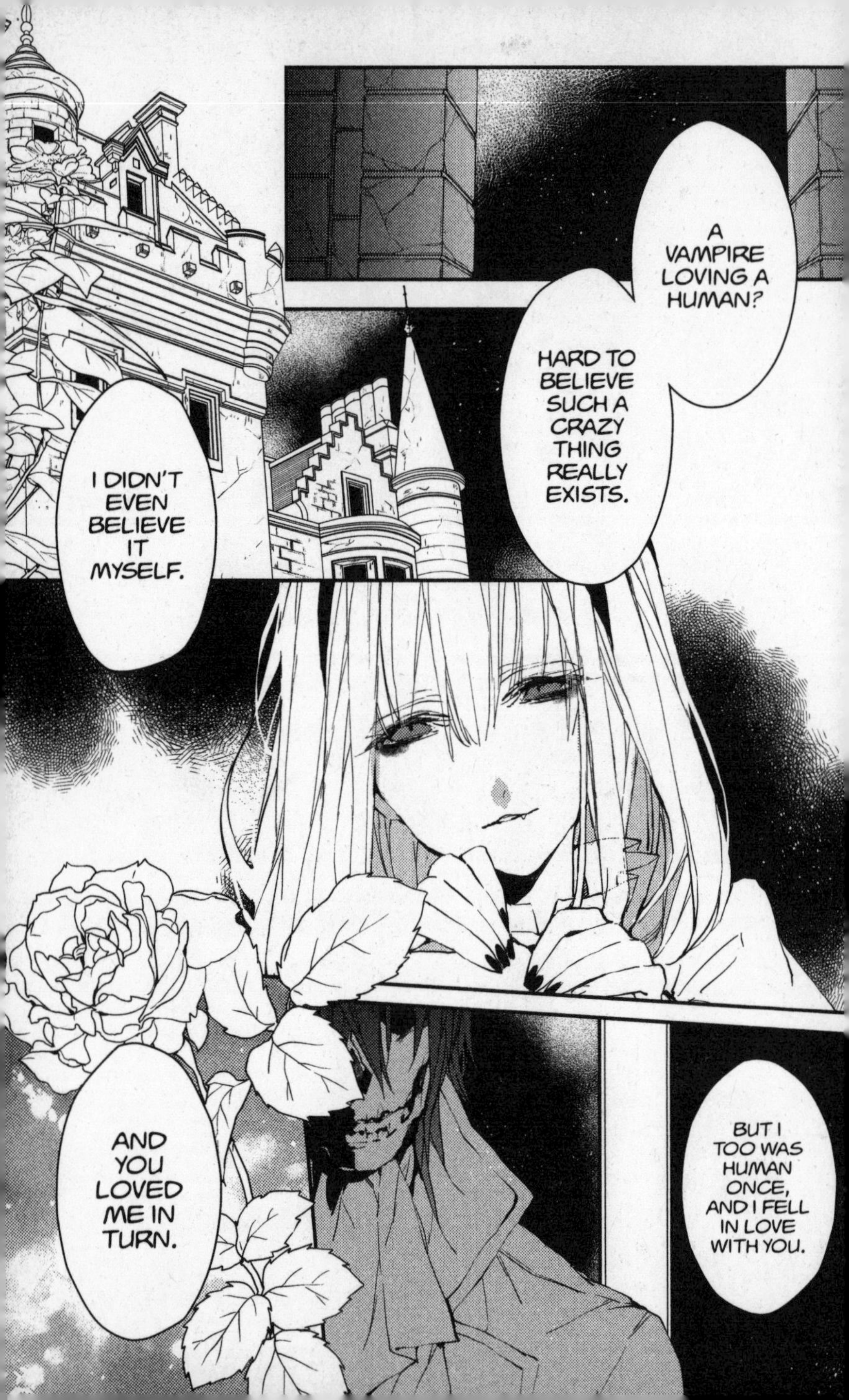
A VAMPIRE LOVING A HUMAN?
HARD TO BELIEVE SUCH A CRAZY THING REALLY EXISTS.
I DIDN'T EVEN BELIEVE IT MYSELF.
BUT I TOO WAS HUMAN ONCE, AND I FELL IN LOVE WITH YOU.
AND YOU LOVED ME IN TURN.

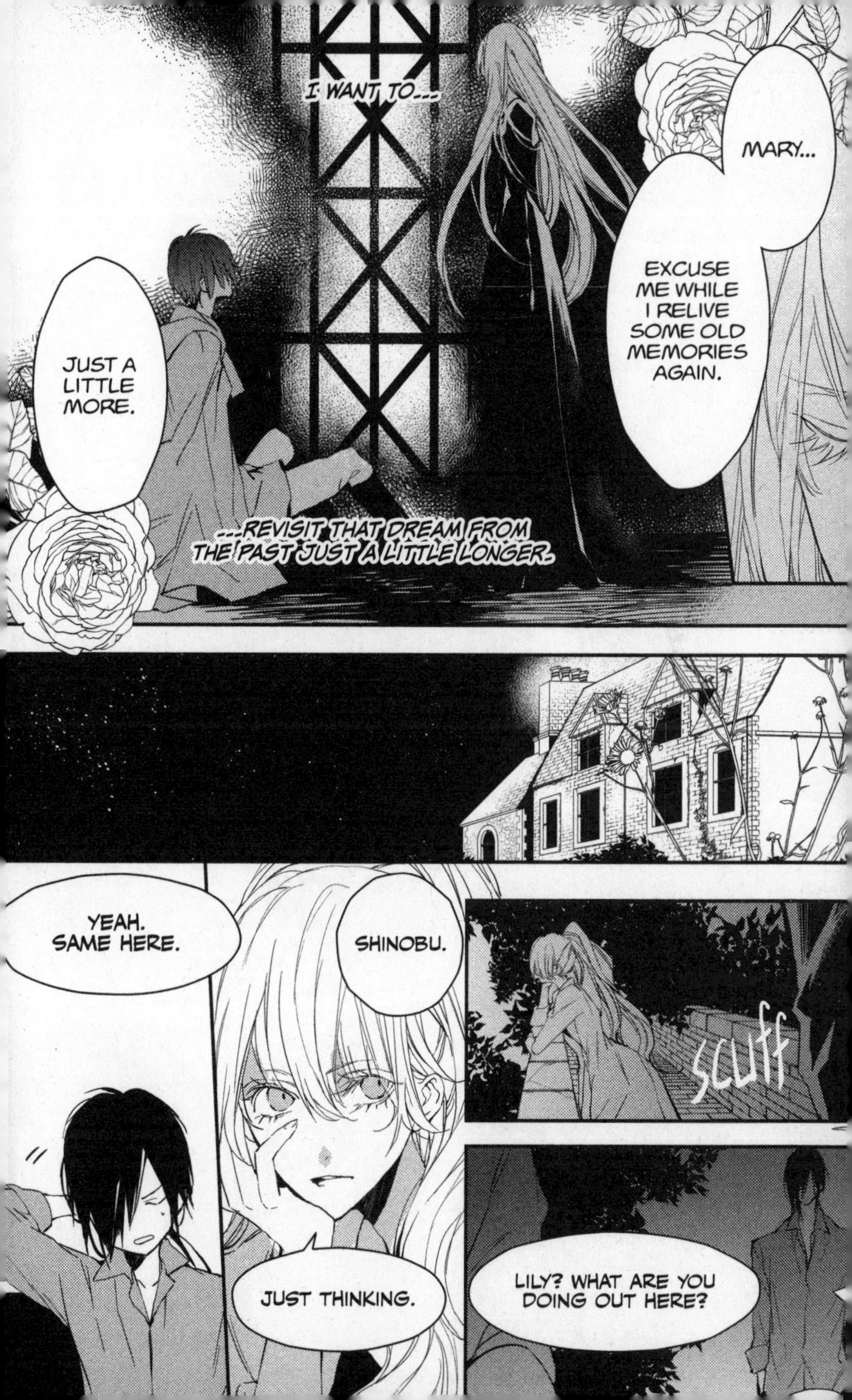

MARY...
EXCUSE ME WHILE I RELIVE SOME OLD MEMORIES AGAIN.
I WANT TO...
JUST A LITTLE MORE.
...REVISIT THAT DREAM FROM THE PAST JUST A LITTLE LONGER.
SCUFF
LILY? WHAT ARE YOU DOING OUT HERE?
SHINOBU.
JUST THINKING.
YEAH. SAME HERE.

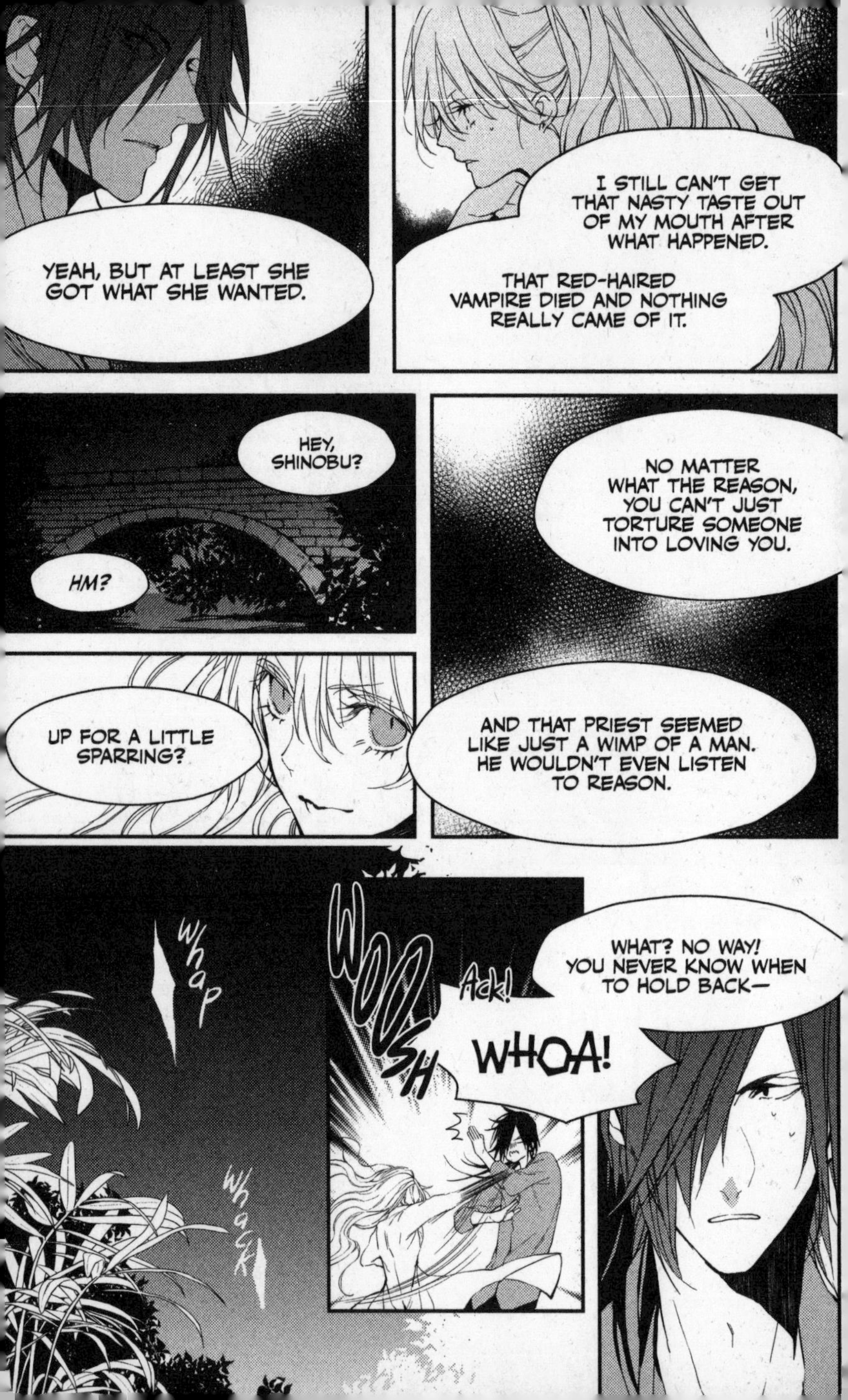
I STILL CAN'T GET THAT NASTY TASTE OUT OF MY MOUTH AFTER WHAT HAPPENED.
THAT RED-HAIRED VAMPIRE DIED AND NOTHING REALLY CAME OF IT.
YEAH, BUT AT LEAST SHE GOT WHAT SHE WANTED.
NO MATTER WHAT THE REASON, YOU CAN'T JUST TORTURE SOMEONE INTO LOVING YOU.
AND THAT PRIEST SEEMED LIKE JUST A WIMP OF A MAN. HE WOULDN'T EVEN LISTEN TO REASON.
HEY, SHINOBU?
HM?
UP FOR A LITTLE SPARRING?
WHAT? NO WAY! YOU NEVER KNOW WHEN TO HOLD BACK—
WHOA!
Ack!
WOOOSH
Whap
Whack

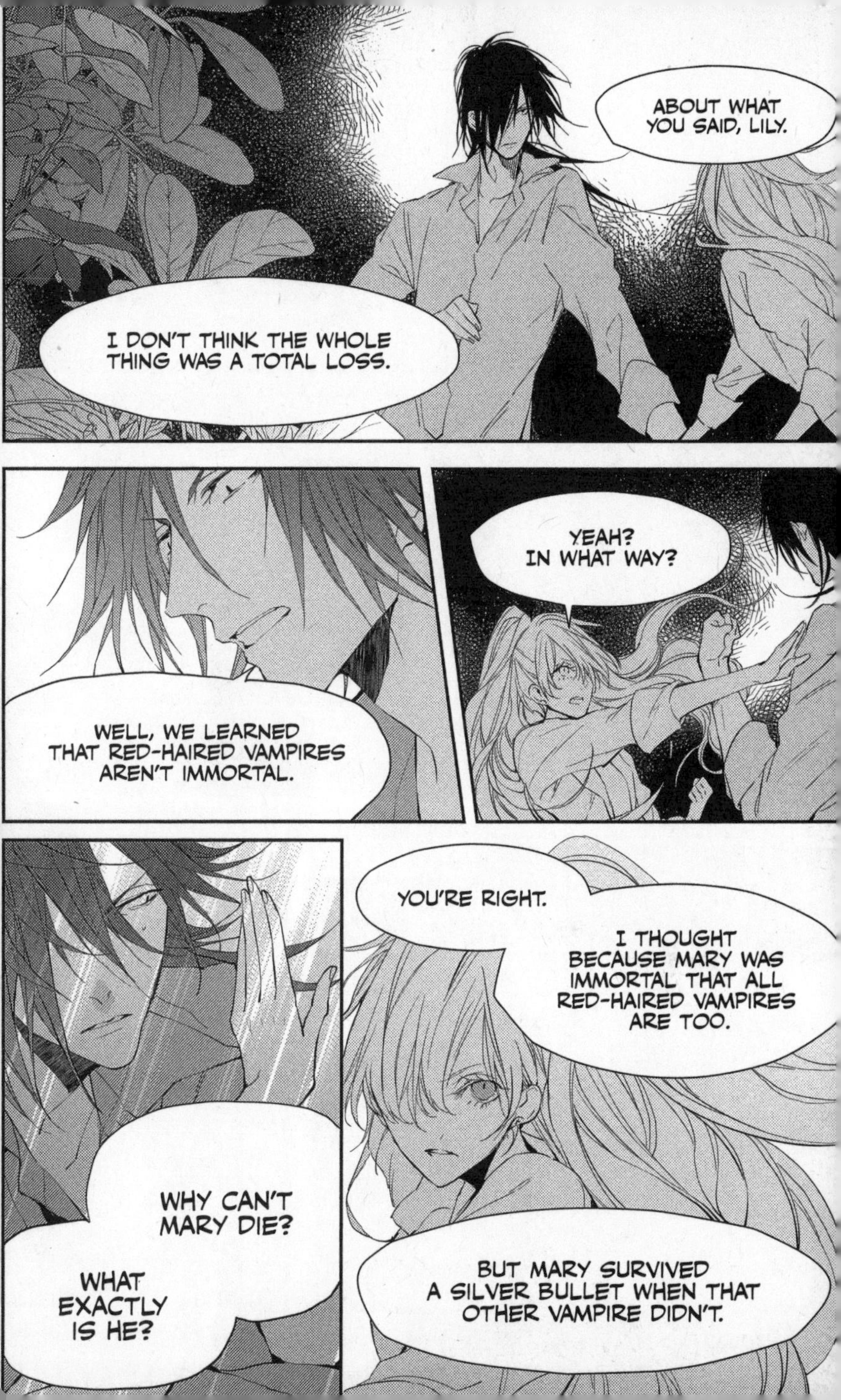
ABOUT WHAT YOU SAID, LILY.
I DON'T THINK THE WHOLE THING WAS A TOTAL LOSS.
YEAH? IN WHAT WAY?
WELL, WE LEARNED THAT RED-HAIRED VAMPIRES AREN'T IMMORTAL.
YOU'RE RIGHT.
I THOUGHT BECAUSE MARY WAS IMMORTAL THAT ALL RED-HAIRED VAMPIRES ARE TOO.
BUT MARY SURVIVED A SILVER BULLET WHEN THAT OTHER VAMPIRE DIDN'T.
WHY CAN'T MARY DIE?
WHAT EXACTLY IS HE?

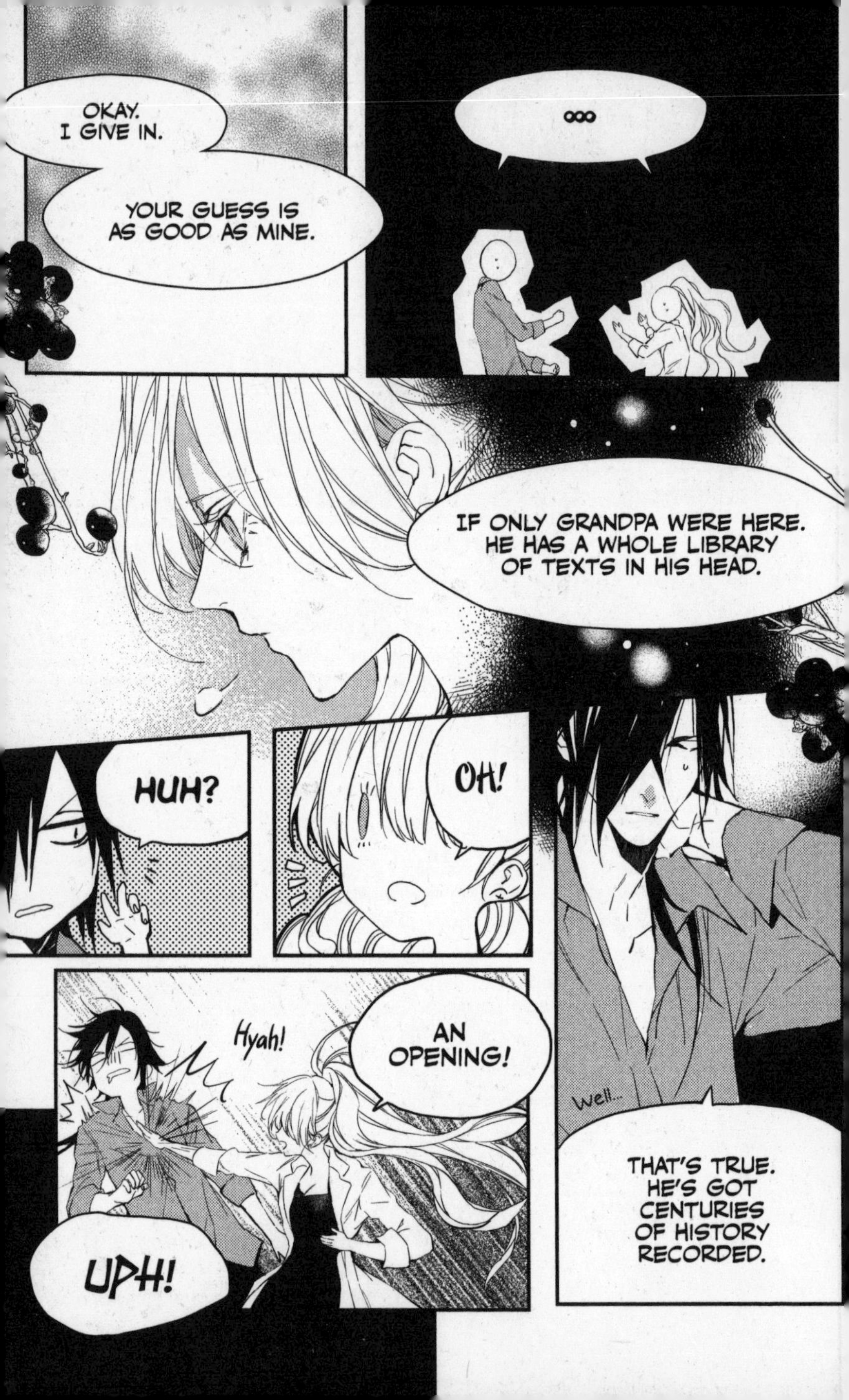
...
OKAY. I GIVE IN.
YOUR GUESS IS AS GOOD AS MINE.
IF ONLY GRANDPA WERE HERE. HE HAS A WHOLE LIBRARY OF TEXTS IN HIS HEAD.
Well...
THAT'S TRUE. HE'S GOT CENTURIES OF HISTORY RECORDED.
OH!
HUH?
AN OPENING!
Hyah!
UPH!

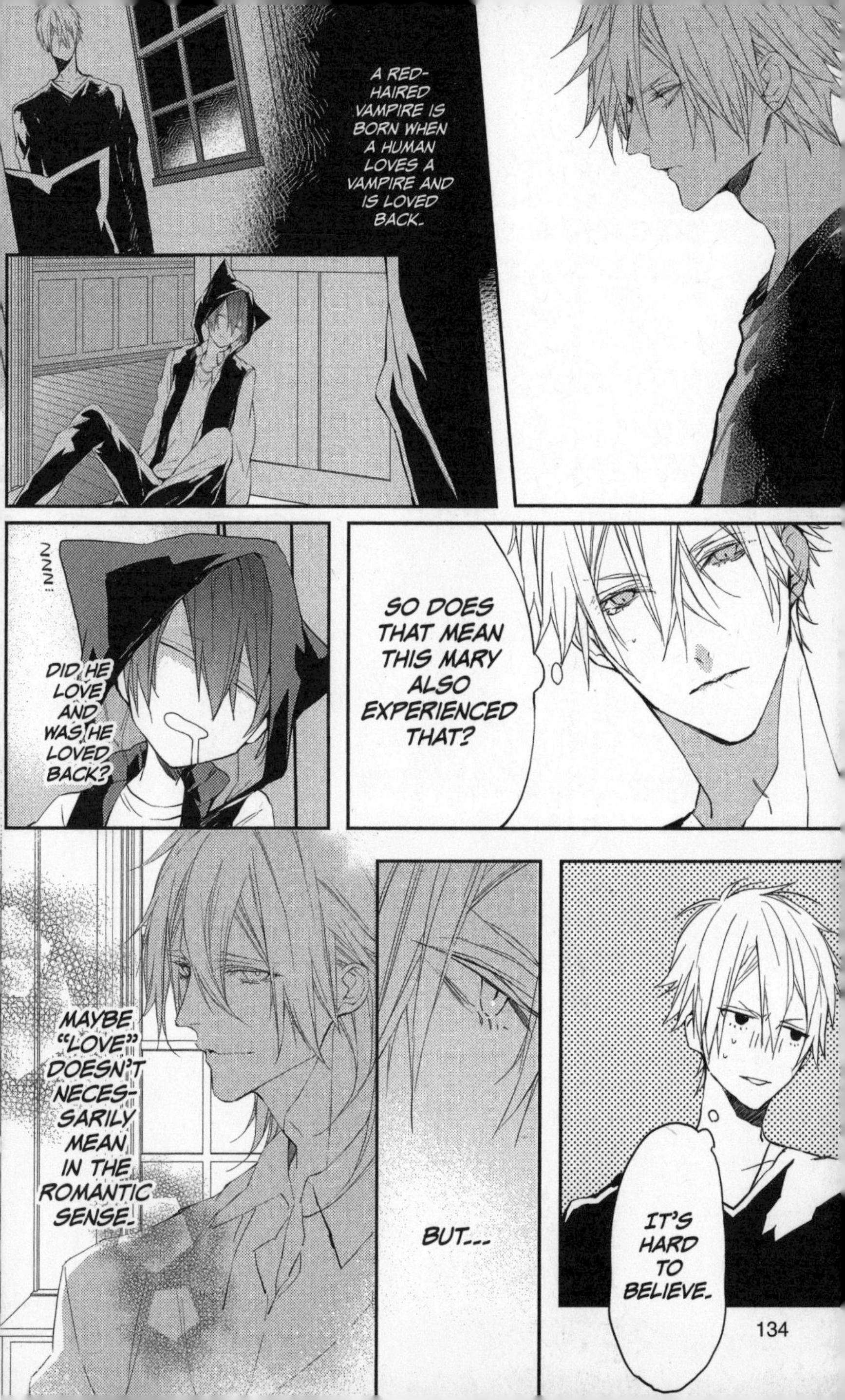
A RED-HAIRED VAMPIRE IS BORN WHEN A HUMAN LOVES A VAMPIRE AND IS LOVED BACK.
SO DOES THAT MEAN THIS MARY ALSO EXPERIENCED THAT?
ZZZ...
DID HE LOVE AND WAS HE LOVED BACK?
IT'S HARD TO BELIEVE.
BUT...
MAYBE "LOVE" DOESN'T NECES-SARILY MEAN IN THE ROMANTIC SENSE.

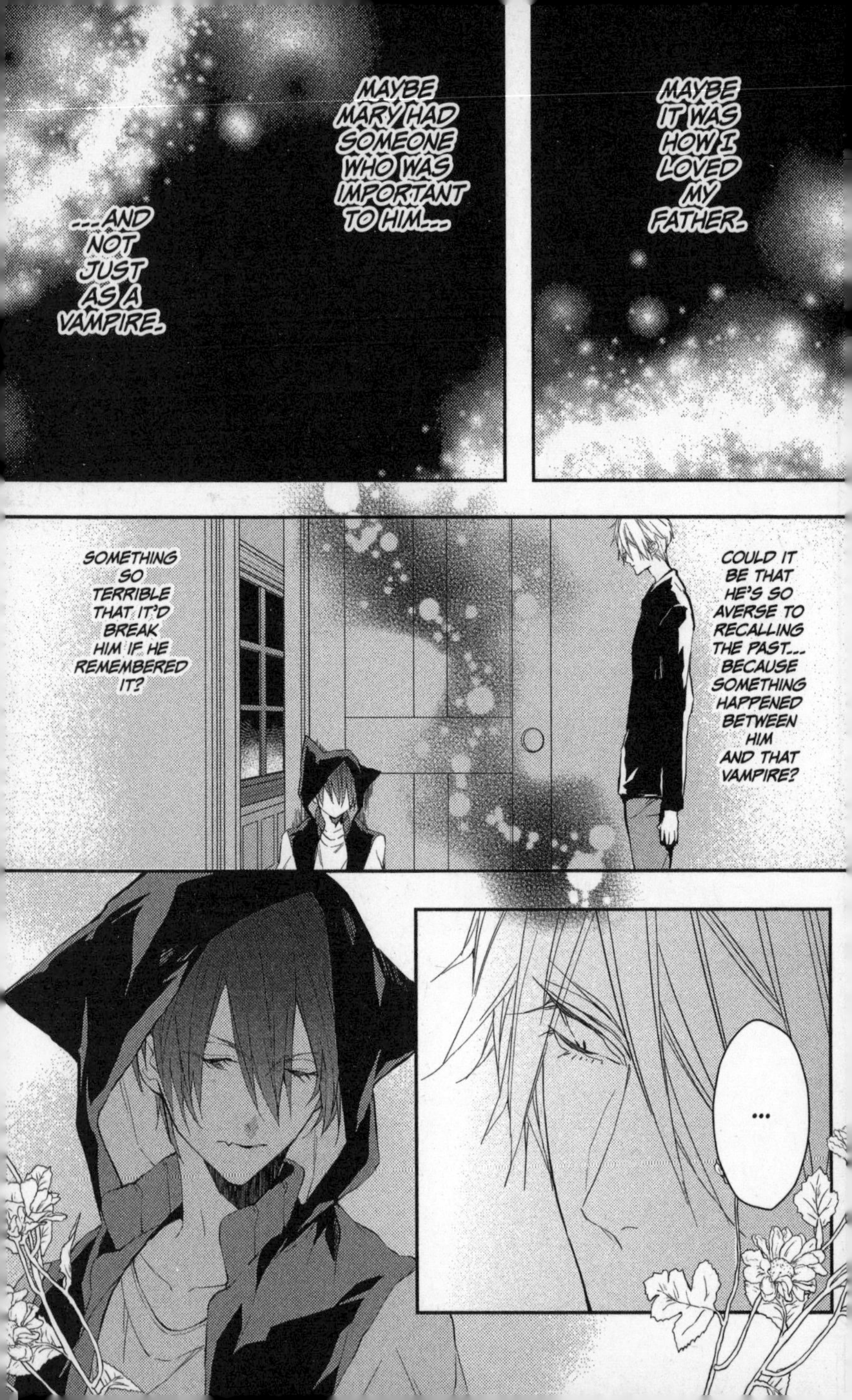
MAYBE IT WAS HOW I LOVED MY FATHER.
MAYBE MARY HAD SOMEONE WHO WAS IMPORTANT TO HIM...
...AND NOT JUST AS A VAMPIRE.
COULD IT BE THAT HE'S SO AVERSE TO RECALLING THE PAST... BECAUSE SOMETHING HAPPENED BETWEEN HIM AND THAT VAMPIRE?
SOMETHING SO TERRIBLE THAT IT'D BREAK HIM IF HE REMEMBERED IT?
...

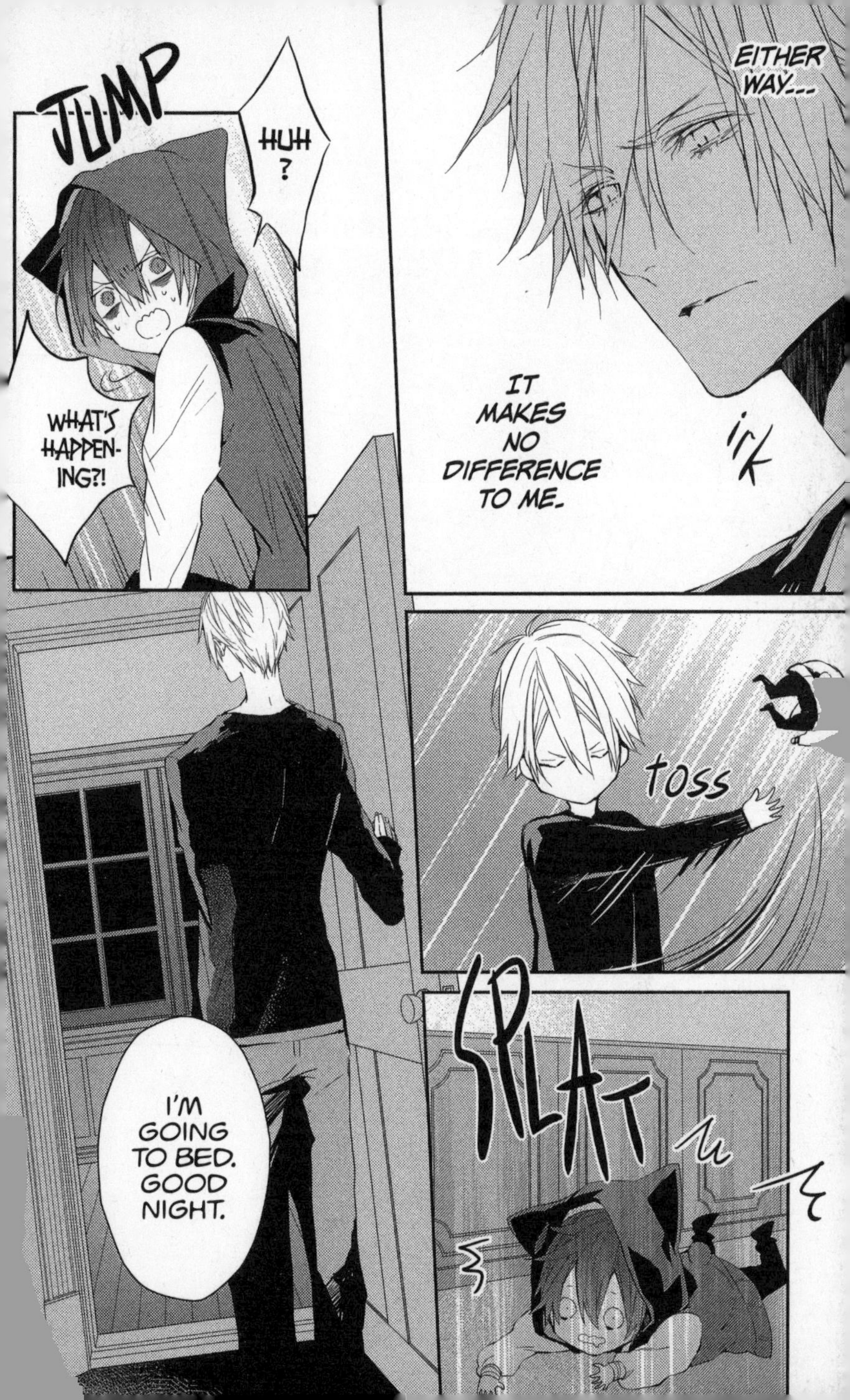
EITHER WAY...
IT MAKES NO DIFFERENCE TO ME.
irk
JUMP
HUH?
WHAT'S HAPPENING?!
toss
SPLAT
I'M GOING TO BED. GOOD NIGHT.

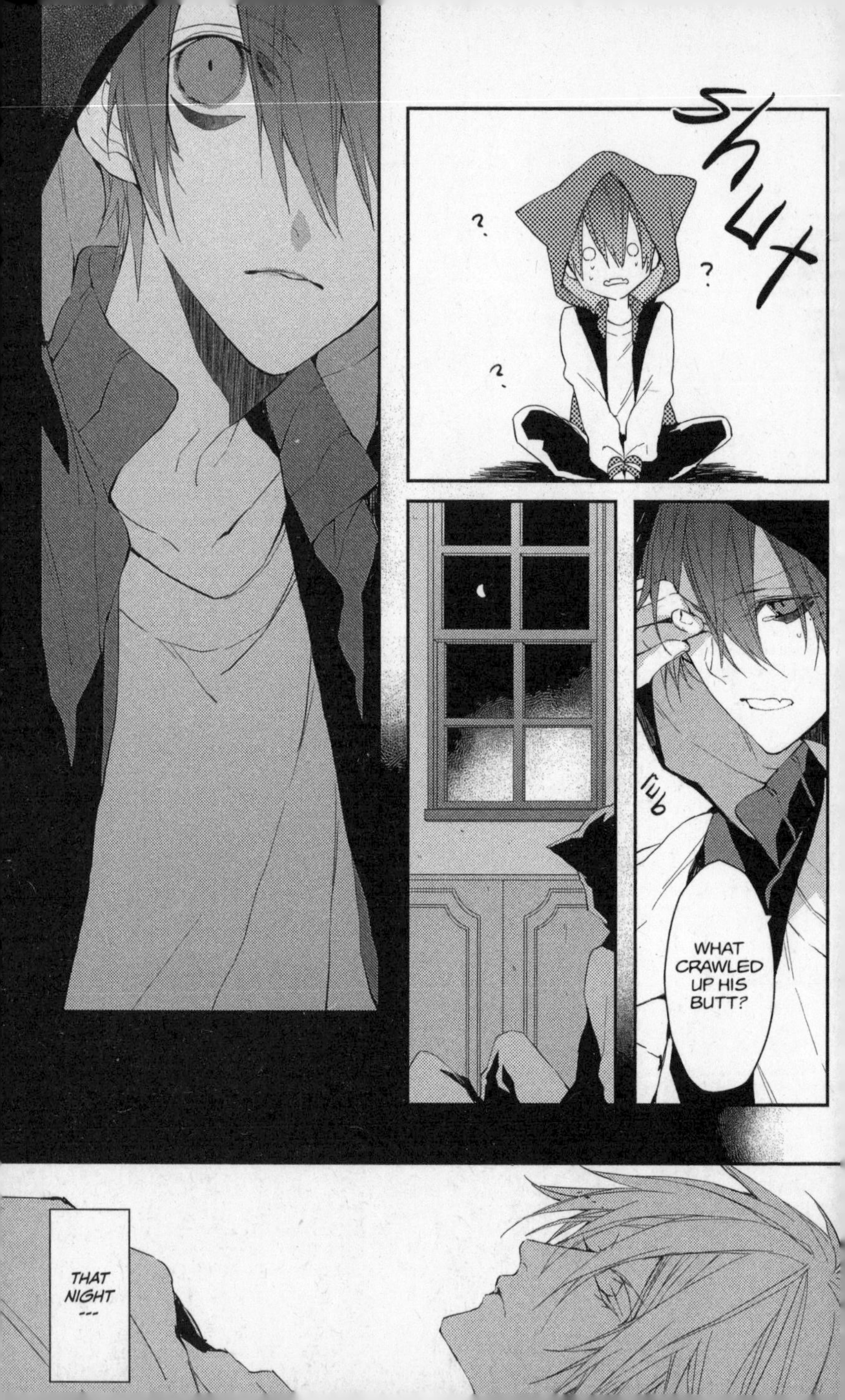
SHUT
?
?
?
rub
WHAT CRAWLED UP HIS BUTT?
THAT NIGHT ---

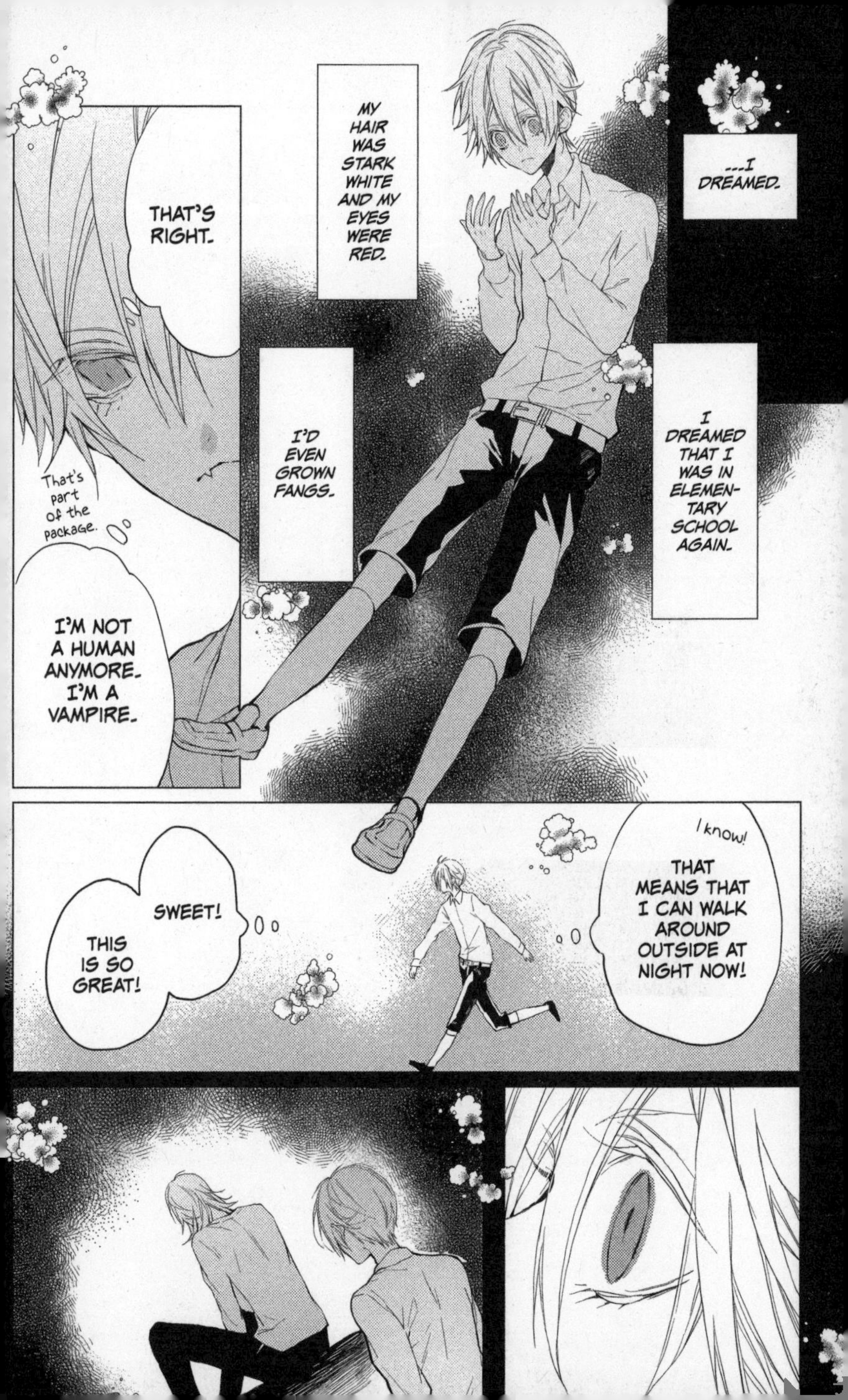
...I DREAMED.
I DREAMED THAT I WAS IN ELEMENTARY SCHOOL AGAIN.
MY HAIR WAS STARK WHITE AND MY EYES WERE RED.
I'D EVEN GROWN FANGS.
THAT'S RIGHT.
That's part of the package.
I'M NOT A HUMAN ANYMORE. I'M A VAMPIRE.
I know!
THAT MEANS THAT I CAN WALK AROUND OUTSIDE AT NIGHT NOW!
SWEET!
THIS IS SO GREAT!

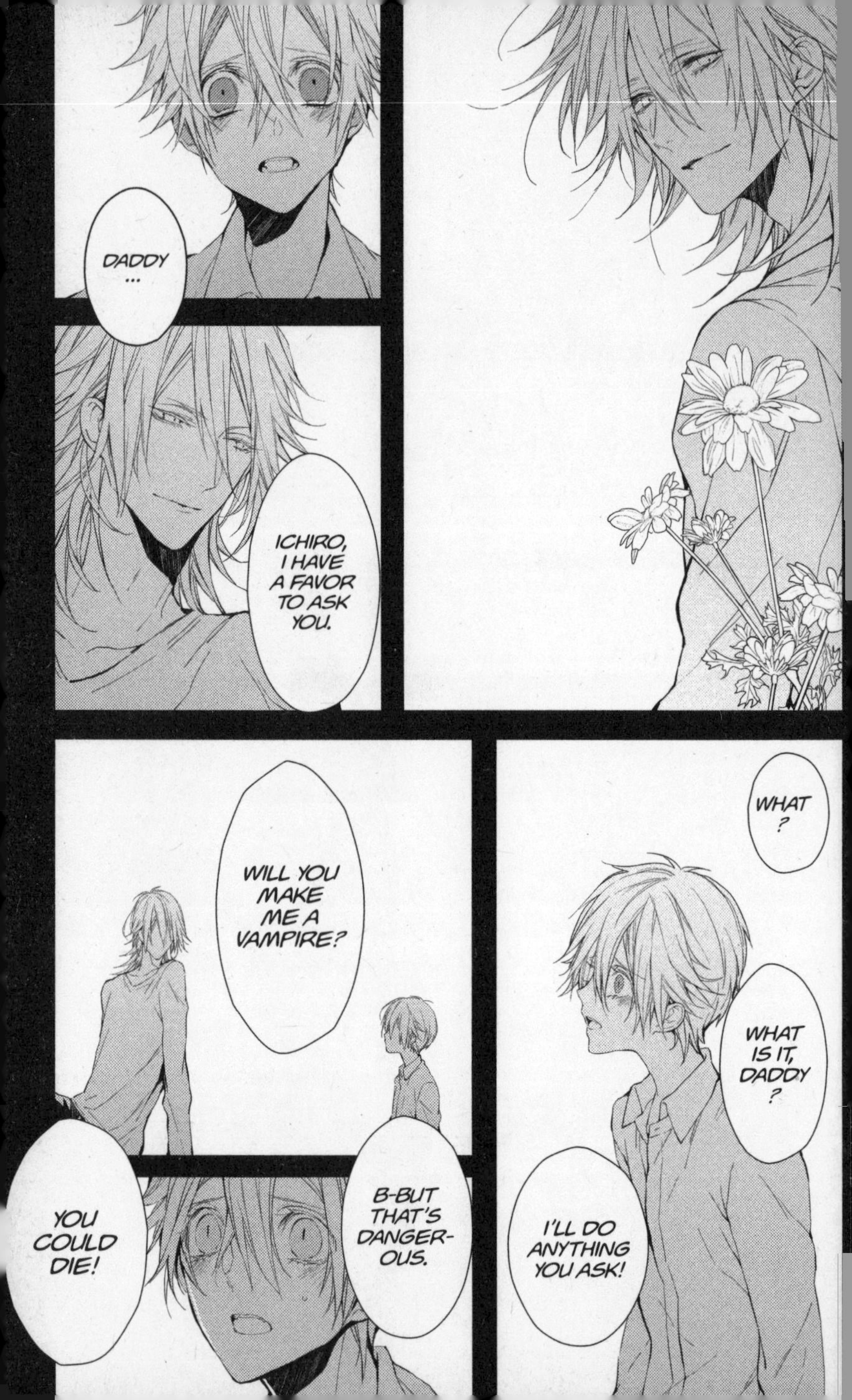
DADDY...
ICHIRO, I HAVE A FAVOR TO ASK YOU.
WHAT?
WHAT IS IT, DADDY?
I'LL DO ANYTHING YOU ASK!
WILL YOU MAKE ME A VAMPIRE?
B-BUT THAT'S DANGEROUS.
YOU COULD DIE!

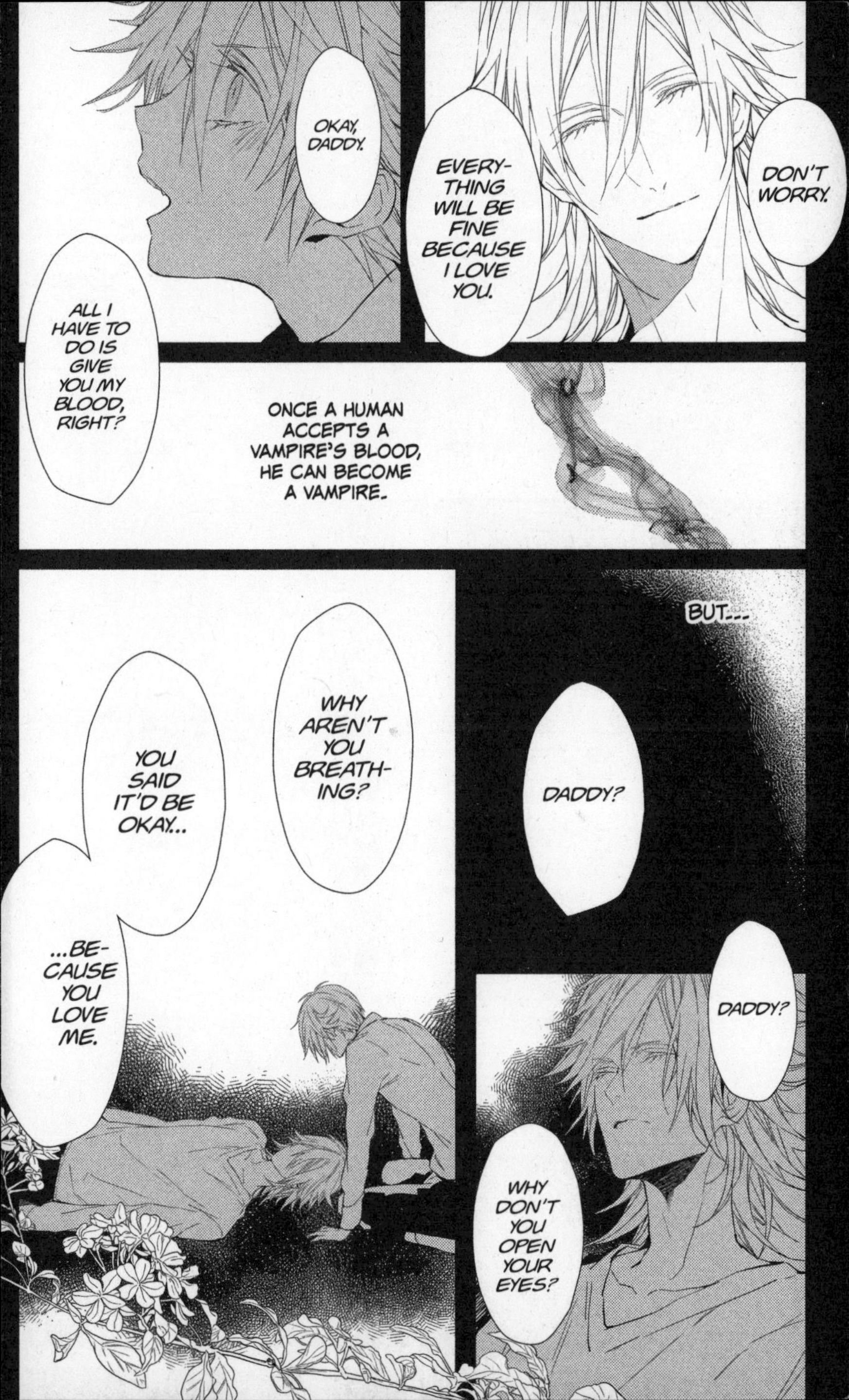
DON'T WORRY.
EVERY-THING WILL BE FINE BECAUSE I LOVE YOU.
OKAY, DADDY.
ALL I HAVE TO DO IS GIVE YOU MY BLOOD, RIGHT?
ONCE A HUMAN ACCEPTS A VAMPIRE'S BLOOD, HE CAN BECOME A VAMPIRE.
BUT...
DADDY?
DADDY?
WHY DON'T YOU OPEN YOUR EYES?
WHY AREN'T YOU BREATH-ING?
YOU SAID IT'D BE OKAY...
...BE-CAUSE YOU LOVE ME.

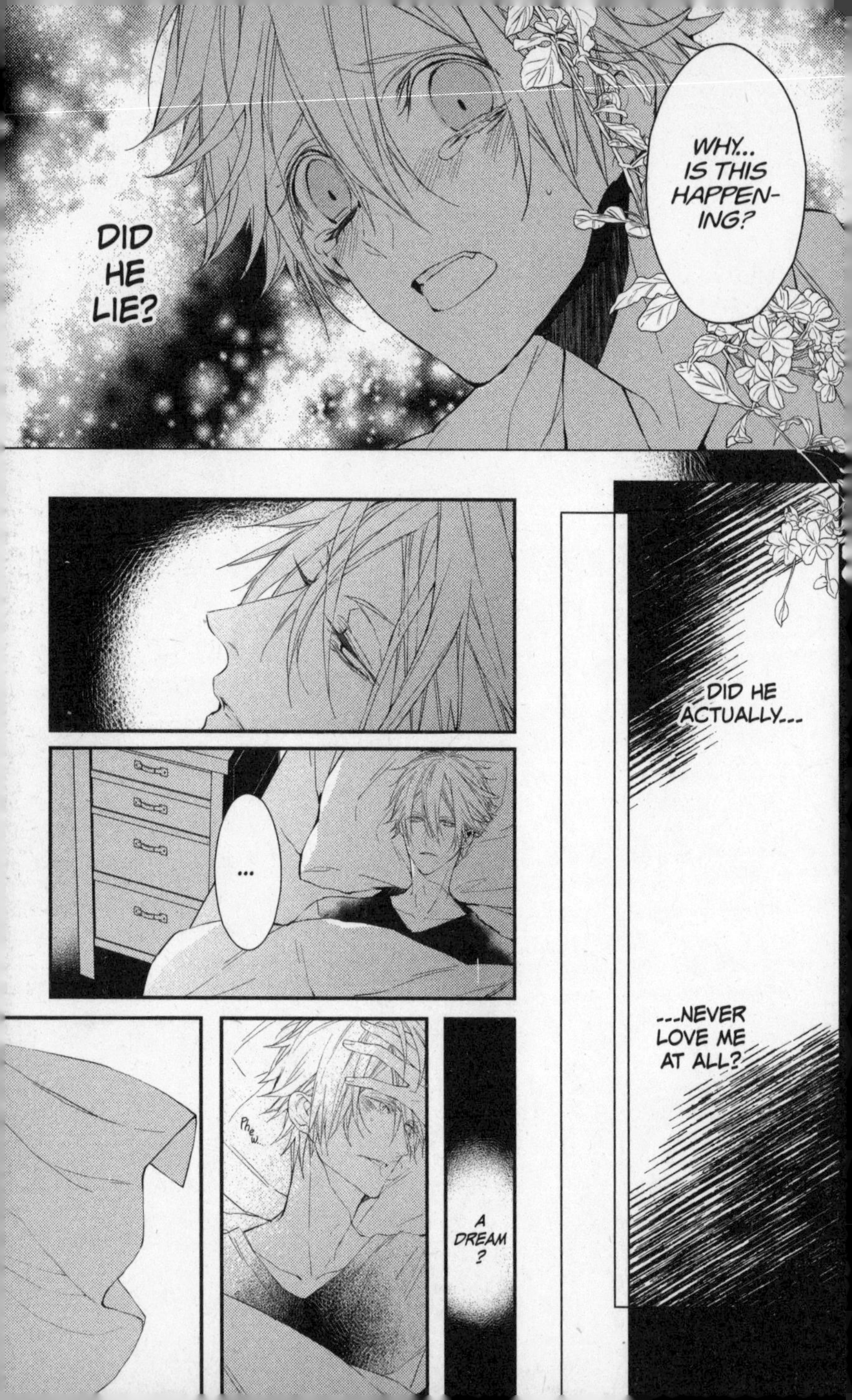
WHY... IS THIS HAPPENING?
DID HE LIE?
DID HE ACTUALLY...
...NEVER LOVE ME AT ALL?
...
A DREAM?
Phew..

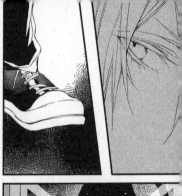

MARY
?

wobble

SLUMP

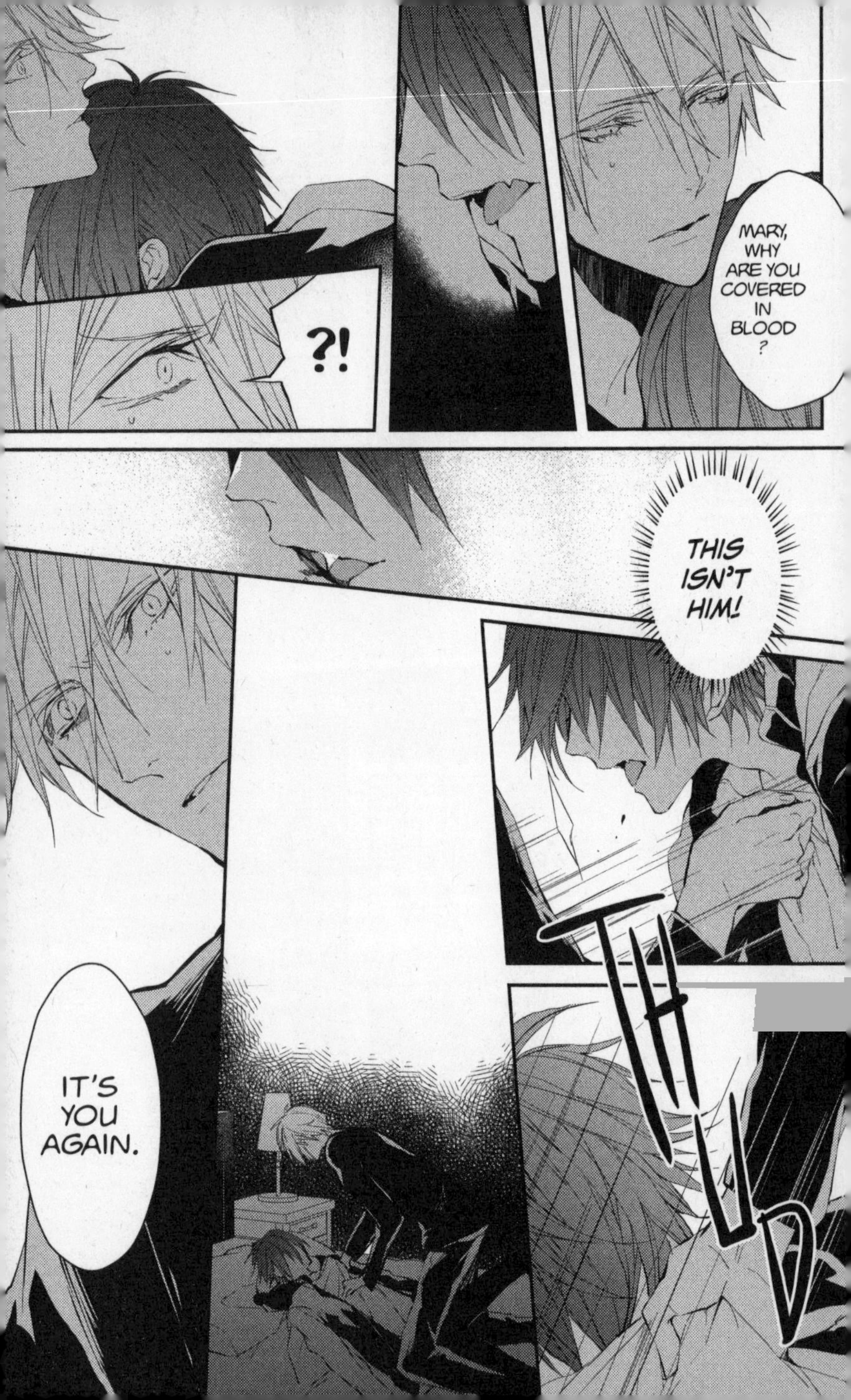
MARY, WHY ARE YOU COVERED IN BLOOD?
?!
THIS ISN'T HIM!
THUD
IT'S YOU AGAIN.

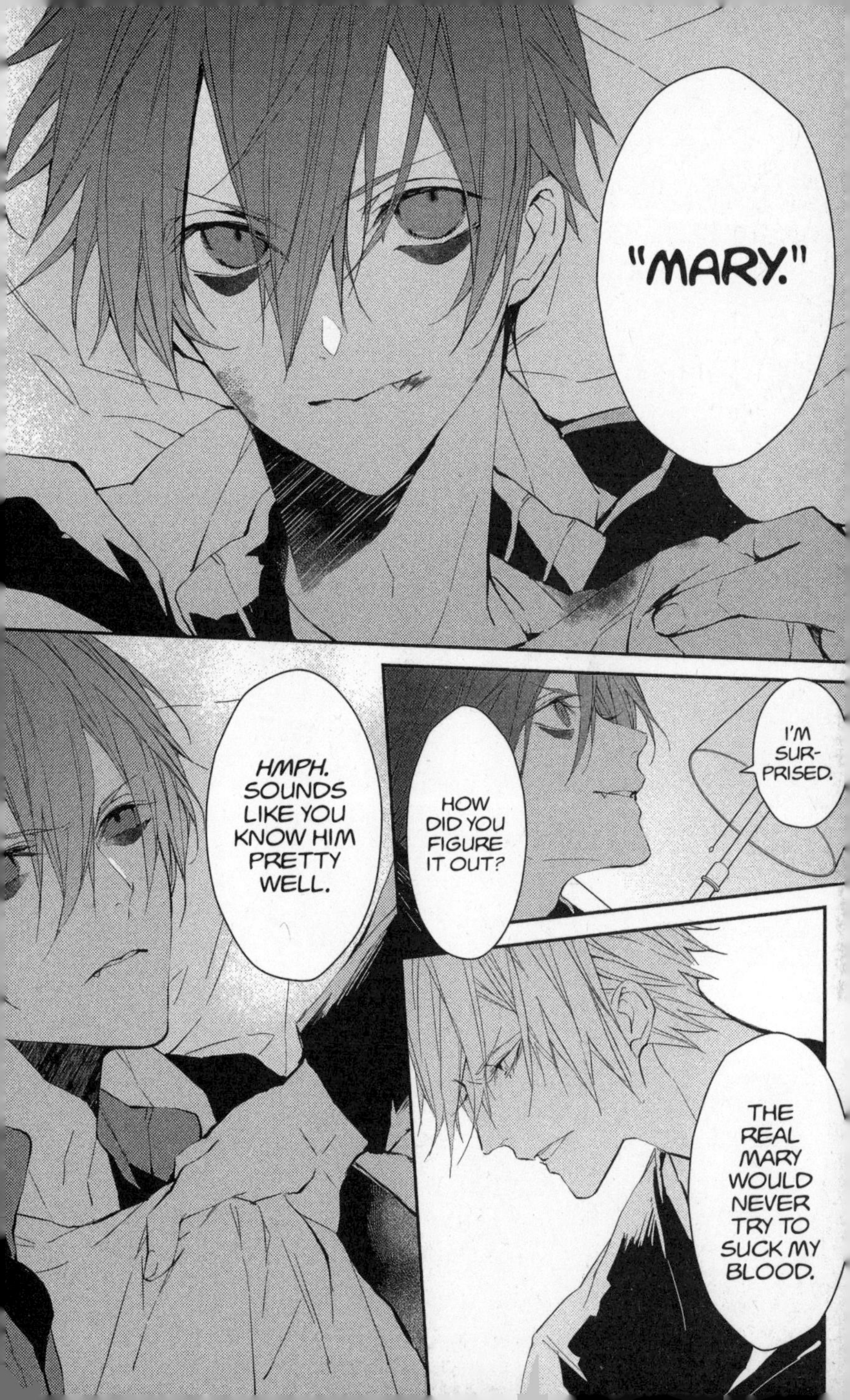
"MARY."
I'M SUR-PRISED.
HOW DID YOU FIGURE IT OUT?
THE REAL MARY WOULD NEVER TRY TO SUCK MY BLOOD.
HMPH. SOUNDS LIKE YOU KNOW HIM PRETTY WELL.

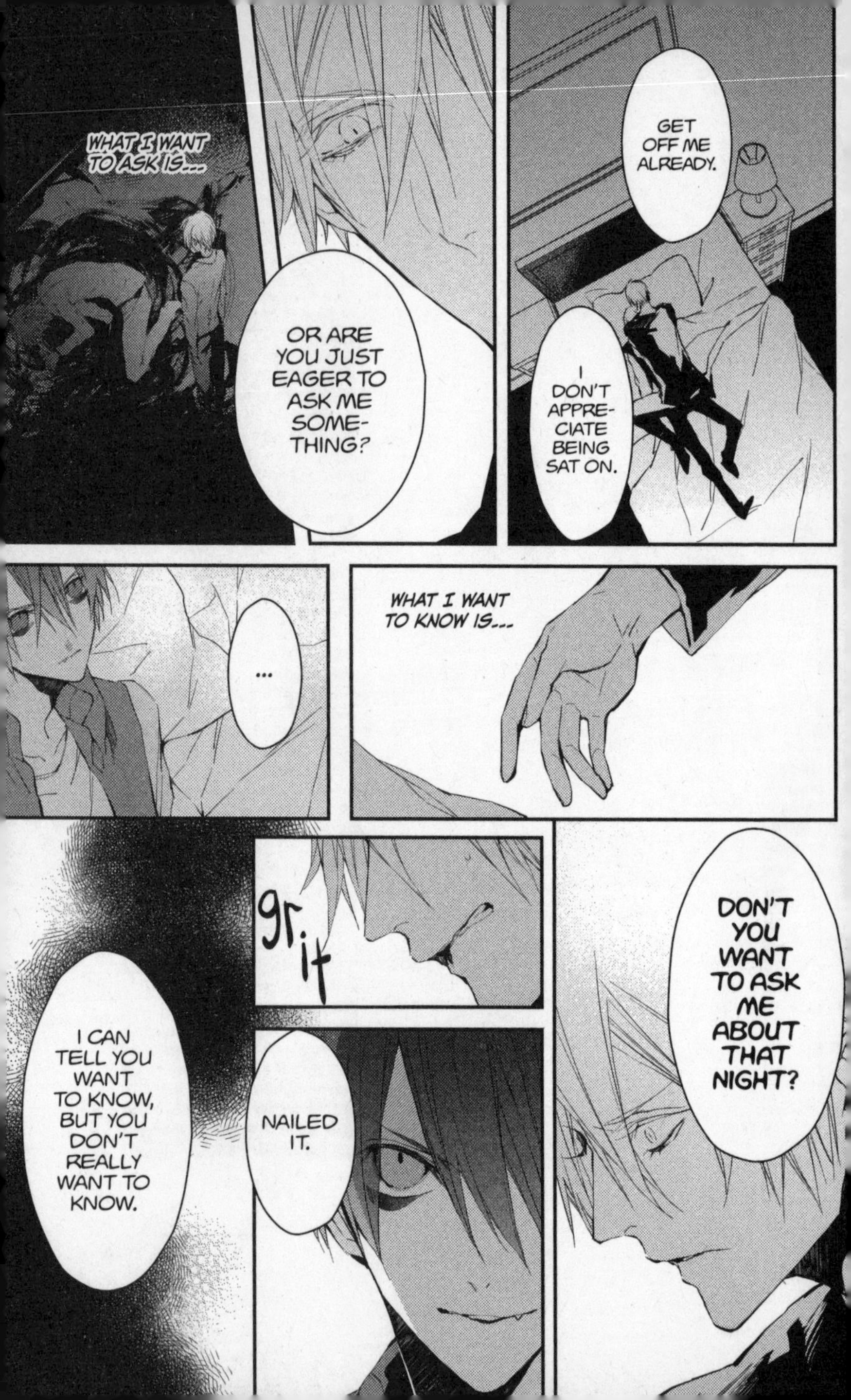
GET OFF ME ALREADY.
I DON'T APPRE-CIATE BEING SAT ON.
OR ARE YOU JUST EAGER TO ASK ME SOME-THING?
WHAT I WANT TO ASK IS...
WHAT I WANT TO KNOW IS...
...
DON'T YOU WANT TO ASK ME ABOUT THAT NIGHT?
grit
NAILED IT.
I CAN TELL YOU WANT TO KNOW, BUT YOU DON'T REALLY WANT TO KNOW.

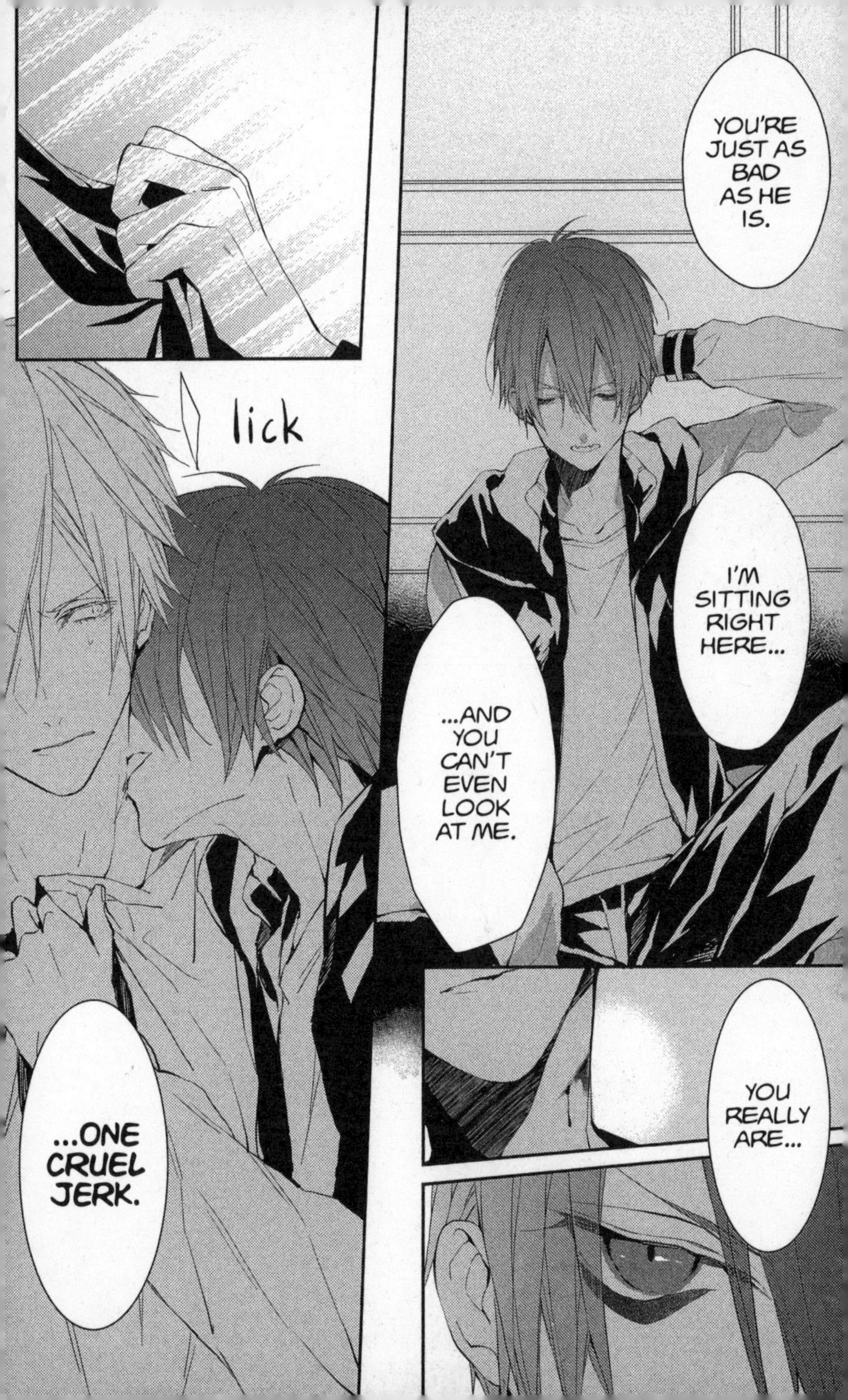
YOU'RE JUST AS BAD AS HE IS.
I'M SITTING RIGHT HERE...
...AND YOU CAN'T EVEN LOOK AT ME.
lick
YOU REALLY ARE...
...ONE CRUEL JERK.

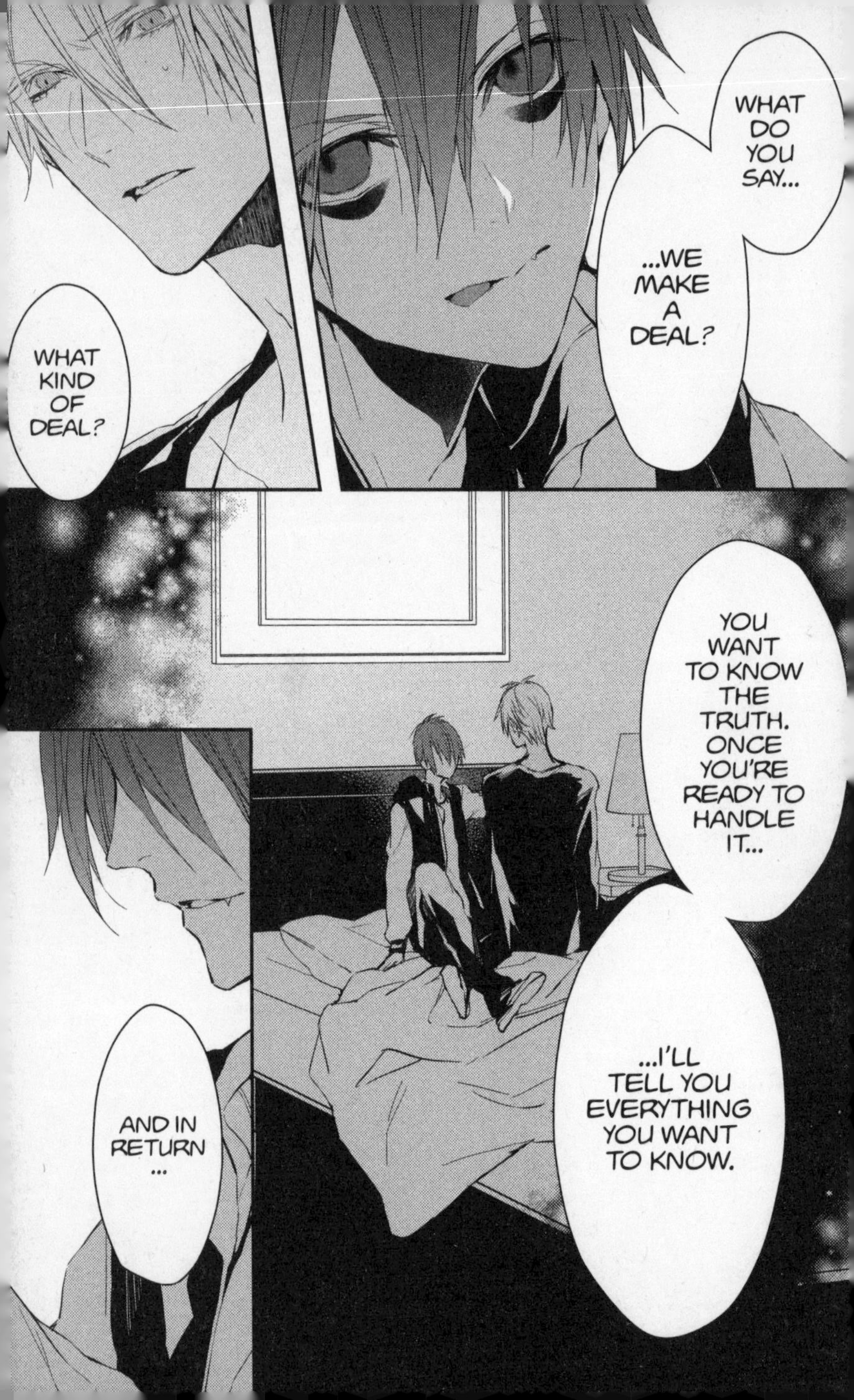
WHAT DO YOU SAY...
...WE MAKE A DEAL?
WHAT KIND OF DEAL?
YOU WANT TO KNOW THE TRUTH. ONCE YOU'RE READY TO HANDLE IT...
...I'LL TELL YOU EVERYTHING YOU WANT TO KNOW.
AND IN RETURN ...

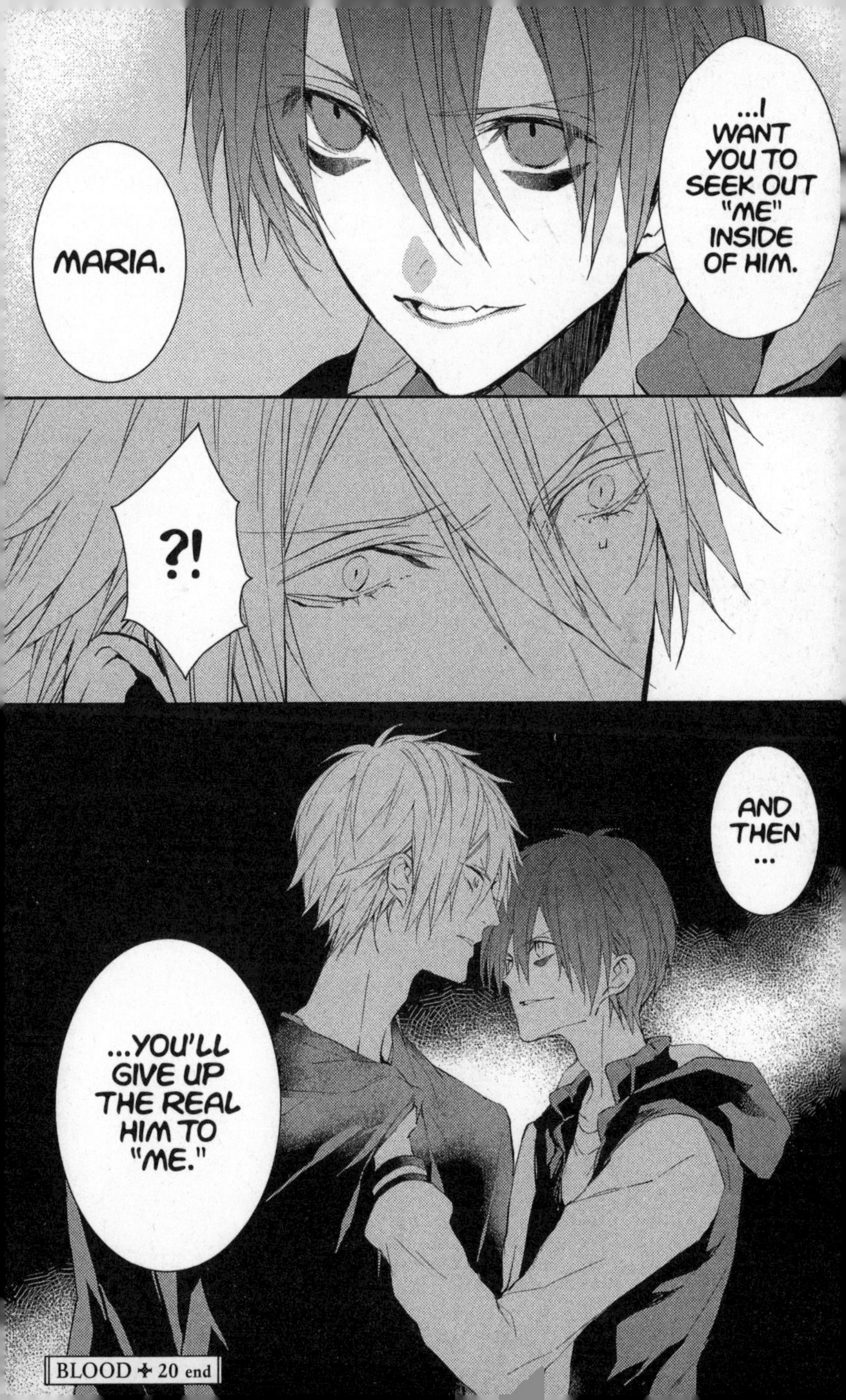
...I WANT YOU TO SEEK OUT "ME" INSIDE OF HIM.
MARIA.
?!
AND THEN...
...YOU'LL GIVE UP THE REAL HIM TO "ME."
BLOOD ✢ 20 end

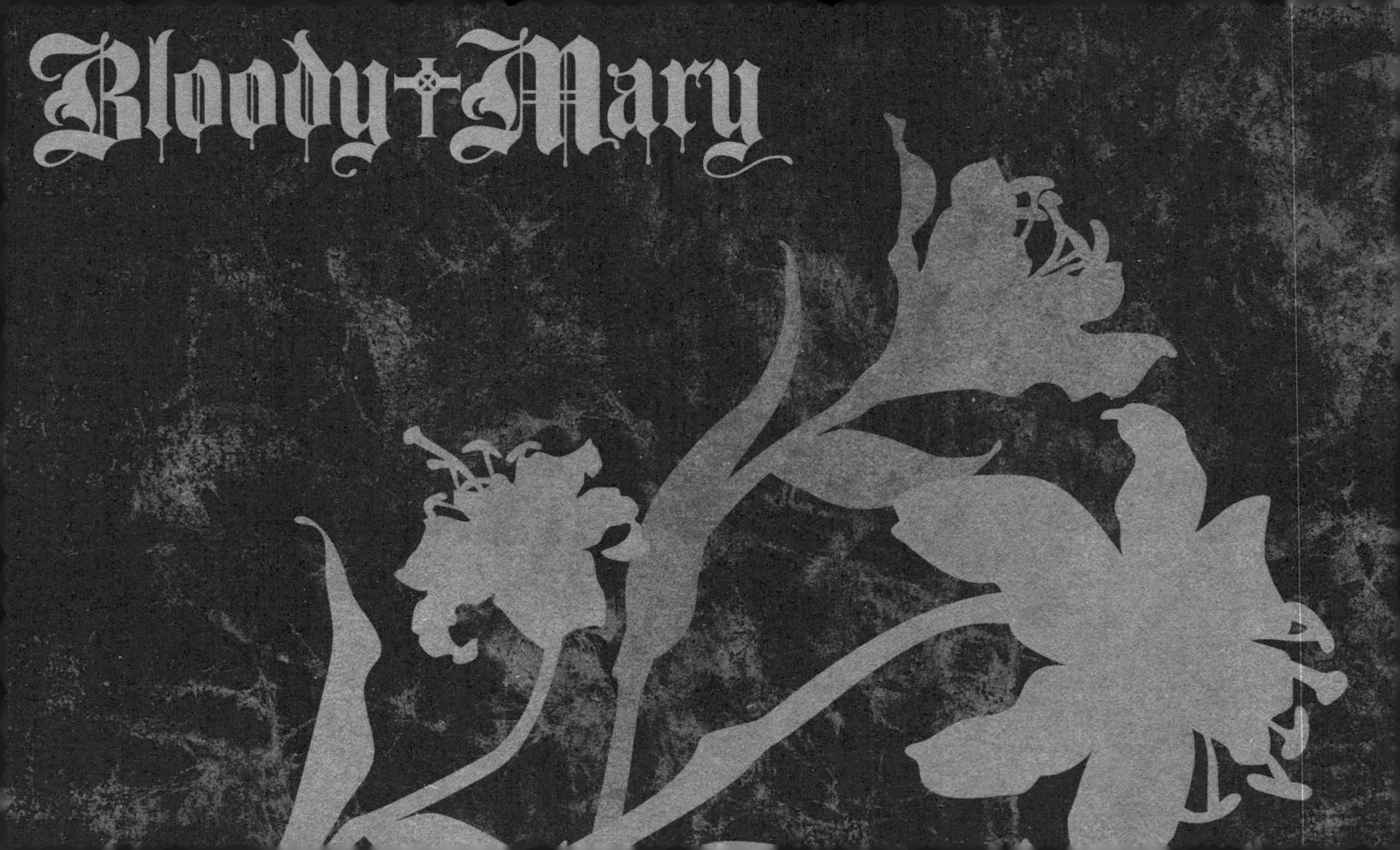
Bloody+Mary

Bloody✝Mary

HASEGAWA Presents
"USAMIMI" Collection

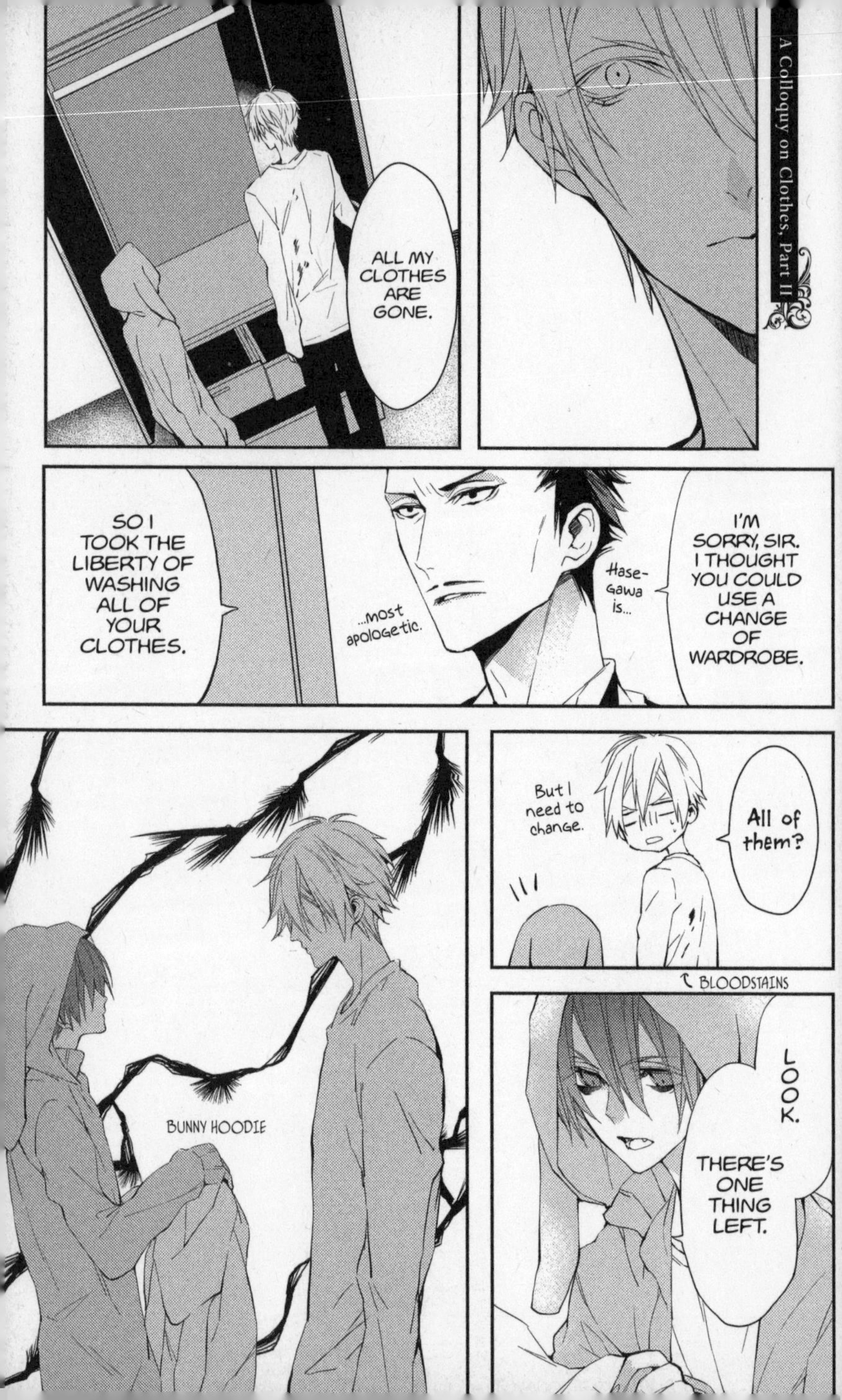
A Colloquy on Clothes, Part II
ALL MY CLOTHES ARE GONE.
I'M SORRY, SIR. I THOUGHT YOU COULD USE A CHANGE OF WARDROBE.
Hase-Gawa is...
...most apologetic.
SO I TOOK THE LIBERTY OF WASHING ALL OF YOUR CLOTHES.
All of them?
But I need to change.
BLOODSTAINS
LOOK.
THERE'S ONE THING LEFT.
BUNNY HOODIE

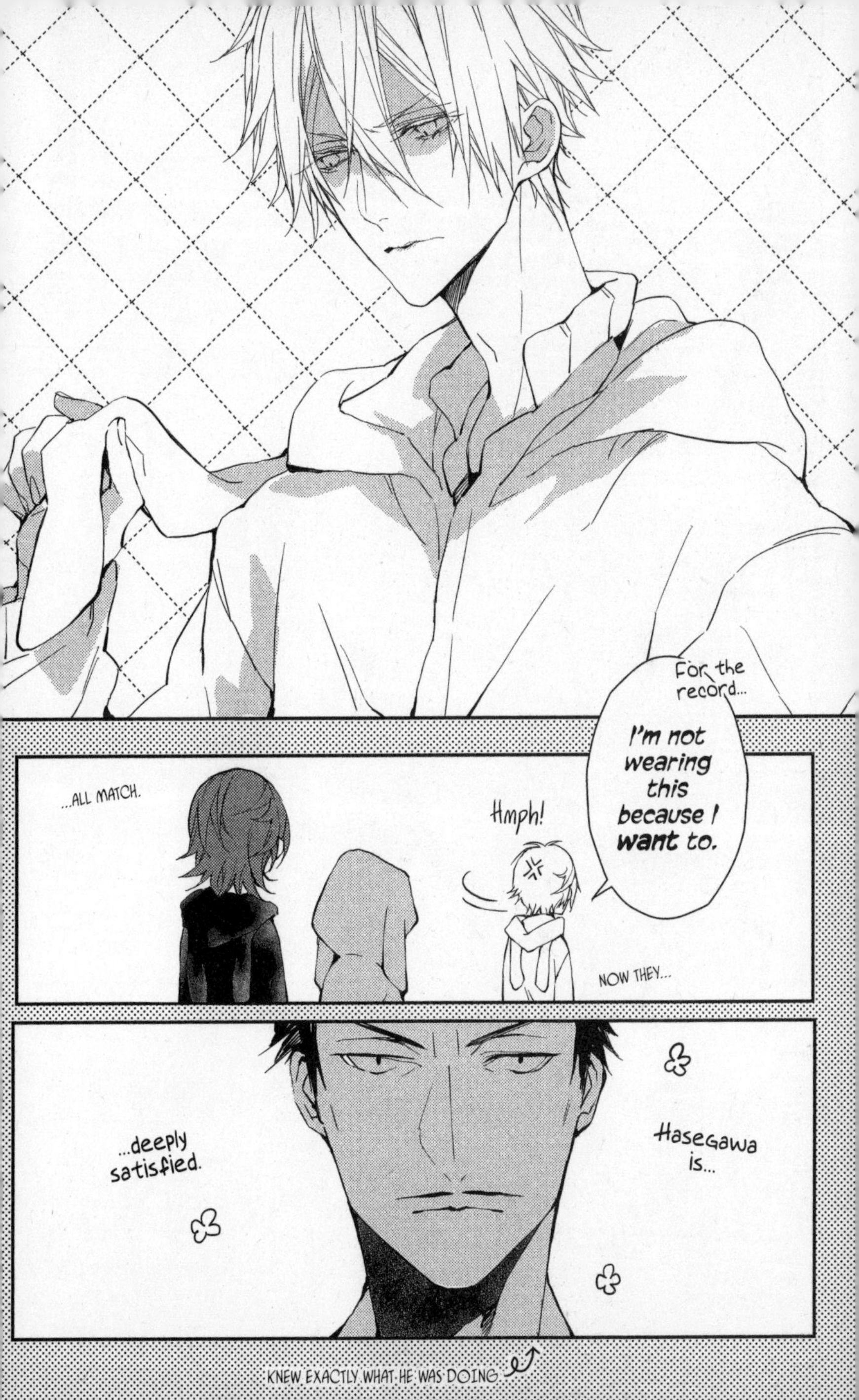
For the record...
I'm not wearing this because I want to.
Hmph!
NOW THEY...
...ALL MATCH.
Hasegawa is...
...deeply satisfied.
KNEW EXACTLY WHAT HE WAS DOING.

A Colloquy on Names

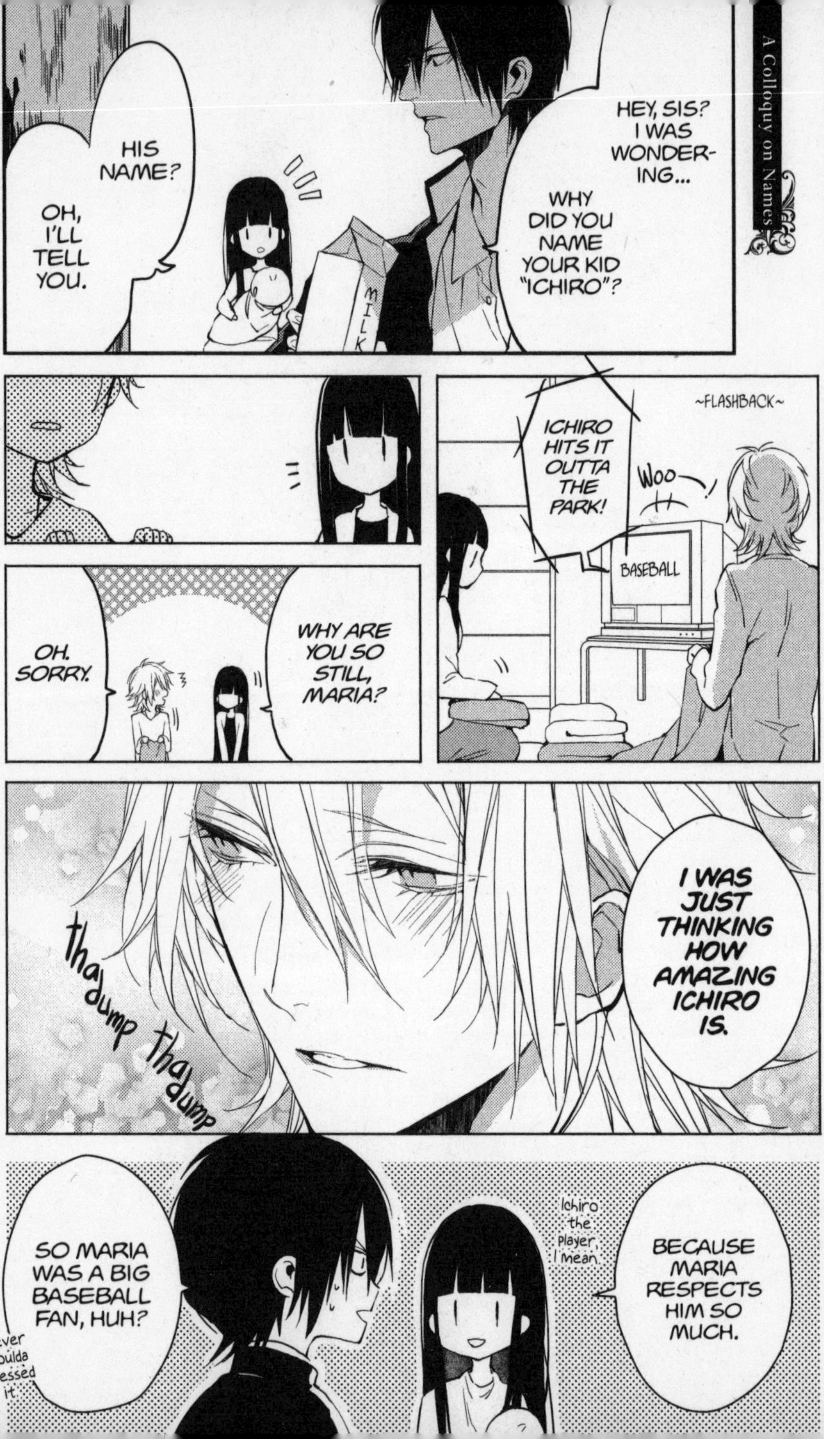
HEY, SIS? I WAS WONDERING...
WHY DID YOU NAME YOUR KID "ICHIRO"?
HIS NAME?
OH, I'LL TELL YOU.
~FLASHBACK~
ICHIRO HITS IT OUTTA THE PARK!
WOO—!
BASEBALL
WHY ARE YOU SO STILL, MARIA?
OH. SORRY.
I WAS JUST THINKING HOW AMAZING ICHIRO IS.
thadump thadump
BECAUSE MARIA RESPECTS HIM SO MUCH.
Ichiro the Player, I mean.
SO MARIA WAS A BIG BASEBALL FAN, HUH?
Never woulda guessed it.

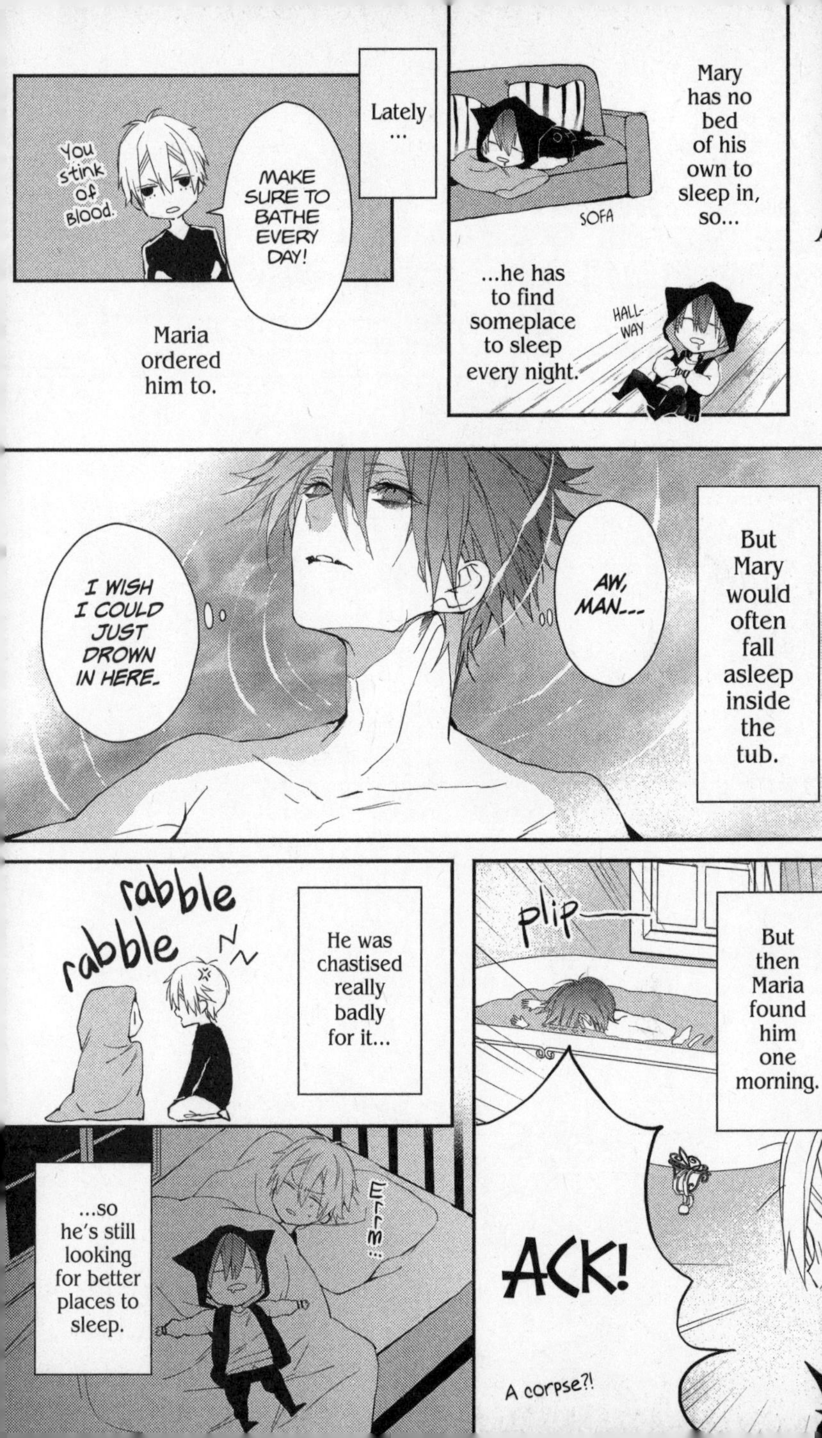
Mary has no bed of his own to sleep in, so...
SOFA
...he has to find someplace to sleep every night.
HALL-WAY
Lately...
MAKE SURE TO BATHE EVERY DAY!
You stink of blood.
Maria ordered him to.
But Mary would often fall asleep inside the tub.
AW, MAN...
I WISH I COULD JUST DROWN IN HERE.
plip—
But then Maria found him one morning.
ACK!
A corpse?!
He was chastised really badly for it...
rabble rabble
...so he's still looking for better places to sleep.
Errrm...

Bloody✝Mary

Masochistic one

nuzzle

But the Bed's too soft. It makes me uncomfortable!

nuzzle

Postscript

Thank you so much for picking up volume five of *Bloody Mary*. This is Samamiya. It feels like volume four just came out the other day. Time seems to be going by so quickly these days! Despite being a Yokohama story, this entire volume was set in London, so we're losing that Yokohama feeling. Mary was also asleep during most of the volume, but I hope to change that for the next one. So I hope you decide to stick around for it!

✝ As for the drama CD...
Chara-ani Corporation just released a drama CD for *Bloody Mary*! I got to attend the recordings, and I was blown away by all the voice actors! They breathed so much life into each and every character!
I really hope you check it out! It comes out July 25, 2015. Thank you so much for the wonderful cast and supporting staff that made it possible!

⇦ The following pages are an AU story that I got to write for the magazine ASUKA. The theme was "old-fashioned courtesan"!

SPECIALTHANKS

Mihoru, H-saka, M-fuchi,
H-gawa, T-mizu, Ezaki

Production Team/Support
Haruo, Sumida, M-ika, Morinaga

Editor S, designers,
everyone who supported me

And the readers

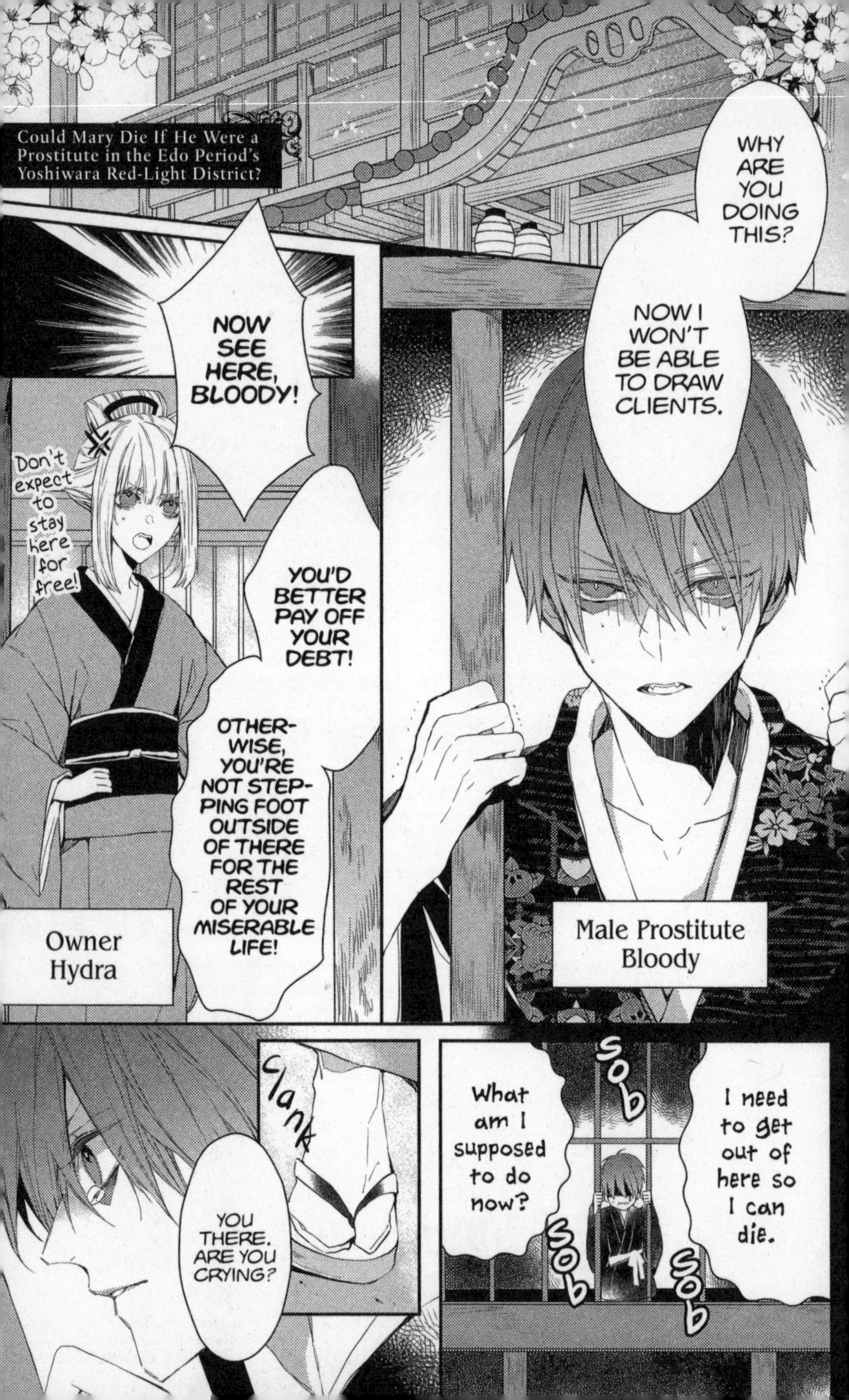
Could Mary Die If He Were a Prostitute in the Edo Period's Yoshiwara Red-Light District?
WHY ARE YOU DOING THIS?
NOW I WON'T BE ABLE TO DRAW CLIENTS.
Male Prostitute Bloody
NOW SEE HERE, BLOODY!
Don't expect to stay here for free!
YOU'D BETTER PAY OFF YOUR DEBT!
OTHER-WISE, YOU'RE NOT STEP-PING FOOT OUTSIDE OF THERE FOR THE REST OF YOUR MISERABLE LIFE!
Owner Hydra
I need to get out of here so I can die.
Sob
What am I supposed to do now?
Sob
Sob
Clank
YOU THERE. ARE YOU CRYING?

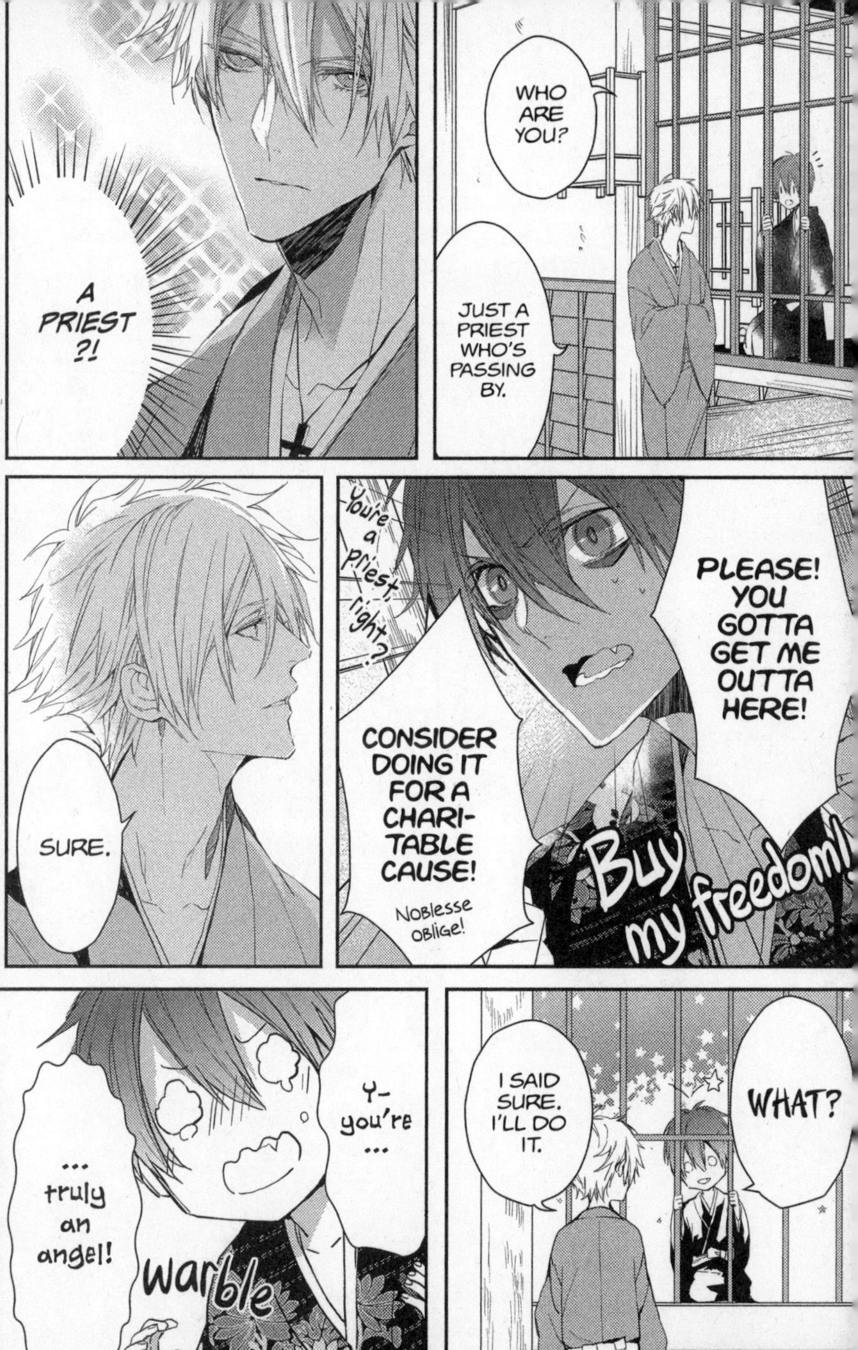
WHO ARE YOU?
JUST A PRIEST WHO'S PASSING BY.
A PRIEST ?!
PLEASE! YOU GOTTA GET ME OUTTA HERE!
You're a priest, right?
CONSIDER DOING IT FOR A CHARI-TABLE CAUSE!
Noblesse oblige!
Buy my freedom!
SURE.
WHAT?
I SAID SURE. I'LL DO IT.
Y-you're ...
... truly an angel!
warble

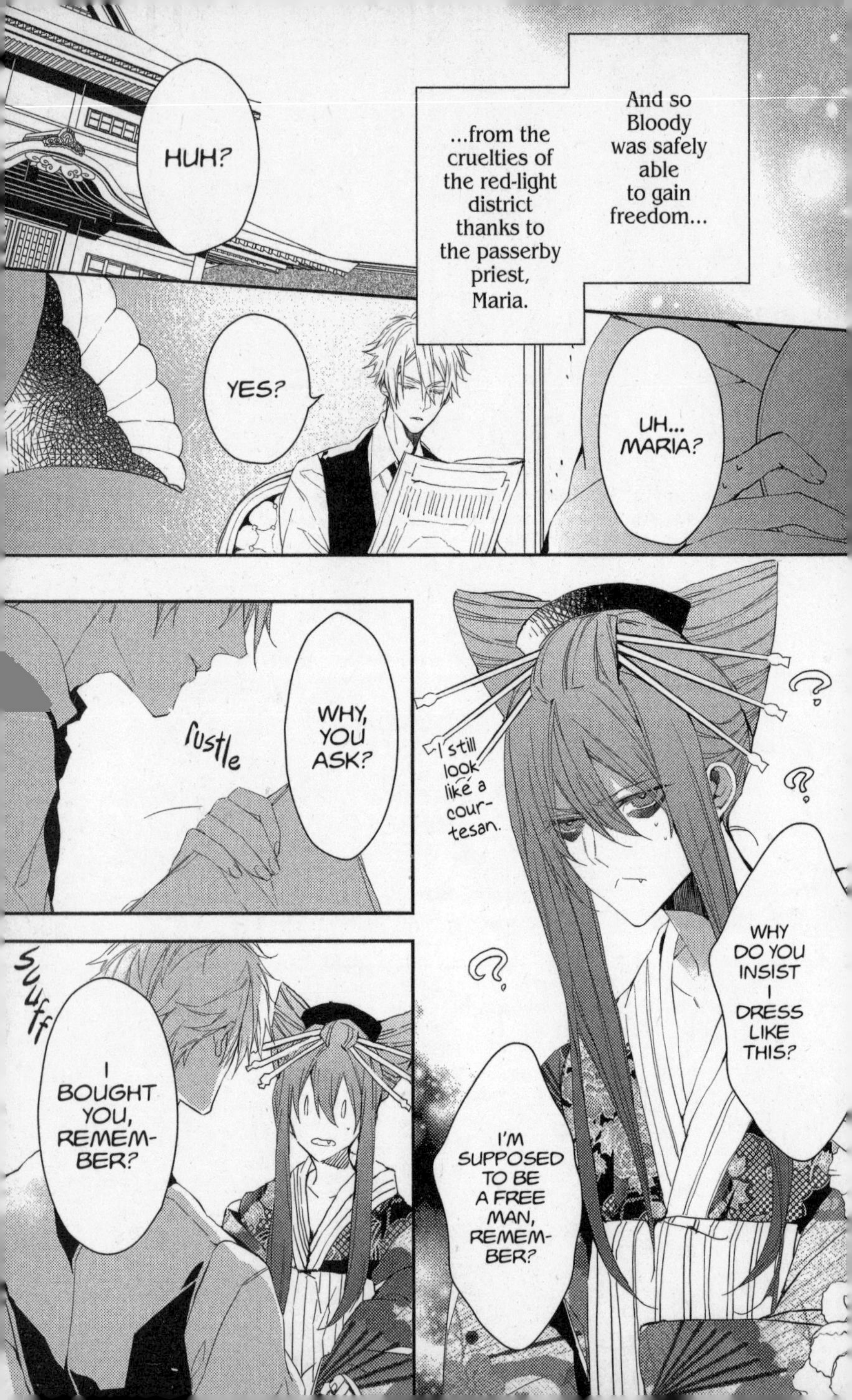
And so Bloody was safely able to gain freedom...
...from the cruelties of the red-light district thanks to the passerby priest, Maria.
HUH?
UH... MARIA?
YES?
?
?
I still look like a courtesan.
WHY DO YOU INSIST I DRESS LIKE THIS?
?
I'M SUPPOSED TO BE A FREE MAN, REMEMBER?
rustle
WHY, YOU ASK?
snuff
I BOUGHT YOU, REMEMBER?

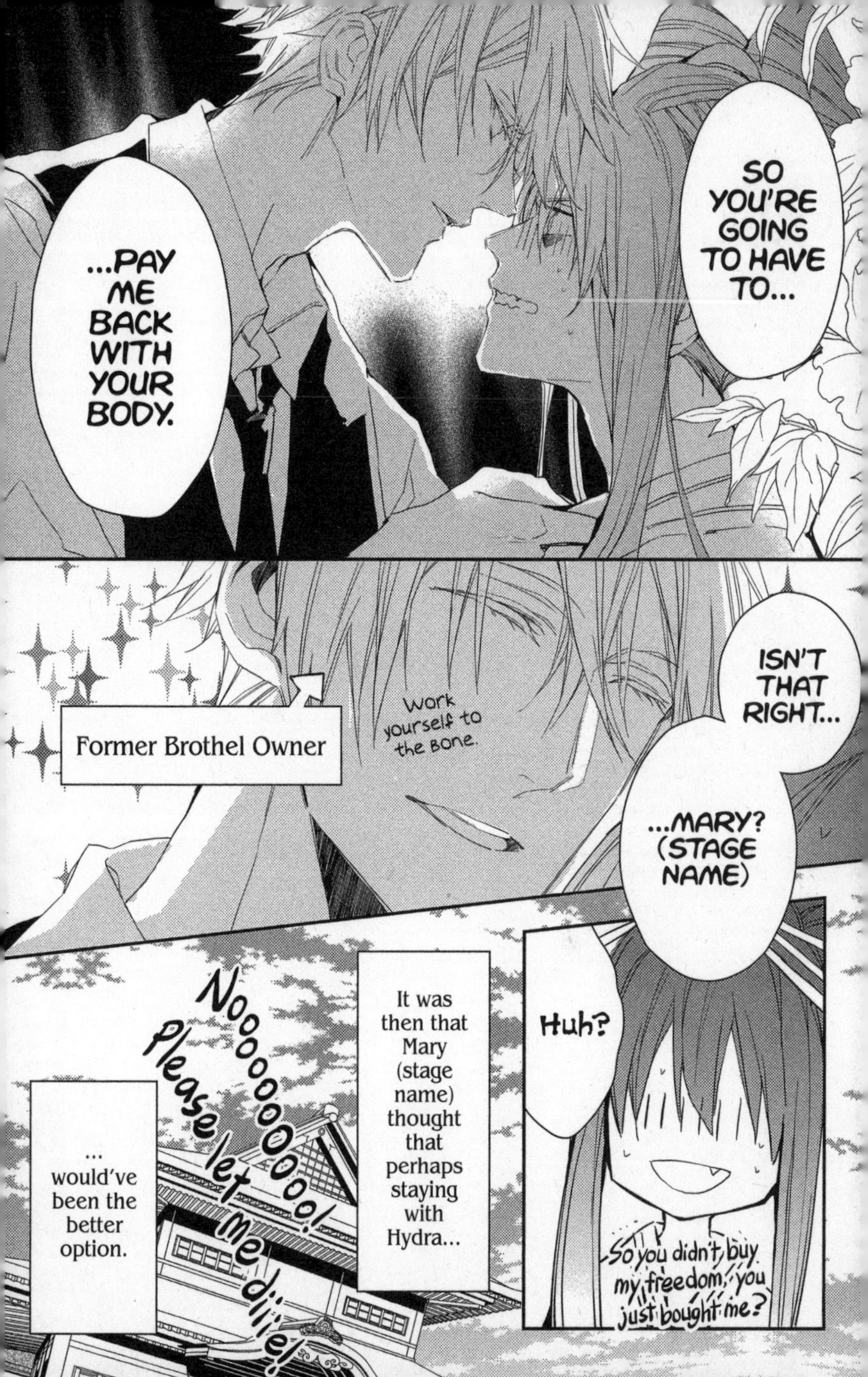
SO YOU'RE GOING TO HAVE TO...
...PAY ME BACK WITH YOUR BODY.
ISN'T THAT RIGHT...
...MARY? (STAGE NAME)
Work yourself to the bone.
Former Brothel Owner
Huh?
So you didn't buy my freedom, you just bought me?
It was then that Mary (stage name) thought that perhaps staying with Hydra...
Noooooooooooo! Please let me diiie!
...would've been the better option.

Could Mary Die If He Were a Prostitute in the Edo Period's Yoshiwara Red-Light District? end

akaza samamiya

Born November 7, Cancer, blood type B. I'm not a very good cook, but I imagine that Maria could whip up anything because he lives alone.

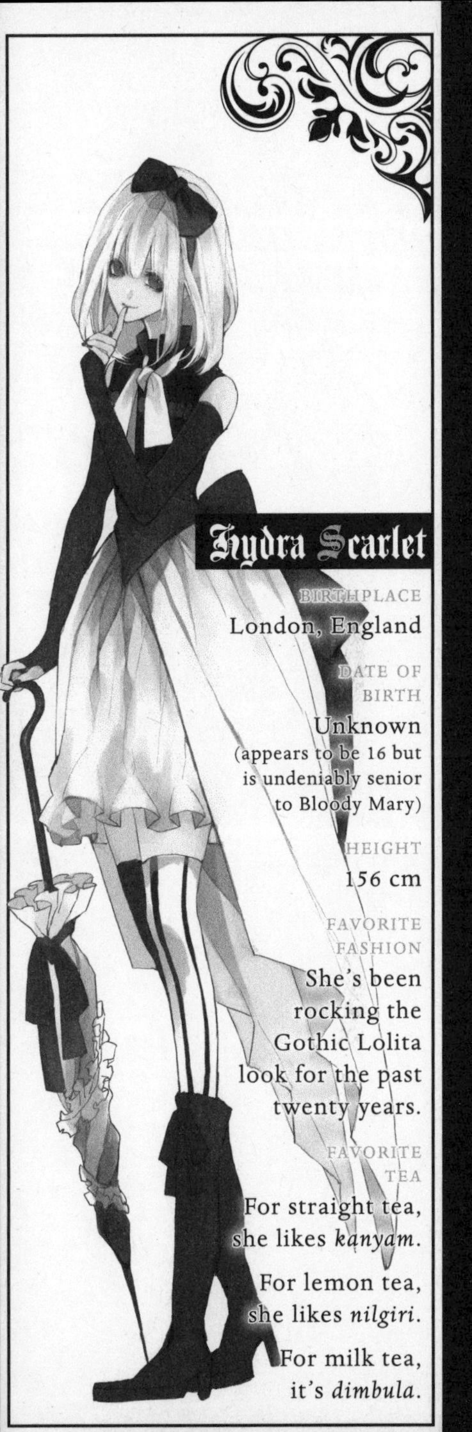

Hydra Scarlet

BIRTHPLACE

London, England

DATE OF BIRTH

Unknown
(appears to be 16 but is undeniably senior to Bloody Mary)

HEIGHT

156 cm

FAVORITE FASHION

She's been rocking the Gothic Lolita look for the past twenty years.

FAVORITE TEA

For straight tea, she likes *kanyam*.

For lemon tea, she likes *nilgiri*.

For milk tea, it's *dimbula*.

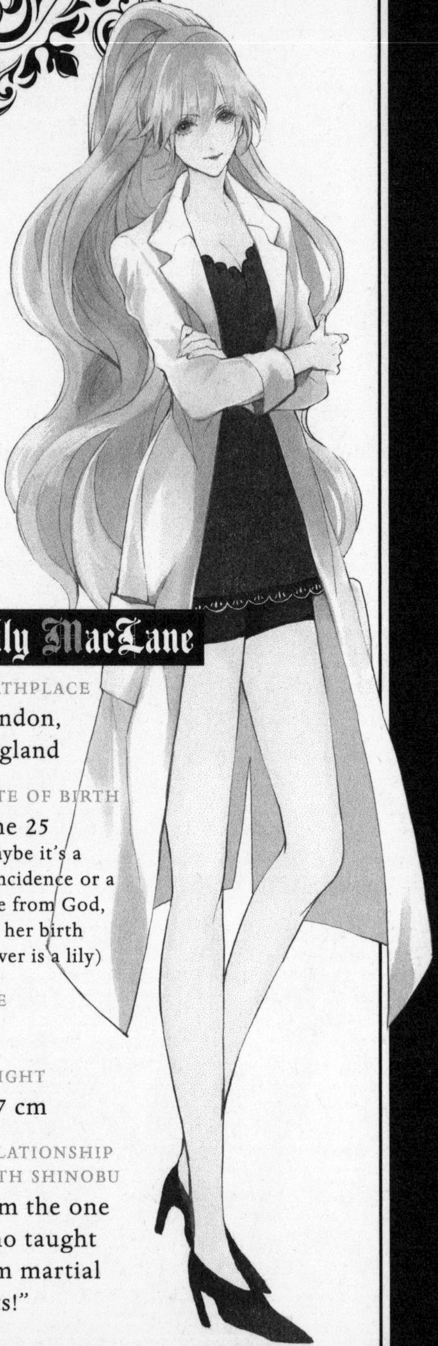

Lily MacLane

BIRTHPLACE
London, England

DATE OF BIRTH
June 25
(maybe it's a coincidence or a joke from God, but her birth flower is a lily)

AGE
27

HEIGHT
167 cm

RELATIONSHIP WITH SHINOBU
"I'm the one who taught him martial arts!"

Mary

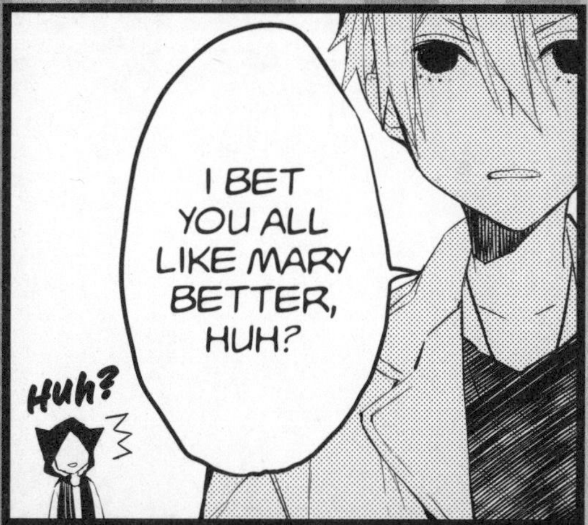
I BET YOU ALL LIKE MARY BETTER, HUH?
HUH?

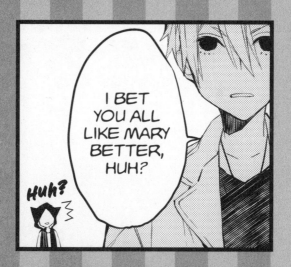

Bloody

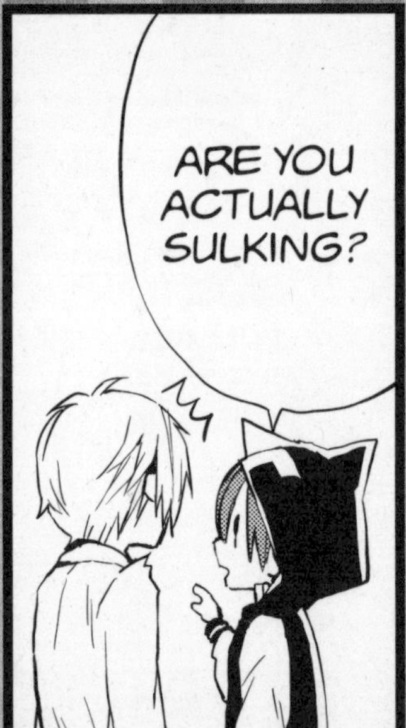
ARE YOU ACTUALLY SULKING?

Bloody Mary

Volume 5
Shojo Beat Edition

story and art by Akaza Samamiya

translation Katherine Schilling
touch-up art & lettering Sabrina Heep
design Fawn Lau
editor Erica Yee

BLOODY MARY Volume 5
© Akaza SAMAMIYA 2015
First published in Japan in 2015 by KADOKAWA
CORPORATION, Tokyo.
English translation rights arranged with KADOKAWA
CORPORATION, Tokyo.

Printed in the U.S.A.

Published by VIZ Media, LLC
P.O. Box 77010
San Francisco, CA 94107

10 9 8 7 6 5 4 3 2 1
First printing, December 2016

www.viz.com   www.shojobeat.com

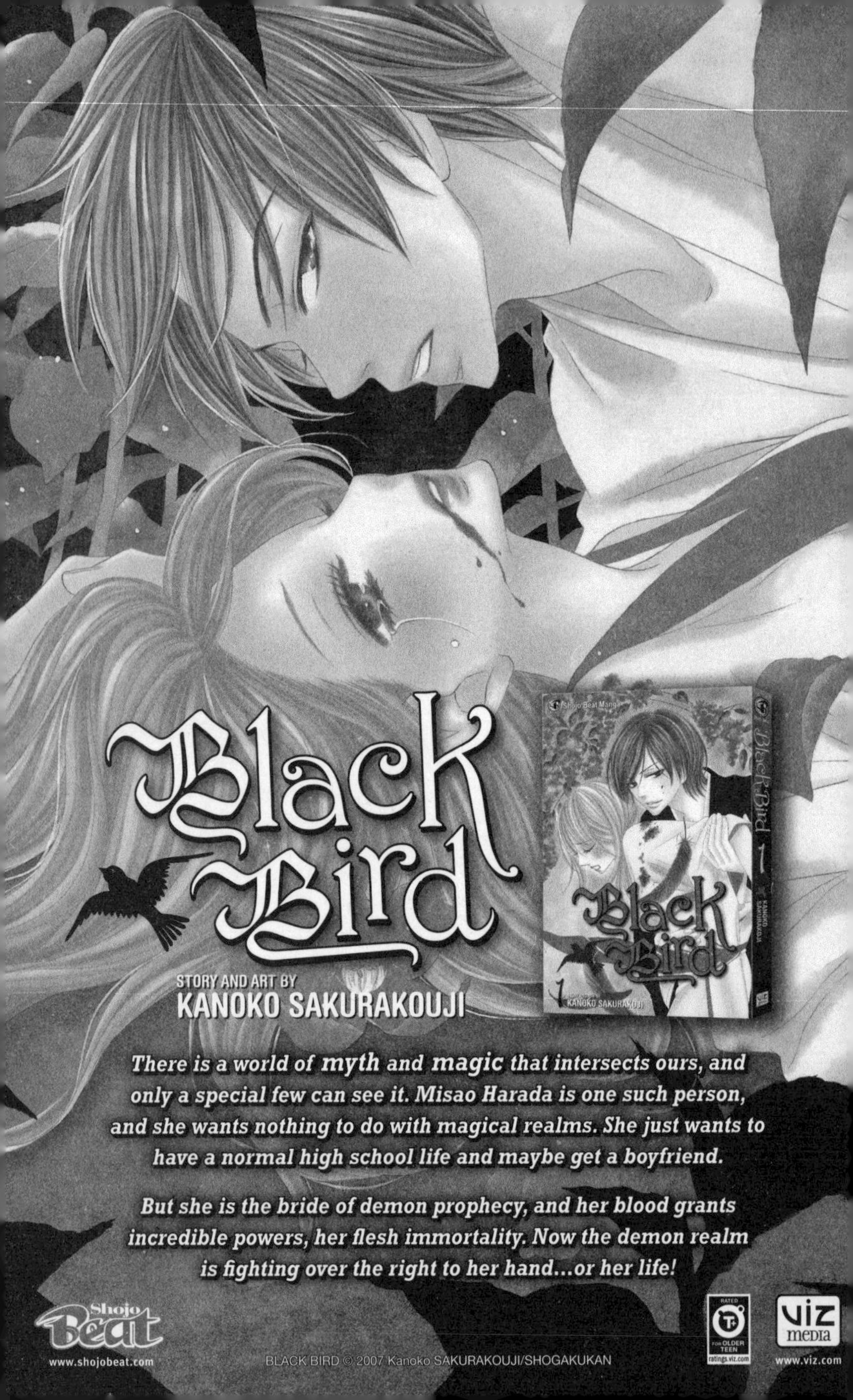
Black Bird
STORY AND ART BY
KANOKO SAKURAKOUJI
There is a world of myth and magic that intersects ours, and only a special few can see it. Misao Harada is one such person, and she wants nothing to do with magical realms. She just wants to have a normal high school life and maybe get a boyfriend.
But she is the bride of demon prophecy, and her blood grants incredible powers, her flesh immortality. Now the demon realm is fighting over the right to her hand...or her life!
Shojo Beat
www.shojobeat.com
BLACK BIRD © 2007 Kanoko SAKURAKOUJI/SHOGAKUKAN
RATED T+ FOR OLDER TEEN
ratings.viz.com
viz media
www.viz.com

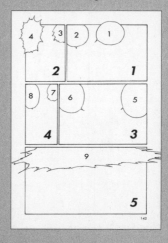

YOU MAY BE READING THE

wrong way

IT'S TRUE: In keeping with
the original Japanese comic
format, this book reads from
right to left—so action, sound
effects and word balloons are
completely reversed. This
preserves the orientation of the
original artwork—plus, it's fun!
Check out the diagram shown
here to get the hang of things,
and then turn to the other side
of the book to get started!